LISTENING
AND
RESPONDING

A. JANN DAVIS, R.N., M.A.

Human Services Educator,
Satellite Continuing Education, Inc.,
Charles City, Iowa

With **84** illustrations

The C. V. Mosby Company

ST. LOUIS   TORONTO   1984

MOSBY

A TRADITION OF PUBLISHING EXCELLENCE

Editor: Alison Miller
Assistant editor: Susan R. Epstein
Manuscript editor: Robert A. Kelly
Book design: Jeanne Bush
Cover design: Diane Beasley
Production: Carolyn Biby

Printed in the United States of America

The C.V. Mosby Company
11830 Westline Industrial Drive, St. Louis, Missouri 63146

Library of Congress Cataloging in Publication Data

Davis, A. Jann.
    Listening and responding.

    Bibliography: p.
    Includes index.
    1. Communication in nursing. 2. Interpersonal communication. 3. Nurse and patient. I. Title.
[DNLM: 1. Communication—Nursing texts. 2. Nurse-patient relations.   WY 87 D261L]
RT23.D38   1984   610.73′06′99   83-4238
ISBN 0-8016-1230-6

GW/VH/VH 9 8 7 6 5 4 3 2 1   02/A/237

TO MY FAMILY
who supported me through the writing of this book
and through the experiences shared within

Preface

Communication is the sending and receiving of attitudes and emotions as well as information, and when it is considered that these messages influence all actions, listening and responding skills deserve more emphasis than they normally receive. *Listening and Responding* focuses on the importance of these skills throughout the various levels of human development.

In this book the term "client" rather than "patient" or "resident" is used to refer to the person interacting with a member of the helping professions. Within the health care system, the responsibility and the autonomy of the health care recipient is being acknowledged. Therefore it seems only appropriate to drop the passive title of patients or residents and recognize clients who employ the help of professionals and have the right to make decisions concerning their body, their life, and their death.

The examples in this book are realistic and relatable because they are true. Only the names have been changed to protect the privacy of those involved. In many cases they are my own experiences during the 3 years that systemic lupus erythematosus threatened my being and taught me to appreciate life.

Chapters 1 through 3 deal with the first three levels of communication: verbal communication, nonverbal communication, and the effects of space on human interaction. Until recently the interrelationship of linguistics, kinesics, and proxemics received little attention, but now it is realized that

understanding is not possible unless this total message is perceived. By becoming more aware of actions and sounds that surround words and silences, care givers can take both the responsibility and the opportunity to listen, understand, and respond in a way that focuses on the client.

Throughout life individuals communicate to themselves about themselves, and this internal message—called body image—is discussed in Chapter 4. In an already complex society the developing body image is bombarded by physiological, psychological, sociological, and cultural pressures. Illness or disability also threatens or alters this image of the self. When body image adjustment is considered too great, the individual may retreat rather than adjust. With overwhelming change some choose to die, whereas many others are able to adapt to their new image and then assist others in adapting to them. In the midst of technology the modern miracle may be human interaction and support as people survive change, restructure their body image, and look to tomorrow with hope instead of dread.

Chapter 5 deals with the communication process between children and their parents. This process begins before birth and continues after birth during the development of a parent-infant bond. Through warmth and human understanding, this emotional tie between parent and infant can be enhanced following birth and nurtured while the child is growing up. As children grow from one stage of cognitive development into another, ways of effective communication also change. Sometimes children are unable to put feelings into words and may instead express their needs nonverbally through their art. Professionals aware of features and emotional indicators in children's art may be able to recognize a child's needs that might normally go unnoticed.

Growing up is more stressful than it once was, and it is up to parents to help their children learn to cope with stressful situations. Through the use of stress scales designed specifically for children and adolescents, adults are better able to offer support during these formative years. Sometimes the difference between coping with the stresses of growing up and developing maladaptive behavior is a caring adult who listens and reponds to the child.

Chapter 6, "Growing Old," is the counterpart of "Growing Up" but, unfortunately, does not bring with it the positive attitude associated with the earlier part of life. Myths and prejudices about growing old cause more harm than does the aging process, and many people begin to act old because they are expected to act old. Others consider staying young a challenge, and they are encouraging the public to reconsider what "old" really is.

Biomedical advances are increasing the percentage of the population composed of those who are 65 years and older. As these numbers increase, so does the recognition that to be old is not necessarily to be frail or senile. Many of the elderly population lead comfortable, independent lives. The health care provider's goal is to make freedom and dignity a right of every elderly person.

Chapters 7 and 8 discuss the relationship of stress and disease and the experience of pain. Emotional well-being and physical health are so interwoven that to ignore one is to neglect the other. As more is learned about stress, disease, and pain, it is also learned that there are few limits to an individual's responsibility for personal health. Americans treat their bodies like machines with replaceable parts and do not really accept that the ultimate responsibility for their health is in their hands. For years there has been increasing evidence of a relationship between personality and disease and that disease

is the body's way of saying, "Enough is enough." The discovery of endorphin, the body's own pain-killer, added further evidence of the powers within the body. Biofeedback, therapeutic touch, imagery, meditation, and relaxation are all part of maximizing a realistic potential of holistic health. Ultimately it may be recognized that the best of medicine is the client who is fully involved in the health care process and that preventive medicine is more effective than trying to cure disease once it is established.

Chapter 9, "Until Death," deals with the ability to postpone the end of life, often resulting in legal and ethical dilemmas. Whereas some accuse physicians of overtreatment, others threaten with malpractice if everything possible is not done. Legislation is encouraged when the real solution may lie in education. Living wills make it possible for people to make their wishes known while they are competent rather than leaving these decisions to family, physicians, or the courts. "Until Death" presents facts about active and passive euthanasia, the inhumane results of postponing death at all cost, and the humaneness of hospice care.

The special considerations involving a child's concept of death are included in Chapter 10. Inside many adults are the emotional scars left from childhood bereavement when parents thought they were too little to understand or be included. Many times the adult regresses back to magical thinking "If only. . . ." As with the child, adults need help in accepting that wishes are not deeds and that angry feelings do not cause death. By understanding a child's concept of death, the adult is better able to respond to a child's needs when a loved one dies. This understanding also helps adults cope with deaths that may have occurred when they were growing up.

Just as death has been included within the normal phase of growth and development, Chapter 11 presents bereavement as a normal part of life. Few people are psychologically prepared for this experience, and when death comes to an infant or child or when it occurs suddenly, survivors are frequently overwhelmed. Although bereavement is a normal process, people need help adjusting. Life is not changed by the loss of something insignificant, but it is never the same after the loss of a loved one. This significant loss produces the pain known as bereavement.

The essence of any helping process is communication, and it is this basis on which the helping relationship is established. Understanding comes from listening and responding in a way that reflects concern, sensitivity, and compassion. Methods and theories are important, but without recognizing the human element and the uniqueness of each person, communication falls short. The matrix of communication unites people in the experience of life. Throughout growing up and growing old, saying hello and good-bye, in sickness and in health, and from life until death, effective communication leaves behind understanding and a feeling that makes people glad that their lives have touched.

Thousands of helping professionals across the country have indirectly contributed to this book. They have attended my workshops and many have shared their feelings and their lives with me. Their courage and faith have added a dimension of sensitivity that is apparent in my work.

It is theorized that laughter is good medicine. If this is true, people should find and experience humor whenever they can. Tom Weinman's outstanding talent is visible throughout this book and his insightful, humorous illustrations enhance the written material. If his illustrations add a little humor to your life, they have served their purpose.

Writing this book has taken more than a year, and it would have been much longer if it were not for many people who helped me during this time. Without the support and encouragement from my husband Charles and our teenagers Kris and Bill, this book would never have been possible. I am deeply grateful to Jan Crawford, who was able to track down information with all the skill of a detective. Cindy Cronin, Pamela Rees, Joy Averill, Mary Dales, Janet Davisson, Thomas Eggars, and Lucille Lettow spent countless library hours researching the literature and locating elusive articles. A special thanks to A.-J. Levinson from the Concern for Dying for her help, and to Dame Cicely Saunders who welcomed me at St. Christopher's Hospice in England. Peg Sinnwell's help gave me more time to concentrate on my writing, and Gayle Hoy's expertise proved invaluable during the writing process. Last but not least is Nancy Evans, former senior editor of nursing science at The C. V. Mosby Company. This book was her vision, and her encouragement turned it into a reality.

A. Jann Davis

Contents

1 • Communication skills

I'm supposed to do what?

Illustration by Tom Weinman.

People talking without communicating.
People hearing without listening.
People responding without caring what was said.

Have people forgotten how to communicate with each other, or is it just that they do not take the time to talk together anymore? Ray Birdwhistell,[1] a speech communications expert, has found that a typical husband and wife spend an average of 27½ minutes a week talking to each other. That is less than 4 minutes a day. Some say that people are so busy coming and going that they do not have time to talk, and when they do, there is not any energy left. Others say that the American family is too involved watching 6 hours of television a day to ever learn the art of communication. Although the older generation tends to look back on the "good old days" when people talked with one another, the same criticisms that are now directed against television were once targeted toward radio. A shortage of conversation persists, regardless of the cause. People pretend to be listening while waiting for their turn to talk, and they respond without ever hearing what was said.

Listening and responding are the cornerstone of a helping relationship that is based on a foundation of understanding. When interpersonal communication breaks down, clients fail to understand, misconstrue what was said, and are confused and bewildered by what are considered to be perfectly simple instructions. What is completely clear and routine to a health professional may be nothing less than foreign to a client, and what the client thinks the professional understands may be entirely different from the message received. The need to improve communication skills becomes evident in helping relationships, for without understanding, helpful interactions are difficult to achieve.

THERAPEUTIC COMMUNICATION

Eric Fromm identifies man's greatest need as the "need to overcome his separateness, to leave the prison of his aloneness."[5] This is difficult to achieve without someone to talk to and someone who will listen. Normal, everyday conversation begins on a nonthreatening level with exchanges involving irrelevant issues such as the weather, food, and clothing. It takes time to establish a rapport of trust so that deeper issues can be discussed. This same foundation of trust must also be established in a hospital or other health care facility, and such a relationship is more likely to develop between the client and the primary care giver than with someone who spends relatively little time with the client. During the client's bath, linen change, mouth care, and back rubs and during pain, fear, and nausea the basis for a therapeutic relationship develops. Not enough emphasis has been placed on the importance of this relationship, and sometimes a member of the multidisciplinary team who has spent very little time with the client walks into the room, sits down, and expects the person to be able to jump into gut-level issues.

Health professionals are good at specific, detailed, and routine actions, but the emotional aspects of illness are sometimes neglected or placed low on the hierarchy of assessed needs. In 1959 a survey among nurses pointed out that nurses considered administering medications their most important activity.[8] Even today some nurses feel guilty if they are seen talking with clients, and most will agree that it is the nurse talking to a client who is assigned an unexpected task. Current research validates the interrelationship between medical treatment and what is communicated to the client, and communication is a vital part of the therapeutic regimen. It does not require more time but rather better use of communication skills during the time spent with clients.

Being therapeutic is not equated with being a therapist. Psychiatric nurses, counselors, psychologists, psychiatrists, and others trained in mental health are able to deal in depth with personal concerns and personality-structure changes, and they may spend a large amount of time delving into the client's past or subconscious. Not that it is not important for an individual to work through these feelings, it is just that the primary care giver seldom has the time or the expertise to become involved beyond the client's present concerns. Consultations with those specially trained in mental health should be obtained whenever time or capabilities are surpassed.

Most clients are capable to some degree of making decisions for themselves, and many have significant others they can turn to for support. However, there are times when clients may not want to worry their family, or they need someone other than a significant other with whom to share fears and feelings. It is up to the health care worker to provide a nonthreatening environment of acceptance and trust so that the door to therapeutic communication is always open. It is also important to maximize a client's coping abilities so that whenever possible the person can function independently. Nothing is gained if dependency is taught. For example, Mrs. Henry is a client who continually asks the nurse to relay questions to the physician. By complying with Mrs. Henry's wishes, the nurse encourages dependency. On the other hand, if the nurse encourages Mrs. Henry to talk to the physician and then supports her during this conversation, independence has been promoted.

Helping professionals also have needs that must be satisfied before they can feel fulfilled in their profession. The need to be needed must not get in the way of the client's need for independence, and self-awareness helps to prevent the achievement of personal needs at the expense of the client. There are times when others inadvertently contribute to a client's fear and weakness by assuming responsibility for something the person is capable of doing alone or with a little assistance. Even those with extreme mental or physical stress should be allowed as much freedom in the decision-making process as possible, with assistance given only when it is absolutely necessary. The most successful answer to a problem is one that the person ultimately works out for him or herself, and the helper who does a good job promotes this independence.

During therapeutic communication the professional is a helper with the resources of support, information, and clarification, which is quite different from making decisions for, giving advice about, placing judgment on, or taking responsibility for another's problem. It is up to the care team to create an atmosphere of trust and respect in which therapeutic communication can take place and coping can be achieved.

Listening

Helping is not a process of solving problems for others. Rather, helping is assisting people to use their own resources to solve their own problems. An individual involved in a helping role is basically concerned with letting the client do the talking. This means giving up the role of the conversationalist and assuming the role of the listener while others share what is central to and of concern to them. Most people are able to determine a solution to their own problem; they simply need someone who will listen with understanding while they are in the process of determining what to do next.

When care givers first become involved in therapeutic communication, they may be unsure enough of themselves to want to prove their ability. They concentrate on knowing how to act and what to say next. They plan their next words at the expense of not hearing the client. After awhile helpers learn that what they have to say is not as important as what they initially thought, and they become more willing to focus on listening.

Listening is hard work. It requires wholehearted concentration that is not in the least passive. The

Listening is receiving with nothing to prove.
Photograph by Martha S. Hennessey.

listener must let go of hopes and fears and concentrate on the present moment. This is much the same as the typist who attends to each letter and word as it appears, rather than trying to determine what a word is by looking at the first letter. Supposition creates error. The helper pays attention to what is said, how it is said, and the accompanying nonverbal expressions and gestures. Equally important is what is not said, alluded to, or held back. Sometimes hidden messages are evidenced through their effects. For example, when profanity is used, others pay attention; words of endearment prompt compliant behavior; ''Why?'' may mean, ''I disagree''; interrupting another says, ''I already know,'' or ''I'm not interested.'' ''Yes, but . . .'' often means, ''No.'' Words of sympathy are commonly used as restraints.

The average person talks at the rate of approximately 150 words per minute, whereas the brain is capable of processing information several times this rate. This leaves the listener with free brain time to use all the senses, including intuition and gut feelings, to understand more fully what is really going on with the individual. To be therapeutic a listener needs to possess the following attitudes and skills:

- Wants to listen
- Has a desire to help
- Gives undivided attention to what the client is saying
- Is patient and does not interrupt the client
- Listens for central themes
- Monitors personal emotions
- Accepts the client's feelings
- Recognizes each client's potential for problem solving

Before people can listen objectively, they must know themselves so that their values, judgments, and needs are not imposed on the client, and nothing within them gets in the way of what the client shares. Because no one is perfectly adjusted, helpers must increase their awareness of behaviors and situations that bother them most. It is impossible to be compassionate, friendly, warm, accepting, and patient with everyone, and instead ot trying to ignore negative reactions, it is necessary to pay attention to what these emotions are saying. What effect do the client's tears, anger, or helplessness produce? Do these emotions result in patterns of behavior from others? When emotions are repeatedly triggered by a client, the situation needs to be assessed. A person who is good at manipulation is able to find another's weak spot and code the message in a way that control can be achieved without the other person being aware that it is happening. A perfect example is the client in the nursing home who has learned that certain nurses will respond to flattery by giving extra attention. Each of the nurses involved believes the client who says, ''You are the best nurse here.'' This reciprocal behavior is likely to continue until one nurse overhears the client use the same flattering phrase with another nurse. This not only points out the needs of the client but also should give some insight into the nurses' susceptibility to flattery.

Listening is receiving without the need to prove anything. If caregivers can disengage themselves from personal needs, an environment is created in which clients can express thoughts and feelings and be assured of continued respect.

Understanding

During therapeutic communication the client tries to verbalize feelings that may be difficult to identify or to share. The helper's role is to assist the client in clarifying these unmet needs and determining how they can best be met. Understanding is a key element in this helping process, for without understanding, the client's coping abilities cannot be maximized.

Numerous psychologists have identified three ways of understanding another person. The most basic understanding comes from secondhand information that is obtained by reading about or hearing others talk about the individual. For example, a health professional receives information concerning a client from other members of the health care team or from reading the client's chart. This information serves as a basis for understanding, although most professionals agree that forming assumptions or understandings based solely on secondary or tertiary sources is not therapeutic.

A second way to understand a client is from a personal frame of reference. In other words, the helper uses him or herself as a guide for understanding a client. Included within this internal frame of reference are the helper's knowledge, experience, skills, values, morals, and ethics. When understanding is based on such personal resources, it is limited to what the individual has experienced or can imagine. In addition, personal feelings may obstruct therapeutic interaction.

The third level of understanding comes from using the client's frame of reference. This requires the helper to view the situation from the perspective of the client—the way the client thinks, feels, and responds. Personal feelings of approval or disapproval, agreeing or disagreeing, and confirming or denying must be eliminated and exchanged for openness and acceptance. Some refer to this as empathetic understanding since the helper imagines as well as possible what the client is experiencing and from this perspective is able to achieve a more accurate understanding of the client. This level of understanding is considered the most therapeutic but also the most difficult to achieve.

I hope you get well soon.

Fig. 1-1. Understanding with secondhand information.
© 1979 A. Jann Davis.

Examples of these three levels of understanding begin with an entry from Mr. Edison's chart that reads, "Good night. Slept well. No complaints." From this information, a care giver has a basic understanding about Mr. Edison. The nurse on the next shift may decide to go beyond this secondary source of information and use a personal frame of reference to determine if Mr. Edison had a good night. The nurse may observe the client's appearance and actions, and if he looks and acts rested, the nurse is likely to concur that, indeed, he had a good night. However, the nurse may prefer to use the client's frame of reference, which is central to the third level of understanding, and ask Mr. Edison, "How was your night?" If the client answers, "Terrible!" the nurse does not argue, "The night nurse said . . ." but instead attempts to understand what has made the client interpret his night as terrible.

The way an individual responds to another readily shows the level of understanding being used as a reference point. These different levels are illustrated in cards written by grade school students to a classmate's mother. The youngsters who wrote the cards did not know anything about their classmate's mother except that she was sick and in the hospital. Most of the cards were written using only this secondhand information, which provided a basic understanding about the classmate's mother. Fig. 1-1 is typical of such a response. However, some of the children began to wonder what it would be like if it were their mother in the hospital, and

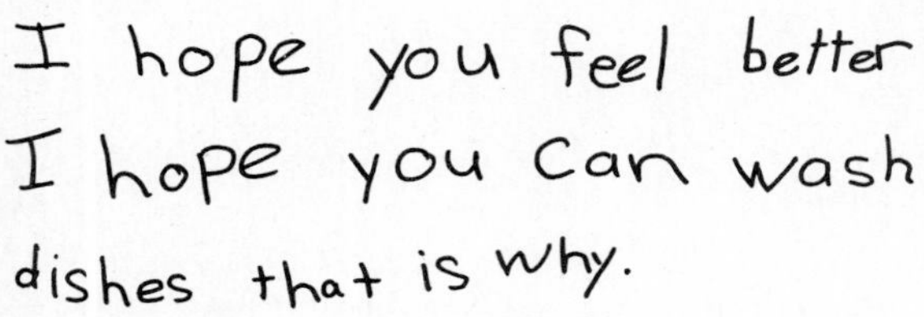

I hope you feel better
I hope you can wash
dishes that is why.

*Fig. 1-2. Understanding with personal frame
of reference.*

© 1979 A. Jann Davis.

Fig. 1-2 is one of the cards illustrating this personal
frame of reference. The woman who was hospitalized had a dishwasher in her home, which further
verifies that the child had thought about his or her
own personal situation rather than that of the classmate or the classmate's mother. The child who
wrote the card in Fig. 1-3 moved beyond a personal
frame of reference to try to understand what it must
be like for the classmate and the classmate's mother
to be separated from each other. Empathetic understanding can be achieved at any age, and it is
one of the greatest gifts that anyone can give. When
this level of understanding occurs between client
and helper, the basis for therapeutic interaction has
been established.

There is always the concern that the helper will
become so engaged in the client's message that it
is difficult to tell one from the other. When the
helper becomes emotionally engaged, objectivity
is lost and the insight on which the client depends
is gone. This does not mean that a care giver cannot
shed tears with a client. There are times for sharing
and there are times when it is necessary to disengage so as not to become absorbed totally in the
client's problem.

■ Mrs. S. was a member of a support group for
parents of infants who died of sudden infant death
syndrome. When anyone in the group became upset
or was close to crying, Mrs. S. would quickly move
next to that person to provide comfort. Everyone
liked Mrs. S. and knew that she always carried an
ample supply of tissues. It became apparent to the
group leader that Mrs. S. was preventing people
from working through their grief. Her need to
"mother" the group members was standing in the
way of their need to grieve.

The next time the group met, the leader began
the session with a discussion about crying and
asked each member to tell the group how it felt
when he or she or someone else cried. Many people
shared that crying made them feel better but that
they were uncomfortable when someone else cried.
When it was Mrs. S.' turn, instead of answering,
she began to sob. It was the first time she had cried
in the group, and the members were somewhat
taken aback to see this happen. Several started to
move toward Mrs. S. to offer her the comfort she
had given them, but the leader waved them aside
and encouraged Mrs. S. to share her feelings. Between sobs she revealed, "My baby cried, and I
didn't get up to check on him. The next morning
he was dead."

Since her baby's death 3 months earlier, Mrs.
S. had lived with the haunting guilt that her failure
to check on her infant had somehow contributed
to his death. She had not been able to accept that
sudden infant deaths occur without warning and
without a known cause, and her feelings of guilt
had completely blocked her grieving. During group
sessions, she had unconsciously tried to turn back
the clock and respond to her baby's cries by responding to the crying group members. Once Mrs.
S. was able to acknowledge her feelings of guilt,
she was able to move past them and grieve for her
loss.

This example underlines the necessity for care
givers to remain themselves so that clients can have
the freedom to get closer to their problem. During
therapeutic interaction, what frequently cannot be
seen in close proximity becomes more visible at a
distance.

It is difficult to hear another cry without rushing
in with tissues and support in an attempt to smooth

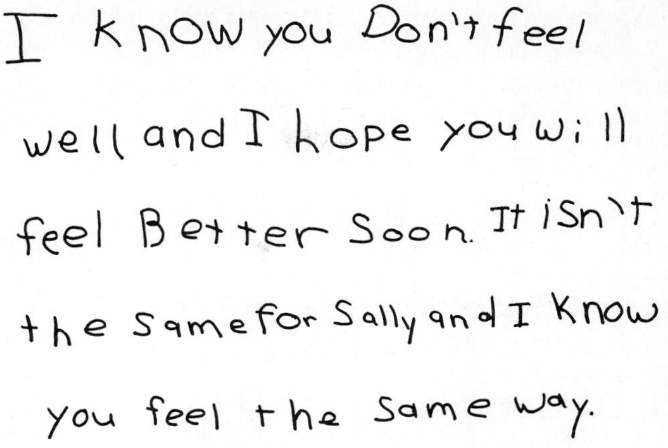

I know you Don't feel well and I hope you will feel Better Soon. It isn't the same for Sally and I know you feel the same way.

Fig. 1-3. Empathetic understanding.
© *1979 A. Jann Davis.*

things over and make the person feel better. A helper who tries to stop a client's tears may be placing personal needs over the client's. Tears serve as an emotional release, and the client may need to cry. Rather than wiping the tears away, it is more helpful to find out the meaning of the tears: "What are your tears saying?" "Tell me about your tears." "What's behind your tears?" In the following narration, all the anger, sadness, and isolation that was hidden behind a facade of smiles found freedom through the expression of tears.

Tears of a Survivor

I clutch at time. Because I know that mine is limited, I squeeze each minute with every ounce of my strength. I have been so busy grasping that I lack both the strength and moments to enjoy, and I have gained little.

During the past few years everything about my life has changed, and I have changed. I have pushed away the tears and anguish that I truly felt and in so doing pushed away those who reminded me of my feelings. I built a protective bubble and wore a mask that stated, "Everything's fine!" The mask hid the tears—and the laughter and radiance that people used to talk about.

Rather than let my friends exclude me from activities once shared, I excluded them first. The bubble became a fortress, preventing me from seeing others doing the things I ached to do. It also prevented me from seeing my friends' extended hands.

I thought of my family and the many times that they put my needs before their own. *How long will it be before they hate me?* So I began to "protect" my family by doing the treatments and surgeries alone. All the while I wanted my loved ones but told myself this was best. *No one wants to be around a person in misery. I can spare them this out of love.* They were not allowed to share my pain, but they felt my resentment for not being with me when I needed them.

From isolation I learned that sorrow cannot be ignored without also missing joy. Unspent tears drown laughter. Only a small part of the real me is gone, although I have said good-bye to far more. I know that I cannot and do not want to live in a world apart. People need people. The sharing of joy increases its rapture. The sharing of pain diminishes the hurt.

I am crying for all the sadness I have felt and for the companionships I have lost—many of which were self-imposed instead of being caused by illness. The most awesome thing that I have learned is that protective bubbles, fortresses, and masks, which take so much work, time, and energy to construct, can be dissolved with something as gentle as tears.

For some, tears are a necessary part of saying good-bye to the past before being able to say hello to the present. When the feelings behind the tears are shared, they have a potential for healing.

Responding

Responding therapeutically requires honest, concrete, and empathic reaction to the client's verbal and nonverbal messages. Before this can be done, the helper must make the transition from social conversationalist to therapeutic communicator, which is easier to understand theoretically than it is to put into practice. An individual's way of communicating is highly personal and has developed gradually over the years. Techniques that promote therapeutic communication require the individual to concentrate on communicating behaviors that in the past have been taken for granted.

Responses and leads are two general ways of responding to a client. A helper's reflection on the ideas and feelings that a client has expressed is called a response. Responses reflect the most therapeutic level of understanding because they keep the clients' ideas and feelings the center of the interaction. When leads are used, the helper's frame of reference becomes the focal point and the helper's ideas and feelings become the center of the interaction. Although leads are used during therapeutic communication, there is always concern that through leads the helper may impose personal beliefs and values on the client. For this reason, leads may contribute to communication blocks rather than therapeutic interactions.

Responding techniques are presented here to help caring professionals become more aware of their own verbal responses and to help them become more sensitive to the ways in which these responses affect clients. With practice, these techniques can help care givers respond more therapeutically to their clients.

Reflective responses. A helper's response to a client's message depends on hearing the cognitive content of the message as well as the affective message of feelings, attitudes, and behaviors. Verbal messages concerning things, people, and events are easier to share and to recognize. However, if only the content of the message is responded to, the underlying feelings and concerns are never dealt with. To be effective, communication skills must be used that involve hearing content, perceiving feelings, and responding to this total message.

Although there are numerous ways to effectively respond to a client, a reflective response deals with both idea and feelings and is especially helpful when a client has underlying emotions that are not being dealt with. Reflection requires the helper to use sensitive and empathic understanding in perceiving the total message and verbalizing it without distortion. The client then has the opportunity to verify or clarify the helper's understanding. Without this type of feedback there is never any assurance that the message received is the same as the message conveyed.

Carkhuff and others[2] suggest a basic format for reflective responses: "You feel _____ because _____ ." The helper fills in the first blank with whatever the client is feeling, and the second blank is used to describe the content of the client's message:

> CLIENT: If I don't see my doctor today, I'm going to walk right out of this hospital.
> NURSE: You feel angry because you haven't seen your doctor.

The helper communicates understanding of the content and by recognizing affect, gives permission for the person to experience and express the accompanying feelings. If instead the nurse uses a defensive remark such as, "Your doctor has a lot of people to see," communication is likely to be blocked.

Feelings cannot be labeled as right or wrong or good or bad. To recognize feelings in an accepting, nonjudgmental way is the beginning of helping a client understand and cope with these feelings. In describing emotions it is important to select words that accurately match what the client is experiencing. The words must be comfortable for the helper to use but must also be words that the client can relate to. To try and use slang or profanity only because the client does will make the helper look and feel phony.

As an individual becomes more proficient with reflective responses, the format can be changed as long as the context of ideas and feeling are included.

> CLIENT: I don't know if I can go through with the surgery tomorrow.
> NURSE: You sound concerned about having surgery tomorrow.

With the reflective response, the client is encouraged to share feelings. If instead the nurse uses false reassurances such as, "Everyone's nervous before surgery; it's perfectly normal," the client will be less likely to share personal concerns about having surgery.

Reflective responses give people the chance to hear what they have said but in different words, and sometimes this in itself is very helpful in clarifying thinking.

Clarification. Techniques of clarification make it possible to clarify messages so that misinterpretations do not occur. Reflective responses are one way of verifying accurate understanding, and clarification can be further enhanced by prefacing statements with phrases such as, "I think you're saying . . ." "Do I understand . . ." and "Let's see if I have this right. . . ."

> CLIENT: Our baby is so tiny I don't know if I can take care of him at home.
> NURSE: You seem to be saying that you're insecure about taking care of your baby after you go home.

Restatement is another effective technique of clarification. During restatement the helper remains emotionally and intellectually uninvolved and simply repeats exactly what the client has said or summarizes the most significant part of the message.

> CLIENT: I didn't sleep at all last night.
> NURSE: You didn't sleep at all last night.

Restatement must be used judiciously; otherwise this clarifying technique begins to sound more like an echo than a form of communication.

Summarization is another effective clarifying technique, and it is also a method that helps to bring an interaction with a client to a close. Highlights of the discussion are presented, and the client has the opportunity to accept, reject, or modify what the helper understood.

> NURSE: Ms. K., I need to leave in a few minutes, but before I go, I want to briefly go over what we've talked about. Let me know if I've misunderstood anything, or if you have additional questions.

Sometimes clients will submit new material just as the helper is about to leave. Material introduced at the last minute may be very important to the client, but the helper's other commitments may mandate that unfinished material be left for a later time or discussed with someone else who is currently available. Usually a client will accept a tactful reminder from the helper, such as, "I really wish I could stay and talk with you longer, but I must go. Let's talk more about this at a later time." Whenever possible, this time should be specified.

Giving information. In the past clients made few demands for information, and health professionals were reluctant to volunteer it. Within the last 10 years individuals have begun to participate more in their own health care, and it is now generally accepted that information concerning the client belongs to the client. Some health care professionals still maintain that clients do not want to know about their illness or treatment and that providing such information serves only to upset or confuse them. Studies have pointed out just the opposite. Most of the time clients do want to know, but what they are told must be administered in dosages that can be used. What is a therapeutic dose of information for one client is an overdose for another, and at different times the same client can tolerate different amounts of information. The following hypothetical client demonstrates this:

■ Mr. Smith is admitted to Room 222 for tests. He hears the words, "upper GI series," "CBC," "UA," "stool specimen," and, "NPO." Undoubtedly, a nurse acts as an interpreter for this foreign language, but what is said and what is heard may be entirely different. During the stress of hospital admission the man's comprehension level will not be up to par. His identity is reduced to an arm band, and his clothing may be limited to a gown that resembles a pillowcase split down the back. Under these circumstances compliant behavior is more likely than assertive behavior, and what is not understood may not be questioned. _____

A lack of understanding about condition, treatment, or hospital routine is a major cause of anxiety for hospitalized clients. Hospital jargon in itself creates a communication fog that may contribute to the misconception that information is precious and sacred to the professional. Clients as well as their significant others filter information through perceptual screens according to what they want to hear, what they think they will hear, and what they expect to hear. For example, one woman had a tumor removed, and although she was told that the tumor was benign, she asked what would be done to stop the cancer. Finally it was understood that the woman thought having a tumor meant having cancer, and she had no idea what the word *benign* meant.

Two major considerations must take place when information is presented to the client or the client's significant others. The first deals with the amount of information given, and the second is evaluating understanding of this information. De Long[3] identifies a relationship between a client's coping style and the amount of information that benefits the client. Three basic coping styles were identified among clients who were to have surgery. Before surgery these individuals received either general information concerning the hospital and operative procedures or specific and detailed information. Following surgery it became apparent that the coping style and the type of preoperative information affected recovery time. "Copers," identified as clients who attempted to deal with stress, recuperated faster when they were given specific information rather than general information. These individuals considered themselves in charge of the situation, and detailed information helped make them feel more in control. "Avoiders" tended to use denial in stressful situations and did much better following surgery when they received general

preoperative information rather than specific details. Since they considered their physician in charge of the details, they preferred not to know anything more than was absolutely necessary to get them through their surgery and hospitalization. The third personality type was identified as "nonspecific defenders," and this included individuals who used both coping and avoiding strategies. These clients had the fastest recovery from surgery regardless of information received. From this study it is apparent that too little or too much information can produce anxiety that may have a deleterious effect on a client. Because people may be copers at one time and avoiders at another, a care giver will need to be flexible in the amount of information presented to clients. Initially general information should be presented, and then, according to the questions and receptiveness of the client, more specific, detailed information can be added.

Half of the process of providing information to clients is to verify that understanding has taken place. This assessment of understanding can take the form of verbal recall or demonstration. Clients seem to be better able to recall information that they believe will be of importance to them. Therefore, as a client's needs change, information already presented may have to be repeated. People are more likely to remember what they hear than what they read, and what they say seems to be retained longer than what is read or heard. Written material helps to enforce verbal instructions, and having clients recall information through verbalization or demonstration not only assesses learning but also helps the client to incorporate this new information.

Information affects a client's health. It is the responsibility of the health professional to verify that information presented is understood, for without understanding, information is useless.

Questions. Many interactions between medical personnel and clients involve obtaining information through questioning. Because asking questions tends to place the recipient of the question on the defensive, a warm, positive relationship may be hampered by the repeated use of questions. However, a certain amount of questioning is necessary for health care to be carried out. Learning how to effectively use questions to gather accurate information without producing blocks is a valuable communication tool.

Questions may be either open or closed. The open question asks for views, opinions, thoughts, and feelings and allows the client to elaborate, discuss, or describe in detail. Because questions beginning with "how" or "what" are more difficult to answer with a yes or no, they stimulate a more in-depth response and are among those considered open. Questions such as, "How can we make you more comfortable?" "What did you do at home when you were hurting?" and "How was your night?" encourage descriptive responses.

Closed questions ask for facts and limit the client's answer to yes or no or to a few words: "Has your doctor been in?" "Do you need anything for pain?" "Have you walked in the hall today?" Closed questions beginning with "who," "when," "where," and "which" prompt brief answers and are used when specific information is needed: "Where are you hurting?" "When did the pain begin?" "Which medication helped the most?" Too many closed questions may make the client feel or believe that the nurse is too busy to listen.

The leading question is a form of closed question that contains its own answer. For this reason it is considered a communication block and is considered in the following section.

Communication blocks

Certain ways of interacting with clients help more than others, and when interaction is effective, the experience is therapeutic. As discussed earlier, two ways of responding to a client are through responses and leads. When responses are used, the client's ideas and feelings are the center of the interaction and it is the helper who reacts. When leads are used, the helper's thoughts and feelings become the focal point and the client reacts. Although there are times when leads are entirely appropriate, such as when information is requested

or given, there are also times when leads result in communication blocks. These include improper use of questioning, use of reassuring cliches, moralizing, defending, interpreting, reassuring, and in general any communication technique that prevents therapeutic interaction from taking place.

Questions that block. Whenever a helper asks a client a question, the interaction becomes helper oriented rather than client oriented. Clearly, questions that result in needed information are important in a helping relationship. However, those that hinder communication should be eliminated.

The leading question blocks communication rather than prompting information. It directs the recipient toward a predetermined answer:

SPOUSE: You're doing so much better today, don't you agree, Dear?
CLIENT: If you say so.

Nothing new is learned from this type of question, and the only needs that are being met are the needs of the person asking the leading question.

Another question that often blocks communication is the "why" question. Most of the time "why" probes for answers that the client may not have: "Why did you wait so long to come to the hospital?" "Why didn't you follow your diet?" Although the frequent response is either silence or, "I don't know," the more assertive adult or the uninhibited child is likely to answer, "At this point, what difference does it make," "Who cares," or "Because." The "why" question can produce facts, or it can produce frustration. Because of this risk, it should be used as sparingly as possible and only when cognitive information is needed. When used to encourage explanation of emotions or feelings, it serves only to add to the client's frustration.

Perhaps the greatest abuse in the use of questions is asking question upon question without waiting for the individual's answer:

NURSE: How was your day?
CLIENT: Well . . .
NURSE: Was it a good one?

In this situation the nurse's open question was not immediately answered and was rephrased into a closed question. Sometimes people get so preoccupied with forming the next question that the respondent's answer is not heard or not considered as a basis for the next question.

Another common occurrence is to interject another question if the respondent pauses while answering the first.

PHYSICIAN: Are you having any pain?
CLIENT: Well, perhaps a little . . . it's just . . .
PHYSICIAN: And how's your appetite?

By the time thoughts and answers are formed, it is difficult to know which question to answer first or whether the answer is worth the effort or even wanted.

Giving advice. Giving information that the client needs is entirely different from giving advice that includes personal opinions and attitudes. These phrases indicate that the listener is judging, comparing, or interpreting: "If I were you . . ." "I feel that . . ." "If you ask me . . ." "My opinion is. . . ." By giving advice helping professionals reinforce clients' feelings of dependency rather than encouraging them to use their own abilities in the decision-making process. Professionals can assist clients by providing relevant information and by encouraging them to examine the factors involved. Questions such as, "What are some good things about that choice?" "Can you give some examples of that idea?" "What other possibilities or alternatives have you considered?" and, "What do you think would be the outcome?" encourage consideration of all aspects of the problem. Being asked for advice may be an ego boost that hides the no-win situation it creates. When advice is sound, clients lose confidence in themselves. When it is erroneous, clients lose confidence in others. The outcome creates a problem greater than the advice was intended to solve.

Approval and disapproval. Although approval can be a useful response to motivate or encourage a client, both approval and disapproval rely on the helper's values, opinions, and goals to set standards of behavior for the client. The client is pushed and pressured by what the authority figure says is bad or good rather than being encouraged to rely on personal strengths. In a hospital this external influence sets the client up to achieve the "good client" role and is likely to block therapeutic communication. Giving recognition is more therapeutic than using approval or praise: "Miss Carpenter, I noticed that you walked all the way down the hall." "You've eaten your meal without any help." Disapproval can be replaced with reflecting on comments or sharing observation of behavior in an attempt to ascertain the meaning of or motivation behind the statement or action: "You seem upset." "You've pulled out your IV."

Agreeing and disagreeing. Agreeing and disagreeing use value judgments involving right and wrong or correct and incorrect. Once a helper agrees with a client, it becomes difficult for the client to make another choice or choose another option. To do so would admit personal error in addition to acknowledging the helper's error. Sometimes clients do not mean what they say, and if the care giver agrees with them, the real message is blocked. The client who tells the nurse, "I don't believe in sex before marriage, do you?" may mean, "I would like to ask about contraceptives, but I'm not married and I need to know if I can talk to you about this." If the nurse agrees or disagrees, the communication is stopped. If, however, the nurse clarifies, "Sounds like you have some concerns about premarital sex," the client may feel more comfortable about asking questions.

Disagreeing with a client may cause the person to withdraw or to become defensive and angry. Rather than weakening the individual's convictions, disagreeing tends to strengthen them. For example, a woman is admitted to the obstetrical department after a spontaneous abortion and shares, "It's all my fault that I miscarried." If the nurse answers, "It's not your fault," the client is likely to defend her statement, "Yes it is." The more people hear themselves say something, the more they believe it. It would be more therapeutic for the nurse to restate, "You feel it's your fault that you miscarried," or question "What's happened to make you feel this way?" thus giving the client the encouragement to share without having to defend. When a helper agrees or disagrees with a client, the helper assumes responsibility for evaluating ideas, feelings, and actions of the client. This responsibility therapeutically belongs to the client.

Defending. When a client criticizes and the care giver defends, communication is blocked. It is virtually impossible for even the most sensitive and caring of nurses to meet the needs of all their clients during an 8-hour shift. There will be complaints. Some are justified, and some are not. When these are voiced to nurses on the same shift, defense is likely to occur because the recipient of the criticism often knows if there was an omission or commission and the reason behind it. When complaints are voiced to nurses on another shift, they are less likely to defend and more willing to agree since it is difficult to appreciate a situation in which one is not involved. Either way, communication is hampered. Clients are encouraged to keep their negative comments to themselves or to wait until the next shift and play one shift of nurses against the others. When complaints are voiced, it is more therapeutic to acknowledge the client's feelings without agreeing, disagreeing, or making excuses. This leaves both the client and the nurse open to explore and remedy the problem:

CLIENT: I've never had such bad nursing care.
NURSE: You've had bad nursing care?
CLIENT: I put on my call light and no one ever answers it.
NURSE: You sound frustrated because your call light isn't answered.
CLIENT: Well, I guess I shouldn't say never, you came right in, but some of the time, mainly in the evening, it stays on a long time.
NURSE: Your call light is on longer in the evening?
CLIENT: Yes, especially when I'm hurting. Maybe it just seems like it's longer because of the pain.

This nurse was able to determine that the client experienced more pain in the evening after her visitors had left and that sometimes when she wanted to report this pain, her call light was not promptly answered. This information was given to the evening nurse, who commented, "She's probably right. Once in awhile, things get a bit hectic in the evening and we're not able to answer a light immediately. I'll talk to her and see if we can't work something out." In their discussion it was concluded that the delays occurred between 8 PM and 10 PM. The medication nurse agreed to check on the client more frequently during these hours, and the client was encouraged to ask for her medication before the pain was severe. Because of the open attitude of the care givers, a complaint that originally included all nursing care was pinpointed to a few incidents in the evening and was corrected. Had the nurses defended, agreed, or offered excuses, the client would have been convinced that her nursing care was terrible. Care givers are less tempted to defend when they remember that the more words used to defend an action, the more unnecessary was the action.

Inappropriate phrases. Clichés, empty reassurances, and generalizations are phrases that fit all stressful situations, but therapeutically they are appropriate for none. Examples of such inappropriate phrases include "It's probably for the best." "The Lord only gives us what He thinks we can handle." "You'll be back to normal in no time." "It's God's will." "You have nothing to worry about." "I know how you feel." "Everything's going to be fine." "You'll get over it." "It'll be better tomorrow." The list could go on and on. These overworked sentences are often prompted by an anxious situation in which an individual does not know what else to say. Most people mean well when they use these phrases; however, such general responses tend to ignore or minimize the uniqueness of feelings. Instead of communicating understanding, clichés, empty reassurances, and generalizations communicate a lack of understanding and a lack of interest in learning more about the situation.

Practicing communication techniques

Listening and responding skills must be practiced before they can be used therapeutically in a helping relationship. It is useful to practice the role of the helper as well as experiencing the role of the client, and role playing is a good way to begin. Rather than dealing with personal problems, participants should pick a topic that is general and nonthreatening. Tape-recorded and videotaped practice sessions are an invaluable teaching tool that is challenging and exciting. During replay participants are encouraged to stop the tape at any time and share what they were thinking or feeling at the particular moment. The client can share what the helper said or did that was helpful or harmful, whereas the helper can evaluate what he or she would do differently if the session were to be redone. Initial comments center around the way the participants look and sound, the later attention is directed toward behavior and technique. The following comments are frequently heard: ''I asked a million questions.'' ''When the client gets upset, I try to smooth things over.'' ''I anticipated what he was going to say and then said it for him.'' ''I forgot to zero in on feelings.'' ''At the time, I thought I was silent for an eternity; now I realize I should have kept quiet longer.'' ''I look like I'm scared to death of her.'' ''Will I ever learn to not interrupt!'' With practice the helper is able to progress from playing a role to discussion of real problems. Through observation and comments from others helpers are able to identify which of their behaviors are an asset to therapeutic communication and which of their behaviors should be discarded.

The fundamental basis of the helping relationship is therapeutic communication. Sometimes care givers become overly concerned with what to say and how to help when frequently clients just want the opportunity to share their concerns and do not expect someone else to solve their problems. Listening in itself is an effective tool that is not used enough in helping others. Sensitivity and self-awareness enable the care giver to understand both content and feelings and respond in a reflective way that helps clients to clarify their thinking. By communicating respect for clients and their values, helpers encourage them to use their own strengths and capabilities to act and overcome obstacles to the best of their abilities. Listening and responding are the corner-stone of effective helping, which depends on a genuine, empathic relationship and communication skills that all care givers possess and need only to improve.

UNDERSTANDING ANGER

Of all the behaviors within the adaptive process, anger is the most likely to block communication. Rather than being considered an expression of an unmet need or a frustrated goal, anger is often viewed as a personal threat that prompts retaliation. When this potent expression of anxiety and frustration is misunderstood, it spreads like an epidemic, affecting innocent people along the way. Instead of reacting to anger, health care personnel can learn to respond in a way that assists the client in identifying the cause of the anger. Once this is determined, energies can then be directed toward coping with the problem.

Defining anger

Anxiety and frustration produce energy, and only so much energy can be accumulated by an individual before a saturation point is reached. Once this occurs, additional input cannot be received without some compensating output, which may be manifested in the form of anger. Anger consists of four factors: (1) a goal that is blocked, a reduction in self-respect, or expectations that are not met, (2) a powerless feeling of being unable to produce an effect, which is a part of the concept of anxiety, (3) powerlessness changed to feelings or actions of power directed against the object, a substitute, or the self, and (4) the subsequent feelings of relief.[6] Although anger and hostility are frequently seen together, anger is usually short-lived and contains an element of powerlessness, whereas hostility has a destructive component that may be more enduring. Both emotions are normal behaviors within the adaptive process, and they reveal a sense of frustration from having needs unmet or goals obstructed.

Society determines appropriate ways of expressing anger. The child uses play to vent anger. Spectators at sports scream and yell at the players or shout at the umpire or referee. The hospitalized person is not immune to anger; the problem is finding an acceptable way of dispersing this energy. Although it is considered therapeutic for the hospitalized child to express anger, care givers are less accepting of the adult client who vents anxiety through angry outbursts. These emotions are often treated as something to be prevented rather than symptoms to be dealt with. The following excerpt from a letter illustrates the need to recognize anger as a symptom rather than a problem:

A crazy Hindoo is my Dr. here but we don't get along. He hasn't said anything to me for three weeks which suits me fine. They have quite a few foreign Drs. here that don't speak so you can understand them. This Hindoo is trying to give me tranquilizer pills but I haven't taken them. If the nurse hangs around I just put them in front of my teeth and spit them out. I have a whole bottle full of them.

A failure to understand creates anxiety that in turn may be reflected in hostile or angry behavior. To treat the behavior and ignore the underlying problem is poor medical management. The treatment for blocked communication is understanding, and understanding can best be achieved through human interaction rather than pharmaceutical action.

The angry client

When a previously healthy individual is confronted with illness or injury, a tremendous amount of stress is experienced. The individual is thrust into a dependency role with hopes and expectations that may not be met. Being sick, limited, disabled, or disfigured is a very threatening experience, and anxiety is produced whenever a situation is perceived as threatening. The powerlessness of anxiety may be masked by defense mechanisms of anger that the individual is likely to experience because of the illness and in response to the illness.

The experience of hospitalization adds to the anxiety of illness. Amidst uniformity and standardization, the client becomes one of a series of cases to be treated. Routine aspects of hospitalization reinforce that the hospital is an impersonal and complex system. For example, the necessary checking of arm bands for identification points out that the client is one of many and that care must be taken or mistakes can be made. Although the client interacts with numerous medical personnel, the majority of these conversations are superficial and centered around the client's physiological function. One hospitalized child kept track of the number of people that had been in his room during the day. By 5 P.M. the count had reached 141, and each person had asked, "How are you feeling?" When this number was questioned, the child produced the paper on which he had kept the traffic tally, and the child's mother verified the accuracy of his figures.[4]

The experience of illness and hospitalization creates anxiety that may take the form of anger. This anger may be turned toward the self or dissipated into the environment.

Internalized anger

Because it is socially unacceptable to express anger overtly, these energies are often turned inward. Some clients avoid their own feelings and withdraw; others create indirect means of coping. The hospital experience recreates childhood feelings of being weak and inadequate, surrounded by authority figures. Illness transfers individuals from a role of independence to one in which others decide when to eat, have visitors, and go to bed. In some cases going to the bathroom also involves permission. This dependent status may intensify anxiety and the need for love and approval. In an effort to please the care giver, the individual may assume the "good client" role of not being too demanding or too dependent. This creates a particularly difficult situation because it requires the person to control behavior when fears and tensions are great. Clients may accept the model client role

"I am not a big brave man. I'm a scared little kid, and I want my mommy."

Illustration by Tom Weinman.

because they do not want to risk offending health care workers. Respect for health professionals may prevent any questioning by the client, and some clients are not aware that they have any say about what happens to them. Care givers may also encourage this compliant role because it helps to maintain the efficiency of hospital routine.

Feelings of powerlessness, regression, and dependency reflect a threat to oneself, and the client may be totally unaware that these feelings are causing anger or hostile reactions. The problem becomes even more inaccessible if the individual considers these emotions unacceptable and represses them. Before the underlying problem can be identified, the person needs to know that these emotions are normal and that it is alright to express them. Care givers can facilitate this expression with comments such as, "It must be difficult always having someone tell you what to do and when to do it," or, "So many things have changed in your life—what's the most difficult for you?" Sometimes clients test the water with statements such as, "Things aren't going so well." By using reflexive responses the care giver may encourage the client to continue: "You sound discouraged because you feel things aren't going so well." Sitting down without saying anything communicates, "I have the time to listen to you." Clients often feel relief in finding a care giver who accepts and encourages expression of these feelings, and sometimes just talking about them helps to disperse energy that otherwise might take the form of anger.

■ Mr. E., a produce manager at a large grocery store, had been hospitalized several weeks for treatment of bacterial endocarditis. He was a quiet man who accepted limited activities without complaint. One morning during his bath he commented, "I feel like a wilted piece of lettuce on the produce floor."

The nurse wasn't sure if he was talking about his loss of energy or perhaps even death, so she asked, "What does it feel like to be a wilted piece of lettuce on the produce floor?"

His comment was somewhat of a surprise. "It feels like I'm being stepped on by everyone, and I'm helpless to prevent it."

The nurse realized that beneath the mask of the perfect client was an individual very frustrated by powerlessness and asked, "How can I help you get off the floor?"

His response was hesitant. "By leaving me alone for awhile."

The nurse gathered the bath things. "Would an hour help?"

Mr. E. gave her a surprised look, brightened, and responded, "Really? That would be nice. I'm very tired and would like to rest."

Through discussion with others involved in his care, it was determined that Mr. E. had never openly objected to anything that was done to or for him since his admission to the hospital. Medical treatment and hospital routine were accepted as though he had no choice. Whenever an option was given, he always said, "Whatever's best for you," and left the decision to the care giver. The staff had unknowingly reinforced Mr. E.'s powerlessness by making all of the decisions. Once this was realized, it was determined that whenever possible, Mr. E. would be encouraged to make choices and take responsibility for some of his own care. The staff reinforced his assertiveness with their prompt response. When a request was made that could not be carried out, he received valid reasons for why it could not be done. On the rare occasions when he was able to express anger, he quickly apologized. Care givers stressed that it was normal to feel and to express anger. One nurse commented, "If you were the nurse and I was the client, would you understand if I was angry?" Mr. E. smiled and answered, "I'd understand if you felt as bad as I do."

Mr. E. progressed and was able to be dismissed from the hospital to continue his intravenous treatment at home. He left behind a note to a special nurse: "Thanks for helping me off the floor." It was signed, "Mr. Lettuce." _____

Externalized anger

Anger is a process of coping with a threat, with the intensity of the anger associated with the degree of threat. Even those clients who are critically ill reach a point when they no longer are able to internalize their anxiety. This built-up energy is dissipated externally, producing a feeling of power and strength that is quite the opposite of the feeling of anxiety for which it is substituted. Because society disapproves of outright behavioral expression of anger, it may be channeled through demanding or uncooperative behavior. Expression may also be in the form of sarcasm, verbal attack, or rudeness. This energy may be directed at members of the health care team or even family members, with the recipient of the anger not necessarily the cause.

Since health professionals may remind the client of illness, it is not uncommon that illness-created anxiety be displaced on them.

■ Mr. Frank was one of those clients that makes nurses glad that they can go home at the end of the shift. One minute he was complaining and demanding to the point that we were all ready to choke him, and the next minute he would withdraw and we would feel guilty. We knew that our responses contributed to his behavior, and still he continued to hook us with his behavior. I guess we cooperated by allowing ourselves to be manipulated. Part of this was because he was young and his prognosis was poor.

During team conference we decided to try and remain objective with Mr. Frank. When we felt ourselves becoming angry, we would leave his room until we were cool, calm, and collected again. The head nurse asked for someone to accept the challenge of being his primary nurse, and I volunteered.

The first couple of days were not so difficult, but then he doubled his efforts at being unpleasant. I did a lot of counting to 10 and had to leave the room several times. Finally, I leveled with him, and said that my getting angry and then feeling guilty because of my anger did nothing to help him. I even went so far as to say, "I can understand why you're angry."

He went into a rage and shouted, "You understand? You all understand nothing!" When he had calmed down a little, he took two pieces of paper from his writing tablet and asked if I would take the paper home and make two lists. His instructions were explicit. "On one paper list five activities that you enjoy the most, and on the other list the five most significant people in your life—number one is the most important and number five the least."

I did not question his instructions but simply took the paper, agreed to make the lists, and left the room.

The next day he told me to look at my list of activities and asked if number five was something I did alone or with someone else.

I told him that the last activity on my list was tennis.

He continued, "Pretend that you can't play tennis anymore. You're too sick. Mark it off with a pencil. Now do you think you will be seeing much of your former tennis partner?"

I scratched out tennis and after thinking it over for awhile realized that the only thing my tennis partner and I had in common was tennis. Mr. Frank instructed me to do the same with number four and number three on my activity list.

I tried to make a joke to cover my discomfort, but he interrupted, "Almost every day, you people come in here and make me mark something off my list."

Then he asked if I had ever had anyone special to me die and how I had felt. I shared that my father had died when I was younger and that I was devastated. He told me to take out my list of significant others and asked, "When was the last time you told these people that they are special to you?"

I looked at my list and realized that with the exception of my husband and our children I could not remember when I shared my feelings with the others. He did not wait for me to answer, but continued, "I don't have much time to tell my people how special they are. I'm on about number ten of my list, trying to work my way toward the top five. Outside I'm saying to them, 'You're special, I love you,' and inside I'm saying, 'Good-bye.' You said you were devastated having to say good-bye to your dad when he died. I'm having to say good-bye to a lot more than just one person."

I sat without speaking. No anger. No guilt. In a healthy body I had thought I understood. We all did. No wonder he tried to punish us. We understood textbook psychology and stages, but reality was too real to comprehend. I did not have any words. Finally, I reached over and squeezed his hand.

He turned toward me and smiled, "That's the nicest thing you've ever said." _____

Helping professionals agree that it is difficult to take care of the angry, hostile client, but most contend that they would rather deal with this kind of behavior than have a client remain silent and turn away. Although care givers may complain in terms of time and energy spent on trying to please the person, the underlying frustration comes from not being able to please the person. The frustration created from perceived lack of effectiveness may be masked with inappropriate niceness or avoidance. This behavior only magnifies the problem because clients must then deal with rejection without the opportunity to know what is behind it. They may conclude that they were right or that no one cares without being aware of their own contribution to this self-fulfilling prophecy.

A great amount of tact allows the nurse to express feelings without burdening or attacking the client. "I" statements that express internal thoughts and feelings, such as, "I really feel frustrated . . ." are less threatening than "you" statements that attack and prompt defensiveness, such as, "You make me feel frustrated." If the nurse can openly and honestly share personal feelings and reactions with statements such as, "I really feel frustrated that everything I do seems wrong; can you help me help you?" clients may be more willing to disclose the cause of their behavior. Revealing authentic feelings may prevent anger and resentment from developing into maladaptive behaviors.

Rather than directing anger at members of the care team, clients may displace their anger toward significant others who are considered less threatening and less apt to retaliate. A client's spouse may be the recipient of this excess energy because the role of a spouse is to love in sickness and in health. On a cognitive level family members may understand that the anger is because of the illness but may still have difficulty not responding to displaced anger on an affective level.

In addition to dealing with the frustration and anger expressed by a loved one, family members have their own feelings to deal with. There are times when health professionals inadvertently contribute to anxiety by failing to explain everything to both the client and the client's family members.

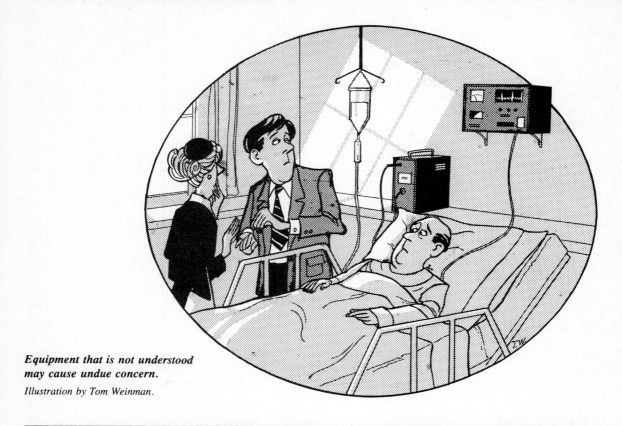

*Equipment that is not understood
may cause undue concern.*

Illustration by Tom Weinman.

Explanations should include information about the
client's condition and what is being done to the
person. Monitors, suction machines, and something as simple as an intravenous set-up can be
very frightening to those who do not know the
reason for these devices. This fear and concern is
often apparent when family members enter a
client's room. They walk hesitantly, tense their
muscles, and move as far away as possible from
foreboding equipment. They are reluctant to touch
their loved one for fear of disconnecting something
that might be keeping the person alive. If family
members are anxious, this anxiety may be passed
on to the client, who certainly does not need additional stress.

Care givers sometimes fail to notice a family
member's need for emotional support or recognize
the person's exhaustion. At the time of crisis, all
energies are focused on the individual who is injured or ill, and family members may hesitate to
ask for help because they do not want to be a bother.
They also experience a dichotomy between the
need for support and a willingness to accept support: they hope that everything is going to be fine,
and reality questions this pretense. Sometimes
loved ones sit by the client's bed hour after hour
while their own coping energies slowly deplete.
They use all their strength offering encouragement
and support while sheltering the pain and emotional
suffering they experience. The following example
depicts illness from a family member's point of
view.

■ Mrs. N. stayed at her elderly husband's bedside day and night. His condition was poor, and she was afraid to leave for fear that he would die while she was gone. Although a reclining chair was in the room, she was unable to sleep soundly at night and spent most of her time sitting next to her husband, who seldom responded. The more exhausted Mrs. N. became, the more she complained to the staff about her husband's care. Finally a nurse sat down beside her, took her hand, and shared her concern. "You look so tired, why don't you go home and rest for a few hours?"

"I can't," the older woman answered, "he might get worse."

The nurse continued, "I'm afraid if you don't get some rest, you'll end up sick."

"I am tired," Mrs. N. admitted. "Can you promise that he won't get worse if I go?"

The nurse was honest in her reply. "I can't be sure that his condition won't change while you're gone, but we'll keep a close eye on your husband and if there's any change, you'll be called right away."

The older woman hesitated and finally agreed to go home for a rest.

In this situation the woman's lack of sleep diminished her adaptive energy, and the anxieties surrounding her husband's poor health were displaced on to the staff. Although she had wanted to go home to rest, she was afraid to make this decision alone and then risk having to deal with her guilt feelings in the event that her husband should die while she was gone. Since the nurse shared in the decision-making process, it was easier for Mrs. N. to leave her husband's bedside.

The nurse asked other team members to help her keep a close watch on Mr. N. She also made a notation of Mrs. N.'s telephone number and taped this on the front of Mr. N.'s chart with instructions that his wife be called in the event that his condition changed. These two steps ensured that the nurse's promise would be kept in the event that she was involved in an emergency elsewhere. Mrs. N. returned to the hospital after 2 hours and was pleased to hear that her husband's condition was not any worse. With encouragement and support from the staff, she gradually increased her time away from the hospital until she was able to spend some nights at her home. A week later Mr. N. died quietly in his sleep. As promised, the nurse called his wife, who responded, "He's gone, isn't he?" The nurse verified that Mr. N. had died quietly in his sleep. She called a cab for Mrs. N. and met her when she arrived at the hospital. Mrs. N. shared, "I've been saying good-bye to him this last week, and I've been practicing being without him. It hurts, but I'll be okay." _____

Without help, some individuals simply cannot deal with the emotional repercussions of a family member's illness. When breaks in communication occur, caring professionals may be able to provide support for resolution and adjustment before these feelings become displaced onto the client, other family members, or medical personnel. Time spent with a client's loved ones is a vital part of client care, for indirectly it is the client who benefits.

Some of the most stressful professions are in the health care field. Members of the health professions experience frustration when they cannot help, when cure is not possible, and when caring becomes difficult. Being a member of the helping professions demands an immense and constant emotional commitment that requires both personal and professional support. There are times when this support can best be provided by not responding personally to a colleague's displaced anger. This is exemplified in the following incident experienced by a nurse who worked the day shift in a small, Midwestern hospital:

■ Following morning report I began my nursing rounds. At the end of the hall I noticed Dr. D., and as soon as he saw me he started yelling about something that had happened on the night shift. Fortunately, I hadn't worked the night shift and had a good night's sleep instead. I knew that Dr. D. wasn't angry at me, but I also knew that he was upset about something that happened earlier. Finally he slowed down, and I said, "I know that you're not angry at me, but if it helps, it's okay."

He stopped short, as if he had just realized where he was and what he was doing. Tears filled the corners of his eyes. Slowly he reached into his hip pocket and took out his handkerchief. After wiping his eyes and blowing his nose he returned the handkerchief to his pocket. "I'm sorry," he said. "I'm okay now. Two of my favorite patients died last night." He turned and walked down the hall to see the rest of his clients.

I have often wondered what would have happened if I had taken his anger literally or personally. I have also wondered how many people have allowed me to vent my displaced anxiety before it exploded onto someone more vulnerable, such as the client. _____

All behavior is meaningful and must not be considered a stage or a phase but rather a symptom that needs attention. When anger is considered a symptom of a problem rather than the problem itself, it loses its destructiveness. Anger requires cooperation to exist. No one can make another person angry, people make this decision for themselves. When confronted with angry or anger-provoking situations, people can decide to respond with anger or use an alternate behavior. Anger reciprocated with anger is similar to fire—it finally dies out, but first it spreads.

A PATIENT'S BILL OF RIGHTS

Too many people feel that once they have been admitted to the hospital, they lose both their rights and their clothes. Hospitalized adults frequently hide their fears and questions behind a facade of calmness and trust when they would be better off to show their concerns and ask their questions. Some of the most stressful events associated with hospitalization are caused by a health professional's lack of communication with a client or a failure on the part of the client to understand what was communicated.[7] Some clients become compliant because they do not know what is expected of them, what they can expect from others, and what they can object to.

In 1973 the American Hospital Association published "A Patient's Bill of Rights." The intent of the document was to make both clients and members of the health care team aware of the rights a client could expect, and implementing these rights depended on effective communication between health professionals and clients. Information contained in the bill was to be posted in hospitals, distributed to employees, and given to clients on admission. In the case of a minor or an incompetent adult, information was to be conveyed to the family member or the client's guardian. In reality the goal has fallen short.

Until recently individuals were willing to leave everything in the hands of their physicians. The age of public awareness and consumer rights and action has arrived. This awareness revolution has produced increasing confrontations between consumer and provider, making a dramatic impact on health care. The ultimate confrontation is in the form of malpractice suits, which are on the rise. It is time to bring out "A Patient's Bill of Rights," post it in hospitals, hand it out to care givers, and make certain that clients know about their rights. By making this bill public, care givers are reminded that clients have rights, and clients are encouraged to assert these rights. Clients need not be intimidated by hospital routines, procedures, or the health care worker, and if health professionals provide proper, humane, and equitable care, they need not be intimidated by "A Patient's Bill of Rights."*

1. *The patient has the right to considerate and respectful care.* This involves courteous behavior such as not being called "pops" or "sweetie" or being treated in a condescending manner. Considerate and respectful care includes being treated with dignity while being provided basic human rights of safety and freedom from unnecessary chemical and physical restraints. This equitable and humane treatment must be available without discrimination to all people.

2. *The patient has the right to obtain from his phy-*

_____

*Reprinted with the permission of the American Hospital Association. Copyright 1975.

sician complete current information concerning his diagnosis, treatment, and prognosis in terms the patient can be reasonably expected to understand. When it is not medically advisable to give such information to the patient, the information should be made available to an appropriate person in his behalf. He has the right to know, by name, the physician responsible for coordinating his care. Clients have the legal right to information concerning their illness, treatment, and expected outcome. Although it is the physician's responsibility to tell the client about the diagnosis, alternatives of treatment, and prognosis, the nurse is alert to the individual's lack of understanding and is responsible for bringing this to the attention of the physician.

3. *The patient has the right to receive from his physician information necessary to give informed consent prior to the start of any procedure and/or treatment. Except in emergencies, such information for informed consent should include but not necessarily be limited to the specific procedure and/or treatment, the medically significant risks involved, and the probable duration of incapacitation. Where medically significant alternatives for care or treatment exist, or when the patient requests information concerning medical alternatives, the patient has the right to such information. The patient also has the right to know the name of the person responsible for the procedures and/or treatment.* Informed consent is the legal right to understand what is involved in a procedure, the consequences, risks, options for alternative treatment, and benefits expected. This information makes it possible for the client to become a partner with the physician in the decision-making process. Any consent for treatment that is obtained by coaxing or coercion or when the client is sedated is considered invalid. A client also has the right to withdraw a consent at any point and be assured that treatment will be prevented or discontinued if it was already started. Many malpractice suits involve an element of informed consent, such as when individuals sue because of complications experienced of which they were not forewarned.

4. *The patient has the right to refuse treatment to the extent permitted by law and to be informed of the medical consequences of his action.* Competent clients have the right to accept, reject, or terminate treatment without punitive action being taken against them. This right has been upheld in court.

5. *The patient has the right to every consideration of his privacy concerning his own medical care program.*

Case discussion, consultation, examination, and treatment are confidential and should be conducted discretely. Those not directly involved in his care must have the permission of the patient to be present. This ethical and legal consideration is easily overlooked in large teaching hospitals in which there may be more invasion of a client's privacy than is necessary for medical care needs. Clients have the right to refuse to submit to treatment, examination, or observation by students or those not directly involved in their care. This provision serves to remind students and faculty that behind the "case" is an individual with needs of privacy that should be met. Clients also have the right to privacy during interview, examination, and treatment and in communicating and visiting with persons of their choice. These rights should be enforced without respect to the individual's economic status or the source of payment for care.

6. *The patient has the right to expect that all communications and records pertaining to his care should be treated as confidential.* The right of confidentiality of all communication and records is a legal obligation. This confidentiality should be maintained except as otherwise provided for by law or when the client signs a written release, allowing information to be transmitted to another physician, hospital, or insurance company.

7. *The patient has the right to expect that within its capacity a hospital must make reasonable response to the request of a patient for services. The hospital must provide evaluation, service, and/or referral as indicated by the urgency of the case. When medically permissible, a patient may be transferred to another facility only after he has received complete information and explanation concerning the needs for and alternatives to such a transfer. The institution to which the patient is to be transferred must first have accepted the patient for transfer.* This right involves courteous care and is not legally binding. A hospital has an obligation to provide service that meets professional standards or to transfer the client to a hospital that can provide this service. An individual's lack of money to pay the bills may prevent admission to some hospitals. Those who are unable to depend on personal assets or private insurance and are ineligible for government-funded plans may be helped by Hill-Burton funding. Hospitals who used Hill-Burton grants to build or upgrade their facilities are required for 20 years to provide a certain percentage of free or below-cost care to people who qualify. Turning people away because of

lack of money creates moral, ethical, and sometimes legal problems.

8. *The patient has the right to obtain information as to any relationship of his hospital to other health care and educational institutions insofar as his care is concerned. The patient has the right to obtain information as to the existence of any professional relationships among individuals, by name, who are treating him.* A part of courteous care is that clients have the right to information about qualifications, names, and titles of those responsible for their care and information that might point out any conflict of interest. For example, the individual may wish to have a consultation from a physician not affiliated with the primary physician or may question a relationship between ownership and a physician's recommendation of a particular extended care facility.

9. *The patient has the right to be advised if the hospital proposes to engage in or perform human experimentation affecting his care or treatment. The patient has the right to refuse to participate in such research projects.* The client has a legal right to be protected against experimentation affecting care or treatment without informed consent. For all clients, regardless of the source of payment for their care, participation in research and experimentation should be a voluntary matter. The National Institutes of Health mandate that hospitals conducting research have institutional review committees for protection of subjects in medical research.

10. *The patient has the right to expect reasonable continuity of care. He has the right to know in advance what appointment times and physicians are available and where. The patient has the right to expect that the hospital will provide a mechanism whereby he is informed by his physician or a delegate of the physician of the patient's continuing health care requirements following discharge.* Continuity of care is another aspect of courtesy, involving the planning of a discharge program so that the client has the names of physicians, the place and time of follow-up appointments, and prescriptions for needed medication. In addition, the individual should receive adequate instruction concerning self-care and basic health needs so that an optimum level of wellness can be achieved. Discharge planning may also involve other agencies, such as the social service department and home-nursing services.

Another client aspect of continued health care that is not included in the bill has to do with the client's med-

ical record. Some hospitals allow clients to read their charts, and there are physicians who have their clients keep their own charts. Others are adamantly against allowing a person any access to their records unless subpoenaed through a malpractice suit. It is generally recognized that the information written in the client's record is the property of the individual; however, the record is the property of the hospital or physician. Several states allow clients access to their records, and the Freedom of Information Act and the Privacy Act require most federal institutions and some state hospitals to allow clients access to their records.

11. *The patient has the right to examine and receive an explanation of his bill regardless of source of payment.* Another aspect of courteous care, clients should have the right to see their hospital bill and, when they have questions, receive help in examining and understanding the charges. They also have the right to challenge these charges. The Health Care Financing Administration reported that in 1981 clients paid only 10 cents of every dollar spent on hospital care, with the remainder being paid by private insurance companies or government-supported programs. Many times the bill is never seen by the individual, who may end up with the atittude that medical care is free or cheap.

12. *The patient has the right to know what hospital rules and regulations apply to his conduct as a patient.* In addition to receiving an explanation of rules and regulations, another aspect of considerate and respectful care includes an explanation of the hospital routine. The client should be given the opportunity to ask questions and express any problems anticipated. Whenever possible, changes in the routine should be made to meet the individual's needs, and when changes cannot be permitted, the reason behind the denial should be explained. Most people are less stressed and more accepting if they know in advance what to expect and also have been given the opportunity to assert their needs and have their questions answered.

Violations of a client's rights should be reported to the physician, the proper supervisor, the hospital administrator, or through whatever channels are necessary to remedy the condition. Amidst the hospital functions of prevention, treatment, education, and research, the dignity and individuality of the person must be maintained. The hospital and members of the health care team must dare enough to care about the human rights of the individual client. This obligation begins by communicating these rights to each client and then following through by honoring these rights.

• • •

Good institutions of health care are not made by massive and impressive equipment but by the helping professionals who balance technology with the warmth and humaneness of therapeutic communication. Therapeutic communication is a process that is complex yet basic to all helping relationships. It is more than listening to what someone else is saying and responding in a way that clarifies thinking. This interaction requires sensitivity and at the same time objectivity. It involves listening as clients share their needs rather than continually telling clients what they need. Therapeutic communication psychologically supports the client until the individual can achieve maximum autonomy.

REFERENCES

1. Birdwhistell, R.: Personal correspondence.
2. Carkhuff, R., Pierce, R., and Cannon, J.: The art of helping, Amherst, Massachusetts, 1977, Human Resource Development Press.
3. De Long, R.: Individual differences in patterns of anxiety arousal, stress-relevant information and recovery from surgery, doctoral dissertation, Los Angeles, 1970, University of Southern California.
4. Eland, J., and Anderson, J.: The experience of pain in children. In Jacox, A., editor: Pain: a source book for nurses and other health professionals, Boston, 1977, Little, Brown & Co.
5. Fromm, E.: The art of loving, New York, 1956, Harper & Row, Publishers, Inc., p. 9.
6. Hays, D.: Anger: a clinical problem. In Burd, S., and Marshall, M., editors: Some clinical approaches to psychiatric nursing, New York, 1963, The Macmillan Co., Publishers.
7. Volicer, B., and Bohannon, M.: A hospital stress rating scale, Nursing Research **24:**352, 1975.
8. Whiting, J.: Patients' needs, nurses' needs, and the healing process, American Journal of Nursing **59:**661, 1959.

BIBLIOGRAPHY

Benjamin, A.: The helping interview, ed. 2, Boston, 1974, Houghton Mifflin Co.
Henrich, A., and Bernheim, K.: Responding to patients' concerns, Nursing Outlook **29:**428, July 1981.
Jourard, S.: The transparent self, ed. 2, New York, 1971, Van Nostrand Reinhold Co., Inc.
Kelly, L.: The patient's right to know, Nursing Outlook **24:**26, January, 1976.
Kiening, Sister M.: Hostility. In Carlson, C., and Blackwell, B., editors: Behavioral concepts and nursing intervention, ed. 2, Philadlphia, 1978, J.B. Lippincott Co.
Nierenberg, J., and Janovic, F.: The hospital experience, Indianapolis, 1978, The Bobbs-Merrill Co., Inc.
Pavalon, E.: Human rights and health care law, New York, 1980, American Journal of Nursing Co.

2 · Nonverbal communication

Actions speak louder . . .

Illustration by Tom Weinman.

An introduction to nonverbal communication would not be complete without the story of Clever Hans, the horse who brought nonverbal behavior into acute awareness. Mr. Von Osten purchased Hans in Berlin in 1900 and trained the horse to count and relay the answers by tapping his front hoof. Rewarded with carrots and bread, Hans became an avid pupil and a quick learner. Each new concept was coded into numbers, and with the help of teaching apparatus, he was taught advanced math, the German alphabet, words, colors, and musical tones. To the delight of audiences all over the world Hans accurately tapped out answers to questions of all kinds.

Although other clever animals of that time were obviously and intentionally cued by their trainer, Hans' cleverness did not depend on the presence of his master, Mr. Von Osten. Almost anyone could present a question to this unique horse, and chances were good that the correct answer would be forthcoming. He became known as Clever Hans because it appeared that, indeed, this horse was capable of rational thinking.

In 1914 an investigating committee was formed to determine whether any deceit was involved in Hans' performances. Nothing in the way of movements or expressions that might have served as a signal to the horse could be discovered. The commission concluded that no trickery was involved.

Three months later a second commission was appointed. This time two individuals whispered different numbers to Hans, and he was instructed to add the numbers—an answer that was unknown to the experimenters, to Mr. Von Osten, or to the onlookers. Hans failed. His cleverness was further reduced when he was fitted with large blinders that prevented him from seeing his questioners. Ultimately it was understood that Clever Hans was clever only when someone in his visual field knew the answer to the question and subconsciously and nonverbally alerted him when to start or stop tapping.

During the long periods of training, this horse had learned on his own to attend to the slightest muscle movement—the raising of eyebrows or the dilation of nostrils—as a signal to begin or end tapping. Even after the cuing system was understood and questioners consciously tried to suppress sending the crucial visual messages, Hans was still cued unintentionally.[4]

The phenomenon of nonverbal communication, so effectively demonstrated by Clever Hans, is experienced consciously or subconsciously each time people interact. Even when an attempt is made to suppress these movements, they tend to escape and communicate. It is estimated that as much as two thirds of the time, verbal and nonverbal messages are incongruent, and when this discrepancy occurs, more credence is apt to be placed on the nonverbal message. Psychologists maintain that between 55 and 65 percent of conveyed messages are via nonverbal cues. Obviously the human aspect of communication is vital.

At no other time is accurate communication more important than when health or life is in jeopardy. There is a preponderance of nonverbal messages in a setting such as an emergency room as verbal and vocal sounds blend with silence, body movements, gestures, and posture all sending their messages. The importance of these cues becomes apparent when one observes the frantic mother who is desperately trying to explain what has happened to her injured child or when one becomes cognizant of the silence as the frightened spouse reaches toward his wife when she is quickly ushered out of the treatment room.

This chapter is designed to emphasize the non-verbal aspect of communication and at the same time stress the interdependence of verbal and non-verbal messages. By becoming aware of nonverbal cues in everyday life, helping professionals can use this perception in therapeutic interactions in which accurate communication is a vital component of helping.

COMMUNICATION STRUCTURE

Communication is an integral process involving both verbal and nonverbal messages with one essential to and completely dependent on the other. One of the most fascinating components of non-verbal communication is called kinesic behavior, or body motion. Without saying a word an individual conveys information, attitudes, and feelings with body movement, facial expression, eye behavior, and posture. These nonverbal messages serve to repeat, contradict, clarify, regulate, or take the place of verbal messages. They have advantages over words in that they have a stronger and more immediate impact, and they are effective outside full conscious awareness. A fleeting look of anger may last only one fifth of a second, barely perceptible to the conscious awareness, yet fully acknowledged subconsciously. Whereas nonverbal cues may or may not support the verbal message, actions do speak louder than words.

Kinesics can be viewed as having the same structure as spoken language, with gestures like words combining into clusters to form a nonverbal sentence. Just as a change in one letter can change the meaning of a word and the same word can have a different meaning in another culture, body movements also acquire meaning in their particular contexts. A congratulatory pat on the rump of a football player who has just scored a touchdown is an acceptable gesture, whereas the same action at a different time and place might be frowned on. Omitting a nonverbal act, such as refusing to shake hands, constitutes its own message, just as small differences in the same nonverbal act—the direction of a person's gaze—can change the meaning.

Paralanguage is usually considered under non-verbal communication although it includes vocal cues surrounding words as well as the silent pauses that separate messages. Rather than dealing with the verbal content of a message, paralanguage deals with the way something is said. The client who hesitantly responds in a whining voice, "Well, (sigh) I guess, uh, I'm okay," uses paralanguage to convey a message that is quite different from the verbal message.

Although the interdependence between verbal and nonverbal communication is recognized, it is also understood that comprehension of nonverbal cues and paralanguage precedes understanding of their relationship in the verbal context. Therefore aspects of nonverbal communication will be emphasized in this chapter and studied within the total communication process.

DEVELOPMENTAL PERSPECTIVES

Verbal behavior has been studied for over 2000 years, whereas the study of nonverbal communication began primarily in the 1950s and grew in the 1960s. A popularized account of nonverbal skills (Fast's *Body Language*) became a best-seller in the 1970s, followed by a steady stream of books on nonverbal skills pertaining to everything from sales to sex to assertion. Too often these books are misleading, especially when a particular behavior is presented outside the context in which it occurs (for example, arms folded across the body could indicate defensiveness or may simply be a position for comfort or warmth).

This new interest has prompted a field of research on the nonverbal aspect of communication. Laboratory experiments are conducted in a reconstructed atmosphere relevant to the study so that the experiment is not artificial or does not produce spurious phenomena with important features of the real world omitted. Research usually takes place in a large, furnished room with a one-way screen from which videotape recordings can be made. Although the subjects are aware that it is a laboratory, they are not told the purpose of the experiment until afterward. They are asked to take part in a conversation, an interview, or some other familiar social task while recordings of their body movements are made.

It became apparent that experimenters, and everyone else for that matter, differed in their clarity and effectiveness of sending and receiving nonverbal messages. In 1974 the Profile of Nonverbal Sensitivity (PONS) test was developed to measure sensitivity to nonverbal messages. This test revealed that younger people were less sensitive to nonverbal messages than older people, and females were better than males at detecting these cues. However, men working in or trained for occupations considered to require nurturant, artistic, or expressive behavior tended to score as well as women on the PONS test. Actors, artists, interior and industrial designers, teachers, and members of the helping professions were among those more sensitive to nonverbal messages, and this ability was independent of general intelligence or test-taking ability.[5]

At exactly what age this ability appears is not known since the youngest group tested with PONS were third-graders, and these girls were already scoring higher than boys. The developers of the PONS test offered the following hypothesis for the females' higher scores:

One purely social explanation would derive from the premise that women are socially oppressed. If women, as well as other oppressed groups, must "read" the expressions of others with great accuracy in order to advance or even survive, then they could become nonverbally sensitive at an early age.[5]

The fact that older people are sensitive to nonverbal messages is particularly noteworthy to care givers since elderly people are admitted to general hospitals over twice the rate of young adults and account for a significant number of the outpatient visits to health care facilities. One wonders if elderly people become more astute at perceiving nonverbal messages because of experience or if this is another area in which nonverbal skills are developed as an aid to survival.

Scientists have long contended that the left hemi-sphere is involved in verbal, analytical, and objective functions. Recently, there has been accumulating evidence that the right hemisphere is involved in nonverbal, creative, and subjective functions. Therefore a peson with a dominant right hemisphere might be more perceptive to nonverbal cues. During mental activity there is consistent movement of the eyes to the right or to the left depending on which side of the person's brain is dominant. Because the right side of the brain controls the left side of the body and the left side of the brain the right, consistently shifting the eyes to the left during reflective thought would indicate right cerebral control and therefore more acute nonverbal perception.

If this theory is correct, it would be safe to assume that leaders who gain their positions through public impressions—based in part on nonverbal messages—either have dominant right brains or have received instruction to compensate for a lack of nonverbal know-how. It is well known that politicians are schooled in the use of nonverbal cues, and as much attention is given to the way they present a message as to the contents. Television has become the political arena, and according to the Nielsen Media Research, more than 55 million households watched the October 28, 1980, presidential election debate. The candidate who knows how to communicate nonverbally is at an advantage in capturing the public's vote. A frightening example of the role of television in politics is found in McGinnis' book *The Selling of the President 1968:*

Television seems particularly useful to the politician who can be charming but lacks ideas. . . . His personality is what the viewers want to share. He need be neither statesman nor crusader; he must only show up on time. . . . The T.V. candidate, then, is measured not against his predecessors—not against a standard of performance established by two centuries of democracy—but against Mike Douglas. . . . Style becomes substance. The medium is the massage and the masseur gets the votes.[3]

As hospitals and clinics use closed circuit television as a medium for client teaching, the nonverbal actions of the educator play an important role in health education. Many facilities have the equipment to make their own videotaped presentations and therefore are able to save on the cost of software and create teaching material unique to their own setting. These advantages will be lost if the educator is tense and nervous about being on television and nonverbally relays this message. One can picture the client tuning in to a preoperative teaching program, hearing reassuring words, and watching a wide-eyed nurse who looks as though she has just witnessed her first operation. Videotape is an excellent teaching tool, but first it should teach the educator before teaching the client.

As interest in nonverbal communication is growing, recognition is being given to the importance of this aspect of communication. From infancy to old age people send wordless messages that range from the tenderness of touch to the power of politics. Heightened awareness of nonverbal cues helps to ensure accurate understanding of the total message.

REPERTOIRE OF NONVERBAL BEHAVIOR

There are two opposing views on the origin of nonverbal behaviors. One side states that these behaviors are instinctive and innate, whereas the other maintains that they are culturally taught, imposed, or imitated. In the cultures studied few nonberbal cues have been found to be universal, and within one culture the same cue has a different meaning at different times. For instance, a smile can portray friendliness or flirtation in one situation and embarrassment in another or even serve as a warning or appeasement. The dichotomy of nature versus nurture is without solid scientific evidence to substantiate either side. To follow one dimension and exclude another would fail to realize the interactions and interrelationships between the biological, psychological, and cultural dimensions of behavior. Since nonverbal expressions appear to be specific to the situation as well as to the culture, the following discussion of nonverbal cues includes those used primarily within the North American culture.

Nonverbal behaviors occur in many types, and although many are used in conjunction with words, others are completely unrelated to verbal behavior. In an effort to make some order of the vast system of nonverbal behavior, Ekman and Friesen[1] have outlined five categories for classifying nonverbal behavioral acts: emblems, illustrators, affect displays, regulators, and adaptors. These are discussed here in an attempt to distinguish the different messages that these nonverbal acts directly or indirectly communicate.

Emblems

Nonverbal gestures that can be translated into a word or two without changing the information conveyed are classified as emblems. These movements are used intentionally within the person's awareness and with a deliberate effort to communicate. Like words, emblems are learned, and the time and place to use an emblem are usually chosen with some care. They serve to repeat, substitute, or contradict some part of the accompanying verbal message and are most often used when verbal exchange is prevented by noise, external circumstances, distance, agreement, or organic impairment. Examples of emblems include sign language used by the deaf, signals between hunters, and gestures exchanged by students in a classroom when the teacher's back is turned. When used as a substitute for words or to contradict words, the gesture is considered to be more effective or safer.

Within the North American culture the approximately 100 emblems with specific, agreed-on meanings are primarily shown by the face and hands. The thumb and index finger drawn into a circle is interpreted in the United States as meaning A-okay. In some cultures this same nonverbal expression has sexual connotations. Different cultures seem to have emblems for similar classes of messages, including insults, directions, greetings, departures, certain responses, physical state, and emotion. Although the classes are similar, the emblems may be entirely different.

Facial emblems are more dramatic than spontaneous facial expressions. For example, an exaggerated drop of the jaw or an overdrawn smile may indicate surprise or happiness. A wrinkled nose may communicate, ''I'm disgusted!'' or, ''It stinks!'' Shrugged shoulders or palms turned upward might convey, ''I don't know,'' ''I'm helpless,'' or ''I'm uncertain.'' Clients may use emblems when communicating discomfort. A holding or rubbing gesture is sometimes combined with exaggerated facial features showing forehead furrowed, eyebrows drawn together, eyes narrowed, mouth drawn to the side or downward—often more extreme on the side of the discomfort.

Children understand more emblems than they can demonstrate, and by the age of 4 years most children are able to interpret the following: ''yes,'' ''no,'' ''stop,'' ''come here,'' ''quiet,'' ''naughty,'' ''good-bye,'' ''two,'' ''out,'' ''I won't listen,'' blowing a kiss, ''hello,'' ''I'm tired,'' ''I don't know,'' and, ''I won't do it.''

Illustrators

Illustrators are primarily hand movements that are directly linked to or accompany speech and are used to emphasize or illustrate what is said verbally. Unlike emblems, illustrators have no precise semantic content. They are learned and are culturally specific. Although they are used intentionally to help communicate, their use is not as explicit as emblems. Illustrators tend to accent or emphasize a particular word or phrase, and they also serve to repeat, substitute, or contradict verbal information. Used more in face-to-face conversation, illustrators may even be evident when individuals talk over the telephone or an intercom. Since children primarily learn illustrators by imitating others, variations in using these behaviors occur because of differences in socialization.

People who are excited and enthusiastic may illustrate more. When a person is demoralized, discouraged, tired, or feeling dominated in a formal interaction, the rate of illustrators is less than usual for that person. A depressed client uses very few hand gestures, as though the message is not worth emphasis or the energy to do so is lacking. When

people are at a loss for words, hands may illustrate the message for them. There are individuals who rely so heavily on illustrators that they have great difficulty talking if their hands are not free to join in the conversation. As one man commented about his wife, ''If you want her to shut up, don't bother to tape her mouth. Just tie her hands.''

Affect displays

Affect is described as an emotion, feeling, or mood in behavior that is displayed according to socially and culturally learned rules. These rules have well-established social norms to prescribe which affect displays are appropriate in various social contexts. By the age of 1 year, most children are capable of displaying happiness, sadness, anger, and surprise, and until the child is older such expressions are spontaneous and not governed by social rules.

Affect is primarily displayed in the face. Although the entire face may give evidence to the emotion, particular areas carry more information for identification. The face often expresses a blending of several kinds of emotions, such as in this situation: The expectant father is very happy to learn that the baby has arrived, but at the same time, he is surprised to learn that the baby is twins! In a fraction of a second affect can change from happiness to concern and may go unnoticed to the observer.

What an individual is feeling is not always the affect displayed, for example, the adolescent who is extremely fearful about his pending tonsillectomy but shows only slight to moderate fear or the grade-school child who exaggerates her school fears to gain attention and be allowed to stay home from school. People may be feeling great emotion but look affectless or neutral, for instance, the man who refrains from all emotional display to ''protect'' his wife after the death of their child or the elderly client who waits anxiously for a letter and then hides her disappointment when the letter does not arrive.

The affect displays of the major emotions anger and fear are quite often misinterpreted. Both are

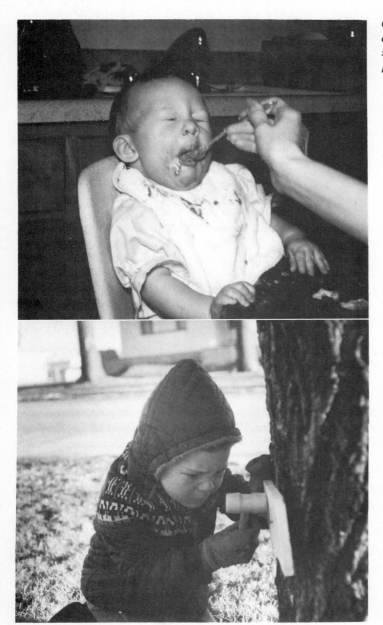

Children are spontaneous in their affect displays, and it is only later that such expressions are governed by social rules.

Photographs by Charles D. Davis.

accompanied by epinephrine, causing increased heart and respiratory rates and muscle tone. During fear there is reduced blood flow to the skin—hence the white face. Anger produces more epinephrine and an increased blood supply to the skin that is usually apparent in a red face.

Affect displays can repeat, qualify, or contradict a verbally stated affect or can be an unrelated channel of communication. They carry more personal information than illustrators or most emblems and are usually emitted without intending to communicate or to transmit a message.

Regulators

The expression, "It's like talking to a brick wall," is what verbal communication is like without the nonverbal cues and sounds that serve as feedback and keep the conversation moving smoothly. During conversation the rapid sequence of facial expressions and other signals, such as hand movements, nods, and shifts of gaze, are dependent on the verbal messages for their organization. These cues, called regulators, carry no message content in themselves but convey information necessary to maintain the back-and-forth rhythm of conversation. The listener uses regulators to nonverbally tell the speaker to continue, repeat, elaborate, hurry up, stop talking, and so forth. The speaker sends nonverbal cues instructing the listener to pay special attention, talk, or wait just a minute. Reinforcers to continue the conversation are slow, deliberate nods, mm-hmmm or other such verbal sounds, leaning forward, smiling, eye contact, raised eyebrows, and a host of other nonverbal acts.

The eyes play an important role in communication. The speaker glances at the listener for feedback approximately one half of the time, whereas the listener looks at the speaker about three fourths of the time. Part of the listener's visual vigilance is in response to the message but also to catch the nonverbal cues indicating that it is the listener's turn to talk.

Speakers make the decision to keep talking or to give the other person a chance to talk, and listeners determine if they want to talk or if they would prefer to just listen. This back-and-forth exchange of conversation is kept more orderly by nonverbal regulators.

When the speaker is ready to turn the conversation over to someone else, the intent is signaled by making eye contact with the potential speaker, decreasing voice loudness, and slowing the speaking tempo. Another nonverbal cue that the speaker has wound down is a posture change from alert to relaxed, with a drop in the position of the hands, the head, and the eyelids. Naturally, silence is used to signal that it is someone else's turn to talk; however, the speaker is not entirely off the hook until the next person starts talking. Any awkward silence is likely to be filled in by the speaker with words such as, "you know," "or something," or, "anyway." If all else fails, the speaker may try to entice someone into talking by asking a question.

The speaker who does not want to stop talking indicates this reluctance by avoiding extended eye contact and by maintaining a more alert posture. Illustrators increase, as do the volume and rate of speech, reducing the frequency and duration of silent pauses. If the listener makes a comment, the speaker merely pauses without a drop in voice or a change in posture. This "holding pattern" is emphasized with extended gaze and a hand held in the air. When the speaker is interrupted by a passerby who commands a brief interchange, the speaker may actually hold the arm of the waiting participant—symbolically holding the conversation—while turning to address the person passing by.

Signals indicating that the listener wants to take over communication include a more alert posture and increased eye gaze. Nods and verbalizations such as, "mm-hmm," and, "yeah," become more rapid and increase in number, as though to say, "Hurry up and get it said, it's my turn." The listener may attempt to break in by gesturing with an index finger or a raised hand that may be accompanied with an audible inspiration of breath in preparation for speaking.

On the other hand, the listener who does not want to speak has some options when handed the conversation. The listener can decline the turn non-verbally by remaining relaxed and silent while avoiding eye contact, or the person can restate what the speaker has just said, which is a verbal way of declining the speaking role.

Children are less likely to use regulators such as eye contact or position change to mark the beginnings and endings of their conversations. When children want to talk, they are more apt to interrupt by tugging at the speaker, jumping up and down, or calling out the speaker's name in an effort to be recognized. Listener responses, including nods and "m-hum," are nearly absent in young children even when they are listening. The lack of these cues frequently leads adults to question, "Are you listening to me?" It is not until early adolescence that the use of regulators increases dramatically.

Regulators are socially and culturally learned, and although on the periphery of awareness, most are involuntary and difficult to inhibit. These subtle cues play an important role in managing the immediate social situation, and even though most people are not consciously aware that they are receiving this information, its significance is demonstrated in the total system of communication.

Adaptors

This group of nonverbal movements is perhaps the most speculative but may offer some psychological meaning to seemingly random movements or to movements people pretend they did not do or do not see. For instance, most people have caught themselves rubbing their hands together for no apparent reason or scratching their heads when there is no itch. Another classic example is when an individual tries to rearrange undergarments in public and if noticed quickly changes to a smoothing or brushing movement. These actions all fit into the last category of nonverbal movements identified as adaptors.

It is thought that adaptors are learned in childhood and are related to the satisfaction of bodily needs. In adults these childhood habits are triggered by something in the current environment that serves as a reminder of the time when the original

behavior was learned. Adaptors serve a purpose, and whether they should be considered an overflow of emotional tensions or as an expression of self-attitudes, they are not intended to communicate except perhaps to the self.

The most common adaptors involve manipulations of one's own body and include touching, holding, rubbing, scratching, pinching, or picking. These are used with more conscious awareness although people pretend they do not know when they are grooming in public. If someone is noticed engaging in a personal adaptor, such as picking the nose or scratching the genital area, people look away since it is considered just as rude to publicly observe these behaviors as it is to engage in them. Personal adaptors are more apt to be carried out to satisfaction when the person is alone. An itch may just be brushed or touched when in public; privacy allows the full act rather than a fragmented act or adaptor. About the only comments made about such actions are from parents concerning how improper it is to perform them in public places.

Many personal adaptors are performed with little awareness and are related to the satisfaction of bodily needs. These increase as a person's psychological discomfort and anxiety increase. However, if the anxiety level becomes too high, the person may move little if at all. There may be a close link between body touching and preoccupation with oneself. Face touching gestures can be interpreted in terms of what has been done to the person, what the individual wants done to the self, or what the person is doing to oneself. Picking and scratching can be forms of self-attack; holding may be giving support; rubbing or massaging may be for reassurance. Rubbing, scratching, or wiping the forehead and back of the scalp often connotes thinking activities. Covering the eyes with hands occurs more often when a person is experiencing shame or negative feelings toward the self. Aggression may be indicated with fist gestures, shame signified by fingers at the lips, and frustration represented by an open hand dangling between one's legs.

Sometimes restless movements of the hands,

feet, and legs are not indicators of anxiety but are fragments of body movements that for some reason cannot be completed. These movements may take the place of kicking aggression, sexual invitation, or flight. Rather than the full activity, all that is apparent is the restless movements. For example, clients waiting to see the physician may make repetitive foot movements, shuffles, or cross one leg over the other and swing the free leg back and forth. These movements may indicate a wish to withdraw that is adapted because of the need to stay.

Another type of adaptor involves the manipulation of objects more than is necessary for the performance of some instrumental task (for example, a person playing with a pencil while in the process of writing or manipulating a cigarette, ashtray, or lighter while smoking). Because these objects are used in a task, there are fewer social taboos against these adaptors than there are against personal adaptors. Worry beads and other items are marketed solely for the purpose of manipulation and the calming effect that touching produces. Lonely people may stroke or hold an inanimate object, usually of sentimental value, when the need for touch is great. This is demonstrated by an elderly lady who strokes the vase given by her daughter whom has not visited for some time or the little boy who carries his mother's picture during her absence.

• • •

Emblems, illustrators, affect displays, regulators, and adaptors are basic categories of nonverbal behavior acts. These implicit behaviors deal with the transmission of emotions and attitudes, serve as social reinforcers, and regulate interactions. Although normal 6-year-old children are still in the process of learning and practicing communication skills, they have a repertoire of nonverbal behaviors that enable them to function within the communication system of their society. These nonverbal skills increase throughout life and ultimately provide insight to the fact that the nonverbal message is often more important than the verbal.

ATTITUDES

Blends of body movements and posture combine to create feelings, impressions, and preferences that have a direct effect on the outcome of communication. Specific blends of nonverbal cues influence the following attitudes: (1) like/dislike, (2) dominance/submissiveness, and (3) deception.

Like/dislike

Orientation. Body orientation, or the degree to which an individual's body is turned in the direction of rather than away from another, communicates attitudes of liking or disliking about the other person. People generally want to be close to something they like, whether it is an object or a person, and they tend to turn away when something is disliked. There is a tendency for people who have an intimate relationship to assume an indirect positioning of shoulders and legs so that they can be closer to each other.

Open/closed body positions. Open or closed body positions also contribute to the formation of impressions and attitudes. Positions that are perceived as being warm or open include various combinations of the following: relaxed posture, knees and feet apart, and arms and hands relaxed or held away from the body. Closed positions include elbows next to the body, arms crossed, hands folded together, knees and feet together, and legs crossed. A more positive impression is created with open positioning than with closed. In a helping relationship the professional is able to create a more relaxed and therapeutic milieu with open posturing. It has also been found that when the client displays very closed, defensive positioning, the therapist's open posture may facilitate a more relaxed open interaction. Whenever open or closed posturing is considered, it is imperative that the leg and arm positions are considered within the context of the situation. Open posturing or body accessibility may simply mean relaxation. The seated individual with arms supported or propped on furniture is perceived as more relaxed and therefore more open. Usually, leaning sideways is considered more negative than leaning back or forward, and a man will usually

Open and closed body positions.

Illustration by Tom Weinman.

T.W.

remain more alert—as though on guard—when conversing with an individual he dislikes, whereas a woman will lean away when interacting with someone she dislikes. This positioning also changes to reflect agreement or disagreement with what the speaker has said.

Courtship/quasi-courtship. Being able to distinguish between courtship and quasi-courtship behaviors will help care givers avoid misunderstandings. Although the two behaviors are very similar, quasi-courtship is initiated during situations inappropriate for courtship or with incompleteness in the gestures and is used to satisfy needs other than sexual.[7] People of all ages use slight and covert quasi-courting behaviors to foster rapport in settings that vary from therapeutic encounters and business meetings to social interactions.

The nonverbal signals that indicate courtship and courtship readiness are a part of and unique to the broader cultural orientations of which each individual is a member. The Portuguese indicate pas-

sage of an attractive woman by an ear-pinching signal. In the United States the hour-glass shape made with both hands serves the same purpose.

A number of different signals used to communicate courtship interest are also variants of affiliative signals: direct orientation, gaze, positive facial expression and tone of voice, proximity, bodily relaxation with open arm position, and bodily contact. Normally a person will use some or all of these cues to communicate a positive attitude, and when one of these signals is not possible, another is used in its place. When a couple is separated in a room but the two persons are able to see each other, extended gaze substitutes for proximity.

A woman communicating courtship readiness holds her head high and cocked while looking at the person of interest from the corners of the eyes through narrowed eyelids. The chest is brought out to display the breasts; the legs are presented in a suggestive manner with the foot extended and the calf musculature tightened. Hand and wrist movements are slow and flowing, with the palm of the hand displayed, for example, when covering a cough, brushing back the hair, or smoking.

A man's courting behavior may resemble that used in dominance. He draws himself up to full height, stands close with spread-legged position, belly sucked in, chest expanded, shoulders squared, jaw protruded, hands on hips with elbows turned outward, and displays what is known as the typical masculine stance.

In Victorian traditions a woman was to reciprocate to this dominant male behavior with submissive display. These behavior patterns included shrinking, lowering the eyes, and a drop in voice loudness and tone until the sound emitted had almost a whisper quality. Times have changed.

When people are together for social interaction, there is an initial time of covert "looking each other over." If eyes meet during this scanning, it is usually not sustained and is only part of the once over. When there is interest in pursuing the relationship, a more lasting eye contact will be established. Sexual attraction is signaled by pupil dilation giving the bright eye appearance that is apparent in sexually interested men and women in this and many other cultures. In times past women used belladonna to dilate their eyes in an attempt to look more alluring.

Nonverbal cues accurately communicate whether couples are content or in conflict within their relationship. A woman who takes the arm of a man when assistance or protection is not necessary, fusses with his tie, or flicks a speck of lint from his clothing communicates the bond between them. Couples experiencing conflict tend to cross their arms and legs, have less eye contact, and touch themselves more frequently than they touch each other. Happy couples sit closer, look more frequently into each other's eyes, touch each other more than themselves, and spend more time talking to their partner than do couples who are unhappy.

Quasi-courtship is comprised of courtship behaviors that are tempered by certain behavioral qualifiers indicating that the person is not to be taken literally. These qualifiers shift the behavior to a more playful encounter or one for a purpose other than courtship. Such disclaimers may be touching a wedding ring, initiating courtship behavior in inappropriate situations, keeping arms folded, or giving incongruent verbal and nonverbal messages. The hospitalized client who flirts with his nurse may be using quasi-courtship in an attempt to bolster an insecure self-image or to gain attention. He may ask, "How would you like to go out tonight, baby?" knowing full well that he cannot even get out of bed. The nurse who understands the concepts of quasi-courtship will not coldly respond, "No thank you," but perhaps, "Mr. H., you're such a flirt." She acknowledges that the individual is not serious, and by referring to him as "mister" keeps the relationship on a more formal basis.

Dominance/submissiveness

Within the hospital walls is a constant scramble for position, status, and influence. Professionalism has prompted an ongoing redefinition of function and status. Those who used to be ancillary personnel are now an accepted part of the medical care profession. Nurses are giving up the role of unquestioned subservience in exchange for independent judgment with direct responsibility to the client. Physicians and hospital administrators vie for a position once belonging to the physician alone. While the hierarchy battles on armed with degrees, experience, and rights, the question of dominance or status continues to be debated at the nonverbal level.

When two people meet, there may be a rapid and subtle exchange of signals that negotiates nonverbally the precise relationship between the two. Equilibrium is very difficult or impossible to obtain if both want to dominate, which may explain why some people have trouble getting along from the first time they meet.

Attitudes of dominance are partly communicated by general patterns of relaxation, which include arms held in asymmetrical position with one arm hooked over the back of the chair or in a pocket, feets and legs positioned differently, and hands, neck, and general posture relaxed with the person leaning back from the vertical. Leaning sideways with hands on hips is frequently used by a person of higher status when communicating with a person perceived of lower status. A dominant display may also consist of standing erect, hands on hips, serious expression, and speaking loudly.

People of higher status are allotted more space, are usually faced directly regardless of personal feelings toward the person, and are usually the initiators and terminators of conversation. In an informal meeting situation it is higher status individuals who occupy the best seats at the front of the room. They sit in a relaxed position and may even put their feet on the table. Seated rocking movements are indicative of relaxation as well as dominance. When the meeting is around a rectangular table, the leader of the group tends to select the head position at the table and the others arrange themselves so that they can see the leader. For the

leader visual access is considered more important than proximity.

Those assuming submissive roles more often lower their heads, maintain a more alert position, and when standing, sometimes have their hands clasped behind their backs. When communicating with a person of higher status, it is the subordinate who adjusts posture to facilitate the conversation; for example, when two are conversing while walking, and the person of lower status walks backward to be visible to the other.

When a dominant person encounters a subordinate at close quarters, feelings of flight may be precipitated but may be difficult or impossible for the person to carry out. The subordinate remains almost motionless until the dominant person leaves or directs attention elsewhere. Two physicians on either side of a client may produce a certain degree of immobilization. The ''victim'' is unable to relax and except for brief approval

Dominant-submissive expressions.
Illustration by Tom Weinman.

sounds and one-word responses is likely to remain quiet until the dominant individuals leave. Later the client may say, "Why didn't I ask about . . .?" "I should have . . ." or, "I forgot to. . . ." Clients report that they go blank, get tongue-tied, or lose their memory when their physician comes around, and this is why clients are encouraged to write down their questions before the physician arrives. Otherwise, they may forget more questions than they remember.

In a mental hospital clients in touch with reality tend to be more dominant than those who have a poor reality base. They are given more responsibility, both for behavior reinforcement and as a method of control, and are therefore more visible to the other clients. This encourages the dominant role since these individuals at times will be able to issue directives to others with the support of the staff. If a dominant client encroaches on a submissive client's space, flight behaviors such as retreat, bodily evasions, closed eyes, withdrawing the chin into the chest, hunching, and crouching may be seen. Some overt signs of tension that usually precede flight include rocking, leg swinging, or tapping. The person may rock back and forth and then on one of the forward movements get up and move away.

Being called to someone else's office is an indication of the other person's higher status. The timing sequence of entering, being seated, and leaving is determined by the power role between those involved. A wide variance between roles and interests is illustrated in the following meeting.

■ The individual arrives at another's office, checks with the secretary, takes a seat, and waits. When given permission to enter the office, the person stops just inside the door and waits to be recognized by the dominant figure behind the desk, who is in the process of something more important and therefore does not rise. The longer it takes to be addressed, the more status variance between the two. The dominant person indicates for the other to be seated since standing and height produce psychological power. The designated chair is across the room from the desk, with both the desk and the distance serving as a barrier between the two. The higher status person initiates and terminates any discussion. Telephone calls and other interruptions further indicate that the meeting is not considered important by both parties. Termination is nonverbally communicated when the higher status person gathers up papers, closes the file, stands, or simply concludes the conversation by saying, "That's all," and directing attention to other matters at hand. _____

Deception

The idea that nonverbal behavior reveals true feelings even when an effort is made to conceal these feelings is not new. It is the underlying emotional state of the person who is being dishonest that is ultimately communicated in the nonverbal message. If there is guilt, shame, or anxiety about engaging in deception or the possibility of being discovered, these feelings are more apt to be expressed than if the person engages in deceit without experiencing these emotional states.

Characteristics identified with deceit—guardedness, discomfort, tension, vigilance, and anxiety—may be part of the normal behavior pattern of an honest person. Before any conclusions regarding deceit can be reached, it is necessary that the person's behavior under honest message-sending conditions be compared with that which is considered dishonest. Even then, dishonesty cannot be assumed. Inconsistent messages may also be attributed to social pressures against expressing negative attitudes or emotions that may be concealed or masked, causing behaviors normally associated with deceit.

Since people are more aware of monitoring their facial expressions, most masking occurs here. Deception in the face may be in the form of a fake smile or a frown that does not fit with the other facial expressions. Unless there is much anxiety, the deceitful communicator often smiles more than the truthful communicator. The person usually speaks more slowly and because of tense vocal cords, the voice is often higher than normal. Although words are chosen carefully, there are frequently more speech errors.

Other signals such as a tense posture and the body directed away from the questioner make it possible to see through some masked facial expressions. The dishonest communicator tends to nod and gesture very little and whenever possible avoids looking at the person he or she is trying to deceive.

The hands are monitored less often than the face and may offer clues of deception. Possibly in response to the discomfort created by dishonesty, the individual is apt to engage in more self-touch gestures such as hands to mouth or nose and clenching or wringing hands together. There may be more scratching, rubbing, picking, and holding gestures and more preening adjustments with hair and clothing. Although an effort may be made to hold the hands quietly on the lap, the need for touch is often stronger and the hands escape to offer security.

Deceptive clues are usually more apparent in feet and leg actions because they are monitored less than the face or hands. Occasional adaptors of aggressive or flight movements may appear as foot kicks or restless, repetitive leg and foot movements.

Discrepancy between verbal and nonverbal messages is estimated to occur as much as two thirds of the time, and adults are more likely to attend to the nonverbal message. Children identify negative expressions more readily and accurately than positive expressions. Therefore when interacting with a child and positive information is to be communicated, both verbal and nonverbal messages must be congruently positive.

An individual may pointedly use overall body gestures to communicate information that might otherwise be unavailable. This is illustrated in the following situation.

Someone leaving the meeting early may perform the behavior sequence of giving an apology signal to the chairman or speaker and then half tiptoe out, all the while wearing the look of someone already half-involved in business vital enough to warrant his leaving early because of it, this purposefulness only disappearing from this appearance when he has shut the door behind himself and can no longer be seen by those whom he has left to listen to the bitter end.[2]

Once again to reiterate an important point, these and all nonverbal behaviors must be kept in a contextual perspective. Just because deceitful characteristics are apparent does not mean that the individual has engaged in deceit.

POSTURE

In recent years social scientists have become more interested in the interaction between people and how posture and body positioning contribute to different outcomes of communication. Posture may be directly linked to speech—similar to illustrators—or completely independent of speech, "He kept his back turned," "Never looked up," "Kept to himself." Body positioning is also an important means of conveying interpersonal attitudes and emotional states. A depressed client displays a more drooping, listless posture and spends time looking at the floor. Manic individuals maintain an alert and erect posture with their bodies in a high degree of arousal. There is a tense-relaxed dimension, characteristic of euphoria, which differs from the continuous muscular tension of anxiety.

A great deal can be found out about a situation by noting posture or body positioning. A kaleidoscope of information awaits observation in a setting such as the waiting area of an outpatient clinic. Posture varies from tension to relaxation, with matching attire that ranges from prim and proper to comfortable and convenient. Individuals "going through the clinic" or those who have tests or appointments on successive days usually show more relaxed posture and dress with each visit. The jumpsuit-clad man soundly sleeping across two chairs was probably awake half the night after taking laxatives in preparation for X rays. His posture and dress will become more rigid when he returns for the test results. Posture changes can be dramatic within a short time as is demonstrated in the following vignette from the outpatient clinic.

■ A middle-aged woman checks in with the receptionist, finds a vacant seat, and sits down. She sits erect in the chair and positions both feet on the floor—as though for a quick exit. Both hands clutch her purse, and her eyes map out the route to the physician's office. As she becomes more relaxed, she leans back in the chair, places her purse aside, and begins to glance through a magazine. When the appointment time approaches, she closes the magazine, retrieves her purse, glances expectantly at the receptionist, and slowly assumes an alert, tense posture. ———————————

Although some believe that posture occurs in an infinite variety of forms, there are approximately 30 postural configurations that are easily recognized by most North Americans. Scheflen[6] identifies the three basic dimensions of postural information as orientation, congruence, and inclusion. Although much of the postural information is used on a subconscious basis, a conscious knowledge of these postural functions is of great value to the individual studying human behavior or conducting therapeutic interactions.

Group orientation

The smallest possible group of two people will orient their bodies to each other in one of two basic ways. They can face each other, or they can adapt a side by side positioning, facing the same direction with orientation toward a common task, object, or person.

The face-to-face position requires interaction to take place. Commonly thought of as involving an exchange of information or feelings, this positioning is used for such reciprocal activities as teaching, nurturing, confrontation, conversation, and courtship.

Side by side positioning is seldom used for direct interaction. This parallel positioning usually involves two persons whose interests are mutually directed toward an object, a task, or a third person. A teacher and student may work side by side if there is a shared item involved in the teaching. For the most part, activities carried out by a group in parallel orientation are activities that could be achieved by one person. The group members tend to complement the individual who acts as the leader. A physician making rounds may be flanked on either side by an intern or resident with the group's attention directed toward the client. The physician will do most of the talking, with the intern or resident giving nonverbal or brief verbal reinforcement or summary. During a counseling session, family members may sit adjacent to those persons from whom they seek support, affection, or approval. This positioning may change as counseling progresses.

When it is inconvenient for participants to adjust their bodies to a configuration of face-to-face or side by side, they tend to orient the upper part of the body in the direction of choice. A group therapy leader can facilitate group stability by dividing body attention with the upper half of the body in one direction and the lower half in another, thereby including all members.

Congruence/noncongruence

Individuals in agreement in view or role will often hold their heads and extremities in the same position. Direct posture involves the same extremities, whereas mirrored posture involves opposite extremities. For example, two people in agreement may assume a direct posture by placing their right hands to their faces. If they mirror each other's posture, one will use the right hand and the other the left. When one takes into account the limited number of postural configurations, position likeness would appear on the surface to be coincidental rather than an indication of agreement. However, when on numerous occasions one member of a congruent set shifts posture and the others quickly follow suit, it is questionable that this is attributed to coincidence.

When different views are presented at a meeting, members in agreement tend to adopt affiliative posturing by direct body orientation, leaning close, and increasing eye gaze. A woman may communicate attentiveness by holding very still and cocking her head; a man may signal thoughtfulness by chin stroking and head scratching. Opposing views often prompt decreased eye gaze and distancing posture such as turning or leaning away with arms positioned across the body. Frowning and picking imaginary lint from clothing may also communicate disagreement or disapproval. This activity may be symbolic of getting rid of the disagreement.

Because two people engage in the same postural behavior does not necessarily mean that they have copied or identified with the other. People do respond to their own physical comfort needs, and their positioning may be irrespective of others. When several in a group shift posture at the same time, it is not uncommon to feel a strong desire to adjust accordingly, regardless of agreement. There is also a tendency to split postural congruence, with the upper part of the body in agreement with the representative of one idea or role and the lower body congruent with another.

Status difference may also account for postural differing, with a member of higher status maintaining a posture unlike that of the others. For this reason, congruent posture is less likely in teacher-student or physician-client interactions.

Inclusiveness/noninclusiveness

Members of a group tend to demarcate the limits of their group by the placement of their bodies or extremities. When people are standing or have the freedom to move furniture, they tend to form a circle with their bodies. If space or furniture is such that a line configuration is necessary, the end members turn inward and extend an arm toward the back or a foot across the front as if to limit access in or out of the group. If the group is comprised primarily of men, those doing the "bookending" with arms or legs are usually of higher status. A line grouping is not conducive to conversation because individuals are not able to see each other. When seated on a davenport or couch,

the group members bob back and forth a great deal to include each member.

Members within a group who are expected to engage in disruptive activities may be denied access to each other with body placement of a third participant. This occurs when arguments between two persons are expected and a third person stands or sits between, such as parents separating squabbling siblings. This protectiveness also happens when a newcomer is perceived as a threat, as is the case when an attractive single man or woman joins a group of couples.

Barrier behavior will appear when tighter spacing is forced on group members. When two people are seated in close face-to-face proximity for other than intimate situations, they are likely to cross their arms and legs and lean away from each other. Eye contact will be noticeably less than if the two were comfortable with their distance. When people cannot create more physical space, they distance themselves with their eyes, extremities, or posture to provide psychological space.

A person indicates that he or she is waiting for another by assuming an alert posture and by frequent, wide, expectant glances, and when posture and actions are relaxed and directed toward others, an invitation for companionship is communicated. In contrast, the individual who wishes to be left alone sends this message by directing actions and posture toward the self.

These basic dimensions of postural relations are neither unique to each individual nor universal to a culture. They are varied by cultural subgroups, personality, age, social class, gender, status, occupation, health, and temporary conditions such as hunger and pain. In social interaction if another does not behave in the desired way, posture or body positioning becomes an ongoing corrective action directed toward producing the desired response.

PATTERNS OF SOCIAL BEHAVIOR

Patterns of social behavior are standardized, have similar consequences, and create a sense of security for those involved. Rituals, ceremonies, routines, greetings, and farewells serve to affirm social relationships and to express beliefs. These patterns depict what is difficult to put into words and provide guidelines that help to regulate social interactions.

Rituals and ceremonies

Rituals and ceremonies rely heavily on symbolic, nonverbal patterns of social behavior and involve changes of social relationships or states of mind rather than physical effects. A ritual uses a programmed use of time, with those involved gaining security from doing the same thing toward a predictable outcome. Ceremonies differ from rituals in that rituals usually involve religion or the occult, and ceremonies do not. For the most part both are referred to as rituals and include governing rules such as when to use silence or words, appropriate facial expression, and proper behavior for each stage of ritual. For example, acceptable behavior at a wedding would be considered inappropriate at a funeral. A birthday, christening, graduation, engagement, wedding, promotion, decoration, and funeral all involve changing social relationships. Because it is difficult to express these subjective experiences with words, nonverbal expression is used.

Routines

Most people have routines they follow that give order to their lives. Mealtimes, personal grooming habits, waking up, and going to bed all occur at fairly consistent times for each person. In many instances, it is necessary that hospitalized clients adapt their normal routines of daily living to meet the care givers' schedule. Whenever possible, this schedule should be adjusted to meet the client's needs because the more closely a hospital experience resembles a person's home routine, the easier it is for the person to adapt. The client who is accustomed to taking a shower or watching Johnny Carson before sleeping should be encouraged to do so. Most toddlers have specific routines that they follow before going to bed, and it is important for care givers to retain as much of the original pattern

as possible. Bedtime routines tend to disengage the mind in preparation for sleep, and when they are allowed, the need for sedation is greatly reduced.

Another routine that helps to maintain social order is used when a minor mistake has been made or someone has offended another in some way. The offender gives an explanation or an apology, which prompts a reply of verbal acceptance. In minor instances a simple, "Excuse me," may be acknowledged with an, "It's okay," or a nod, without feeling the need to converse further. If the infraction is more severe, this acceptance is sometimes followed with the offender expressing ap-

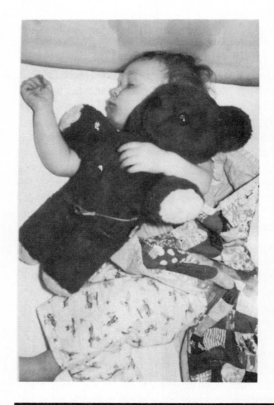

Bedtime routine.
Photograph by Charles D. Davis.

preciation for the other being so understanding, which is then followed by the appreciation being minimized:

■ The medical student, staring off into space while waiting in the cafeteria line, bumps into a physician, spilling coffee over the tray. "I'm sorry," offers the embarrassed young man.

The physician begins to sop up the coffee with her napkin. "That's all right," she responds.

As the last of the mess is wiped up, the student adds, "I appreciate your being so understanding."

The physician proceeds with arranging her tray and without looking up concludes, "Think nothing of it." The two have cleared their obligations in this social discord and are now free to continue on their individual ways. _____

Greetings and good-byes

Even to pass close by another on the street involves unspoken rules. In crowded and hurried conditions people tend to regard each other as physical objects or "nonpeople" and limit interactions to the minimum. A client will often make comments about the physician who "remembers my name—even when I'm in the hall—and takes the time to ask about the family. He's such a busy person, too."

In a large city strangers avoid each other's gaze and glance toward another just long enough to determine the direction of movement. Passing occurs without verbal or nonverbal acknowledgement. In rural communities the spontaneous impulse to exchange greetings with passing strangers may be very strong, and if an exchange takes place, it is relatively muted. The standard minimal middle-class recognition is eye contact, a brief smile, and the eyebrow flash—during which the eyebrows are raised to maximum extent for about one-sixth of a second.

Minimal acknowledgments are, "How are you?" and, "Fine," at approximately 8 to 10 feet from where paths will meet. Whatever is said is a greeting and not a question or statement for gathering or providing information. To stress the fact that

most people do not care what is responded to the greeting, "How are you?" one person answered a few friends, "Dying, and you?" Most of the time the friends replied, "Fine," and went on their way without any verbal or nonverbal acknowledgment of what had been said. Because this phrase is so overworked, it may be necessary to repeat the question again before an honest response is received, "Seriously, how are you?"

After greetings have been exchanged individuals glance in the direction of intended passing. Sometimes preoccupation prevents one of the individuals from subconsciously registering this glance, and the two will do an embarrassing jig before going on their way.

When individuals sight each other, a distant wave or smile initiates the greeting sequence. As the two approach, their gaze is averted as they groom themselves by adjusting clothing or hair. If a formal greeting is desired, a protective arm is drawn across the front of the body. Arms left free anticipate a warmer greeting. As the individuals draw closer they make eye contact, smile, and extend a hand for a handshake or both arms for an embrace. The longer the separation and the closer the emotional ties, the more expansive the greeting. Each successive greeting within a short time frame results in a reduced version of the initial display until eye contact and a smile suffice.

Farewells follow rituals similar to greetings with the extent of the farewell dependent on the relationship and the expected time apart. For those expecting to see each other soon, a wave or a phrase such as, "So long," or, "See you later," may be used. Saying good-bye on the telephone is usually, "B'bye," or, "G'bye," with, "Good-bye," being used for formality or when continued conversation becomes unwanted or costly.

Bodily contact is more readily seen when separation involves greater distance and longer time periods. Failed departures have a disordering effect on those involved. The experience of forgetting an item and having to return for it after going through the farewell is one most people have encountered. The host or hostess, caught off guard with this surprise greeting—which in itself causes a certain amount of fumbling and embarrassment—realizes the recently performed farewell was in vain. The second parting ritual will be a lesser version of the earlier farewell.

Sometimes a client is hospitalized long enough or the circumstances surrounding the hospitalization are such that a close relationship is formed with the nursing staff. Understandably, the individual receives extra attention from care givers at the time of dismissal. If readmission becomes necessary within a short period of time, the person may experience all the awkwardness of a failed departure. The feeling that an agreement was not kept can be minimized if nurses share with clients at the time of dismissal, ''We're here if you need us.''

A farewell that has no emotional parallel is the parting before the separation of death. The poignancy of this ritual cannot be duplicated. In cases of sudden death or when the significant others are not able to be present or cannot accept the pending death, the farewell may take place following the death. The rituals of the funeral and the bereavement period are beneficial to the bereaved in their readjustment period partly because open grieving is allowed and also because of the social support. Having the opportunity to share memories and to talk about the deceased person's last days helps in bringing to reality the finiteness of death. In the United States public support and publicly approved grief are often removed at the time the ''supporters'' no longer feel the need to support, leaving the bereaved alone to work through a period of withdrawal and the transition to normal life.

Patterns of social behavior are the result of cultural development that are passed on by tradition and learning from generation to generation. Although the benefits of these social behaviors are difficult to measure, it is agreed that they reduce anxiety by bringing about social cohesion. These stereotyped sequences function like a language, expressing things nonverbally when words do not suffice.

PARALANGUAGE

Paralanguage, or the vocal cues that accompany spoken language, includes tempo, pitch, intensity, vocal sounds such as laughter and sighs surrounding words, and the pauses that space words and word groups. People also react to dialects or accents, nonfluencies, latency of response, duration of speech, interaction rates, and silence. These and other acoustic phenomena influence the way something is said, which at times is more important than what is said.

Vocal cues

Characteristics of paralanguage begin to make their appearance before spoken language is learned. A 3-month-old infant playfully experiments with babbling sounds, and those not reinforced receive minimal use later in life. By their sixth month infants are able to respond to and purposefully create different pitch levels and soon learn to imitate the sounds made by others. Pausal patterns, tempo, and loudness seem to be well established by the time children enter school. These vocal nuances are influential throughout life not only in conveying message content but also in making judgments of emotion, personality, and attitude.

Message content. Just as the word, ''Sweetheart,'' can be a word of endearment or sarcasm depending on the way it is said, numerous distinct responses can be evoked from the same message content by manipulating the voice. The physician who responds, ''I wouldn't want to guess,'' can be interpreted as saying different things according to which word receives emphasis. An accent on the, ''I,'' implies that the doctor does not want to guess. When emphasis is placed on the word, ''guess,'' the physician indicates that guessing would be wrong. It is estimated that over 30 percent of conveyed messages are attributed to paralanguage, and when such things as fatigue, anxiety, fear, and pain are present, nuances of paralanguage may not be heard at all. Nurses fatigued from working double shifts may miss these subtle messages. Clients experience high stress during times of admission and dismissal from the hospital, and during stressful times they are likely to suffer a depressed responsiveness to the emotional stimuli of paralanguage. It is not that clients ignore information relating to their own best interest, it is just that what was said or implied was not heard. This emphasizes the necessity of a follow-up assessment to evaluate what the client has or has not understood and also the importance of providing written information whenever possible.

Emotion, personality, and attitude. Inferences are made from vocal cues people are largely unaware of. Psychiatrists report critical insights into emotional states and problems from the client's vocal cues. People who are depressed or dependent use a flat voice described as flabby, sickly, and helpless. Weakness, debility, and fatigue are indicated with a hollow voice using few high frequencies. Highly nervous individuals use a sharp voice that is interpreted as complaining, helpless, or infantile.

Psychologists have found a correlation between vocal expression and personal characteristics. The low-pitched voice often is equated with security and a positive manner, and although exceptions occur, there tends to be less favorable reaction to speakers with a dialect or accent other than the listener's. With amazing accuracy, social class or status has been reported on the basis of voice alone since individuals tend to form speech patterns similar to the people with whom they associate. Age can also be assessed from vocal cues since pitch tends to lower from infancy through middle age. Although the pitch level in women's voices varies little throughout adult life, men's voices raise somewhat with advanced age.

Effects on communication. Variations of volume, rate, pitch, and articulation tend to produce higher audience comprehension or retention. Although poor vocal qualities and hesitant speech do not interfere with comprehension, they do contribute to a listener's perception of the speaker's credibility. Persuasion is signaled by variation of vocal tones as well as a louder and faster speech rate.

Analysis of speech patterns shows that fluency in speech may be more an illusion than fact since two thirds of spoken language comes in chunks of less than six words. Approximately one half of the pauses during spontaneous speech occur at grammatical junctures (for example, at the end of sentences and clauses), with the rest occurring at midsentence. Speech delays may be prompted by thought processes or an emotional state and are varied by individual differences, the verbal task, situational pressures, and many other factors.

The two major types of pauses are the silent pause and the pause filled with, "um," "uh," stutters, repetitions, and other phonations. Silent pauses allow the speaker time to prepare a better response, but listeners may equate too many unfilled pauses with anxiety, anger, or contempt. Some helping professionals tend to think that silent pauses will be followed by messages that are more revealing about the client. Filled pauses, which may be used to control the conversation, tend to block the speaker's thought and also create the impression that the speaker is anxious or bored.

Silence

Silence is defined as the lack of sound or noise. Yet in a world polluted with noise, silence has become a resource that is not only scarce but uncomfortable for many even when it is approximated. If there is a pause in the conversation, the gap is quickly filled with meaningless drivel; people go to sleep and awaken to music; stereo or television is continual background sound in most homes. The jogger, the paper carrier, bicyclists, and people walking along the street are wearing headphones that keep them in touch with stereo or radio. Music is changed into noise when it is imposed in elevators, over the phone, and in other public places.

In health care settings personnel become inured to the sounds that are unique to this environment. They are able to tune out what clients and visitors consider to be distracting noises and are alerted only when these sounds change or stop.

Each person's environment is filled with noises that might cause concern to another. The contrast between a home environment and that of a hospital or nursing home is seldom considered by anyone except the individual who experiences this transition. Mrs. Jackson, alert and 79 years old, describes what "peace and quiet" is like in her home:

■ I've lived alone for 15 years 'cept for Jadda, my cat . . . only he doesn't know he's a cat. I mostly stay at home 'cause most of my friends are gone. . . . And when it's quiet, I hear my rocker squeaking and Jadda's purring . . . unless I rock on his tail, and then what a yowl! I hear the clock a ticking, and the refrigerator's humming away until just before it shuts off, and then it rumbles somethin' fierce. The bathroom faucet . . . it's dripped for years. I love to hear the children playing outside and the birds a singing. . . . I saw a cardinal yesterday. _____

When Mrs. Jackson is admitted to the hospital or nursing home, she is surrounded by machines that whirr, click, swish, or beep; people talking, laughing, and crying out all hours of the day and night; paging systems and intercoms delivering announcements, messages and pages; carts and equipment rumbling down the hall; sounds of metal, glass, and footsteps. Sometimes care givers do not understand why Mrs. Jackson slips back into her own peaceful world.

Whether silence is welcome and comfortable or obtrusive and distracting depends on the person's mood and point of view at the time. Some well-meaning care givers add to the machinery of sensory overload by bobbing in and out of clients' rooms during the rush traffic of a hospital day without regard to the individual's cues and needs and filling what privacy and quiet is available with trite talk. Yet in the middle of the night when external stimuli have quieted and internal needs surface, the overwhelming need for another human being may go unheeded in the silence of darkness.

Using silence. Silence is a form of nonverbal communication that is therapeutic only when it serves a function that is not frightening to the client. Some nurses comment that handling silence is one of their greatest problems in working with clients, and this discomfort is often shared by other members of the helping professions.

There are times when an individual simply needs the presence of another human being without feeling compelled to maintain another's interest. Verbally or nonverbally helpers can relay the message that it is not necessary to talk and that they will sit quietly in a silence that goes beyond words. Too often incongruent messages are sent by squirming in the chair or busying oneself with an available task.

Pause with a purpose. Usually longer in duration than the pauses that surround words and sentences, the pause with a purpose is a silence that gives people time to sort out thoughts and feelings and to decide where to begin and what to discuss. Respect for this thought time is important. If the client becomes uncomfortable with the silence, sometimes a brief comment may encourage response, "What concerns you most right now?" or, "From the expression on your face, it looks like you are dealing with a lot of things; can you share them with me?" Some people simply cannot pinpoint their concern although they display nonverbal signs of anxiety or depression. General questions that tend to encourage communication include, "If you had your choice, where would you like to be right now?" or, "What would you like to be doing?" or, "Whom would you like to be with?" People and events are then prioritized, with the individual encouraged to compare these "wishes" with the current situation. Ultimately the person may be able to identify his or her own source of concern.

Too many people fear that if they release the anger they feel, they will be destructive to themselves or others. Tears and emotions of sadness, disgust, fear, or love may be protected with silence, "I'm afraid if I let go, I'll break down, fall apart, lose control, and go to pieces."

Confusion or lack of situational structure may also lead to silence. Some individuals are inherently shy and inhibited and will not verbalize their concerns, but sometimes these concerns and questions are nonverbally expressed:

■ The diabetic client who is receiving meal planning instruction from the dietitian suddenly becomes silent. He does not understand what the dietitian has explained, but to admit that he doesn't understand would imply that either he is stupid or the dietitian is a poor teacher. The dietitian noted that before the silence, he glanced up and then changed positions. She recognizes these nonverbal cues as a question and goes over her instructions until verbally and nonverbally she is assured that the client understands what is presented. _____

Silence can also be used to evaluate and respond to information or another person. It may be easier for a client to sit in silence than to disagree with the physician, who is considered an authority figure. Lack of response may represent an "ah-ha!" enlightenment as the pieces begin to fall mentally into place.

Silence that is indicative of resistance is the most difficult to deal with because the helper may tend to feel rejected and thwarted. A client in psychotherapy may use silence as resistance or revenge against the therapist. A hostile person may direct displaced anger at the care giver in the form of the "silent treatment." A student may use silence as a power play against the counselor, "You made me come in here, but you can't make me talk." It is important that the situation be accepted for what it is and that the therapist not respond as if personally attacked. Sometimes, accepting and responding to the silence will prompt communication, "It's okay if we don't talk, but it may help if you will share what you're feeling so that we can examine it together." Talk that is used as a mask to avoid or camouflage the real issue may actually be more indicative of resistance than is silence.

After a few seconds of silence if the client is the first to speak, the length of the response is usually longer than if the helper had broken the silence. Longer silences are less effective.

Shortcomings in handling silence need special attention. Even if this discomfort does not verbally interrupt, nonverbal interruptions will be perceived. Once silence can be handled comfortably, each situation must be objectively appraised before a decision is made to interrupt the silence or allow it to continue. The proverb "silence is golden" is true only if silence is used as a therapeutic tool and not as a weapon.

• • •

Nonverbal communication supports, sustains, and is closely intertwined with speech. Influenced by personality, culture, and psychophysical and developmental traits, nonverbal signals convey emotional states, attitudes, and information. The shrug of the shoulders, a tensed mouth, or a nod of the head each send their message. In ritual, ceremony, politics, and courtship actions communicate. Words are wrapped in sound and in silence, and there are times when words intrude and it is silence that binds. Members of the helping professions are more capable of realizing their true potential as helpers by becoming aware of that aspect of language that everyone uses but no one speaks.

REFERENCES

1. Ekman, P., and Friesen, W.: The repertoire of nonverbal behavior: categories, origins, usage, and coding, Semiotica **1**:49, 1969.
2. Goffman, E.: Relations in public, New York, 1971, Basic Books, Inc., p. 133.
3. McGinniss, J.: The selling of the President: 1968, New York, 1969, Trident Press, pp. 29-30.
4. Pfungst, O.: Clever Hans: the horse of Mr. Von Osten, New York, 1965, Holt, Rinehart & Winston. (Edited by Robert Rosenthal.)
5. Rosenthal, R., and others: Body talk and tone of voice: the language without words, Psychology Today **8**:64, September, 1974.
6. Scheflen, A.: The significance of posture in communication systems, Psychiatry **27**:316, 1964.
7. Scheflen, A.: Body language and the social order: communication as behavioral control, Englewood Cliffs, New Jersey, 1972, Prentice-Hall, Inc.

BIBLIOGRAPHY

Argyle, M.: Bodily communication, New York, 1975, International Universities Press, Inc.

Argyle, M., and Ingham, R.: Gaze, mutual gaze, and proximity, Semiotica **6**:32, 1972.

Bakan, P.: The eyes have it, Psychology Today **4**:64, April 1971.

Beier, E.: Nonverbal communication: how we send emotional messages, Psychology Today **8**:53, October 1974.

Benjamin, A.: The helping interview, ed. 2, Boston, 1974, Houghton Mifflin Co.

Birdwhistell, R.: Kinesics and context, Philadelphia, 1970, University of Pennsylvania Press.

Collins, M.: Communication in health care, ed. 2, St. Louis, 1983, The C.V. Mosby Co.

Dittmann, A.: Developmental factors in conversational behavior, The Journal of Communication 22:404, 1972.

Ekman, P., and Friesen, W.: Unmasking the face, Englewood Cliffs, New Jersey, 1975, Prentice-Hall, Inc.

Ekman P., and Friesen, W.: Measuring facial movement, Environmental Psychology and Nonverbal Behavior 1:56, 1976.

Henley, N.: Body politics: power, sex, and nonverbal communication, Englewood Cliffs, New Jersey, 1977, Prentice-Hall, Inc.

Knapp, M.: Nonverbal communication in human interaction, ed. 2, New York, 1978, Holt, Rinehart & Winston.

Kumin, L., and Lazar, M.: Gestural communication in preschool children, Perceptual and Motor Skills 38:708, 1974.

McGinley, H., LeFevre, R., and McGinley, P.: The influence of a communicator's body position on opinion change in others, Journal of Personality and Social Psychology 31:686, 1975.

Mehrabian, A.: Silent messages, ed. 2, Belmont, California, 1981, Wadsworth Publishing Co.

Mysak, E.: Pitch and duration characteristics of older males, Journal of Speech and Hearing Research 2:46, 1959.

Nash, H.: Perception of vocal expression of emotion by hospital staff and patients, Genetic Psychology Monography 89:25, 1974.

Ostwald, P.: Soundmaking: the acoustic communication of emotion, Springfield, Illinois, 1963, Charles C Thomas, Publisher.

Richardson, S., Dohrenwend, B., and Klein, D.: Interviewing its forms and functions, New York, 1965, Basic Books, Inc., Publishers.

Sethee, U.: Verbal responses of nurses to patients in emotion-laden situations in public health nursing, Nursing Research 16:365, 1967.

Spitz, R., and Wolf, K.: The smiling response: a contribution to the ontogenesis of social relations, Genetic Psychology Monographs 34:57, 1946.

3 · Space and communication

Illustration by Tom Weinman.

Table 3-1. Distances for interaction

Intimate distance	Physical contact-$1\frac{1}{2}$ feet
Personal distance	$1\frac{1}{2}$-4 feet
Social distance	4-12 feet
Public distance	12 feet and beyond

*Data from Hall, E.T.: The hidden dimension, Garden City, New York, 1966, Anchor Books.

Space cannot be seen and is without substance, yet this invisible power influences all life. When thinking or talking about space, people think of "empty" and refer to the intervals or distance between objects. The Japanese are trained to give meaning to spaces and have a special word, *ma*, to refer to these intervals. In the United States the word *proxemics* is used to identify the social and personal use of space.

The study of proxemics is largely concerned with the spatial needs exhibited by people and the way these needs are shaped by culture, sensory perception, and the environment. In a subtle though persistent way surroundings affect both implicit behavior and social interaction. Additionally, the use of space can have a dramatic effect on the achievement of therapeutic communication goals. An understanding of the theoretical framework of proxemics is needed before conversational space is examined. This framework will provide a useful perspective for a later discussion of the therapeutic milieu.

SPATIAL DISTANCES

People have uniform spatial distances in handling interactions with others, and this distance is determined by the way the individuals are feeling toward each other at that time. For instance, if intimacy is desired, a much closer proximity is necessary than if a social interaction is the goal.

The simplest breakdown of situational personalities is identified by Hall[4] as intimate, personal, social, and public (Table 3-1). This is not to say that all people use the identical amount of space for a specific type of interaction but rather that these are generalities that are affected by many factors such as personality, culture, and environment. These guidelines help to explain the implicit and explicit spatial behaviors that occur in both personal and professional interactions.

Intimate distance

Close phase. The close phase of intimate distance involves physical contact and is reserved for such activities as lovemaking, comforting, care giving, and protecting. For the care giver, the close phase of intimate distance involves touching the client's skin. Whether the contact is for physical assessment, care, or assistance, it still requires invasion of the person's intimate space. Sometimes members of the health care team forget to announce their presence, fail to state their intentions, or neglect to ask for permission before touching a client. Touch, whether it be for comfort, assessment, or treatment, may be reassuring and pleasurable or a source of stress and fatigue. Several interruptions for procedures that could be accomplished at one time not only prevent the client from relaxing and falling asleep but also serve as a reminder of illness. Frequent intrusions on a client's intimate distance may be met with hostility or anger.

When the dentist is working on someone's teeth, a very close proximity exists between the two individuals. Because the dentist is positioned to the side and behind the client, eye contact can be avoided. Some clients close their eyes to create an illusion of privacy or distance. This same closeness is also experienced at the barber shop or hairdresser, and if it were not for practical reasons, interaction at such close distance would not be allowed.

Far phase. The far phase of intimate distance leaves a space of 6 to 18 inches between individuals, which is close enough for touch. Crowded subways, busses, and elevators bring strangers into intimate spatial distance, but those involved have learned that regarding others as objects or "nonpeople" makes this proximity less intimate. Maximum physical distance in crowded conditions is realized by being as immobile as possible, placing arms at sides, and tensing muscles. If touch inadvertently occurs, withdrawal is immediate, and when this is not possible, muscles in the affected areas are tensed.

Passengers on an elevator assume a defensive position facing the door and the floor-indicator panel. They attempt to protect their personal space without displaying avoidance behavior and at the same time allot the available space equally. Those wearing strong perfume, having unpleasant body odor, or infringing on others' space with cigarette or cigar smoke are considered rude. Because of the brief encounter, the offender seldom receives verbal reprimands. Psychological distance is provided by refraining from eye contact and conversation.

Public conveyances such as trains, busses, and cabs create a greater discomfort because more time is spent in closer confinement. People busy themselves with tasks such as reading and sleeping and avoid acknowledging the presence of others. Acknowledgment changes "nonpeople" into people, which heightens the discomfort of sharing intimate space with strangers.

In a hospital setting a space of 6 to 18 inches between client and care giver is close enough to see, hear, and touch but also distant enough to refrain from contact. Following painful treatments and examinations, clients may want care givers close but at the same time may not want to be touched. The far phase of intimate distance allows clients to psychologically recover from intrusive touch before other procedures are initiated.

Personal distance

Close phase. Personal interaction between family and friends or people well-known to each other occurs at a distance of 1½ to 2½ feet. At this distance, people can still touch or grasp one another, but they are too far apart for much body contact.

When working with elderly clients, it may be necessary for care givers to interact at this closeness to help compensate for visual and hearing loss. If the individual is unable to get out of bed, items such as glasses, a clock or watch, pictures, cards, and flowers should be kept within close personal distance on the nightstand or overbed table.

Far phase. Contact between individuals at an arm's length of 2½ to 4 feet is limited to touch. The conversation that takes place at this interval centers around topics of personal interest and involvement.

In a hospital or nursing home the curtain separating beds is at an arm's distance, and closing it can help to create a sense of personal distance and privacy. Clients may be afraid that drawing the curtain will offend their roommate and may instead turn away and face the wall. When care givers observe this nonverbal behavior, they can check with the client to see if the curtain should be pulled. Partial closure allows for visual privacy but prevents what some people describe as a "hemmed-in" feeling.

Social distance

Close phase. Social distance of 4 to 7 feet is outside the limit of touch. People who work together tend to maintain this spacing as do those attending a casual social gathering. To stand and converse with a seated person at this distance not only creates a domineering effect but also causes neck discomfort for the seated person.

Clients in a nursing home or hospital are more likely to consider a space as social if the area is close to their rooms. Sitting areas at the ends of

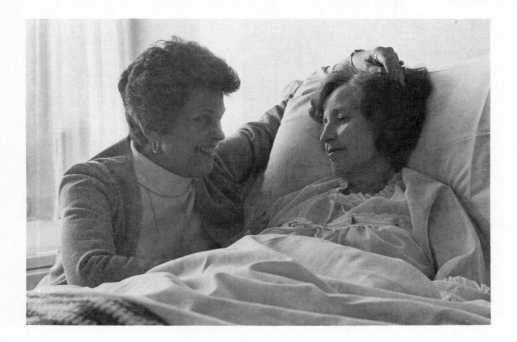

Personal distance.
Courtesy of Riverside Hospital Hospice Program, Newport News, Virginia.

corridors are used primarily by those whose rooms are adjacent. The farther the individual's room is from the area, the more the area is considered public. Despite the fact that most semiprivate rooms lack adequate space and privacy for socializing, most clients prefer to visit with people in this area rather than a public area such as the lobby.

Far phase. Formal transactions are carried out at a distance of 7 to 12 feet. Desks in offices help maintain this separation between the person behind the desk and those who interact with the person. This separation can be used as a screen between people without appearing to be rude. The receptionist's area in a physician's office is spaced about 10 feet from the chairs in the waiting area, allowing the receptionist to continue working. A closer proximity would mandate conversation. When individuals converse at the far phase of social distance, their voices are noticeably louder and visual contact is more important than when people are closer together.

In most open intensive care units approximately 7 to 12 feet separate the nurses' station from the clients' rooms. Although the nurses and clients have visual access to each other, glass partitions prevent the transfer of sounds beyond the immediate area. This separation allows both to retreat into their own personal spaces when they are not interacting.

Public distance

Close phase. A distance of 12 to 25 feet places people well outside the circle of involvement. People are perceived as less than life size, and any verbal exchange is loud but not full volume.

The distance between client rooms and the adjacent hallway or corridor is public distance, and clients may elect to close their doors so as not to be disturbed by noise or people within this public area. A closed-door phenomenon exists in health care settings, which recognizes closed doors as necessary and reasonable in theory but difficult to achieve in reality. Members of the care team sometimes respond to closed doors as though they have been closed out of their territory. Some visitors expect the hospitalized person to be host or hostess and ever receptive at a continual open house. Visitation hours, Do Not Disturb signs, or obvious physical discomfort may fail to deter visitors, and clients are left to endure when they are too sick or too sensitive to repel the inconsiderate visitors. One client summed up his needs with, ''God bless the nurse who will see to it that I get some peace and quiet and rest.''

Some extended care facilities are providing their clients with Do Not Disturb signs that they can use at designated times during the day when care or treatment is not usually scheduled. If the sign is hung on the closed door and for some reason the care giver is concerned about the individual, the room is entered only if the client does not respond to the care giver's knock.

Far phase. Beyond a distance of 25 feet subtle shades of meaning are lost that are usually conveyed by the vocal tones or through subtle expressions and movement, and nonverbal emphasis shifts to overall body posturing. As distance reduces people to minute size, involvement with them as human beings also diminishes.

Clients awakening from anesthetic report distorted visual and auditory perceptions ''like everyone is far away.'' Faces are blurred, and words if heard are likely to be forgotten. Physical contact is important, and sometimes all that clients remember of the immediate postoperative experience is the fact that they were sick, they hurt, and someone held their hand.

SPATIAL NEEDS

People have spatial needs that are important to a healthy existence. The minimum amount of space necessary under given conditions before negative psychological and physiological effects are produced is difficult to determine. Short-term anterospective studies do point out environmental influence on behavior, but causality between space and morbidity and between space and mortality cannot definitely be determined because of legal, moral, and ethical implications against this type of research. Understandably, much of the effects of environment on humans is learned retrospectively, and frequently causation is only theorized because of the myriad of factors involved.

Although it is recognized that the environment does influence behavior and health, seldom is its importance included within the treatment plan. Because many individuals in hospitals and nursing homes spend a great deal of time in their rooms and many spend extended time in bed, the topic of spatial needs is presented here.

Minimal spacing

The interrelationship of limited space, behavior, and health was the focus of a prison study published by the National Institute of Justice. This study pointed out that long-term inmates housed in overcrowded prisons become ill, die, commit suicide, and create disciplinary problems more frequently than those confined in private cells of at least 50 square feet. More space was considered necessary when inmates were confined for large parts of the day to their housing units, although inmates included in this study were confined to their cells only during sleeping hours.[7] This study included prisons across the United States with inmates that differed in age, racial or ethnic identification, and the type of crime committed. Whereas it is not known if these spatial behaviors can be translated to the general population, it is known that some institutionalized people outside of prisons do not have the benefit of 50 square feet of living space, which was considered minimum for inmate population.

Although extreme behavior associated with inadequate space may be prevented by providing a minimum of 50 square feet of space per individual, Altman and Haythorn[1] found that abnormal behavior was still evident when people were isolated in an area of 72 square feet per person. Their research involved the spatial behavior of nine pairs of volunteer sailors who were socially isolated in dyads in 12 by 12 foot rooms (72 square feet per person) for 10 days. These men gradually became more possessive of fixed areas in the room, personal objects, and finally more mobile, less personal objects. At the same time there was also a general pattern of social withdrawal. These behavior patterns were not apparent in the control group members who had access to other people and outside facilities.

Researchers have concluded that the minimum personal space for living is 8 to 10 square meters (86 to 108 square feet) per person, and when this available living space is lacking, it is found that there are twice as many social and physical disorders. Most current standards for institutionalized persons mandate 80 square feet for multibed rooms and 100 square feet in one-bed rooms. New additions on old buildings reveal the striking contrast between these current minimum standards and previous ones. When compared with the old rooms, the new ones are described as huge. The concern is for clients who do not have minimal personal space, and it is these individuals who desperately need the benefit of space outside their rooms. Unless care givers recognize the relationship between adequate space and physical and psychological health, the client may end up with problems that additional space could have prevented.

When clients begin to spend more time in their rooms, there is an increased incidence of withdrawal behavior and at the same time clients exhibiting greater control and defensive behavior involving items and space within the room. In the following example nursing intervention is directed toward increasing mobility and reducing the effects of isolation.

■ Mrs. D. and Mrs. J. had shared a room together in the nursing home for almost a year. They got along well and tolerated any idiosyncrasies the other might have. Both ladies were social and spent most of their time out of the room.

Mrs. D. experienced a brief illness during which she was confined to her room. Following recovery, she began to be socially withdrawn, and unless care givers walked with her down the hall, she stayed in her room. The more isolated she became, the more she complained about her roommate, "She's always leaving her stuff on my side, and she wakes me up at night, clomping through my part of the room to the bathroom." Although the two used to spend time visiting with each other, Mrs. D. began to treat the television as her best friend, and Mrs. J. commented, "That suits me fine, the old crab."

Within a few days Mrs. D.'s irritation changed to psychological withdrawal, and she wanted to be left alone. When a physical examination revealed no organic basis for her behavior, nurses began to intervene. They realized that getting Mrs. D. out of her room several times a day was just as important as position changes are for bedfast clients. The more she stayed in her room, the more withdrawn she became, to the point that her behavior was pushing others away.

Nurses shared this information with Mrs. D., who said it was "hogwash" and accused the staff of being cruel and inhumane by "kicking a sick old lady out of her room." Staff members helped Mrs. D. with walking, and when she complained of weakness, they offered a wheelchair, which she said was for "old fogies." At first Mrs. D. just sat in front of the television in the lounge, but with encouragement she slowly became more interested in others. Within a week her normal behavior began to return. ───────────────────────

For the institutionalized person few sleeping rooms provide adequate space for extended healthy existence. Lack of personal living space produces feelings of crowding, loss of control, physiological stress, and illness complaints. Bedfast individuals are desperately in need of increased visual area, and the view from a window can create this much-needed psychological space. Clients able to spend time outside their rooms benefit from this additional area but may not be aware of these spatial needs. Visitors are usually anxious to help by taking a friend or relative on walks or brief outings in a wheelchair. One client commented, ''I didn't know that I needed to get out, but I must have because I felt so much better when I got back.'' When limited space prompts social and psychological withdrawal, physical or psychological morbidity may follow.

Factors affecting spatial needs

Situations contribute to different spatial needs, and many researchers have found that persons under a great amount of stress possess or prefer a larger personal or social environment than do persons with little stress. This brings up questions about the spatial needs of people during disaster, especially when being sheltered in limited areas. Although shelters have been designed according to the needs of people during simulated conditions, a real disaster might prompt spatial needs entirely different from those experienced in practice situations.

Personality abnormalities such as claustrophobia (fear of closed spaces) and agoraphobia (fear of open spaces) show contrasting spatial behaviors. Clients with schizophrenia require more space and seem to withdraw from interpersonal relationships and intimacy. Kendall[5] demonstrated a relationship between locus of control and interpersonal space. Individuals with external locus of control perceive themselves as less able to control what happens in social interaction and therefore maintain a greater distance with others than do those with internal locus of control, who recognize inner control in social interactions.

Psychiatrists report that emotionally disturbed children require more interaction distance. These youngsters may be less trusting and more distant because they have had experiences of being hurt by others. Adolescents described as hostile, defiant, and aggressive demand more personal space than normal adolescents. Prisoners who commit crimes against other people need approximately twice the amount of personal area as prisoners who commit victimless crimes such as possession of drugs.[2]

When personality is considered a variable affecting spatial needs, it becomes even more evident that spatial needs are unique to each person and to each situation.

CRITICAL SPACE

All vertebrates have an essential component of aggression that is controlled by the development of hierarchies and by sufficient space. When density and crowding preclude adequate space, the survival of the species is threatened. Much of the insight into the effects of density and crowding on humans is obtained from research done on animals. Unless animals have adequate space, survival is impossible, and when the animal population builds up so that this critical space is no longer available, a situation develops that results in removal of some of the animals. It was first theorized that die-offs in animal groups were related to a decreased food supply; however, following mass suicides of lemmings, rabbits, and rats, carcasses revealed no signs of starvation.

Endocrine studies before, during, and after animal die-offs have shown that as density increases, stress builds up until an endocrine reaction is triggered that contributes to population reduction. Calhoun[3] raised three generations of Norway rats in a stressful situation of crowding. In addition to physiological effects evidenced on autopsy, he observed disruptions of nest building, reproduction difficulties, and gross negligence in the care of young. Courtship patterns were totally disrupted, as male rats frequently mounted other rats regardless of age, sex, or receptivity. Aggressive behavior increased significantly, and only the most dominant males were able to maintain their own personal space. Hyperactive males ran in packs, disregarding all spatial rights and boundaries except those backed by force. Mortality and morbidity increased dramatically in what Calhoun described as a behavioral sink.

The increased knowledge of the effect of density on animal behavior leads to concern about the outcome of crowding and density on human behavior. How much of the information gained from animals can be related to conditions of human density and crowding is not known. Mass suicides have also

The 1972 demolition of the Pruitt-Igoe housing project in St. Louis.
From the St. Louis Post-Dispatch.

been evidenced in human beings, but endocrine studies are not available and autopsies were not performed. Many factors contributed to these deaths, but it is entirely possible that density and crowding were among the stressors.

The Pruitt-Igoe housing project that opened in St. Louis in the 1950s turned out to be a human behavioral sink. Approximately 12,000 people were crammed onto 57 acres of land, with little regard for play areas, proper maintenance, or security. The project has been described as boxes stacked into 11-story vertical neighbor-

hoods, without money for landscaping, painted walls in general circulation areas, or even ground-floor toilets. Elevators were installed on alternate floors, and elderly people who were unable to climb steps became prisoners in their own apartments. Without play areas children either wandered the streets unsupervised or were kept inside.

What was to have been low-income dwellings turned into a fortress of crime and a ghetto for drug addicts, drunks, rapists, and derelicts. Ultimately an 18-year-old housing project that cost 36 million dollars to build was demolished in 1972 by the city. Unfortunately, a regard for human spatial needs may not appear important or necessary until after the damage has been done. The needs of people are of utmost importance whenever physical and social environments are created. Rather than expecting people to change to fit the environment, it is the environment that must be changed to meet the needs of people.

Density and crowding

In any discussion of spatial needs, it is important to clarify the difference between density and crowding. Density is the number of people in a given space, whereas crowding is a subjective state that may develop in either high- or low-density situations.

An individual's perception of being crowded is influenced by a multitude of things, among which are space, noise, personality, past experiences in similar situations, and the number and relationship of people involved. On university campuses across the country, many dormitory rooms that were designed for double occupancy are housing three students. Without question density exists in these living conditions. Parents call the situation "crowded." Student reaction to the tripled rooms varies from, "It's a blast!" to, "It's fine if you're a sardine."

Density does not automatically mean increased stress or antisocial behavior. Millions of people each year elect to sit in a packed stadium and watch a sports event rather than viewing it on television. Many will admit that they could see it better at home and that they miss the instant replays but, "The crowd is what makes the game. The excitement is like electricity. It makes me feel alive." Density is not usually considered undesirable if presence in a highly populated situation is by choice and if the amount of time in such conditions is limited.

High density contributed to a tragic outcome when on December 3, 1979, 8,000 rock fans stampeded to get first-come, first-served seats to The Who's concert in Cincinnati. Ticket holders waited in line as long as 7 hours in a crowd that was described as being too dense to light a cigarette. When this intenseness was added to fatigue, hunger, drugs, and alcohol, aggressive forceful behavior resulted in the death of 11 young people and the injury of 22 more.

When stress increases, people need more space, and if this space is not available, further stress is created. People insist on having their own territory as a way of minimizing stress, and therefore when people experience displeasure and high arousal, they may become more forceful.

High-density living

Studies in social psychology point out that the larger the group, the more likely that people will experience lack of privacy and the loss of self-identity. The preservation of privacy and self-identity can be achieved in institutions by replacing open wards and dorms with separate cubicles and providing individuals with their own cupboards and shelves to place personal items.

If human beings have the choice, they do not passively accept long-term high density without trying to cope with or offset potentially harmful effects. City dwellers cope with high density by tuning out those things that do not directly effect themselves. Students in crowded dormitories spend more time outside their rooms. Although it is difficult to isolate the effects of density and crowding, people do have spatial needs and these needs account for certain important patterns of behavior.

Part of helping is being alert to the client's need for space. If individuals are physically and psychologically able, they will attempt to alter the environment to meet these needs. As capabilities decrease, manipulating the environment becomes less possible. Apathy, withdrawal, and aggression may be ways of responding to inadequate space when physical response is not possible.

TERRITORIALITY

Homeowners all over the country have decided that the invisible boundaries between properties are not enough. Tree or plant groupings serve as a subtle lot line reminder, with continuous hedges and shrubs planted for the purpose of separating properties. Of greater interest is the fact that more and more homeowners are fencing themselves in. The November 7th, 1966, issue of *Newsweek* reported that a Boston fence maker estimated a sales increase of 45 percent a year and Washington fence makers described their business as fantastic. At that time Houston's Yellow Pages listed 62 fence companies, with advertisements ranging from waist-high chain-link to 6-foot cedar fences. In 1982 Houston's Yellow Pages advertised fences described as ornamental, iron, wood, and chain link for 123 fence companies. In 16 years, the number of fence companies almost doubled. The word for this need to gather, demarcate, and protect is territoriality—a behavior by which an individual claims and defends a specific area against others.

Purpose of territoriality

The possession of a territory fulfills a basic need in humans for security or freedom from anxiety that can be achieved in an area where one holds mastery and is surrounded by familiar people and things. So strong is this need that even the newly admitted client possessively refers to areas and items in the room as ''mine'' and begins to personalize the area with placement of items, cards, and plants. This structuring of space and the arrangement of objects within this area is unique to the person and is a visible symbol that says, ''This is *my* area.'' Following surgery or treatment, clients frequently ask to be returned to their rooms, where they are able to relax their defenses and rest. If a client's territory is reduced because of immobility, personal items are brought within reach for use, enjoyment, and also for protection. It is not uncommon to find dentures, letters, and pictures tucked within the covers of an elderly person's bed, and if the person asks that these be left, the request should be honored. The further away territorial boundaries are, the less direct control the owner has in defending them.

Types of territories

Basically territories are either permanent or temporary and differ in terms of purpose and organization. Permanent territories are geographically outlined areas such as houses, yards, and other property that are protected by law and its courts. Within a home there are areas identified as belonging to family members, such as Mom's kitchen, Dad's shop, the boy's or girl's room, or the family room. Within a health care setting permanent territories are assigned to multidisciplinary groups, and within each group there usually are other claimed spaces. Clients also establish territory in their rooms; however, this claim is not as strong as the territories of the professional groups within the hospital. For example, health care workers often enter the client's territory without permission, whereas the client's entry into the professional's territory is only through invitation.

Temporary territories are within a setting that is available to the public, and park benches and restaurant tables are examples of this type of territory. Some public places arrange chairs in a manner that is *not* conducive to comfort or conversation, minimizing territoriality in these areas. This may be experienced in airport terminals in which the chairs are bolted to the floor and arranged side by side facing the ticket counter. The next row might be directly behind the first and facing the opposite direction, and if rows do face each other, there is usually a room's distance between. These arrangements make it virtually impossible to converse comfortably for any length of time, and this discomfort is capitalized on to encourage people to leave the waiting areas and go into cafes, bars, and shops where they will spend money.

Functions of territories

According to Lyman,[6] territories can be classified by their use or function. Public territories provide freedom of access and are available to almost anyone for temporary use. The lobby of a hospital or nursing home is an example of public territory, although some clients frequent the area enough that they establish a kind of personal territory and become upset or dismayed if someone uses "their chair" or "their space."

Home territories allow for freedom of behavior as well as a sense of control and intimacy. Normal emotions can be expressed without fear of losing the love of others. In a hospital the same behavior may prompt the words "depressed" or "hostile" to be written on the chart.

Interaction territories are areas for social gatherings, and those involved set their own boundaries and duration and decide who is welcome and who is denied access. This type of territory is often seen in hospital or clinic waiting rooms outside treatment areas. Clients and family members form an informal interaction group to support each other as they experience a stressful time. Seldom is a health professional included in the interaction, and the appearance of a physician or nurse will probably interrupt conversation temporarily.

Body territories include the human body and the space it encompasses. Theoretically the body is the most private territory belonging to an individual, and for others to view or touch one's body is subject to great restriction. Clothing, jewelery, and personal items carried with the person are also included in this type of territory, and to clients these items are a symbolic link to home. Once a client is settled following an emergency admission, one of the questions frequently asked is, "What did you do with my clothes?" It is necessary for care

"She's in my chair!"
Illustration by Tom Weinman.

givers to take the time to let the individual know exactly where these items have been placed and that they are safe.

Territorial encroachments

Territorial encroachments exist in different forms. Violation is the unwarranted use of another's territory and may be done with eyes, with voice or other sounds, or with the body. Having a roommate that snores may be considered a serious violation of territory by some clients. Invasion of someone else's territory is more encompassing and permanent in nature. Sometimes clients will feel that their territory has been invaded when a roommate crosses over their space on the way to the bathroom. Contamination of another's territory is not done by a person's presence but rather by what is left behind. This infringement may be in the form of litter, stains, excreta, odor, and body heat. Finding food on clean silverware or lipstick stains on a clean glass are examples of territorial contamination.[6]

Obviously, not all territorial encroachments produce a defensive response. The reaction to territorial infringement depends on who did the invading and where it occurred, how and why it was done, the type of territory involved, and how long the trespass lasted. A nurse may quietly enter a client's hospital room in the middle of the night to check on the individual's condition and not be considered a territorial threat. The client who mistakenly enters another person's room in the middle of the night will create quite a different response.

Defending a territory. Temporary territory such as space located in a public place is more difficult to defend than is permanent territory or property, which is backed by law. To prevent invasion of temporary territory an effort is made to personalize the territory so that others will recognize it as taken and go elsewhere. Claiming a territory can be achieved in a number of ways. A person's presence is the most effective way of convincing others that the territory is taken. If the owner's continual presence is not possible, another person may be asked to hold a public space until the owner returns. Peo-

ple who are frequently present in a certain area can establish a type of tenure that will be supported by their neighbors in their absence. The newly admitted nursing home client may have difficulty finding a chair that does not already "belong" to someone else. Almost as if he or she were involved in an initiation, the person moves from chair to chair only to be told, "That's Mr. Jones's chair." "And that's Mrs. Jones's chair." The nurse can prevent such an interaction by pointing out a chair that has not been claimed.

A second way of marking a temporary territory is by leaving behind a personal item, called a marker, on the empty place. A jacket will usually hold a public seat in a person's absence, but the individual must consider if saving the space justifies the possible loss of the jacket.

The third way to identify a space as taken is with a marker of little value, such as a newspaper. If conditions of density do not occur, the newspaper will probably save the seat, particularly if the newspaper is a current one.

Permanent territories are also easier to defend when they are personalized, and clients in many nursing homes are allowed to bring small furniture and special items from home that help in marking their territory. Multioccupancy rooms in health care settings lack many of the visual boundaries and markers that make territorial defense easier, so Nelson[8] conducted a study in two nursing homes to see if visibly defining each client's territory would have any effect on behavior. Wide strips of yellow vinyl adhesive tape were placed on the floor of double-occupancy rooms in such a way as to mark each client's territory and a common space. When the territories were visibly defined, clients showed reduced anxiety and improvements in self-satisfaction and general adjustment. Fifteen days later the tape was removed, and client behavior returned to prestudy baselines. For many clients, the tape had made the double-occupancy rooms more like single rooms, and they responded positively to this perceived territory.

Responding to territorial trespass. Even though people are involved in the same type of interaction,

Staking out a territory.
Photograph by A. Jann Davis.

they will require different amounts of space to feel comfortable. Minimal space can be determined by having a person walk toward another individual and stop when he or she feels uncomfortable. The space separating comfort from discomfort is a person's personal boundary, and invasion occurs whenever this invisible boundary is crossed.

Persons with schizophrenia have been shown to require more personal space than other psychiatric clients, and if this space is violated, the flight response may occur. This flight response can be eliminated by simply providing a larger amount of interacting space.

Almost all nursing home clients establish territories within their rooms, and many express anxiety toward territorial invasion. A certain amount of staff intrusion is anticipated and tolerated; however, intrusion by other clients produces more anxiety. Long-term clients and those who share space usually show less anxiety toward territorial invasion than do new admissions or those who have private rooms. Apparently, clients either become accustomed to intrusions or learn to accept them because they feel they can not be prevented.

Territorial invasion of personal space prompts behavior that ranges from aggressive defense to apparent apathy. One client found another in *his* chair "for the umpteenth time!" and whopped the offender over the head with his cane. Another person may have responded to the same situation by glaring at the offender or quietly finding another chair. Regardless of the overt response, a certain amount of anxiety usually accompanies territorial intrusion.

Both defensive and offensive nonverbal displays to territorial trespass include the use of position, posture, and gesture to maintain a comfortable distance between the individuals. The person may look away (except for an occasional hostile glance toward the intruder), turn or lean away, position books or other objects between him or herself and the intruder, cross arms to form a frontal barrier, or gather in personal objects. Flight is more likely to occur if the invader is perceived as being more dominant or of a higher status.

Russo[9] spent 2 years studying the response of women college students whose territories in the college library were invaded. Invasion techniques consisted of sitting next to or across from these students. Flight responses were prompted most quickly by sitting beside and moving the chair closer to the subject. Whereas, women react more unfavorably to adjacent invasions, other researchers have noted that men feel more stress from frontal invasion. Few subjects in these experiments asked the invader to move.

Not only do people dislike having their territories invaded but also they do not want to play the role of the invader. A person usually prefers to walk around rather than walk between two individuals who are conversing. When it is necessary to cross another's territory, head and eyes are lowered, apologies are offered, and the trespass is completed as quickly and quietly as possible.

On admission to a hospital or nursing home, the individual perceives this area as the nurses' terri-

Territorial invasion.

Illustration by Tom Weinman.

tory because of their 24-hour presence. Feeling somewhat like an intruder who is not sure what to expect, the client is likely to be tense, hesitant, and apologetic about inconveniencing the staff. In the following example the nurse minimizes this behavior by acknowledging the territory as the client's, explaining routines, and assuring the client that privacy will be respected.

■ Mr. Thomas, nurses will be checking your blood pressure every few hours for awhile. If your door is closed or the curtain is pulled around your bed, we'll let you know before we enter. At night you'll be reminded about the blood pressure before it's taken, but the nurse won't awaken you completely. Throughout your stay, we'll try not to disturb you more than is necessary. Because we're here to help you, please let us know if there's anything you need. _____

If the client is to share a room, hesitant behavior may be directed toward a roommate who is perceived as being dominant in established territory. Before long the newly admitted client begins to manifest territoriality with identification of bed, bedside stand, closet, overbed table, and the placement of personal items. Many disagreements between roommates are prompted by territorial invasion: "He always sits in my chair." "That television is so loud, how could anyone sleep!" "Her visitors smoke, and it about chokes me to death." When clients are unable to reach an amenable agreement over territorial disputes, it may be necessary to separate those involved. This example illustrates territorial concessions.

■ Mrs. Smith is admitted to a semiprivate room 2 days before her scheduled surgery. Her roommate, Mrs. Johnson, is also a new admission undergoing a series of tests. Both ladies are up and about in the room and make a special effort to share space and items such as furniture, the telephone, and television.

After her surgery Mrs. Smith asks to have the phone positioned on her nightstand, and she leaves her robe draped over the large comfortable chair. Mrs. Johnson is willing to make these concessions and is careful not to disturb her roommate with television or conversation.

As Mrs. Smith becomes more mobile, her roommate begins to reassert her territorial rights. She removes Mrs. Smith's robe from the chair and transfers the phone to her bedside table—with the excuse that she is expecting a call. Almost as though to compensate for the times when she was quiet, she talks louder and turns up the volume on the television. Mrs. Smith decides that she's never seen anyone so inconsiderate, and Mrs. Johnson comes to the conclusion that her roommate is demanding.

It is unlikely that either will understand that these defensive feelings are the result of territorial invasion. After a day or two of verbal and nonverbal negotiation, territory is reestablished and the discord between the ladies disappears. _____

If an agreement cannot be reached over variables such as heat and lighting, the one able to adjust these controls without crossing into the other's space will have the advantage. Even with ample amount of space, some individuals seem oblivious to others' territorial rights. Although people have psychological advantage in their own territory, it is usually the dominant person who is willing to fight back. The submissive victims quietly relinquish their claims or move on to new territories, with the hope that elsewhere privacy and belongings will remain undisturbed.

PRIVACY

Privacy constitutes a basic form of human territoriality that involves the right of the individual to decide when, where, what, and with whom personal information should be shared. Privacy allows for autonomy, emotional release, self-evaluation, and limited and protected communication that can be achieved by the temporary and voluntary withdrawal of an individual by physical or psychological means.[11]

Functions of privacy

The first function of privacy is personal autonomy—the desire to be independent without being manipulated or dominated by others. An individual needs the opportunity to be alone with thoughts and feelings in privacy, where the uniqueness of the person can be explored and developed. Independent from others, an individual tests ideas and practices thoughts before expressing opinions. Privacy makes it possible for the client to consider alternatives, think about outcomes, and make decisions.

A second function of privacy is to allow for emotional release that may not be achieved if others are continually in the person's presence. A client is virtually front and center as professionals come and go at all hours of the day and night. A perpetual audience creates an emotional mask that takes valuable energy to wear, and individuals cannot continue to play roles indefinitely. They need a chance to put down their guard, be themselves, and take off the mask. Care givers recognize the importance of emotional release but sometimes fail to acknowledge that for some this release may require the privacy of aloneness. Few clients will be as frank and honest as Mr. G. was when he announced to the nurse, "Don't expect me to be pleasant today. I'm tired, I don't feel good, and I have very little energy. My family's coming later today, and I want to save what energy I have for them. I hope you will understand if I seem rude or unpleasant."

A third function of privacy is self-evaluation—the need to integrate experiences into a meaningful pattern in the person's life so that actions can be as consistent and appropriate as possible. One client confided, "My life is like a soap opera, only I can't turn off the set. Just about the time I'm starting to figure out one problem, I get dumped on again. Just leave me alone. I need to think things out." This request for privacy may leave a helper not knowing whether to encourage the client to talk or to honor the request and leave the room. When-

ever a member of the helping professions is not sure what the client really wants, the client can be asked, "Would you like to talk about it, or would you prefer that I leave?" One of the kindest, most appreciated messages is one that conveys respect for privacy and at the same time extends an offer of support. "My name is J., and if you decide you would like someone to talk to, you can ask for me."

The last function of privacy is to allow for limited and protected communication. This confidence may be with a member of the health care team, minister, significant other, or friend. Without privacy, information becomes available to everyone, and in a computerized world these concerns are justifiably magnified.

Degrees of privacy

There are varying degrees of privacy that allow an individual to control the quality and quantity of social interactions. A person or persons in complete privacy cannot be seen or heard by others, making it possible for a close and frank relationship to take place. For the institutionalized person the nearest thing to complete privacy is in a private room when the door is closed. However, since there is always the possibility that intrusions may occur, intimacy is not likely. If this complete privacy is imposed, such as in protective isolation, the individual may be overwhelmed by a lack of sensory stimuli, which can be just as harmful as sensory overload.

Visual privacy or the protection from being seen by others can be achieved in a semiprivate room when the curtain is pulled between the beds or through the use of screens.

When an individual is unable to achieve the privacy needed, psychological privacy may be created through withdrawal. The person tunes out visual and auditory stimuli and retreats into a self-made solitude.

Ultimately people have to deal with themselves without the distraction of others and without certain social constraints. It is through privacy that an individual is able to attain self-understanding and self-identity.

Territoriality, space, and privacy contribute to an individual's physical and emotional well-being. Each person's attitude toward space changes with age, health, and living conditions. To ignore these spatial needs is to deny the person an environment conducive to health, identity, and a meaningful life.

CONVERSATION AND INTERACTION

Finding a comfortable distance for conversation and interaction is more difficult than it sounds. When standing, individuals move slightly backward or forward until just the right distance is achieved, and then the topic changes and the spatial transaction begins all over again. Some people want to be close during conversation, and others need more space. This creates an advance and retreat tactic that can end with one person cornered or talked right out of the room. People who are seated will attempt to adjust either their chairs or themselves to meet their proxemic needs, and when people are seated around tables, the seating arrangement usually reflects personal and spatial needs. Comfortable interaction distance is determined by many factors, and an understanding of these variables is both enlightening and relevant to therapeutic interaction.

Conversational distance

When people have the choice of sitting side by side, around corners, or face-to-face, subconsciously many things are considered before a seat is selected. It has been repeatedly proven that side by side seating is the most intimate, followed by corner and face-to-face seating. Distance between seats is usually more important than the type of seating. For example, if individuals want to become friendly, an approval-seeking distance of approximately 4½ feet is selected, and when polite social conversation is desired, a distance of 5½ feet is more appropriate. If, however, avoidance is the message, sitting a distance of 8 feet or more from the other person will send the nonverbal message of disinterest.

Table tactics

When seated at a rectangular table, individuals usually prefer a corner or opposite seating for impersonal conversations and side by side seating at round tables. When in a restaurant, intimate friends usually choose side by side seating, whereas others are more likely to assume opposite seating.

A home health care nurse made the comment that she did some of her best nursing at the kitchen table over a cup of coffee. "I really don't need the coffee or the cookies," she admitted, "but my clients want to talk, and they need something to do with their hands. At the table they talk about things they won't anywhere else." The kitchen table symbolically represents an informal location where people gather and personal topics can be discussed. It also provides an ideal distance of 4 to 6 feet between individuals, depending on corner or opposite seating. Distance or proximity can be easily achieved, making it possible for the persons to adjust the space to fit the topic.

Sooner or later most health professionals are involved in meetings that relate either directly or indirectly to client care. Some behind-the-scene psychology of small groups may benefit the outcome of this structured gathering. If the meeting is formal, it is apt to take place around a rectangular conference table with chairs positioned along the sides. The end positions carry with them a status or dominant factor partially because the individuals seated in these positions have greater visual access to others around the table. A task-oriented leader, flanked by a hierarchy of personnel, may be attracted to this head position. Relative status of those around the table can be determined by the number of seats between the person and the leader. A leader who is interested in group relationships and involvement may prefer the middle-side position, which is a secondary dominant position. This type of arrangement is common in a meeting of colleagues or peers who have an appointed chairman.

Opponents in a meeting prefer to keep an eye on each other and are therefore apt to sit opposite one another. A middle-side position can also be used for active defense or disagreement with a leader seated at the end. Conversation usually flows across the table rather than around it, so it is not surprising that most of the talking comes from the dominant personalities strategically seated in either the end or the middle-side position. The weakest positions are the seats between the powers or those the farthest from the leader. When people want to be active participants in a meeting, they select end or middle-side positions. Those who want a more passive role sit in between.

Seating behavior is not accidental, and the more that is known about face-to-face groups, the more that becomes apparent about the people within these groups.

Dimensions affecting self-disclosure

Both physical and phenomenological distance affects a client's anxiety, communication ease, and sharing of personal fears and feelings. Phenomenological closeness can be achieved through touch or by brief self-disclosure by the helper, which in turn may promote positive feelings and increased client self-disclosure. However, the care giver should be cautioned about revealing too much personal information, or the interaction becomes a social relationship involving the matching of experiences, stories, and ideas. When personal information is given, it must be determined if it is to benefit the client or the helping professional.

Physical distance of approximately 5 to 6 feet encourages a client to talk longer than if the distance is closer or further away. For each interaction the appropriate distance, both physical and psychological, plays an important role within the interaction of a therapeutic relationship.

When a client is interviewed, a face-to-face arrangement produces a stimulus value that facilitates an exchange of factual information. This positioning is particularly useful during the admission interview, and an overbed table positioned between the nurse and the client makes this arrangement less confronting.

If there is to be an exchange of feelings or affect, sitting at a 45 degree angle is encouraged. When the interaction takes place within the client's room, the helper seeks permission before sitting down and selects a chair that will leave the client enough space to get up, walk around, or leave the room. Sitting on a client's bed not only hems the person in but also prevents the helper from looking at the person without staring. When the care giver is seated first, the client has more freedom to adjust his or her chair for comfortable spacing. Throughout the interaction, the proxemic behaviors of the individual may nonverbally express more than the person is able or willing to express verbally.

Variables affecting conversation

Spacing of individuals is affected by a number of things, including cultural background, personality, the task at hand, and the nature of the physical setting. Proxemic behaviors of several cultures outside the United States will be considered in a separate section (pp. 69-72).

Culture. Generalizations from different cultures within the United States are presented here to help make the reader more aware of proxemic similarities as well as differences. These descriptions must be viewed as tentative because cultural practices evolve continually.

Watson[10] has conducted some of the most extensive studies on cross-cultural proxemics and identifies cultures as "contact" or "noncontact" according to the way members within group interact with one another. Persons within the contact group face each other more directly, interact closer, touch more, use more eye contact, and speak in a louder voice. Within this contact group are Arabs, Latin Americans, and Southern Europeans. Noncontact, or more distant groups, include the Asians, Indians and Pakistanis, Northern Europeans, and Americans, and these individuals usually try to avoid touching when in crowds and apologize if touch accidently occurs.

Groups from all over the world have brought their practices, beliefs, and life-styles to the United States. Although there has been some degree of acculturation, a great deal of diversity exists. Proxemic behaviors do differ and although much of this diversity can be attributed to culture, some may be prompted by socioeconomic difference rather than ethnic background. The difficulty arises in trying to separate these two factors. For example, studies comparing the spatial patterns of Afro-Americans with European Americans have produced contradictory findings, and it is theorized that any differences that do exist may be attributed to socioeconomic factors rather than ethnic background. The need for space may be similar, but minority cultures typically do not have the personal living space afforded European Americans. Another example involves Asian Americans whose noncontact cultural heritage is like that of European Americans. Yet many of the Asian Americans in the United States live in conditions of great density and crowding that are prompted by economics, not cultural heritage. The negative effects of forced density and crowding are reflected in higher stress levels, and in the San Francisco area several investigators have reported suicide rates among Chinese that are two to three times the national average.

What is comfort in one culture may be crowded in another, and what is too close in one may be distant in another. Most of the time Afro-Americans and European Americans maintain greater spatial distances than do Mexican Americans. During conversation Afro-Americans and European Americans usually stand just beyond touching distance, whereas Mexican Americans arrange themselves within tactile range and use touch during conversation. Individuals in the Middle Eastern or Oriental cultures are taught humility and modesty and value individuals who subordinate themselves. Interaction distance is determined by status, and when conversing with someone who is older or of a higher social position, people from Asian cultures allow more space and display passive behaviors such as keeping the head low, speaking softly, and averting eye gaze. Because people in the United States achieve psychological distance by decreasing eye contact with others, they tend to view individuals who avert gaze as being distant, submissive, or evasive. Hispanic people usually like direct eye contact, but Afro-Americans are more apt to consider face-to-face gazing as a putdown or a confrontation.

Most researchers agree that when individuals of dissimilar ethnic groups are interacting, greater personal space is required than when persons share the same ethnic group. For example, when a European American approaches an Afro-American or Mexican American, more space is necessary than if the person were approaching a European American.

Broad cultural generalizations are too imprecise, and small studies may not be representative of the cultural group. Through observation and study it is the health care provider who attempts to identify consistent cultural patterns so that these variables do not block communication.

Personal characteristics. Usually a man and a woman will converse at a closer distance than two women, and men require more conversational space than women. Individuals are more likely to interact at closer distances with those of their general age group; however, the very young and very old encourage interaction at closer range. The elderly person's sensory loss may contribute to this need for closeness, which may be misunderstood by some. In a helping relationship, the least inhibited communication occurs when both the helper and client are young and of the same sex, and the most inhibited communication is likely to result when the helper and client are of the same age and the opposite sex.

Physical characteristics such as height and weight necessitate changes in interaction distance. Trying to converse with a very tall person requires a greater distance so that eye contact can be made without straining neck muscles. Obvious handicaps initially cause people to be more distant, but this distance does decrease as the length of the interaction increases.

Attitudes and prejudice also affect conversation. If an individual expects another to be warm and friendly, a closer distance is initiated than when an unfriendly interaction is anticipated. Subjective negative behavioral reports concerning clients may result in more distant proximity, causing the client to decide that it is the care giver who is cold or unfriendly. Obviously this type of misunderstanding could perpetuate problems. In most instances people who interact at a closer distance are evaluated as being warmer and liking each other more and are considered more empathic and understanding. When approval is desired, a closer proximity is combined with increased smiling, eye contact, and use of gestures.

When friends interact, they stand or sit closer together than acquaintances, and acquaintances stand or sit closer than strangers. Status is associated with greater space and the freedom to move about, and the greater the status discrepancy, the more the distance between communicators.

In lounges of hospitals and nursing homes people who do not want to interact will communicate this by their selection of seating. The person who sits in the middle of a couch is communicating, "Don't sit here," whereas sitting toward the end invites another to interact.

Personality characteristics such as introversion, extroversion, and traits of dependence and independence are other variables considered subconsciously during interactions. Some have found that introverts are more distant, whereas extroverts use closer proximity and allow others to approach them more closely. Dependent individuals tend to be more affiliative when anticipating an unpleasant experience than those who are independent. This may explain why some clients prefer to be alone before treatment or surgery and others want each and every one of their loved ones with them. In general there is more of a desire to be with others when anticipating a pleasant rather than an unpleasant experience regardless of personality type.

Topic. Pleasant topics encourage proximity; however, close distances that are inappropriate for the situation can elicit negative attitudes and decrease the amount of conversation regardless of the topic. People who are stressed require a greater conversation distance, whereas those who are happy and excited move closer.

Forward or backward movements during conversation identify beginnings, endings, and topic changes. People move closer when initiating conversation or a new topic, followed by mutual spatial adjustment until comfort is obtained. When the topic or conversation is exhausted, the individuals once again increase distance.

When people are talking about personal topics, they tend to need more space. This can be achieved by distancing the entire body, leaning away, or by looking less often at the listener. The conversation may be directed at the ceiling or the floor with only brief glances toward the other person.

Physical setting. Numerous environmental factors, such as lighting, temperature, noise, available space, and amount of privacy, will influence interaction distance. Dim lighting encourages people to move closer and speak more quietly. Restaurants often depend on this response to increase the number of patrons that can comfortably be served in one area. A formal or unfamiliar setting will produce greater distances between strangers and closer proximity with familiar individuals.

In a large room people sit closer together, and a small room invites more distance that may not be available in areas such as a hospital room. Two people can sit in close proximity at a 45 degree angle if there is a corner table between them. Another way to create psychological distance is to place an overbed table between the client and care giver when they are seated in direct orientation. When such a protective barrier is not available, the client may display barrier behavior with body and extremities directed back and away and gaze concentrated on items in the room rather than looking at the care giver.

Proximity. Greater contact among persons enhances the possibility of liking and friendship; however, increased contact does nothing to benefit a relationship between hostile people. For the institutionalized person physical closeness may interfere with privacy and in turn impede positive interaction. Nurses in extended care facilities find that conflictual exchanges occur more often between clients sharing a room or occupying adjacent rooms. Positive interaction is more likely between clients who are not too close and not too far, and this ideal distance seems to be at least two rooms away. More arguments and fights are reported when nursing home clients are confined in close spatial proximity, usually in those areas that house clients requiring the most nursing care. Since most interactions between profoundly retarded persons can be characterized as aggressive, those individuals who live next to each other have a greater chance of interaction and a greater frequency of assaults between them. An increase in space produces a decrease in interaction and therefore reduces the frequency of aggression.

The spacing that individuals select for conversation and interaction is not random but the result of personality, cultural and ethnic background, topic, and environment. During any helping relationship proxemic needs must be evaluated and attended to, for something as simple as being too close or too far away may block communication. By understanding the interaction between the physical, social, and cultural aspects of the environment, the care giver can create an optimum human milieu.

CULTURE AND PROXEMICS

The following section is not intended as a comprehensive overview of cultures nor is it meant to be representative of major ethnic groups. Although great diversity exists within any one cultural group, generalities are presented here to contrast different proxemic patterns that emerge from a dynamic process involving structuring of time, space, material, and involvement. This contrast serves not only to highlight cultural diversities in different countries, but also to emphasize some of the major cultural patterns that have been brought to the United States.

The Germans

Although privacy is important to North Americans, Germans will go to almost any length to preserve their private sphere. This desire for privacy is a characteristic that is prevalent both in the environment and in interactions with others. An

American exchange student made the following observation about her new home in Germany:

> This house is so beautiful, but there are many closed doors so that all you see is a family room and no hall. I have my own room and so do each of their four children. There are locks everywhere in this house. I have four: my door, my desk drawer, closet, and my bike. The front door locks behind you.

If the letter were evaluated on the basis of North American proxemic patterns, the environment would appear to be cold, withdrawn, and of questionable safety. When evaluated in view of the German emphasis on privacy and security, a different message is conveyed.

In most homes in Germany family members have their own private space, even though this space may be small. Doors are important in the German culture; they are solid and fit well and have a lock that offers security. Many of their hotel rooms have double doors for soundproofing. Open doors in Germany are considered disorderly and represent exposure. Therefore a closed door does not necessarily mean that the person behind the door wants to be alone.

Yards in Germany are arranged for privacy and are often beautifully landscaped and fenced. When in public, approaching another at a distance of 7 or 8 feet mandates the same personal interaction that would take place at a distance of 3 or 4 feet in the United States. To look directly at a German, regardless of intervening space, is to intrude on that person's privacy, and for the same reason to photograph a German without permission is considered rude.

Germans highly respect another's space and object strenuously to those who do not wait their turn. Order and space are valued, and furniture is heavy, making movement difficult. The invitation, "Pull up a chair," would be inappropriate in Germany, where such adjustment would destroy the sense of order.

Although Germans do not like being approached too closely, they do shake hands considerably more than Americans. To maintain distance and still be close enough to carry out this exchange, Germans may lean forward just long enough for a quick handshake and then step back until a comfortable distance is achieved. In Germany emphasis is placed on human relations, and even in small shops and stores a personal type of atmosphere prevails. On entering the shop an individual is met by a salesperson and extended a "Good morning" or "Good afternoon" before assistance is offered. If another person enters before the customer has made a decision, the salesperson offers a tactful apology and greets the new arrival. The atmosphere is more like that of a social gathering with the merchant as the host. Each person is very quickly acknowledged and made to feel welcome and comfortable until he or she can be helped. When the person leaves the German shop, it is customary to exchange a farewell such as "Goodbye" or "Good day." To leave the shop without such an exchange is impolite.

A German client in an American hospital will undoubtedly experience a great deal of stress from lack of privacy. To meet proxemic needs both auditory and visual privacy are necessary, which can best be met with a private room. Care givers will be considered more polite if they offer some form of recognition any time the German client is within visual distance. Above all else, the client's door is kept closed since people walking in the hall will invade the client's visual privacy.

The English

Rather than relying on architectural features for privacy, the English have learned to be alone by tuning others out, ignoring the phone, and retreating into the self. Raised in a nursery with siblings, an English person seldom expects or feels entitled to a room alone. Even in businesses the English get along without private space by learning to adjust and direct their voices so that they do not intrude on others. When communicating with another, they look straight at the person who is talking and communicate attentiveness by blinking their eyes rather than nodding or using sounds to indicate that they are listening. The use of touch and in-

teraction distances are much the same as in the United States.

The English spend a great deal of time socializing in public places, and English pubs are favorite places to spend an informal evening. Piano music is lively and "sing-songs" are popular. The pubs do not have waiters or waitresses, so there is continual movement of patrons to and from the bar. This activity encourages interaction and also contributes to the relaxed, friendly atmosphere of the pubs. Patrons move from place to place with their drinks and arrange furniture to suit their needs.

Whereas Americans rely on their environment to display their status—such as living in a big house on the right side of the tracks—the English person is born into a social system that is not affected by address, a large house, or other material props.

An English client in an American hospital will probably adjust very nicely. The individual is capable of achieving privacy whenever and wherever, so it is unlikely that the usual hospital noise or activity will bother the person. Care givers may have more of a problem adjusting to the English person who may suddenly become quiet and withdrawn as a way of achieving privacy. This behavior may be repeatedly questioned by the care giver, which is likely to contribute to the behavior rather than solving it. A simple "Would you like to be alone for awhile?" may clear up any concern that the care giver may have and at the same time acknowledge the client's need for privacy.

The French

The French socialize a great deal outside their homes, but unlike the English, who gather indoors, the French congregate in their parks and outdoor open areas. Sidewalk cafes create a relaxed and inviting atmosphere in which the French gain satisfaction from their cities and the people within them. Enormous sidewalks provide ample space to leisurely and openly watch others. If the French want to look at someone, they look as long as they want. This is quite different from the American custom of quickly looking away if an individual is caught staring at another. The French are noted for their warmth and hospitality and offer undivided attention and steadfast eye contact during conversation.

Unlike the "noncontact" Americans, Germans, and English, the French are a "contact" culture who live together more closely than do North Americans. Their crowded interactions suggest high sensory involvement, which is apparent in all areas of their life.

Much of the French culture is established around central areas and figures. Offices may be arranged with the key person in the center rather than in an office apart, and the education system also follows this centralized pattern. In smaller communities the center of the town is the area where loudspeakers present music and news.

The French use a "radiating star" type of transportation system in which different lines or roads come together at central places of interest. The Arc De Triomphe in Paris is the center of one such radiating star at which traffic converges from all directions. Drivers enter the circle at their own

A "radiating star" in Paris.
Photograph by Charles D. Davis.

discretion and travel around the circle until reaching their desired exit. What sounds simple becomes a maze at rush hour. The cars may be six deep at the center, with some moving against traffic, backing up, or trying whatever is necessary to maneuver their way to their exit. Understandably traffic jams frequently occur, and on other occasions cars speed out of the circle as though flung out by centrifugal force.

Small maneuverable European cars are built to fit the needs and personalities of that culture. Within the United States, some cities have devoted over half of their space to fit the needs of cars.

A French client in an American hospital is unlikely to establish social barriers or be reluctant to share concerns with strangers. The client may be confused about hospital routines that the person may not feel are central to the purpose of hospitalization. Routines such as wearing hospital gowns, taking daily baths, and checking blood pressure or temperature may not be considered important to the French client and therefore not necessary. When such routines are added to a lack of touch or undivided attention from care givers, the client may feel unimportant to those who are providing care. To someone from France the person is the center, and all activities evolve around the person rather than the person adjusting to meet what is considered an unnecessary routine.

Although North Americans share portions of other cultures, significant distinctions between cultures do exist. These few examples point out the uniqueness of a culture's spatial orientation and how these spatial patterns can affect client care. Proxemic differences may be outside of awareness, leading individuals to be offended by the spatial behavior of people from cultures other than their own. Without an understanding of these proxemic differences, behavior that differs from the dominant culture may be considered strange, inconsiderate, or just plain rude. To plan effective health care for all people it is up to the provider of health care to attend to the proxemic needs of clients regardless of culture or ethnic background.

• • •

The therapeutic environment is a blending of proximity and distance and privacy and togetherness. These principles are of great importance in institutional settings in which clients have little control over interaction distances and depend on the care giver to recognize spatial needs. A type of environmental docility occurs when a client's spatial needs are overlooked. Many clients ultimately manifest a tendency to accept the line of least resistance, and no matter how unpleasant or unusual the spatial arrangements, these arrangements become fixed and natural. To provide a therapeutic atmosphere those directly and indirectly involved in health and human services must be alert to the spatial needs of those with whom they are interacting. When spatial needs are not met, therapeutic interactions may be hampered.

REFERENCES

1. Altman, I., and Haythorn, W.: The ecology of isolated groups, Behavioral Science 12:169, 1967.
2. Booraem, C., and others: Personal space variations as a function of criminal behavior, Psychological Reports 41:1115, 1977.
3. Calhoun, J.: A behavioral sink. In Bliss, E., editor: Roots of behavior: genetics, instinct, and socialization in animal behavior, New York, 1962, Harper & Brothers.
4. Hall, E.: The hidden dimension, Garden City, New York, 1966, Anchor Books.
5. Kendall, P., and others: Proxemics, locus of control, anxiety, and type of movement in emotionally disturbed and normal boys, Journal of Abnormal Child Psychology 4(1):9, 1976.
6. Lyman, S., and Scott, M.: Territoriality: a neglected sociological dimension, Social Problems 15:236, 1967.
7. McCain, G., Cox, V., and Paulus, P.: The effect of prison crowding on inmate behavior, Washington, D.C., 1980, National Institute of Justice.
8. Nelson, M., and Paluck, R.: Territorial markings, self-concept, and mental status of the institutionalized elderly, The Gerontologist 20(1):96, 1980.
9. Russo, N.: Connotation of seating arrangements, Cornell Journal of Social Relations 2:37, 1967.
10. Watson, O.: Proxemic behavior: a cross-cultural study, The Hague, 1970, Mouton Publishers.
11. Westin, A.: Privacy and freedom, New York, 1968, Atheneum Publishers.

BIBLIOGRAPHY

Amiel, R.: Psychiatric architecture and sociotherapy, World Hospital **12:**69, 1976.

Ardrey, R.: The social contract, New York, 1970, Atheneum Publishers.

Benney, M., Riesman, D., and Star, S.: Age and sex in the interview, American Journal of Sociology **62:**143, 1956.

Chombarte de Lauwe, P.: Famille et habitation, Paris, 1959, Editions du Centre National de la Recherche Scientifique.

Christian, J., Flyger, V., and Davis, D.: Factors in mass mortality of a herd of sika deer, Chesapeake Science **1**(2):79, 1960.

De Julio, S., and Duffy, K.: Neuroticism and proxemic behavior, Perceptual and Motor Skills **45:**51, 1977.

Goffman, E.: Relations in public, New York, 1971, Basic Books, Inc.

Griffin, W., Mauritzen, J., and Kasmar, J.: The psychological aspects of the architectural environment: a review, American Journal of Psychiatry **125**(8):93, 1969.

Hazlewood, M., and Schuldt, J.: Effects of physical and phenomenological distance on self-disclosure, Perceptual and Motor Skills **45:**805, 1977.

Johnson, F.: Response to territorial intrusion by nursing home residents, Advances In Nursing Science **1**(4):21, 1979.

Jones, D.: Spatial proximity, interpersonal conflict, and friendship formation in the intermediate-care facility, The Gerontologist **15**(2):150, 1975.

Kay, J.: Architecture, The Nation, p. 284, September 24, 1973.

Knapp, M.: Nonverbal communication in human interaction, ed. 2, New York, 1978, Holt, Rinehart & Winston, Inc.

McCue, G.: $57,000,000 later, Architectural Forum **138:**42, May 1973.

Mehrabian, A.: Silent messages: implicit communication of emotion and attitude, ed. 2, Belmont, California, 1981, Wadsworth Publishing Co.

Mehrabian, A., and Ksionzky, S.: A theory of affiliation, Lexington, Massachusetts, 1974, D.C. Heath & Co.

Newman, R., and Pollack, D.: Proxemics in deviant adolescents, Journal of Consulting and Clinical Psychology **40:**6, 1973.

Rago, W., Parker, R., and Cleland, C.: Effect of increased space on the social behavior of institutionalized, profoundly retarded male adults, American Journal of Mental Deficiency **82:**554, 1978.

Rierdan, J., and Wiener, M.: Linguistic immediacy of schizophrenics in different proxemic conditions, Journal of Consulting and Clinical Psychology **45:**1209, 1977.

Skowronski, S.: Proxemics and nursing care, Hospital Progress **53**(8):72, 1972.

Sommer, R.: Personal space: the behavioral basis of design, Englewood Cliffs, New Jersey, 1969, Prentice-Hall, Inc.

4 · Body image

Illustration by Tom Weinman.

Mr. and Ms. Commercialized America—preservation of self-image.

CONCEPT OF BODY IMAGE

Body image is the mental picture that people have of themselves. Included in this self-image is the perception of how one's body looks and functions as well as personal feelings about the self. This concept of the self develops from messages received from the internal and external environment. The internal environment includes the biological and psychological changes within the person that are in turn affected by external environmental factors, including sociocultural variables and attitudes of significant individuals in the person's life. During infancy the parental attitudes are paramount, whereas during adolescence more emphasis is placed on peer-group attitudes. Ultimately the individual is affected by society and culture as a whole. This blending of messages communicated through body sensations, experiences, environmental attitudes and variables constitutes the dynamic, ever changing process called body image.

In the United States television commercials overtly and covertly affect body image by telling viewers how to look, feel, and act. Friendly druggists have the solution for health problems, and what they cannot handle is sure to be answered by neighborhood grocers. Catchy little jingles offer savings, health, and beauty, and consumers are led to believe that certain products make it possible to win friends, influence people, and ensure love. Enough Americans follow this pied piper of commercialism to justify advertisers paying 75,000 dollars for an average 30-second prime-time television announcement. The effects on body image are pictured in this hypothetical scene.

■ Mr. and Ms. Commercialized America awaken with the worst breath of the day. They quickly adjourn to the bathroom, where the pasty film is attacked with toothpaste and cleaners that fight cavities and leave everyone wondering where the yellow went and who ate the blueberry pie. After using mouthwash that kills germs and leaves the breath minty fresh, they greet each other with a warm, rousing, affectionate, "Morning."

Mr. America heads for the shower with the smallest bar of soap in the house that promises to bring him back to life as well as provide confidence all day long. Following his shower he uses a 24-hour deodorant and then splashes on cologne that is sure to drive women crazy. He removes the hair from his face, adds a toupe to his head, and begins to select the proper clothing for the business executive look.

Ms. America removes her nighttime bra, chin strap, and the night cream that prevents wrinkles and age spots and adds deodorant strong enough for a man but gentle enough for a woman. She spends an hour transforming her face with the myriad of make-up necessary to create the natural look. Her next goal is to gather all excess weight into a girdle and push it up through the padded uplift bra. Feminine lingerie of satin and lace is followed by a tailored business suit and perfume that never lets him forget that he's a man.

Mr. and Ms. America collect one last look of approval from the mirror before they head into the world of nine to five in which few people really are as they appear. ——————————

Now consider the reaction of Mr. and Ms. America to hospitalization. Many of their props are gone, and their clothing may be limited to the latest style in hospital gowns, which undoubtedly lacks at least one snap and two strings. When the stress of illness, injury, or treatment is added to the already threatened image, it becomes more understandable why some clients flatly refuse to wear a hospital gown, will not remove make-up before surgery, and lie about wearing dentures. These things are central to who they are. Equally important is the ability to control some aspect of their lives at a time when health change and hospitalization create an out-of-control feeling. Because a person's body image both influences and is influenced by the dynamic state of health, a knowledge of the body image process is fundamental to health maintenance and health restoration.

Body boundary

From the surface level of bodily experience comes the important concept of body boundary. This interesting phenomenon refers to a person's perception of the boundary between his or her body and the rest of the world. The infant has an almost indefinite body boundary, and the younger the child, the less clear is the difference between inside and outside the body. A child is abler to understand invasive treatments such as enemas, intravenous infusions, and injections if they are illustrated with a drawing or demonstrated on a doll.

Healthy adults have a more clearly delineated body boundary, although this boundary does not end precisely where the body ends but is likely to include hair and fingernails and items such as dentures and eyeglasses. People differ in what they include in their body image. For example, some clients refuse to remove their dentures because they consider them part of who they are, and others treat their dentures as a tool and retrieve them from the cleaning solution or the drawer only at mealtimes. The same contrast is seen when one individual considers a broken fingernail as a major catastrophe and others bite their fingernails as short as possible.

Clothing is often included in varying degrees in the body image, and some hypothesize that the self-image is expressed in a person's choice of clothing. On college campuses students are more likely to wear a favorite outfit when they feel insecure and to wear more clothing when they are homesick. Occasionally a client will talk about being depersonalized by having to wear a hospital gown. For this person clothing is an important aspect of body image and should be permitted whenever possible.

A certain image is associated with types of clothing that sets expectations for the behavior of the wearer. This is particularly noticeable if the clothing is a uniform of some kind. One hospitalized client commented, "They come and go all dressed up like the militia. The officers wear white and the enlisted wear other colors." The power of the uniform was displayed during a 2-day power outage one summer at a hospital in Texas when a thunderstorm knocked out electricity and damaged the hospital's emergency generators. A young client from the mental health unit had just received a 2-day pass when the power failed, and instead of leaving the hospital, the young man donned a scrub suit and began issuing directives to employees and volunteers and generally took charge during the emergency. With no outside power the hospital was without lights and air conditioning, and the temperature soared. At one point the young man had his temporary charges deliver 2,000 pounds of ice to the hospital lobby to help cool the hospital. Because he was dressed in a scrub suit and looked authoritative, no one questioned what he was doing. The client succeeded in conferring with the county commissioner before his true identity was discovered some 28 hours after beginning his volunteer service.[1]

Terminology

Body image is often confused or used interchangeably with the similar concepts of id, ego, superego, self-image, and self-esteem. These concepts all contribute to a person's body image and they are defined here to clarify and prevent confusion.

Id. The id is the part of the personality that is innate or inborn and ensures survival of the self and survival of the species. The ego and superego develop from the id as the individual progresses through stages of development from infancy to adulthood.

Ego. The ego is a personality part involving reason or common sense that interacts with the person's internal and external environment. Infants do not see themselves as distinct organisms, and it is only through maturation that the child is able to differentiate between body and nonbody parts and begin the process of ego development.

Superego. The internalization of cultural and ethical rules, standards, values, prohibitions, and taboos from authority figures form the superego or conscience. This part of the personality provides the individual with internal controls over thoughts, feelings, and actions and begins to develop around the age of 4 or 5 years.

Self-image. Whenever a person envisions the self, a mental picture is formed called self-image. Relevant to this concept are role, status, goals, and value systems. Self-image includes strengths and weaknesses and is influenced by the appraisals of significant others in the environment.

Self-esteem. A person's evaluation of his or her self—whether positive or negative—is called self-esteem. So important is self-esteem that Maslow identifies it as a basic human need. A person with high self-esteem feels worthwhile in spite of mistakes or defeats, and when people lose their self-esteem, they no longer feel good about themselves.

Body image is a concept central to human experience and is therefore a good indicator of a person's general health. It is important that the helping professional be able to assess the development of body image, promote measures to ensure healthy development, and detect deviations from the normal development of body image. A care giver's awareness of how illness and handicapping conditions affect body image can be valuable in helping others adapt to these changes. Before dealing with alterations in body image, the normal development of body image in the healthy individual will be discussed.

DEVELOPMENT OF BODY IMAGE

Body image evolves slowly through the process of growth and development and through interaction with the environment. This ongoing process—from infancy to death—is central to human experience and progresses chronologically while constantly responding to external and internal forces.

Fetus and newborn

In Memoriam

The baby new to earth and sky
What time his tender palm is prest
Against the circle of the breast,
Has never thought that "this is I."

But as he grows he gathers much,
And learns the use of "I" and "me,"
And finds "I am not what I see,
And other than the things I touch,"

So rounds he to a separate mind
From whence clear memory may begin,
As thro' the frame that binds him in
His isolation grows defined.

This use may lie in blood and breath,
Which else were fruitless of their due,
Had man to learn himself anew
Beyond the second birth of Death.
Alfred Tennyson (written in 1850)

Child care professionals have learned that the newborn is not a helpless blob of clay but an individual with a unique and distinct personality capable of interacting with the environment. This interaction begins before birth with the fetus affected by environmental conditions through its mother's uterus. The mechanical stimulation occurring during a normal pregnancy, labor, and delivery is important to the neonate, and clinicians verify that premature babies who receive additional stimulation from touch, rocking movements, or certain sounds do better than those who do not receive a substitute for lost normal stimulation.

Researchers have found that the fetus is able to hear before birth and will turn and move in response to the sounds of a heartbeat and pulsing blood vessles when a recording of this "womb music" is played against the abdomen of the pregnant woman. Following birth the neonate responds to this same recording by suddenly raising its arms and kicking its legs. An abrupt increase in breathing and heart rate is also noted. Some believe that this womb music may become an accurate way to test a new baby's hearing.

An unsedated newborn is alert for approximately 1 hour following birth and during this time demonstrates both the ability to see and to hear. Eye treatments should be delayed until after this alert time so that visual and auditory interaction can take place between newborns and their parents.

Because neonates are born with tastebuds throughout the mouth, their perception of taste is greater than an adult's, whose remaining tastebuds are located on the tongue. Most newborns react very negatively when fed sterile water, and perhaps if adults had the same capacity to taste sterile water, they too would give a negative response.

Neonates have a keen sense of smell, and by the fifth day of life, breastfed babies are able to discriminate their mother's breastpads from the breastpads of other mothers.[5] There is mounting evidence that adults remember what they smell longer than what they see or hear and perhaps this ability begins early in life.

Personality characteristics are evident at birth as newborns interact differently with their environment. Some are better able to ignore distracting stimuli and soothe themselves in stressful environments, whereas others fuss and cry in the same situation. The Brazelton Neonatal Behavioral Assessment Scale is a tool used to identify the initial temperament of neonates. This valuable resource and guideline can be used in teaching parents more effective and appropriate ways to interact with and adjust to their newborn. For example, a baby who is not cuddly may create anxiety in the parents unless they know that the neonate responds the same with care givers. A quiet baby may be appealing to one mother, whereas another mother prefers a more active baby. By knowing what to expect, parents are given a sense of autonomy and control that they in turn recognize in their baby.

Early detection and treatment of perceptual problems in the newborn reduce the number of individuals who go through life with sensory deficits. If the newborn has permanent sensory loss, health professionals can assist the family in adapting to these problems and in promoting early development of a normal body image for the child.

Infant

The innermost bodily sensations and the way in which these communicate to the total organism form the first component of body image. For the infant these sensations are centered around comfort and relief from pain and anxiety, and being able to rely on others to meet these needs is the beginning of developing trust in other individuals.

The skin forms the outer boundary of the human organism, providing the earliest and most elemental mode of communication. Tactile communication and stimulation are paramount to survival of the infant. This was learned at the turn of the century, when 50 to 100 percent of the infants in foundling homes in Europe and the United States died by the end of their first year. Infants who did survive developed psychiatric disturbances and became asocial, delinquent, feeble-minded, psychotic, or problem children. These effects of institutional care were attributed to lack of stimulation and the absence of the child's mother, who provided more intense stimulation than the best trained nursery personnel.[8]

Harlow's studies[4] with neonatal and infant monkeys further confirmed the need for tactile stimulation. Baby monkeys separated from their mothers and given the option of nursing from a cloth mother surrogate or a wire mother surrogate overwhelmingly preferred the cloth mother. During times of fear they rushed to the cloth mother, clutched her, and rubbed their bodies against her. Although there was no difference in the amount of milk ingested or in weight gain between monkeys fed on the wire or cloth mother surrogate, the softer stools of the wire mother infants suggested psychosomatic involvement. It became clear that contact comfort was an important basic affectional variable, even stronger than the variable of nursing.

The infant's mouth is richly endowed with sensory receptors, and in this area infants begin to differentiate their body boundaries from the outside world. Initially the infant views the mothering figure as an extension of self. By the end of the infant's first year internalization of sensory experiences produces the simultaneous developmental process of ego and body image. As the child's body image gradually evolves—becoming more concrete and distinct from the environment—there is a marked increase in differentiation of self from others.

Toddler

As the child is able to become more independent, the second phase of body image development emerges as the child explores and works at mastering the environment. The mother or primary care giver remains the center of the small child's security; however, mobility and exploration become more important to the child than remaining physically in contact with the mother. The toddler, unlike the infant, is able to actively seek the physical contact that is needed, and although it would appear that the toddler receives less touch than do infants, in actuality toddlers between 14 months and 2 years receive more parental touch than they did as infants.[2]

Two-year-olds know they are either boys or girls and understand that there are significant differences between the sexes. During toilet training the proximity of the orifices may cause children real difficulty in separating them in their thinking. If one opening is considered to be "dirty," so is the other. The way parents handle toilet training and their response to the child's exploration of the genitals influence the child's early evaluation of sexuality.

Toddlers are still uncertain of bodily boundaries and are concerned about body products such as urine and feces, which they consider a part of their bodies that they do not want flushed away. This same concern may be expressed when a child receives a haircut or when a laboratory technician takes a blood sample. Children do not understand that these products can be separated from the body without harming what they believe is part of the self.

As the toddler develops, specific personality traits become more apparent. A certain amount of autonomy is necessary for the youngster to develop a healthy, independent body image, and this control may surface in the form of temper tantrums, toilet training problems, and eating problems. It may be helpful for parents to understand that the behavior specific to the "terrible twos" is an important and healthy display of independence and that compromise solutions may help both the parent and the child satisfy their own needs. The toddler's self-concept reflects the appraisals of significant others, and it is this relationship with significant others that becomes the basis for all future relationships.

Preschool child

Young children have learned to distinguish between their innermost bodily experiences and are able to use language as a tool in requesting help from others rather than crying in response to disequilibrium as does the infant. They know that they hurt but may be unable to localize the pain or use the right words to describe the problem. A 3-year-old may state, "I have a headache in my tummy." By observing nonverbal information the adult is able to determine the location of the problem.

Researchers have identified early behavioral differences between the sexes, and whether these are learned or innate continues to be debated. Girls display a stronger maternal behavior than boys, who show more fascination with machines and wheels. Aggression is also expressed differently, with little boys more apt to physically express their aggression, whereas little girls tend to do so verbally. These differences can be credited to upbringing, education, and social conditioning; however, it may also be that there are minimal differences between boys and girls at birth that are reinforced by their environment. Studies do point out that baby girls and boys use opposite sides of the brain, and although no such differences are found in adults, the exact age when this difference disappears is not known.[7]

Around the age of 2 or 3 years the child begins to show a preference for using the right or left hand, and by the time the child is school age, this preference is established. The exact reason why some children have left-hand preference is not known, although a relationship between birth order or environmental factors operating at any of several points in time during pregnancy is hypothesized. It is important that parents realize that the hand preference of a child is an important part of body image, and forced alteration may result in personality problems later in life.

Children between the ages of 2 and 4 years have difficulty comparing current experiences with what they have experienced in the past. This is important to members of the health team because the child is likely to treat each procedure as a new experience even though it may have been experienced before. When the care giver explains procedures, a comparision can be made, ''This is a shot like the one you had yesterday,'' followed by an explanation of what will happen. When youngsters are able to compare, they are apt to respond, ''I know what it is. I've had it done before.''

Preschoolers have not learned to delay gratification and therefore want immediate results. Because they do not share an adult's time frame, it is difficult to explain how long they must wait. The preschooler is unlikely to comprehend such information as ''Later, this afternoon,'' or ''In a couple of days.'' Short-range goals and 15-minute time segments are usually the maximum that they can understand. By the time children are in school, they have learned to be more patient.

Preschool children become aware of differences in skin color and visible handicaps, and this is an excellent time to teach them about body differences. A listing of books for preschool children on the topics of racial differences and handicaps are included in the suggested readings at the end of this chapter.

School-aged child

There is a tremendous change in the physical, cognitive, and psychosocial factors during the school-age years. Youngsters in elementary grades begin to show a natural interest in learning about their bodies and what's going on inside them. They want to know the names of the sexual organs, the difference between male and female sexual organs, why girls do not have penises, where babies come from, and how babies got in and how they get out. Parents may turn to health professionals for information and resources dealing with the human body. There are suggested readings at the end of this chapter pertaining to physiology and sex education that would be of interest to the school-aged child. By middle-school years, the preoccupation with body characteristics lessens, only to reemerge during puberty.

As children begin to interact with the environment, outside friendships strongly influence both their behavior and their body image. At first, interactions are with one or two friends and later with a group. Children search for a group that they can fit in with and receive the positive feedback concerning self and body that is needed in these formative years.

Adolescent

Adolescence is that special time of life when an individual is no longer considered a child and certainly not an adult. Avalanched by physiological, psychological, sociological, and cultural changes, the person undergoes extreme changes during puberty, experiences a more stable period identified as youth, and then proceeds into the responsibilities of adulthood.

The adolescent is caught up in a struggle for autonomy and self-direction while being practically bombarded by the innermost bodily experiences centered around sex hormones. The rapidly changing level and activity of these hormones produce such dramatic changes in appearance that much time is spent in front of the mirror in an effort to integrate physical changes with the mental image of the self. The concept of speed and power is added to the body image through trail bikes, motorcycles, speedboats, snowmobiles, and automobiles. A noticeable increase in energy level and lessening impulse control may result in a frightening, out-of-control feeling, especially for adolescents who have negative feelings concerning sexuality or their bodies. The high energy level

Responding to a child's natural curiosity.

Copyright by American Nurses' Association. Reprinted by permission.

typical of this period may be dissipated in healthy ways such as sports or unhealthy ways that are potentially harmful or destructive such as playing chicken on the highway.

Because this stage in the life cycle is strongly influenced by sexuality, adults in helping roles must be knowledgeable, open, and articulate with adolescents about such topics as intercourse, orgasm, masturbation, homosexuality, abortion, and contraceptives. All of these experiences have an effect on body image, body boundaries, and sense of the physical self. Adolescents need assistance in predicting and understanding the transitions experienced during this stage of life, and they need to know the biopsychosocial ramifications and how to deal with them. Unfortunately, too many parents consider the topic of sex taboo and want to keep the subject out of the classroom and off the library shelves. If more community health professionals took a stand on the importance of including sex education in the school curriculum, fewer teens would be overwhelmed by feelings that often lead to unwanted pregnancies, sexually transmitted disease, and in extreme cases, suicide. The need for love and acceptance is so strong during adolescence that this need—rather than libido—is often the driving force behind sexual behaviors of teenaged girls. A love-starved teenager with a low self-image is an easy mark for prostitution, drugs, and violence.

Adolescence is an ambivalent time between childlike dependence and complete freedom and independence. Although considered an adult when paying for public entertainment and conveyances, adolescents comment that they are treated as juveniles the rest of the time. Personality development is both chaotic and confusing as the adolescent tries to gain a sense of identity.

This transition into autonomy often produces conflict with parents and increases involvement with peers. Maturation enables adolescents to see things from another's point of view. In fact, they become so concerned about the opinion of their peers that this concern almost governs this period in their lives. Although adolescents are trying to decide for themselves who they are and what direction they are heading, their critical task is learning to develop intimacy with others.

Youth

During the period of youth the wide mood swings and generally disquieting stage of adolescence are gradually resolved as individuals begin to accept both themselves and their bodies. The hormonal levels tend to stabilize, causing a decrease in sex drive and an increase in impulse control. The parental conflict softens during youth and changes into a peer type of relationship in young adulthood.

Young adulthood

The period of life span following youth is marked by major responsibilities and is identified as young adulthood. It is during this time that individuals have enough emotional stability to understand and incorporate the body changes of adolescence into their body image. Many young adults choose mates and begin families. Pregnancy produces a tremendous fluctuation in hormonal balance that may affect the woman's personality and her sex drive. Many pregnant women are initially ambivalent about their pregnancies, and when one considers the tremendous physical and social changes brought about during this time, mixed feelings are not surprising. Many couples head into parenthood with the only lessons on parenting those learned from their parents. Unfortunately, mistakes tend to be repeated generation after generation. Even with the most ideal childhood, what worked for one generation of parents may be completely inadequate for another.

Young adults often find the need to reevaluate the work and home roles taught by their parents. Yesterday it was considered that the woman's place was at home, and today it is becoming more accepted that a woman's place is wherever she wants it to be. Many women have entered the highly competitive business world, combining the roles of wife, mother, and career. The frustration of choosing between a career or children or dealing with guilt from neglecting the job or family are very real issues for today's woman.

Today's man may prefer that his wife and the mother of his children remain at home. His childhood may have been centered around a father as provider and mother as nurturer, but the traditional male role of bread-winner and head of the family is undergoing transition. In many families financial need mandates two paychecks, and balancing the demands of the workplace and the family requires a sharing of family responsibilities that is often more idealistic than realistic.

As an adult the image of the self as an individual is more secure, and the person is freer to express his or her unique self rather than going with the crowd and looking and acting like one of many off an assembly line. Personal needs take precedence over conformity, and rather than depending on peer

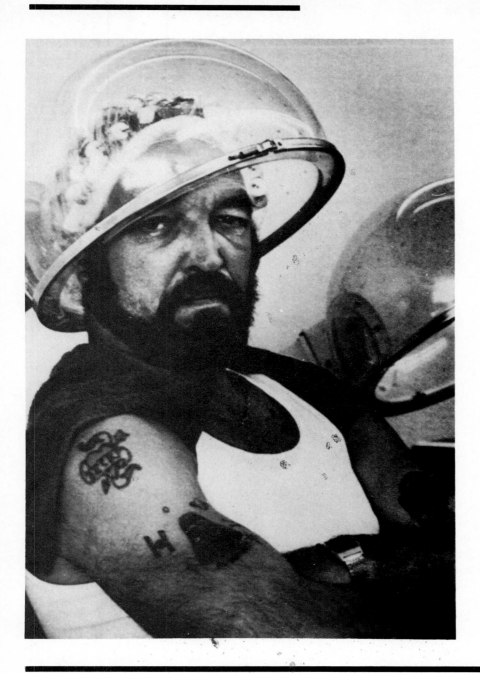

Exchanging conformity for comfort. This man likes to get a permanent during hot weather so that he does not have to bother with his hair.

Wide World Photos.

approval to nurture self-esteem, the adult relies more on inner strength and the support of significant others. The peer pressure of adolescence becomes replaced with influential factors in the environment, one of which is finances and another is raising a family.

Middle-aged adult

Middle age is identified as being those years between the ages of 40 and 65 years, which are sometimes referred to as the prime of life. Few people of this age group want to be young again. "I wouldn't want to go through all that again," is the usual comment. "However, I wouldn't mind a little of the energy I used to have and the good health." Despite this decrease in energy level, a person's most productive career years are during their middle years. It is during this time that people begin to realize that bodily resources are limited and therefore are more interested in preventive health measures.

Hormonal changes occur in both the middle-aged man and woman, resulting in a climacteric, or change of life. Although the man experiences a drop in testosterone, this decline is gradual and does not produce the physiologically based climacteric that is experienced in menopause.

Menopause is the transitional stage in which a woman's ovaries cease to function and her estrogen level drops. Although surrounded by myth and folklore, menopause causes only mild symptoms in the majority of women. The lowered estrogen level may cause hot flashes, which can be both annoying and embarrassing. Vaginal changes ranging from mucosal dryness to atrophy can also be experienced and may lead to dyspareunia, or painful intercourse. Estrogen replacement may be required to alleviate these symptoms; however, oral estrogen medication may also change the acidity level in the vagina, causing frequent yeast infections.

The responsibilities and pressures of midlife are combined with the realization that the clock is ticking and there may not be enough time to do it all. This stress can change to depression as roles in life are changed. Women who have centered their lives around their children are left to face the empty nest when the children leave home. Individuals with identities formed around their careers can experience this same type of limbo when retirement leaves them with an unsure self-image. Counseling and guidance before these major life changes can help prevent midlife depression.

Old adult

Early old age is arbitrarily set at 65 years, and the onset of later old age is around 75 years. The period of old age is receiving more interest in the last several years because the percentage of the population 65 years and older in the United States is increasing dramatically. Senility is an abnormal process of aging identified by failing memory, comprehension, judgment, and mental ability. Although the label "senile" indicates chronic, untreatable states, it sometimes overshadows disorders that are responsive to medical and psychotherapeutic intervention.

Musculoskeletal and perceptual changes progress at a faster rate in later life. Contrary to popular myth, there is no decline in intellectual abilities with advancing age as long as there is good physical and mental health, adequate educational levels, and intellectual stimulation. Although there is a decrease in reaction time and memory, this is compensated by an increase in some abilities such as judgment, accuracy, and general knowledge.

The myth that sex ceases after middle age is still believed in our society. Sex is one of the innermost drives that continues throughout life. Many adults are not knowledgeable about their bodies and may be too embarrassed to ask about or discuss sexual matters. It may be necessary for the physician or nurse to ask if there are any questions or problems concerning sex.

An older person's self-image often does not match what is reflected in the mirror. "I don't feel any older than I did 10 years ago," is a common response of a healthy older person. Even if all diseases were eliminated, undesirable genetic traits nullified, and pathogenic environmental factors removed, the aging process would still continue. It

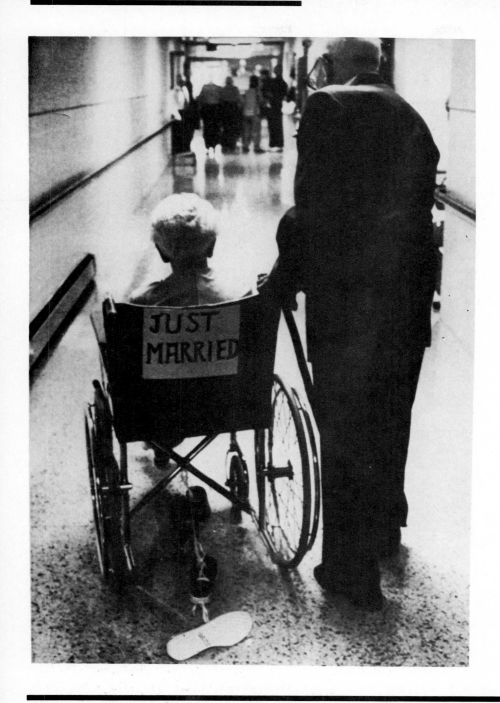

"Just married." **High school sweethearts met again after their spouses died, and at the age of 79 years were married at the nursing home where they reside.**
Wide World Photos.

is a necessary part of the normal development of life, and although it is measured in years, a more accurate appraisal would be, "You're only as old as you feel."

The overall physical health plays a critical role in the adaptive capacities of the elderly. Although 86 percent of the elderly population have one or more chronic health problems, only 5 percent are confined to an institution. The earlier child-parent dependency relationship is often reversed, and adult children may find it difficult to accept their aging parents as sexual beings who need love, affection, and stimulating relationships. Older people need freedom, autonomy, and independence, and when these needs are not met, depression is common.

The physical, social, cultural, and economic aspects of life are all woven into the concept of self. Physical, mental, and social well-being can be realized when the person's strengths and potential are recognized and encouraged. With information and support individuals can be helped to discover who they are, for this image of the self organizes what they will say and do as they find their place in society.

Life Is Full Circle

Children do not know that time is elusive.
They hear, see, feel, and let happen.
Adolescents cram a lifetime of experience into the
    moment.
Then come the years when time is precious,
But physical limitations prevent quest.
Prompted perhaps by frustration or perhaps by reve-
    lation,
The paradox begins.
Once again,
Today justifies today.
Tomorrow will take care of itself.

(© 1982 A. Jann Davis)

ALTERATIONS IN BODY IMAGE

Body image is formed by the interaction between the internal and external environment at a particular time in the life span of an individual. This inner image of self is influenced by the person's percep-

tion of his or her appearance and a multitude of variables that include the person's beliefs, values, and goals as well as such things as intelligence, social status, and profession. An individual's perception of body function, sensation, and mobility also contributes to this mental image, as does physical stamina, physical and mental capabilities, and tolerance to pain. Individuals defend their body image against change, devaluation, and attack, and when illness, injury, or treatment brings about body change, it takes time to assimilate these alterations into the body image.

Body image and physical appearance

A person's body image is affected by the opinion of others, and even though these opinions may be based on prejudice or stereotypes, they do influence a person's self-image. For instance, certain body builds are associated with certain personality and temperament traits. The overweight endomorph is considered good-natured, agreeable, dependent, and trusting; the muscular mesomorph is associated with such traits as adventurous, mature, and self-reliant; the thin ectomorph is categorized as ambitious, stubborn, and quiet.

Theorizing a relationship between appearance and antisocial behavior, several researchers initiated programs to improve the appearance of inmates. Through plastic surgery tattoos were removed, sagging skin tightened, noses reshaped, scars disguised, and other deformities corrected. Although some inmates demonstrated improved behavior following the change in their appearance, most studies failed to show significant changes in postinstitutionalized behavior. Even though the appearance of the convicts was surgically changed, the body image for some may not have changed accordingly.

Body image is more than skin deep. It is a pervasive attitude that may be quite different from the person's physical appearance, and any change in the physical self needs to be incorporated into the mental self. A healthy unity between this visible and invisible image can be achieved by helping people identify and maximize the positive aspects of their lives.

Body boundary disturbances

Body boundary, or the perception of a boundary that differentiates the body from everything else, may at times become distorted. There are two major body boundary disturbances. In the first, the body wall changes, but the individual maintains the mental image of the old body boundary. Phantom limb pain may be a problem of body boundary adjustment in which instead of shrinking to exclude the limb, the body boundary remains the same as before the amputation. In another example, a client with long-standing emphysema is unable to extend the body boundary to include a permanent tracheostomy.

In the second type of body boundary disturbance the person changes the mental image of the body boundary although the body wall remains unchanged. A client who has experienced a stroke may be unable to feel a part of the body, and the person may consciously or unconsciously exclude this body part from the body boundary. In frustration a normally gentle man with a paralyzed left leg shouted, ''I can't feel the damn thing. It's no good to me. Get it the hell out of here.'' Some clients with schizophrenia extend their body boundaries several inches to several feet beyond their actual bodies and therefore require a greater than normal interaction distance.

Body boundary can be measured by such tests as the Rorschach test that yield a penetration score and a barrier score. Low penetration scores and high barrier scores are usually indicative of people with very definite body boundaries, whereas those with high penetration scores and low barrier scores have less definite body boundaries. Some theorize that people with high barriers are more likely to develop periphery physiological problems such as neurodermatitis and arthritis, whereas these with low barriers are more prone to internal physiological problems similar to ulcers or colitis.

Body image and body weight

Obesity. Overweight people are viewed as having both a physical deformity and a behavioral aberration. They are often held responsible for what is considered a voluntary, self-inflicted disability that is indicative of a lack of personal control. This prejudice begins early in life, and investigators have found that kindergarten children consistently rank overweight people more negatively than those with obvious physical handicaps. The attitude that overweight people are socially deviant contributes to behaviors that perpetuate the problem.

For some people the problem of being overweight begins in infancy, when an insecure mother figure offers food as a panacea for frustration and anxiety. The infant never learns to differentiate nutritional needs from tension or feelings of discomfort. The formula-fed infant is at greater risk of being overfed than is the breast-fed infant who determines the quantity of milk consumed. Some mothers equate mothering with feeding, and the more the baby eats, the better the mother feels. Mothers need to be told that they can harm their babies by mixing formula too strong, feeding the infant too frequently, and starting solid foods too soon. They may also need help in differentiating the cry of a hungry baby and one who is communicating other needs.

The overweight adult who has a negative body image is likely to continue to be overweight despite attempts at weight reduction. Dieting without counseling is usually ineffective unless the person has somewhat of a positive self-image or some degree of self-esteem. A weight reduction program is more effective when it is oriented toward promoting self-confident behavior with weight loss as the secondary goal. Overweight persons need help in identifying and concentrating on their worthwhile traits, abilities, and achievements. Independent, assertive behavior is encouraged to help build up self-confidence in preparation for dieting and the physical and emotional changes that occur with weight loss. For some persons being overweight has been a way of life, and weight reduction makes it necessary to learn new ways of interacting with others.

Anorexia nervosa. Men are usually more satisfied with their bodies when they are somewhat larger than normal, whereas women are more satisfied with their bodies when they are smaller than normal. Attractiveness is correlated with thinness, and dieting may be seen as a way to become more appealing. A condition called anorexia nervosa or self-starvation exists when dieting is carried to extremes. Typically those with anorexia nervosa are teenaged girls with a close, involved, and dependent relationship with their families. The onset of the illness may be associated with a time in life when individuals are expected to become more independent.

Although women have a tendency to overestimate their body size, anorexic persons have such a distorted body image that they fail to recognize their starved bodies as too thin. The relationship between body image and anorexia nervosa is so vital that the degree of body image disturbance is related to the severity of the illness. Treatment begins with stabilization of the client's weight followed by therapy directed at improving self-esteem.

Bulimia. Bulimia is a behavioral condition similar to anorexia and is characterized by uncontrollable overeating followed by forced vomiting or overdoses of laxatives. Those typically involved in this dangerous binge-purge habit are single, middle-class women in their twenties, and on some college campuses the practice is considered epidemic. Eating is in response to external signals rather than internal physiological cues, and the person is obsessed both with eating and the desire to stay thin. The long-range side effects of bulimia include gastric problems, hernias, and dangerous blood chemistry imbalance. Treatment is directed at the inner turmoil that finds emotional release through the obsessive binge-purge practice.

The conditions of obesity, anorexia nervosa, and bulimia are all symptoms of poor body image. When self-blame, self-punishment, and guilt are added to the already negative self-image, it becomes even more difficult for the person to initiate positive change. A good dose of self-esteem may be the necessary catalysts before change can take place. Unfortunately, this is not an immediate acquisition but one that takes time and support yet is well worth the effort.

Body image and medical technology

"The miracles of survival are often so spectacular that no one can blame the surgeons for failing to weigh the costs of the procedure against the likelihood of a workable rehabilitation result."[3] Humans are kept alive beyond data available to know the quality of life that is ahead for the survivor. Such an example is a 1-pound 8-ounce infant born 16 weeks prematurely to refugees from Laos, where physical perfection is more highly valued than in America. For months the infant lived among tubes and wires while every innovation of modern technology was used to keep her alive. Because of the infant's extreme immaturity at birth, she is blind and may have cerebral palsy. The infant's future is decribed as an "open book" because there are little data to help physicians know what to expect.

The dynamics of organ loss and replacement must be seen in terms of body image and interpersonal dynamics. Kidney transplants and heart valve replacements have become common. Heart-lung transplants are being performed. The sexual revolution has created more options and problems. Men experiencing impotence resulting from an organic cause can now opt for a penile implant. Women unhappy with breast size may choose to have augmentation mammoplasty. Sex reassignment, artificial insemination, and babies conceived in vitro are raising moral and ethical questions.

Caught up in technology is the human being whose body image is so resistant to change that psychological problems created by science may not appear for months or years after the change has taken place. Whenever possible, in-depth interviews and counseling should precede elective changes so that individuals are not faced with irretrievable loss.

There is no magical adjustment scale that determines whether or not an individual is ultimately able to adapt to a change in body image. Perhaps one of the greatest frustrations known in health care is to maintain life in spite of tremendous odds only to have the person decide that the life saved is not worth living. When this occurs, the question becomes, "Did we go too far with our help or not far enough?" The following narration, entitled "Life and Death as One," is a poignant example of a young woman whose life was compromised by paralysis.

■ Amidst incredible grief I am engulfed in a catacomb of loss. It is incomprehensible that one life can be so ravaged and others continue as usual. People tell me that adversity is the great teacher and I am lucky to be alive. Total paralysis is not alive. The only thing alive in my whole body is my mind. I wonder if it would be better the other way around.

I am a living corpse: too dead to want to live and too alive to die. I witness a living rigor mortis as my body slowly twists, becoming gnarled and rigid while others work diligently to prevent decay. It is awesome that life and death can be so inseparable.

I watch couples hold each other with strong arms and press their bodies close. I remember that warmth. I watch people come and go, laughing and full of life, and I remember that freedom. I remember the dreams and hopes and everything I was and planned to be. In one moment it was gone.

Sleep is a blessed transition, blending memories and plans into fantasized reality. I hold the infant that was to have been—feeding, bathing, and loving. The nightmare begins when I awaken and I am the infant being fed, cleaned, and turned.

Within the order of the universe, there must be a reason for me to be alive. Support me as I search for the purpose of my existence, and please understand if I decide that it doesn't justify life. (© *1982 A. Jann Davis.*) _____

ADAPTATION TO CHANGE IN BODY IMAGE

In illness and health and old age and youth, messages are continually being fed into the human's dynamic body image system. These messages are interpreted and then rejected, revised, or accepted into the person's own unique way of perceiving his or her physical self. When sudden changes are brought on by illness, injury, or treatment, the messages may completely overload the system. The interdisciplinary team members become a support system during this dynamic state of change, lending the additional energy that may differentiate between an emotionally intact or an emotionally devastated person.

Norris[6] states that a person's adaptation to a change in body image depends on the nature of the threat, the meaning of the threat to the person, the individual's coping abilities, the response from significant others, and the help available to the person and his or her family. This framework offers a basis on which to evaluate adaptation to body image changes.

Nature of the threat

An individual's body image is his or her basis of identity, and almost any change in structure or function is considered a threat.

Age. The point in the person's life span when the threat is experienced is important in relation to how great a threat is perceived. Children born with abnormalities incorporate these problems into their original body images unless the abnormalities are corrected or compensated for while the child is young. An adult's body image is well defined and more rigid; therefore it becomes more and more difficult to incorporate an illness or handicap into this original image.

Function. Another influential variable is the functional significance of the part involved. Supposedly the loss of a finger requires less adaptation than the loss of an arm. When a major organ is involved, clients receive more support than when a less vital part of the body is involved.

A person's teeth are highly functional, and although little attention is given to the psychological reactions of loosing teeth, some people relate that receiving dentures was the most traumatic thing they have experienced. In some cases dentures do not fit, and the person either goes through life in discomfort or displays a toothless smile. Dental implants are helping restore the normal function of teeth to many who are unable to wear dentures.

Infants born deaf or blind are likely to live in a world of isolation, rejection, and intellectual obstacles unless thay are taught alternate ways to receive information about their environment. One way of doing this is by stimulating the child's other senses to compensate for the sensory loss.

Visibility. Visibility of the part involved is also an important consideration in body image change. Individuals with obvious handicaps talk about being stared at or having others move away as though what they have is catching. A lady with psoriasis over most of her body joked,'' I just say that I have syphilis or leprosy. I try to laugh it off, but inside I'm not laughing. It's easier to stay home than be treated as though I am revolting, unclean, or infectious.''

Although most will agree that visible handicaps cause more threat to body image than those not easily visualized, this is not true for some. Fear of the unknown or unseen can be disturbing for those involved. ''Everybody thinks it's all in my head,'' one client commented. ''They tell me how great I look. I have a notion to tell them, 'It's not my face that hurts.' ''

Threat to body image may also come from the need to use a highly visible device such as a wheelchair, walker, or cane. Crutches do not usually create a threat to body image since they are associated more with injury than with illness or old age. Because of the connotation between a wheelchair and old age and illness, many clients strongly object to riding in a wheelchair, even if it is just long enough to be dismissed from the hospital.

Meaning of the threat to the person

The meaning of the threat to a person depends in part on the value the individual places on wholeness, independence, and attractiveness and the speed in which changes in these areas are experienced. For a young child mobilization and self-mastery are important for proper development. The adolescent's concerns are centered around attractiveness and normality, whereas adults place less emphasis on the physical self and greater emphasis on psychosocial satisfactions.

Wholeness. An effort to retain wholeness was experienced by a 28-year-old woman after undergoing a hysterectomy. She said she and her husband had two children and was quick to tell the health care team, ''It's no big deal. I don't want any more kids anyway.'' After dismissal from the hospital she was totally unprepared for an avalanche of emotions prompted by seeing a new mother and her newborn infant on television. Although she had appeared to be coping well following surgery, her frequent comments about not wanting more children were an attempt to convince herself—rather than the staff—that her uterus was no longer important. Removal of a superfluous part of the body would not disrupt her wholeness. Counseling was required to help her deal with her loss and revise her body image.

Independence. Independence is a part of a healthy person's body image that is often taken for granted. ''Depending on others is one of the hardest parts of growing old,'' many elderly people admit. ''I was once so active, could do just about anything I ever wanted and whenever I wanted. Now I feel like a child. Everybody else decides what I can do, and I'm supposed to do it whenever they want.''

Physical appearance. The American culture places a great deal of emphasis on physical appearance and physical perfection. Next to death physical disfigurement is one of the hardest realities for many people to accept. The birth of a malformed child may be catastrophic for some parents, with grief over the loss of their hoped-for healthy child chronic and without resolution.

Severe facial disfigurement may create a person who in all reality becomes socially dead. How much of the client's body image can be destroyed before life is no longer meaningful is a question prompted by medical technology. Although some people choose to die, many opt for life, adapt to their new image, and then assist others in adapting to them.

Side effects from drug therapy such as moon face, hirsutism, and changes in body contour may be very threatening to the body image. A 22-year-

A wheelchair may threaten body image.
Illustration by Tom Weinman.

old woman had undergone several series of chemotherapy treatments in an attempt to cure Hodgkin's disease. She experienced a multitude of side effects from these treatments and contended that the worst part was losing her hair. Although her scalp was cooled to protect hair follicles during treatment, hair loss continued. When the conventional treatments failed to control her disease, the young woman was given the option of trying an experimental drug. Her first question was, "Will my hair fall out?" When the oncologist responded that it probably would, she refused to take the drug. Sometimes people decide that the treatment is worse than dying from the problem and this may present both moral and ethical problems for the health professional.

Extent and speed of change. Other factors that influence the degree of threat include the extent of change and the speed in which the change occurs. The following are two accounts of clients who experienced overwhelming physical changes within a brief amount of time.

■ A 19-year-old man awakens in a hospital room, surrounded by people wearing gowns and masks. The last thing he remembers was hearing a loud explosion while he tried to light a space heater. He feels pain everywhere and slowly relates the explosion to what he is now experiencing. Over 40 percent of his body received first- and second-degree burns. Ultimately he becomes deeply depressed and refuses to talk to anyone. _____

■ A 40-year-old man experienced a severe case of endocarditis and subsequent mitral valve damage. Within a few weeks his life-style was changed from being an active businessman to a person on bedrest. Following mitral valve replacement the man angrily snapped, ''I can just see that thing flapping away, 'Lubb dupp, lubb dupp.' The dupp is all mine, the lubb is not.'' _____

Both men experienced life-threatening changes within a brief amount of time. With so much destruction to body schema, it is difficult to integrate contempt of self and acceptance of self. Silence and anger are ways of grieving for loss of valued body image, and the ability to move beyond this grief to body image adjustment depends in part on the person's coping abilities.

Coping abilities

A person's coping patterns before disease or injury contribute to how the individual will adapt to changes in body image. From past experiences a repertoire of coping abilities is established that can be recalled whenever threat is perceived. If the coping strategy is to ignore the problem until it goes away, this type of denial will be apparent when body image is threatened. People who have learned to cope with and adapt to stressful situations are better able to accept body image changes. A chronically ill person is often able to handle stress better than a healthy individual. The individual has developed effective ways of coping in order to live with the disability and these coping skills are applicable in other stressful situations.

Response from significant others

Another variable that affects a person's response to loss is the support received from significant others. One type of family offers encouragement and support while hiding its own fears and feelings. Some families become threatening, attempting to force clients into actions for which they may not be ready. There are also families who completely ignore the client, which may be out of fear or disinterest or because they have rejected the person.

Significant others need help in accepting the physical and psychological changes in their loved one. They too are experiencing changes in their body image because of the illness or injury to the person for whom they care. For this reason many of the same emotional reactions experienced by the client may be experienced by those who are significant to this person. When the client-family is considered as a unit of care, they can be helped to progress together from change to adaptation.

Help available to person and family

Rehabilitation is directed toward treating the problem and preventing it from disrupting the family unit. When the client is a child, special effort must be taken to prevent the problem or treatment regimen from interfering with the development of the child.

The client may benefit from talking to others who have had similar experiences *if* this exchange is arranged when the person is receptive to information. Initially people have difficulty comprehending their own problems and certainly are not interested in someone else's similar experience. As they begin to acknowledge the change, it is often treated as a unique situation, and comments such as, ''They haven't seen too many cases like mine,'' and, ''One in 10,000 and I had to be it,'' reflect these feelings of uniqueness. Since the individual is just beginning to own the problem and probably has not yet come to coping with the problem, it is unlikely that he or she will be receptive to the person who announces, ''I experienced the same thing.'' At some point after clients begin to ask questions and actively learn about the change, they become aware that this same thing has happened to many others. ''I had no idea so many people have handicapped children,'' or, ''A lot of people I know have diabetes, but I didn't know about it until now.'' At this time the person is apt to be receptive to sharing and learning from another who has had a similar experience. As the person and those significant to the person adjust to changes in body image, existence is no longer centered around the illness or injury and the change it created. Life takes on a new meaning with the past serving as a reminder to live life to the fullest in the future.

TRANSITION

The transition that occurs during the process of altering the pre-injury or pre-illness image to include the medical crisis usually includes feelings of shock and withdrawal before acknowledgment and integration take place. This transition does not occur at the time of injury or illness but is a lengthy process that evolves over time.

Psychological shock

Psychological shock is a defense mechanism brought on by anxiety whereby an individual filters information or distorts reality to the point that it can be handled. For some clients this reaction takes the form of selective deafness, allowing the individual to take in what he or she is able to cope with at that moment. The person may be in such stress overload that even good news is missed. For others anxiety may be so great that the person is not aware of anything.

Psychological shock is often the initial emotional reaction when a person becomes aware of his or her problem. This may occur at the time of the injury or illness or at a later time when the person is able to see bodily changes or experience the results of these changes. Clients may initially perceive their situation to be far worse than it really

is, and they have difficulty seeing beyond the immediate loss, surgery, or disfigurement. Faced with the process of adjustment while at the same time experiencing a strong desire to return to the way things were, clients are likely to become discouraged and passively accept events within the environment. The inwardly directed energies of despair may ultimately change to anger and hostility and be directed outwardly toward the staff. A nurse in a burn unit remarked, ''At first they're so down, they won't have anything to do with anyone. They tune me out completely, and I find that very difficult. Then they start to blame me for anything and everything. Even though I don't enjoy being shouted at, I understand that this behavior is simply a projection of what they are feeling, and it is more therapeutic than directing the anger inward.''

Withdrawal

Once the person becomes aware of injury or illness and begins to contemplate future implications, there is an overwhelming desire to move away from the reality of the situation. Since this is not physically possible, the person may retreat emotionally from what must eventually be faced. This withdrawal provides an opportunity to replenish physical and psychological energies used during the shock phase.

During this time clients are careful to keep conversation directed away from self and will talk about other people, pets, the job—anything other than what has happened to them. There is no interest in becoming involved in their own care, and they remain passive and dependent on others. Nurses can present small amounts of factual information without overwhelming the individual with anxiety. Realistic encouragement is also important so that clients do not give up and become severely limited because of their own lack of effort toward rehabilitation. Pushing people to become involved in their care too soon may force them further into denial.

While the individual is withdrawing from body image threats, reminders of bodily changes create anxiety. The client may question, ''Why is all this junk here? People coming and going all the time, it's like Grand Central Station. What do you think I am, a goldfish? Leave me alone!''

The desire to maintain the body image that was held before the illness or injury is so strong that the individual may experience autoscopy, or the hallucination of one's own body image. This vision of the self usually reflects a healthy image that was experienced in the past or hoped for in the future. Although reported cases of autoscopic hallucinations are infrequent, such visions are very frightening to people, who may feel that they are going crazy or have seen a ghost. Some people may be reluctant to talk about these visions for fear of being laughed at or committed. Knowing that this phenomenon is prompted by a drive to be well and is potentiated by stress, fatigue, and worry makes the experience less frightening. Part of helping others adjust to changes in body image is providing the opportunity and the acceptance necessary for the sharing of concerns and fears surrounding these changes.

Acknowledgment

Once individuals acknowledge their loss, they begin to mourn this loss, regardless of its degree of severity. During this phase, clients need time to reflect on the meaning of the change and its implication on the future. This is also a time when medical and nursing activities may be at a height and the person is front and center when the need to be alone is great. Uninterrupted time may be provided if the person is able to tolerate several care procedures at once rather than spreading them over longer intervals.

During shock and withdrawal the person envisions the way things used to be. As the subconscious begins to grasp the body image threat, this acknowledgment may be reflected in the person's dreams. Clients sometimes report that they dream of being in danger but they are unable to flee because of intravenous infusions, catheters, or other such tubes, wires, and equipment. Sometimes a fear of infiltrating an intravenous setup or ''messing up the equipment'' keeps a client almost im-

mobile. They need to know the full range of motion allowed without interfering with monitors, infusions, or treatments. Repeated reassurances from nursing personnel that they are checked frequently and that prompt attention is just the touch of a call light away may help alleviate some of the feelings of helplessness.

Gradually, the client is able to think about what has happened without mentally running from the thoughts. If the body change is visible, the client begins to imagine what it might look like and finally gathers enough courage to peek at the change itself. Ultimately questions are asked about the change. To the health care team these cues are indications that the person is ready to begin integrating the change into the life-style.

Integration

The client begins the long and difficult process of adapting to changes in body image. Through rehabilitation and counseling the client is given the opportunity to project into experiences ahead and prepare for new approaches that must be undertaken. Many individuals are able to assign some meaning for their loss and appreciate the function that they still have.

The following is a true account of a young nurse who experienced dramatic and sudden change in body image. Her narration entitled ''What Does A Miracle Look Like'' includes her feelings as she experienced shock, withdrawal, acknowledgment, and ultimately integration of the changes into her life.

■ I didn't have time to be sick, yet there I sat with other people who probably didn't have the time either. The waiting room was familiar: the stack of magazines I was too nervous to read, the efficient receptionist with a monotone voice.

It had been 3 years since my family doctor had first referred me to this large medical center. I was only 28 then . . . a tender age for a hysterectomy. Now it seemed like a repeat of disrupted plans. I had looked forward to working some extra days during another nurse's absence. I loved nursing and

Peeking at the change indicates transition from withdrawal to acknowledgment.

Illustration by Tom Weinman.

was able to use my part-time wages for extras—like the Disney World trip we planned. "So much for plans," I muttered under my breath.

I thought of the surgery I would soon be having. Anger and anxiety were mixed with thankfulness. My ovaries were enlarged and would have to be removed. The doctors were confident they would find the same type of nonmalignant tumor that had made the hysterectomy necessary. After days of tests and examinations, I was anxious to have the preliminary scheduling over with. Waiting was never easy for me. Especially now.

Looking around the clinic, I saw anxious faces, white-knuckled hands clutching wadded tissue. People waiting in seemingly endless time with concern for living and the quality of life ahead. I looked at each person and wondered about their fear. Was it cancer or heart disease or perhaps the loss of sight or hearing?

I reflected back to my student days when my medical fear was formed. As a queasy young nurse I was unable to care for individuals with a colostomy. I had been fascinated with the surgical process of bringing a healthy section of large intestine—colon—through the abdomen, forming a new opening, or ostomy, for bowel wastes. My interest ended when it came to changing soiled dressings or helping with colostomy care. I knew I would never be able to cope with a colostomy.

I sat secure in the waiting room with the knowledge that my intestinal x-rays were normal. I would not have to face the unfaceable. Others in the room would not be so fortunate. Some would have their fears realized with plans altered or never carried through. By the time I left the clinic I was grateful that our plans would only be delayed.

My surgery went well—no malignancy, home in record time. Then the pain began. Perhaps I had overdone, pulled a muscle, eaten something wrong. I tried desperately to justify the pain and remain in control of my health. Two days later we returned to the hospital.

Hours of pain drifted into days of tests, x-rays, examinations; all were without explanation for my deteriorating condition. Teams of specialists were called in, slowly changing me from a person to an undiagnosed disease. Our children, safe and secure with their grandparents, were out of my thoughts. Days evolved around my illness and my husband. Although our marriage had all the conflicts and turbulent times of any normal marriage, Charles and I were more than husband and wife or intimate friends. We had evolved to that almost psychic state of knowing before sharing. Now when the pain became unbearable, he held me, touched me. Somehow, as though through osmosis, his love made the pain easier to endure.

After almost 2 weeks I was once more lifted onto the surgical cart and taken for exploratory surgery. This time there was no bitterness or even apprehension. I welcomed the anesthetist and his deep sleep.

Only too soon the reprieve was over. Sharp, intense pain seemed everywhere. Even through the haze of anesthetic I sensed something was wrong. Bright lights, a blur of white uniforms. Bits of sentences—intensive care, severe peritonitis, condition critical—increased my anxiety. I knew that peritonitis was massive inflammation in the abdominal cavity. Struggling to gain consciousness, to focus, I wanted Charles. He always made things better . . . more secure. I felt his touch, gently stroking my face, my hands, and I began to relax, drifting back to sleep. But Charles didn't relax with me as he had in the past. His hold on my hand became tighter. He didn't want me to sleep. There

was an undertone of urgency in his voice as he talked about the peritonitis . . . about severe damage to the large intestine. Then finally with his love wrapped completely around me, offering no protection or buffer, I heard the words, ''You have a colostomy.''

My mind whirled, ''Oh no. No!'' I stared in blank horror at the outline of my husband. Knowing how I felt about a colostomy, how could he say the words—allow it to happen to me?

During the past weeks as doctors had fought for my life, Charles was my life. He had fed me when I no longer had the desire or strength to eat. When I became delirious with high temperature, it was Charles who soothed and comforted me back to reality. How could such a love allow such a horrid thing to happen?

Using all the strength I had, I pushed away his hands. ''Go away,'' I cried. ''I'm dirty.'' Closing my eyes, I willingly slipped back into unconsciousness.

The next few days were a blur because I wished them to be. I didn't scream or shout out my grief the way movies or stories portray the remorseful person. There was hardly the strength for words, and my pain threshold allowed only silent tears.

At night, in the sanctum of sleep, my vengence was released. I painlessly tore out the intravenous tubes that fed and medicated me. I pulled the catheter out of my bladder. The stomach tube was ripped from my nose with such force it left my nostril cut and bleeding. I dreamed in horror as a healthy young woman—who loved to sun and swim in a bikini—was taken, strapped to a cart, and permanently disfigured. I awakened sobbing . . . I could not remove what had happened to me. The colostomy was mine. Nurses bathed my feverish body, comforting quietly, allowing me to express my bereavement without question or explanation.

The dreaded dressing change day arrived, bringing vivid all the colostomy memories from years ago. I closed my eyes and sank deep into the bed, trying not to exist. It was over in minutes. No odor . . . no mess. The nurse explained that an adherent, pliant disposable pouch had kept my skin and dressing from becoming soiled. Things had certainly changed since my student days.

I was most fortunate to be in a hospital that staffed professional personnel to teach and help ostomy clients with their questions and care. I read and reread all the colostomy literature that I could get. The more I read, the more questions I asked. The smallest detail was important if it would help me through this new undertaking.

I was amazed at all the products devised to make wearing and cleaning comfortable, convenient, and odorless. With a mixture of fear and determination, I headed for the bathroom. Things didn't go as smoothly as the literature portrayed, but I completed my care alone. My sense of pride was beyond words. I could once more manage my own body functions.

My surgeon assured me that the occasional gurgle-like noise from my colostomy would subside as I healed and became more active. "And until then," he joked, "just look at the guy next to you. Who will know who did what?"

I slowly gained strength and was dismissed from the hospital. Afraid of how I would affect others, I tried to isolate myself. Our 8- and 11-year-old children were curious and blunt with their questions. Ultimately I abandoned my secret in exchange for honest, simple explanations. What I had felt was a horror, they perceived as being something interesting and special. Sometimes it takes a child to see reality.

After a week of hiding I decided the time had come to join grandparents and family at mealtime. Just as things were at the quietest, there was the slightest noise from my colostomy. I froze! Everyone pretended not to hear except my 8-year-old son. Without missing a bite, he sounded out with a loud, "Excuse me." My tears of embarrassment dissolved into laughter. I was accepted.

I gave up my lounging gowns, finding I could wear my outfits over the colostomy pouch. I ventured out into public cautiously at first and then in exuberant gusto. My world was alive again, and I was a part of it. At night my husband held and loved me. The colostomy pouch was between our bodies although it never came between us.

I have learned that the miracle of life comes in many forms and shapes. For me it is a tiny pink section of intestine that forms a petal-like opening on my abdomen. I am one of the fortunate ones. It wasn't necessary that I recognize a miracle to receive it. My colostomy is a gift of life. (© 1979 A. Jann Davis.) ⎯⎯⎯⎯⎯⎯⎯⎯

• • •

The dynamic state of body image is an ongoing communication process between the internal and external environment that continues from birth until death. The health care team can assist in this process by reinforcing the person who is adapting in a healthy manner and intervening whenever unhealthy adaptation is demonstrated. Whereas some clients are able to integrate more destruction into their body image than is considered medically possible, others are unable to assimilate what is considered to be routine. Each human being is unique, and life cannot be measured in terms of pain, function, or appearance. With proper support from helping professionals both client and significant others will be able in time to achieve some degree of acceptance of body image changes brought about by illness, injury, or treatment. This support may mean the difference between life and death and the difference between coping and succumbing.

REFERENCES

1. Associated Press: Mental patient directs hospital in blackout, Fort-Worth Tri-City Herald, p. 11, July 7, 1981.
2. Clay, V.: The effect of culture on mother-child tactile communication, doctoral dissertation, New York, 1966, Columbia University.
3. Hackett, T.: Problems created by advanced medical technology, Psychiatric Annals **6**(10):9, 1976, p. 13.
4. Harlow, H.: The nature of love, The American Psychologist **13**:673, 1958.
5. McFarlane, J.: In Ciba Foundation Symposium 33: Parent-infant interaction, Amsterdam, 1975, Elsevier Publishing Co.

6. Norris, C.: Body image: its relevance to professional nursing. In Carlson, C., and Blackwell, B., editors: Behavioral concepts and nursing intervention, ed. 2, Philadelphia, 1978, J.B. Lippincott Co.

7. Shucard, J., Shucard, D., and Cummins, K.: Auditory-evoked potentials and sex-related differences in brain development, Brain and Language **13**:91, 1981.

8. Spitz, R.: Hospitalism. In Freud, A., Hartmann, H., and Kris, E., editors: The psychoanalytic study of the child, vol. 1, New York, 1945, International Universities Press, Inc., p. 53.

BIBLIOGRAPHY

Allon, N.: Self-perceptions of the stigma of overweight in relationship to weight-losing patterns, The American Journal of Clinical Nutrition **32**:470, 1979.

Bower, F., editor: Normal development of body image, New York, 1977, John Wiley & Sons, Inc.

Casper, R., and others: Disturbances in body image estimation as related to other characteristics and outcome in anorexia nervosa, British Journal of Psychiatry **134**:60, 1979.

Halmi, K., and others: Unique features associated with age of onset of anorexia nervosa, Psychiatry Research **1**(2): 209, 1979.

Kellerman, J., and others: Psychological effects of illness in adolescence. Part I. Anxiety, self-esteem, and perception of control, The Journal of Pediatrics **97**(1):126.

Klaus, M., and Kennell, J.: Parent-infant bonding, ed. 2, St. Louis, 1982, The C.V. Mosby Co.

Kleck, R.: Physical stigma and task-oriented interaction, Human Relations **22**(1):53, 1969.

Lee, J.: Emotional reactions to trauma, Nursing Clinics of North America **5**:577, 1970.

Leviton, A.: Birth order and left-handedness, Archives of Neurology **33**:664, 1976.

Lukianowicz, N.: Autoscopic phenomena, Archives of Neurology and Psychiatry **80**:199, 1958.

Masters, F., and Greaves, D.: The Quasimodo complex, British Journal of Plastic Surgery **20**:204, 1967.

McCloskey, J.: How to make the most of body image theory in nursing practice, Nursing '76, p. 68, May 1976.

Roberts, S.: Behavioral concepts and the critically ill patient, Englewood Cliffs, New Jersey, 1976, Prentice-Hall, Inc.

CHILDREN'S BOOKS ABOUT HUMAN DIFFERENCES
Racial differences

Adoff, A.: Big sister tells me that I'm black, New York, 1976, Holt, Rinehart & Winston, Inc.

Anders, R.: A look at prejudice and understanding, Minneapolis, 1976, Lerner Publications Co.

Cohen, M.: Best friends, New York, 1971, Macmillan Publishing Co., Inc.

Goldin, A.: Straight hair, curly hair, New York, 1966, Thomas Y. Crowell Co.

Merriam, E.: Boys and girls, girls and boys, New York, 1972, Holt, Rinehart & Winston, Inc.

Simon, N.: Why am I different? Chicago, 1976, Albert Whitman & Co.

General handicaps

Greenfield, E.: Darlene, New York, 1980, Methuen, Inc.

Mack, N.: Tracy, Milwaukee, 1976, Raintree Editions.

Stein, S.: About handicaps, New York, 1974, Walker & Co.

Hearing impairment

Levine, E.: Lisa and her soundless world, New York, 1974, Human Sciences Press, Inc.

Litchfield, A.: A button in her ear, Chicago, 1976, Albert Whitman & Co.

Visual impairment

Delaney, N.: Two strikes four eyes, Boston, 1976, Houghton Mifflin Co.

Jensen, V.: What's that? New York, 1978, The William Collins + World Publishing Co, Inc.

Mental disorders

Anders, R.: A look at mental retardation, Minneapolis, 1976, Lerner Publications Co.

Clifton, L.: My friend Jacob, New York, 1980, E.P. Dutton, Inc.

Fassler, J.: One little girl, New York, 1969, Human Sciences Press.

Smith, L.: A special kind of sister, New York, 1979, Holt, Rinehart & Winston, Inc.

CHILDREN'S BOOKS ABOUT THE HUMAN BODY
Physiology

Balestrino, P.: The skeleton inside you, New York, 1971, Thomas Y. Crowell Co.

Brenner, B.: Bodies, New York, 1973, E.P. Dutton & Co.

Gross, R.: A book about your skeleton, New York, 1978, Hastings House, Publishers, Inc.

Showers, P.: Look at your eyes, New York, 1962, Thomas Y. Crowell Co.

Showers, P.: Your skin and mine, New York, 1965, Thomas Y. Crowell Co.

Showers, P.: Hear your heart, New York, 1968, Thomas Y. Crowell Co.

Showers, P.: Use your brain, New York, 1971, Thomas Y. Crowell Co.

Watson, J., Switzer, R., and Hirschberg, J.: My body: how it works, New York, 1972, Golden Press.

Sex education

Andry, A., and Schepp, S.: How babies are made, New York, 1968, Time-Life Books, Inc.

Gordon, S.: Girls are girls and boys are boys, so what's the difference, New York, 1974, The John Day Co.

Helmering, D., and Helmering, J.: We are going to have a baby, Nashville, 1978, Abingdon Press.

Meeks, E., and Bagwell, E.: Families live together, Chicago, 1969, Follett Publishing Co.

Meeks, E., and Bagwell, E.: How new life begins, Chicago, 1969, Follett Publishing Co.

Sheffield, M.: Where do babies come from? New York, 1974, Alfred A. Knopf, Inc.

Showers, P.: A baby starts to grow, New York, 1969, Thomas Y. Crowell Co.

Showers, P., and Showers, K.: Before you were a baby, New York, 1968, Thomas Y. Crowell Co.

5 · Growing up

Turning people into parents is a big task for someone so small.

Illustration by Tom Weinman.

now clamped free. We gently touch her tiny head, and her hair feels like silk. Her arms and legs are unbelievably soft. As her daddy touches her hand, she coils her tiny fingers around his big finger and he whispers, ''We have a beautiful daughter.'' She closes her mouth over my nipple, and as she begins to nurse, I tingle all over my body. At that moment she becomes my child, more beautiful than the Gerber baby, more special than any other child. Changing people to parents is an awesome task entrusted to someone so tiny, and the miracle of birth is made complete by a phenomenon called love. _____

■ Nine months ago it all seemed like a good idea. Parenting comes naturally we had told ourselves. It's an instinct that people are born with; it's something they just know how to do. Right now I'm not too sure. She's so tiny. Here we are mother and father with our newborn, and neither one of us knows how to be a parent. We've never even been around babies before, and now we have a baby who is totally and completely dependent on us. The thought is overwhelming. I'm beginning to wonder if the only instinct involved in parenting is libido.

Somehow she doesn't look like the baby I expected. Maybe it's because she doesn't have much hair. She's so red and wrinkled. I'm wondering if the person who drew the Gerber baby ever saw a newborn.

She opens her eyes and looks at us, and we try to decide if those little eyes can see. Her tiny little face turns into a maze of wrinkles that leads to an open mouth, and she produces a sound humanly impossible from a body that small. Her screams announce to the entire hospital that her parents don't know how to take care of her, and quite frankly she's right. I wait for that flood of maternal instinct to make everything okay, but it doesn't happen. The nurse helps me nestle the baby to my breast, and even though she doesn't nurse, the crying stops.

Our baby with little toes and fingers, and a cord that was once connected to me—a part of me—is

This chapter is about children, about helping them grow up in an environment in which they are loved and cared for and in which they have the security to become their own unique person. It deals with listening to children as they express their needs and fears and responding in a way that nurtures trust, understanding, and self-esteem. Growing up depends on love and security, for without these, children are unable to become physically and mentally healthy adults.

PARENT-CHILD BONDING

Although the traditional two-parent and natural-child families make up the greater percentage of families in the United States, there are many blended families, those created by adoption, and a growing number headed by single parents. A large body of research is directed toward helping families form healthy relationships, but there is little research on effective methods of enhancing relationships between infants and single, adoptive, or stepparents. All family groups need support from caring professionals. A relationship of security and love between child and adult is the ultimate goal, and this goal is not dependent on numbers or a relationship created by birth.

The very early days of a child's life are important in forming a healthy parent-child attachment, and if parents are to parent their child adequately, they must begin by building a firm and close tie with their infant as soon as possible. Preventive and therapeutic measures should be geared to optimum establishment of the healthy parent-child interaction because the strength and durability of this attachment may well determine the infant's optimum survival and development.

ATTACHMENT BEHAVIOR

Maternal-infant bonding was once considered to occur after the infant's birth; however, women whose newborn infants die at birth still have intense grief even though some may not see or have physical contact with their infants. This grief may also be experienced following spontaneous or induced abortions, regardless if the pregnancy was wanted or not. Generally researchers have found that more intense mourning is experienced by those for whom pregnancy was a positive experience and when tactile contact was made with the infant. These behaviors suggest that women begin to attach to their infants before the infant's birth perhaps because during pregnancy the mother perceives the baby as part of herself. It is following birth that interaction with the infant enables the mother to transfer her love for the infant as part of herself to love for the infant as a separate individual.[7]

Only recently has father-infant bonding been recognized as a vital element in healthy family development. Part of this interest has been created by fathers who are not content having their role limited to fathering the child and then handing out cigars after the birth. They want to learn the same information and procedures mothers are learning during the prenatal period, to be present during the birth of their baby, and to be included as a family member in postnatal interactions. Fathers are much more interested in and responsive toward their infants than previously acknowledged, and unless they receive the same child care instructions given to the mother, they do not develop the skills necessary to comfortably care for their infant. Instead, the father feels awkward and clumsy and may ultimately leave the care giving to others. In so doing he misses out on interactions that develop interest

and love and a feeling of what being a father to a child is all about.

Prenatal attachment

In the last trimester of pregnancy, prospective parents are becoming more infant oriented. They choose a name for their baby and begin to make plans for the future. It is during this time that community health nurses can enhance prenatal attachment by having the mother and father listen to the fetus's heartbeat and teaching them how to determine the fetus's position. When they discover that they can hear their child and identify fetal parts, they become more attuned to the reality of the human being that they have created. If the mother has no history of premature labor, the mother and father can be encouraged to touch and stroke the abdominal area over the baby for brief periods each day as a way of communicating with their unborn infant. Simple as this sounds, research has shown that such activities before the birth of the infant more then double the mother's level of attachment with her infant following birth.[2]

Attachment during birth

Across the country alternatives to traditional technologic births are being sought. People are turning away from what was once considered the birthing norm, with fathers excluded and mothers medicated and helpless as the obstetrician delivers the baby. More prospective parents are attending childbirth classes and are learning how to cope with each step of labor and delivery. They want an atmosphere in which they can receive physical and emotional preparation with a childbirth experience that is safe, emotionally meaningful, and rewarding. Mothers and fathers want to be participants in a natural birth without routines such as enemas, perineal preparations, intravenous fluids, or other regimented orders. They want to be assured of maximum emotional support as a new family by not being separated after birth and through active participation in baby care. Single mothers are asking to have friends or significant others attend childbirth classes and to be present during and fol-

Fathers need child care instruction too.

Illustration by Tom Weinman.

lowing the delivery of their infants. For some hospitals this is asking too much, and the requests are denied. There are hospitals available that will respond to the needs of the family, and they are attracting enough clientele to bring about change.

Consumer power has prompted physicians to study alternate birthing techniques in countries that have learned to blend the best in technology and humanity into the birthing process. These techniques are gaining popularity in the United States, and in many areas the labor-delivery room is a homelike atmosphere with one-to-one nursing support. Modern medical technology is readily available, and the obstetrical and pediatric staff are only seconds away. During labor the mother is free to move about or assume a position of comfort. Emotional support, encouragement, and meaningful touch are important aspects of the birthing process, and combined with relaxation and breathing tech-

niques childbirth becomes possible with little or no medication. Assisted by a midwife or a physician, the mother and father or significant others share the exhilarating experience of working together toward the miracle of birth. The new family remains in the labor-delivery room as members become acquainted with each other and begin the attachment process in the immediate postnatal period.

Postnatal attachment

In the typical hospital in the United States the new mother sees her infant briefly following birth and then for approximately 30 minutes every 4 hours for feedings. Fathers are routinely left out of infant care, and the small interaction time permitted between mothers and infants is not sufficient for some mothers to get to know or develop a close attachment with their infants.

Numerous studies conducted in the United States

and other countries indicate the existence of a sensitive bonding period in the first minutes and hours of life, and during this time the mother and father need to have close contact with their infant. They should be brought together for a minimum of 30 to 45 minutes in a private session with as few interruptions as possible. A heat panel maintains the nude infant's temperature so that parents have the opportunity to look their child over, touch and hold it, and confirm the baby's health and sex. If the mother plans to breast-feed her baby, this is an ideal time for the first nursing to take place.

There is a characteristic pattern of touch used when parents first interact with their infants. Initially they use fingertips to touch the infant's extremities and proceed to massaging, stroking, and finally using the entire hand for maximum contact with the infant. If the infant is clothed, this progression from fingertip touching to encompassing palm usually takes longer than if the infant is nude. Maternal touch has also been found to be affected by the quality of touch the mother received during labor and delivery. Mothers who received nurturing touch during labor and delivery use more effective touch with their infants than do mothers who are treated in a distant or impersonal nature.[14]

Immediately after birth, unsedated infants are in a prolonged, alert state, and if eye treatment is delayed, the newborn is more likely to be wide eyed and attentive. Eye contact is particularly important to parents, and they encourage a sleepy infant, "Open your eyes, please open your eyes and look at me." Parents of blind infants miss this visual interaction and may feel more distant with their babies until they learn to substitute other means of communication. One mother commented, "Whenever I talk to my baby, he turns away." What the mother had interpreted as rejection from her blind baby was actually a sign of affection. Since the child could not benefit from eye contact, he had turned his ear toward her voice to achieve sensory contact.

Postnatal parent-child attachment is enhanced by providing as much interaction time as possible. Research findings consistently show that mothers who receive their infants immediately after birth and for additional postnatal time are more supportive and affectionate with their infants than are mothers who have limited time with their infants. Follow-up on some of these mother-infant groups has extended as long as 5 years, and benefits of early and extended contact are still apparent.

Although there is much emphasis on this early sensitive period, obviously, normal healthy parents have been and are able to bond successfully with their infants without spending this sensitive time together. However, for the mother or father insecure with parenting or with giving their love to an infant, this interaction time may be vital to the survival of the family and perhaps even to the survival of the infant. It is not always possible to predict who will need this interaction time, so it is far wiser to ensure that all parents and infants are given the best possible start as a family than to try and repair a relationship that could have been strengthened in the beginning.

SPECIAL SITUATIONS

Prenatal classes should provide prospective parents with information concerning the normal birth and bonding experience and also information about situations that might separate parents from their infant following birth. Bonding can still take place in these cases, but without this understanding, parents may decide that they have missed their chance to bond and then fulfill their own prophecy. Sometimes mothers or fathers start out parenthood feeling like failures because they were unable to live up to their own or their spouse's expectation during labor or delivery. In one case a mother became frantic when she learned that an emergency cesarean birth was necessary, and much of her concern was because she had denied her child a natural birth. "We worked so hard to make sure that our baby would come into this world in a normal, loving way, and now I've ruined everything." A father who fainted during the birth of his child was sure that he would never be able to relate to his baby. Babies need love, and they will adapt and adjust to meet this need. Every effort must be made on the part of the obstetrical and neonatal team to prevent parental feelings of guilt or inadequacy that could interfere with a loving parent-infant relationship.

Brief separations

When it is necessary for parents to be separated from their infant following birth, anxieties about the well-being of the baby may delay the development of parent-infant bonding. Even mild illnesses in the newborn, such as bilirubin elevation, feeding problems, the need for additional oxygen, and incubator care for a day, may cause parents to distance themselves from the infant. If detachment becomes more extensive, one or both of the parents may see the infant as interfering with the fulfillment of their own personal needs. During these early events every effort must be made to include rather than exclude the parents in the care of their infant. Prompt information concerning the infant and reinforcement of the health status will help delay fears and anxieties that prompt detachment.

Premature or ill infant

Parents of a premature or ill infant have the difficult psychological task of simultaneously preparing for the infant's death while hoping the baby will live. Selecting a name or placing any investment into the relationship may be delayed until the parents realize that the infant will survive.

Parents separated from their premature or ill infant may have more problems of attachment following the separation. In the past parents were not allowed to enter the intensive care nursery because of the threat of infection and disruption or interference with medical procedures. Numerous studies have shown that there is no increase in potentially pathogenic organisms when parents take proper precautions, and nurses report that parents do not disrupt the organization or interfere with medical procedures in the unit.

Whenever possible, parents of premature or ill babies are encouraged to interact with their infants. Clinicians have determined that increased stimulus through touching, rocking, fondling, or cuddling increases the infant's rate of weight gain, improves breathing and physical development. This interaction also helps parents feel closer to their infant while at the same time improving their confidence and care giving skills.

If the infant is to be transferred to another hospital, it is important that the parents see and touch their baby before he or she leaves the hospital. Mothers unable to hold their infants talk about how empty they feel inside and how their arms actually ache from wanting to hold their baby. Instant photographs of the infant help the parents adapt their mental image of the infant to reality and help them adjust to the fact that they do have a baby.

It is difficult for parents to feel like parents until they can psychologically and physically move from the role of the observer to the point that they are making an important contribution to the well-being of their baby. Some see their infants as belonging more to the neonatal team than to them, and comments such as, "I have to keep telling myself that we have a baby," indicate the need to involve mothers and fathers more in their infants' care.

Congenital malformation

When a baby is not "perfect" according to the parents' and culture's standards, more time may be necessary before the parents can accept their infant. "Defective" has different meanings to each parent. For some it is something as seemingly insignificant as the sex of the infant or the birth weight. In the United States a great deal of emphasis is placed on the first child being a boy and resembling the healthy, robust Gerber baby. For others "defective" means a child with a major malformation that occurs in 2 of every 100 births in the United States.

Parents have a mental image of their infant before its birth, and following birth this image must be altered by reality before the parents can accept and relate to the infant as he or she really is. When a child is born with congenital malformation, not only is the image of the baby drastically changed, but also that of the parents. They may wonder,

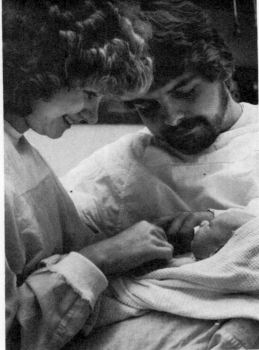

Parents interacting with their premature infant.
Courtesy of Wesley Medical Center, Wichita, Kansas.

"What's wrong with me that made my child this way?" "What did I do wrong?" The parents go through a grieving period for the loss of their "perfect" child and their inability to produce a "perfect" child. The acute grief may last several months before it begins to subside enough to allow full attachment to the living infant. Some parents maintain that the grief never completely goes away. "Every time I see a healthy child about the same age as mine, I hurt inside."

Health professionals have the responsibility of assisting whenever necessary in the reconstruction of the identity of the infant, the individual parent, and joint parental identities. This help is usually in the form of listening, providing information, and support. It does not help parents to be told that their grief is in response to the loss of a healthy child or that their grief is normal and is experienced by all parents of congenitally malformed infants. Although these things may be true, intellectualizing grief deals only with the cause and does nothing to handle the emotions that grief is all about. The feelings that parents experience are almost impossible to describe with words, and when someone who is free of grief attempts to circumscribe another's grief as being routine, more harm is done than good.

The parents will need to be told several times about their infant's diagnosis and what can be done to normalize their child. They fear for their child's life and his or her future and want to know why this has happened to them. Interaction between the parents and the infant is even more important than if the child were normal, and parents who experience a delay in seeing their infant often imagine things as being worse than they really are. Care givers can accentuate the infant's positive attributes and include the parents in the care and planning for their infant.

One mother shared that when her first child was born, she received plants, cards, and phone calls from her relatives and friends. When her second child, Jamie, was born with Down's syndrome, the response was different.

■ The first couple of days we felt virtually alone with this enormous problem. Our friends and relatives acted as though the baby hadn't been born. We began to wonder if they didn't want to associate with us anymore because we had a child that wasn't normal. The second day my Aunt called and asked, 'How are you dear?' I started crying and told her about the baby. That was the first time I had said "Down's syndrome" out loud, and it really hurt. It still hurts, but not so much.

I decided to quit waiting for my friends and relatives to call, and I began to call them. Over and over I made myself tell people that our son Jamie was born, that he had Down's syndrome, and that we all needed love very much. The easier it was for me to talk about it, the easier it was for others to offer the support that we desperately needed.

I can't be critical of the initial lack of response or support from people important in our lives. They didn't know what to say or do, so they did nothing. Before Jamie was born, I might have done the same thing.

Taking care of Jamie is difficult. I don't know what we are going to do in the future. Right now, we are taking one day at a time. Jamie is our son. He is not our joy or our delight, but he is our child and we love him. ──────────────

Ultimately most parents are able to achieve a balance between mourning and acceptance and assimilate the child into the family. Through the ongoing help of an intradisciplinary team the needs of the family unit can be met so that parents are able to care for as well as care about their child. Children can live with a disability, but they cannot live without love.

Death of a family member

Although some parents state that the birth of their child helped them through the loss of a loved one, attachment and detachment cannot easily occur at the same time. While mourning the loss of a loved one, a parent may be unable to complete the process of attachment and therefore be unable to care for a newborn adequately. When one twin dies, parents may find it difficult to mourn this death and at the same time feel attached to the survivor. The same difficulty occurs when a woman becomes pregnant soon after losing a neonate. It is recommended that conception not take place until 6 to 12 months following the death of a loved one so that the grieving process can be completed.

Failure to bond

Child abuse often results from the parents' failure to form an attachment with their child, and the incidence of child abuse is far greater in infants who have been separated from their parents in the early neonatal period.[9] Far too frequently the neonatal team spends weeks saving the life of a premature infant, only to have the infant returned to the hospital as an abused or neglected child.

Many times child abuse and neglect are predictable and therefore preventable. Routine observations of parents as they react and interact with their infants help to identify families that need extra support, encouragement, and help from the staff. Immediately after delivery care givers observe the way the mother and father verbally and nonverbally respond to their infant. They note if the parents are happy with their child and eager to touch to the infant or if their response is one of massive disappointment or filled with negative reactions. They watch for attachment behaviors such as eye contact, close contact during the feeding, fondling, kissing, stroking, nuzzling, talking to, and smiling at the infant.

Parents who may need help in forming a healthy relationship with their infant are those who respond in a passive or negative way or show little interest in touching or talking to their infant. There is little eye contact, and during feedings the baby is held away from the body with the bottle supported by blankets or clothing. If the infant is in a neonatal nursery, the parents seldom visit or phone, and when they do visit, there is little interest or involvement with the infant.

According to several studies, one of the easiest ways to encourage bonding and thereby prevent child abuse has been by increased parent-infant contact through rooming-in services in the hospital. When rooming-in is not feasible, as much parent-infant time as possible should be provided. It is essential that a rapport be established between the parents and a health professional so that feelings, concerns, and questions can be expressed. Sometimes mothers or fathers need help in improving their competence as parents. Through extra encouragement, teaching, and emotional support anxieties may be reduced, ineptness overcome, and parents helped to function on a more nurturing level with their infants. Following dismissal the family's care is continued through frequent phone calls, office visits, and the help of public health nurses and social workers. If at any time attachment behaviors fail to appear, supportive services are mandated.

Sometimes problems are not evident during the immediate postnatal period but may become more apparent at a later time. During a follow-up visit the interaction between the parents and their infant is observed. Mothers are asked if they are enjoying their baby and if they have had someone stay with the baby so that they can have time away. The mother who responds that the baby cries a lot and says that it was great to get away shows less attachment than the mother who shares that she is having fun with the baby and that although she has gone out, she did not want to leave the infant. A mother who appears detached and looks around during the infant's physical examination shows less attachment than the mother who watches the examination and soothes the infant if he or she cries.

Other signals that may indicate that the parent feels inadequate and disturbed are frequent telephone calls to the physician's office with concerns about the infant or more than one visit on the same day to the emergency room with a completely normal infant. These may be cries for help from parents who may be afraid that they will harm their baby. It is mandatory that the infant be admitted to the hospital so that the parents can receive the supportive help necessary to improve their competency as parents.

An infant who fails to thrive in the absence of organic cause may be suffering from maternal deprivation. If there is no weight gain for a month and the infant has no acute or chronic illness, hospital admission may be necessary to determine the cause for the infant's failure to thrive. The mother may be having problems with the baby's formula or feeding schedule that can be taken care of quickly.

Evans and others[6] studied mothers of infants who failed to thrive and identified three basic profile groups. The first profile group revealed that failure to thrive began about the time the mother experienced a major loss in her life, such as the death of a close family relative. This crisis brought about a breakdown in mothering, with symptoms of depression, loneliness, and ambivalence toward the child. These mothers are responsive to help, and most are able to get past this time of crisis and resume a nurturing role with their infants.

In the second group of mothers, psychological problems were compounded by a basic lack of adequate food or shelter. Dramatic changes in family existence needed to be achieved in addition to dealing with the parenting problems that were often a reflection of poor mothering in the mother's own childhood. Through community, county, or state resources the child may be able to grow up with the parents; however, in some cases it is necessary that the child be moved to a foster home.

The third group included mothers who had failed to form an attachment with their infants, and deleterious outcomes with these infants were situations in which the mother had an extreme amount of anger and hostility toward the child. Often the mother reported being abused or neglected as a child and throughout life was unable to establish any meaningful relationships. The mother saw the child as being an unwanted burden and an obstacle standing in the way of her needs. Evans warns that when this type of situation occurs, there is a dangerous potential for child abuse—if it is not already apparent—and placing the child outside the home may be the only way for any normal physical or psychological development.

Evans and others report that the typical child who is neglected or abused is unplanned and unwanted by the parents, is bottle-fed, and has a history of feeding problems. These infants are irritable and difficult to cuddle or hold and are content to stay in their crib. Seldom do they smile or vocalize. They show no objection to being separated from parents and little anxiety when exposed to strangers.[6] As the child grows older, almost a role reversal occurs, with the child picking up after the parents and doing actions such as straightening magazines or emptying ashtrays in an effort to please the parents. Abused children want to be loved and will frequently tell their parents, "I love you." These behaviors may be noticed in a child admitted to the hospital for reasons unrelated to abuse or neglect. Sometimes these children display such atypical behavior as not moving when dressed or undressed and not crying when they receive injections. They have been trained at an early age not to cry when they are hurt.[9]

The infant is totally dependent on parents for survival, and although there are many factors that enter into abnormal parenting, failure to form a bond with the infant may be a contributing cause. For health professionals to deal only with the medical aspect of childbirth and ignore the psychological components of parenthood is as negligent as paying attention to a child's physical health and ignoring the emotional health of the child's family. The child's emotional, intellectual, and physical development is at stake, and it is the responsibility of professionals who work with children and parents to give each infant the best possible start in life. Early and extended parent-infant contact nurtures a relationship between parents and their infant that is an ongoing process throughout life. This process, called bonding, is also referred to as loving.

MENTALLY HEALTHY FAMILIES

One night spent in front of television or at the movies and parents begin to question their parenting ability and kids wonder how they ever were stuck with such unfair parents. On the way out of the movie *E.T.* one child was overheard telling his friend, "And my mom won't even let me have a hamster. How unreal can you get." The typical American family as portrayed in the media is made up of adorable children who know how to communicate their every need and insightful parents who always respond in a loving, helpful way. The illusion is presented in such a way that it is accepted as more real than reality, and many parents conclude, "Either there's something wrong with me or there's something wrong with my kid."

Helping children grow into healthy adults is not an easy task. Parents are not perfect and neither are children. The families portrayed in prime time television and in movies are not an accurate depiction of the real world but illusions produced to entertain. Mentally healthy families do not depend on the traditional structure of two parents and natural children but on the ability to communicate love, trust, and acceptance. Single parents, blended parents, and other caring adults are just as capable as natural parents in creating a healthy psychological home base for children. This psychological security is called self-esteem, and it is the foundation of a mentally healthy family.

Self-esteem

Self-esteem is what people think about themselves—whether or not they feel valued and worthwhile—and when family members have self-respect, pride, and belief in themselves, this high self-esteem makes it possible to cope with the everyday problems of growing up.

Successful parenting begins by communicating to children that they belong, are worthwhile, and are loved for no other reason than just because they exist. Through touch and tone of voice parents tell their infants whether or not they are cherished, valued, special, and loved, and it is these messages that form the basis of the child's self-esteem. When children grow up with love and are made to feel lovable and worthwhile despite their mistakes and failures, they are able to interact with others in a responsible, honest, compassionate, and loving way. A healthy self-esteem is a resource for coping

when difficulties arise, making it easier to see a problem as temporary, manageable, and something from which the individual can emerge.

If, however, children grow up without love and without feelings of self-worth, they feel unlovable and worthless and expect to be cheated, taken advantage of, and deprecated by others. Ultimately their actions invite this treatment, and their self-defeating behavior turns expectations into reality. These youngsters do not have the personal resources to handle everyday problems in a healthy way, and life may be viewed as just one crisis after another. Without a healthy self-esteem they may cope by acting out problems rather than talking them out or by withdrawing and remaining indifferent toward themselves and others. These individuals grow up to live isolated, lonely lives, lacking the ability to give the love that they have never received.

All persons have days when self-esteem is low or damaged. They feel down and may use words to hurt the person who did the hurting or transfer these feelings onto someone or something else. When the child's self-esteem is low, parents can offer love, understanding, and support that enable the child to replenish feelings of self-worth. If the parent's self-esteem is also on shaky ground, the child's symptoms of damaged self-esteem may be misinterpreted and taken personally. An encounter between two people in need of support and unable to recognize this need in each other may result in blocked communication, which compounds problems rather than alleviating them.

Self-esteem is a kind of energy, and when it is high, people feel like they can handle anything. It is what one feels when special things are happening or everything is going great. A compliment, a smile, a good grade on a report card, or doing something that creates pride within oneself can create this energy. When feelings about the self have been threatened and self-esteem is low, everything becomes more of an effort. It is difficult to hear, see, or think clearly, and others seem rude, inconsiderate, and abrasive. The problem is not with others, it is with the self, but often it is not until

Love, understanding, and support help a child to develop a healthy self-esteem.
Photograph by John Hennessey III.

energies are back to normal that the real problem is recognized.

Children need help understanding that their self-esteem and the self-esteem of those they interact with have a direct effect on each other. For example, a little girl comes home from kindergarten, curls up on her mother's lap, and says, ''I need lovings cause my feelings got hurt today.'' The mother responds to her child's need to be held and loved. An adolescent warns his younger sister, ''I flunked my math test, so don't bug me today.'' His sister leaves the room and warns her dad, ''If Jim's a crab tonight, it's cause he flunked a test.'' In both cases the source of the problem was recognized, and each person requested and received what they believed they needed until their self-esteem was restored. If instead the mother said she was too busy to hold the little girl or the younger sister persisted in bothering her brother, the outcome would have been different.

The infant's self-esteem is totally dependent on family members, and it is not until about the time the child enters school that outside forces contribute to feelings about the self. A child must also learn that a major resource for a healthy self-esteem comes from within. Some parents raise their children to depend on external rather than internal reinforcement through practices such as paying for good grades on report cards or exchanging special privileges for good behavior. The child learns to rely on others to maintain a high self-esteem and is not prepared to live in a world in which desirable behavior does not automatically produce a tangible reward such as a smile, money, or special privileges.

Maintaining a healthy self-esteem is a challenge that continues throughout life. A high school counselor encouraged students to keep an ongoing list of things that they liked about themselves. He told students, ''This 'like' list comes in handy when you're down. You can read through the list and say to yourself, 'So today I messed up. I still have good qualities, and I'm still an okay person.' '' One family found that they could help each other identify positive attributes. One evening during an electrical storm the family gathered around the candlelit kitchen table, and each person wrote down two things that they liked about each family member. These scraps of paper were folded and given to the appropriate person, who one by one opened their special messages. The father later commented, ''It was quite an experience, opening each little piece of paper and reading the message. I still have those gifts, and when I've had a really bad day, I read through them and I always come away feeling better.''

The foundation of a healthy family depends on the ability of the parents to communicate messages of love, trust, and self-worth to each child. This is the basis on which self-esteem is built, and as the child grows, self-esteem changes from a collection of other's feelings to become personal feelings about the self. Ultimately a person's self-esteem is reflected in the way he or she interacts with others.

COGNITIVE DEVELOPMENT AND EFFECTIVE COMMUNICATION

Few parents or children start the day determined to make each other's day miserable, but sometimes it happens and many of these situations are the result of poor communication. Effective communication is a challenge in any family situation, for it is a process that continually changes as family members grow and develop.

According to Piaget's theory, a child's cognitive ability develops in stages that emerge in the same sequence with all children. Since communicating effectively with children depends on understanding what they understand, Piaget's formulations provide help in interacting effectively with children as they are growing up. In general this organizational behavior is related to age, with one stage completed before another is begun. Although the sequence seems constant, neither age nor stage is absolute because children vary in their development. With the understanding that each child is unique, Piaget's theory is presented here to establish a reference point from which effective communication can be developed (Table 5-1).

Sensorimotor stage

Piaget identifies the cognitive activity of children from birth to age 2 years as sensorimotor. During this time children learn from immediate experi-

Table 5-1. Piaget's stages of cognitive development

Stage	Age (years)
Sensorimotor	Birth to 2
Preoperational	2-7
Concrete operational	7-11
Formal operational	From 12 on

ences through the senses and are in the process of discovering both the self and the environment. Although it was originally believed that infants behaved as isolates, it is now known that they are acutely aware of their environment. In the first day of life neonates pay close attention to a person who is talking and will synchronize their movements with the pauses and sound segments of adult speech.[5] Although infants have no comprehension of word meaning, they learn to associate pleasure and displeasure with different vocal tones from the way they are touched or handled when these tones are used. By 6 months of age infants are able to purposefully create different pitch levels to express emotions, ask questions, and show excitement through vocal tones alone. They also adjust their vocal pitch to match the person with whom they are "communicating," and when the infant is babbling alone or "conversing" with the father, the pitch level is distinctly lower than when communicating with the mother.[11]

Few new parents are really aware of the difficulty associated with understanding and responding to the needs of a child, and nothing brings this point home any quicker than a crying infant whose needs are not understood. Many new parents have admitted, "I would never have believed that one tiny baby could completely wear out two grown-up adults," and this weariness often comes from being unable to determine what it is the infant wants.

There is a distinct need to label what is not understood or difficult to control, so for the first few months the word "colic" becomes the catch-all word for everything from gas pains to "I don't understand what you want." Somehow labeling reduces guilt and self-blame associated with not being able to comprehend what an infant is trying to communicate or the inability to satisfy this need. After several months the word "colic" is dropped and "teething" takes its place. This label is used to explain both the developmental process of cutting teeth and also the frustrating process of not being able to comprehend or satisfy a fussy, fretful infant.

During the sensorimotor stage the child's world is centered around immediate sensations, and when disequilibrium is felt, restoring equilibrium is all that matters. An adult can go into great detail telling the hungry infant, "Mommy will be there in just a minute," or, "First your diaper must be changed," but until the hunger is eliminated, the infant will continue to communicate awareness of an unfulfilled need.

Touch is paramount to the survival of an infant, who is unable to actively seek this vital stimulation. Without an adequate amount of physical contact, the infant becomes placid, withdrawn, and fails to thrive. Through intervention as simple as being touched and handled by a caring adult, an infant failing to thrive begins to gain weight and interacts with the environment.

Sensations soothing during the sensorimotor phase of life are stimuli similar to those experienced in utero. Rhythmic sounds such as lullabies and nursery rhymes produce the in utero patterns of heartbeat and pulsing blood vessels. Infants are calmed by a metronome, heartbeat recordings, or simply being held in a position so that the adult's heartbeat can be heard. Repetitive or passive movement, such as patting, rocking, walking the floor with the infant, or going for a ride in the car have a soothing effect on babies. Cradles, once discouraged in the early 1900s, are becoming more popular because parents find that infants like this passive motion. The sensations and stimulation associated with a bath are thoroughly enjoyed by most infants, and mothers sometimes resort to bathing the infant almost as a specific quieting remedy when nothing else works.

According to Piaget, children are born seeking information, and their mouth becomes a center for discovering the self and the environment. When infants are not sleeping or eating, they are busy exploring their world visually. They are especially perceptive to the human face and will stare for several minutes at a drawing of a face that has prominent eyes. Infants look to the side more than straight up, so brightly colored items should be tied along the crib or cradle sides to provide visual stimulation. Mobiles will be enjoyed more if the items have broad and colorful undersides and are positioned to the side, approximately 12 inches from the infant. Safety is always first, and mobiles with sharp edges should never be hung over an infant. Numerous infants have been injured or killed after being entangled in items hung across the crib.

Hand coordination makes it possible for babies to move from visually exploring the environment to poking, pulling, and tasting everything they can get their hands on. As they progress from a dependent prone position to mobility, it is imperative that surroundings be made safe for children. A child's natural curiosity is without limits, and it is up to the adult to provide a safe environment for exploration. Toys help children learn about size, texture, and shape and should be purchased for baby appeal rather than for parent appeal. One young couple spent a great deal of time picking out a ball for their 7-month-old baby. The ball was hard plastic and was balanced off center so that it rolled in a zigzag pattern. "We thought she would be fascinated with it," the mother commented, "but it turned out to be a disaster. She pushed the ball, and it rolled back toward her. Her eyes got big as saucers, and she started crying. That was the last time she would get close to the ball." The parents learned that what the baby needed was a toy that she could grasp and control, not something that would threaten her.

During the sensorimotor stage of life infants have a demanding job of exploring and discovering. They communicate their needs as best they know how, and when parents respond with food, a change of diapers, and a little cuddling, infants learn that most of the time their needs will be satisfied. It is this manageable frustration that lets the child know that there is a world apart from the self, which stimulates the youngster to discover and learn more. With love and trust, innate curiosity is allowed to flourish, and the child is prepared to move on to the next stage of development.

Preoperational stage

According to Piaget, preoperational development takes place between 2 and 7 years. The 2-year-old child is able to think about a problem, consider one aspect of a situation at a time, and develop a solution to the problem. Piaget identifies the thought process of this age group as preoperational or intuitive, which is often magical and very egocentric. The 2-year-old child sees a situation from his or her point of view and is unable to comprehend that others do not share the same perspective. This egocentricity combined with the child's venture for autonomy contributes to what one parent called the Jeckel and Hyde personality of her 2-year-old child. It is the onset of this preoperational phase of cognitive development that is frequently labeled the "terrible twos." During this time youngsters do a better job of communicating what they want; however, the problem is trying to convince the child that wants and needs are not always synonymous.

Whereas the discovery of self and environment is the primary task during the first phase of cognitive development, children in this second phase are in the process of gaining control over themselves and their environment. Their understanding and use of language progresses dramatically, with an average 2-year-old child understanding approximately 200 words, and by 5 years of age, word comprehension increases to 2,000 words. Children practice using language and are not hampered by logic or consequences. A 3-year-old thinks nothing of going up to a stranger and announcing, "My Grandma can take out her teeth and gums," or, "You sure are fat." These youngsters use magical thinking and fantasy and are able to carry on long conversations with themselves or with their dolls or stuffed animals. During this period children talk at rather than with others, which gives them a chance to use words without waiting for their turn. They are continually asking questions, and it almost seems that these youngsters do not have an unexpressed thought. A 4-year-old has difficulty distinguishing fantasy and reality, and rather than scolding a child for talking about a lion that he or she saw on the way to Jimmy's house, the adult can ask about the adventure. The child can be coerced into saying there was not a lion, but the only thing that is accomplished is having the child repeat what he or she does not believe is true.

When children are in these formative years, their emotional needs must be met so that they can grow up being happy with themselves. The following are some basic ingredients that nurture psychological safety.

Unconditional love. Learning about love early in life makes it easier for a child to view the world in a positive way. Children need to know that they are loved when they are good as well as when they are bad, and parents verbally communicate this by saying, "I don't like what you did, but I still love you." This is unconditional love. Love is such a confusing phenomenon there is little wonder that children have trouble understanding this emotion. As more families experience divorce, children express the fear, "Will you stay in love with me, or will you fall out of love with me like you did with mommy (or daddy)?" One of the kindest actions parents can do is work out their personal problems in a way in which their child's self-esteem is left intact and the child is free to love and be loved by both parents.

Trust and security. Preoperational children are surrounded by new and strange experiences, and they need to know that they have someone they can trust and rely on for security. There is safety in knowing what to expect in advance of new experiences, and there is security in knowing that adults will be truthful about this information. Parents should refrain from making promises that they cannot keep since repeated broken promises contribute to distrust regardless of how good the parent's intentions were.

Owning feelings. Feelings are a part of life. They are not right, wrong, good, or bad, they just are. Acknowledging a child's feelings and letting the child know that it is okay to feel sad, glad, or mad and that it is okay to be afraid and to cry help the child accept these feelings as normal. Children need to be taught at an early age that emotions such as fear and anger are not bad. Rather than encouraging children to repress these emotions, parents should help children to identify their feelings and to channel them in a nondestructive way. When

a youngster feels angry, the child is encouraged to "talk it out" or to use some nonthreatening physical activity to "work it out." The goal is for children to learn that they can control their emotions rather than have the emotions control them. Suggested children's books about feelings are listed at the end of this chapter.

Nonjudgment. Part of parenting is helping children with their problems, and effective helping withholds blame or judgment and concentrates on the problem. Faultfinding, criticizing, and labeling only serve to reinforce a child's bad feelings about him or herself while leaving the problem unattended. Arguing reinforces a child's original conviction; discussions—listening to both sides—point out alternate ways of looking at a problem and the possibility of a mutually agreeable solution. Blaming hinders, whereas helping the child identify and work out a problem teaches.

"I" statements from parents recognize their feelings without attacking the child's character. In the following example the parents feelings and the child's behavior are focused: "I am really upset because of the window you broke." This is in contrast with: "You make me upset, always breaking things." Another type of label is the use of words such as "always" and "never." For instance, "You never pick up your clothes," and "He's always such a good boy." When describing the action or behavior of youngsters, these words are seldom accurate.

Sometimes adults have the misconception that pointing out a child's faults will bring about improvement. Being called a liar does not make a child honest. Children labeled as lazy have little incentive to become industrious, and youngsters who are called dumb may give up and live the label rather than working toward their true potential. Encouragement works much better than criticism. Parents who recognize the good in their child and then nurture these attributes by treating the youngster as the person he or she is capable of becoming, find that improvement is toward the expected.

Undivided attention. "I remember what it was like before my little sister was born," one 4-year-old child reflected. "Mom used to do things with me, you know, just with me. Now I have to wait until my sister gets what she wants first, and she takes up all the time.'' Sibling rivalry and parents who do not take time with each child may cause a child to feel more like a bother instead of a blessing. Time alone with a child is a gift that is within reach of each parent. A single parent exchanged baby-sitting hours with a friend so that each week she could spend one-to-one time with each of her two children. Sometimes they played games, took a walk, or went on a picnic. Years later the older son reminisced about these special times. ''We didn't have enough money to eat out, but I'll never forget the picnics. Sometimes they weren't any further than the back yard, but it was my time with Mom and it made me feel very special. On those days I thought she was about the best mom in the world, and now I realize that she was.''

If children have to wait until Mom or Dad has time, they grow up while they are waiting. A parent who sets aside one-to-one time for each child gives a gift more valuable than anything money can buy.

Uniqueness. Sometimes parents see in their children the opportunity to become everything they ever wanted to be and the chance to do everything they always wanted to do. Children are not carbon copies of their mother or father, and they need to be allowed to develop into their own unique person. Because of this uniqueness, the child's thoughts and actions are going to differ from those of the parents. A 3-year-old girl asked her father, ''Can mommys and daddys tell what little kids are thinking?'' When the father reassured her that they could not, the little girl responded, ''Good.'' By allowing uniqueness, children know that they are loved and valued even when their behavior has to be limited.

Responsibility. Sometimes a parent can help most by not helping—allowing children to do what they are capable of doing and allowing them to learn from their own efforts. There are a large number of youngsters whose parents do virtually everything for them, and these children have no chance to experience either success or failure. Responsibilities should be appropriate for a child, and

the results should be expected to reveal the child's efforts, not those of perfection. Youngsters can help around the house and with meals. They will not make their beds perfectly, and the job should not be criticized or redone; it is simply the beginning of improvement to come. If a parent negates a child's best effort, the child may decide to avoid failure by not trying.

During the school week mornings are a hassle in many homes as parents take it on themselves to get their children to school on time. Elizabeth was in the second grade, and each morning her mother awakened her in time to eat breakfast before she walked to school. At least one morning each week Elizabeth went back to sleep, or for some reason or another she did not have enough time to eat and still arrive at school on time. On those mornings her mother took her to school in the car. There were usually angry exchanges between Elizabeth and her mother, and the feelings that stemmed from these hassles affected their entire day.

Finally, Elizabeth's mother bought an alarm clock for Elizabeth and after showing her how to work the clock, told her that getting to school on time was her own responsibility. She was warned that if she overslept she would be late to school because the car would not be used to prevent tardiness. The first morning went fine, but on the second Elizabeth overslept and ended up late to school. Her mother reported that it took about 2 weeks before Elizabeth realized that her promptness was her own responsibility and her pleading and crying stopped. ''The change wasn't easy, but mornings are a lot more peaceful now. Elizabeth is also very proud of herself and the fact that she hasn't been late to school in 2 months.''

During the preoperational years children concentrate on gaining control over themselves and their environment. If during this time they are also given the chance to experience responsibility appropriate to their age, they learn that accountability is a part of growing up rather than an addendum to be learned at a later time. Children whose emotional needs are met are better prepared to progress from the preoperational stage of cognitive development toward more intellectual growth during the phases of concrete and formal operations.

Concrete operational stage

Piaget classifies the cognitive processes of youngsters between 7 and 11 years as concrete operational. Capable of thinking concretely, early school-aged children can consider two aspects of a situation at the same time and view the world from an external point of view. They are able to understand another's viewpoint and use logic in their reasoning. Although a 9-year-old child can distinguish between a dream and a fact, the difference between a fact and a theory or hypothesis is not yet clear. Rules are an important part of elementary school children's lives, and they understand the reason for these controls rather than following them without understanding as do preschoolers. These youngsters often spend more time going over the rules of a game than actually playing the game. These literal-minded thinkers see instructions as something to be followed explicitly and become very frustrated with parents who are not in complete agreement with what the teacher has said. "But she wants us to make our 'Ds' this way." Parents do not understand why the teacher has to be so inflexible, and teachers become annoyed at parents who confuse what they are trying to teach.

Communication problems with school-aged children are often attributed to teachers who do not understand and classmates who are insensitive, cruel, and heartless. Parents theorize that without these school problems, home life would be easier, and teachers maintain that without home problems, the child would do better in school. Both sets of adults rationalize what may be produced in part by a literal-minded child caught between equally arbitrary groups of adults.

Childhood is supposed to be a carefree time, and most adults say that it is. Children disagree. Many describe themselves as being unhappy, miserable, and isolated, and they carry around a great deal more stress than most parents recognize. Home and school produce a certain amount of stress for the child that even the best of parents and teachers cannot eliminate. Consequently it would seem prudent to help children learn to cope with stress in a healthy way as they are growing up rather than waiting until stress produces enough distress to govern health and life.

In the past few years numerous stress scales have been developed for children, but many are nothing more than adult stress scales with words such as "spouse" changed to "parent." Children and adults do not react to the same events in the same way. What an adult finds stressful may not be noticed by a child and vice versa. Coddington has spent many years involved in prevention of emotional disorders of children, and his research has identified environmental stressors specific to children and adolescents. The purpose of the Life Event Scale—Children (Fig. 5-1) is to identify children with a high potential for developing some form of maladaptive behavior, although other factors such as the child's coping skills and support systems also affect the scale's predictive efficiency.

Included in this scale are positive as well as negative events since any event requiring an individual to adjust produces a certain amount of stress. Most researchers agree that there is more impact experienced from negative than positive events. Although there is controversy regarding the use of weights to indicate the stressfulness of events rather than simply counting the number of events, some studies have found that weighted scores are more accurate in predicting maladaptive behavior. Coddington points out that these weights are not absolutes, with each person experiencing the same event in the same way, but that they serve as guidelines in estimating the amount of readjustment necessitated by the event.

The scale is broken down into four columns with each column representing 3 months of a 12-month period. When using the scale, the individual enters the weights of the life events that have occurred in the past 12 months in the appropriate column under the month each event occurred. Stressful life events not listed can be added to the appropriate column, and the weight assigned to a similar event on the

LIFE EVENT SCALE — CHILDREN (Age 6 through 11)

NAME: _____ DATE: _____ AGE: ____ SEX: ____ RACE: ____

INSTRUCTIONS:

1. If any of the events listed below occurred in the PAST 12 MONTHS, write the weight in the correct column on the right.

	WEIGHT	SUMMER June July Aug.	FALL Sept. Oct. Nov.	WINTER Dec. Jan. Feb.	SPRING Mar. April May
The death of a parent	109				
The death of a brother or sister	86				
Divorce of your parents	73				
Marital separation of your parents	66				
The death of a grandparent	56				
Hospitalization of a parent	52				
Remarriage of a parent to a step parent	53				
Birth of a brother or sister	50				
Hospitalization of a brother or sister	47				
Loss of a job by your father or mother	37				
Major increase in your parents' income	28				
Major decrease in your parents' income	29				
Start of a new problem between your parents	44				
End of a problem between your parents	27				
Change in father's job so he has less time home	39				
A new adult moving into your home	41				
Mother beginning to work outside the home	40				
Beginning the first grade	20				
Move to a new school district	35				
Failing a grade in school	45				
Suspension from school	30				
Start of a new problem between you and your parents	43				
End of a problem between you and your parents	34				
Recognition for excelling in a sport or other activity	21				
Appearance in juvenile court	33				
Failing to achieve something you really wanted	28				
Becoming an adult member of a church	21				
Being invited to join a social organization	15				
Death of a pet	40				
Being hospitalized for illness or injury	53				
Death of close friend	52				
Becoming involved with drugs	38				
Stopping the use of drugs	23				
Finding an adult who really respects you	20				
Outstanding personal achievement (special prize)	34				

2. List below any events that occured in the PAST 12 MONTHS but were not included in our list and place a check mark in the correct column.

Fig. 5-1. A, Life Event Scale—Children.

	Approximate upper limit scores for seventy five percent of a young population			
	Length of Scoring Period			
Age	Three Months	Six Months	Nine Months	Twelve Months
8 -10	50	95	110	110
11 -13	60	115	130	135
14 - 16	75	140	160	170
17 - 19	90	170	195	200

Fig. 5-1, cont'd. B, Interpretation of scores.
© *R. Dean Coddington, M.D., 1981.*

scale can be used. Three-month scores are computed by adding the numbers in each column. Since a certain amount of attenuation of stressfulness occurs over time, column scores are adjusted according to how long ago the life events occurred. The most recent 3-month score is not adjusted because the stressfulness of these life events is at its greatest. The next most recent 3-month score is reduced by 25 percent, the next by 50 percent, and the most distant by 75 percent. For example, Susan is involved in a mid-January study and reports the following 3-month scores: summer, 28; fall, 40; winter, 20; and spring, 50. Her scores are adjusted as follows:

Quarter	Score	Adjustment	Adjusted score
Fall	40	No adjustment	40
Summer	28	Reduced 25%	21
Spring	50	Reduced 50%	25
Winter	20	Reduced 75%	5

Susan's 12-month score is 91, which is within a range that the majority of healthy children age 8 to 10 years obtain. Some youngsters are able to adjust to more and others less, depending on their coping abilities and support system. The scale does not mandate that more events or higher scores will result in maladaptive behavior but that the potential is there.[3]

Children dealing with a lot of stress are encouraged to reduce those life events over which they have control. Whenever possible, parents should postpone changes that might add stress to a child who is already experiencing psychological trauma. A child's coping abilities can be maximized by support from family members and extrafamilial relationships. The greatest resource for helping a child cope is a sensitive, caring adult who shares the child's problem. Unfortunately, some children lack this support, and they turn to drugs or alcohol to take the place of human understanding.

Formal operational stage

Perhaps the label most synonymous with "I don't understand" is "adolescence." This is a time when teenagers feel out of control amidst a myriad of changes within themselves, and they transfer this anxiety and uncertainty to their parents. Adults maintain that it is impossible to communicate with adolescents, and adolescents say that their parents spend all their time preaching but never listening.

LIFE EVENT SCALE — ADOLESCENTS (Age 12 and over)

NAME: _____ DATE: _____ AGE: ____ SEX: ____ RACE: ____

If any of the events listed below occurred in the PAST 12 MONTHS, write the weight in the correct column on the right.	WEIGHT	SUMMER June July Aug.	FALL Sept. Oct. Nov.	WINTER Dec. Jan. Feb.	SPRING Mar. April May
The death of a parent	108				
The death of a brother or sister	88				
Divorce of your parents	70				
Marital separation of your parents	62				
The death of a grandparent	52				
Hospitalization of a parent	52				
Remarriage of a parent to a step-parent	51				
Birth of a brother or sister	50				
Hospitalization of a brother or sister	49				
Loss of a job by your father or mother	46				
Major increase in your parents' income	41				
Major decrease in your parents' income	43				
Start of a new problem between your parents	41				
End of a problem between your parents	30				
Change in father's job so he has less time home	35				
A new adult moving into your home	34				
Mother beginning to work outside the home	28				
Being told you are very attractive by a friend	26				
Going on the first date of your life	42				
Finding a new dating partner	34				
Breaking up with a boy/girl friend	39				
Being told to break up with a boy/girl friend	35				
Start of a new problem between you and your parents	43				
End of a problem between you and your parents	35				
Beginning the first year of senior high school	19				
Move to a new school district	41				
Failing a grade in school	47				
Suspension from school	34				
Graduating from high school	33				
Being accepted at the college of your choice	39				
Recognition for excelling in a sport or other activity	24				
Getting your first driver's license	32				
Being responsible for an automobile accident	36				
Becoming an adult member of a church	25				
Being invited to join a social organization	18				
Being invited by a friend to break the law	21				
Appearance in a juvenile court	31				
Failing to achieve something you really wanted	32				
Getting a summer job	35				
Getting your first permanent job	40				
Deciding to leave home	41				
Being sent away from home	46				
Being hospitalized for illness or injury	50				
Death of close friend	63				
Becoming involved with drugs	45				
Stopping the use of drugs	30				
Finding an adult who really respects you	22				
Getting pregnant or fathering a pregnancy	Boys 61, Girls 88				
Getting married	78				
Outstanding personal achievement (special prize)	39				
Other events (describe and check column)					

© R. Dean Coddington, M.D. 1981

Fig. 5-2. A, Life Event Scale—Adolescents.

| | Approximate upper limit scores for seventy five percent of a young population | | | |
| | Length of Scoring Period | | | |
Age	Three Months	Six Months	Nine Months	Twelve Months
8 -10	50	95	110	110
11 -13	60	115	130	135
14 - 16	75	140	160	170
17 - 19	90	170	195	200

B

Fig. 5-2, cont'd. B, Interpretation of scores.
© *R. Dean Coddington, M.D., 1981.*

As youngsters enter adolescence, they develop what Piaget identifies as formal operations, or the ability to abstract and hypothesize concepts and consider several aspects of a situation. Literal thinking gives way to logical thinking, and a vastness and complexity of knowledge produces an answer for each question and a question for each answer.

Youngsters of this age are bombarded by potentially stress-provoking situations. They live in a time when they have more choices, temptations, and pressures than previous generations have experienced. In the past teenagers were concerned primarily with the traditional problems of dating, their appearance, drinking, and drugs. Now they worry about schoolwork, exams, finding part-time jobs, and career choices. Because adolescents are faced with the combination of rising educational expectations and shrinking opportunities, it is necessary that they make career decisions at a much earlier age. The Occupational Outlook Handbook of the U.S. Labor Department projects that in 1985 there will be more than 10 million bachelor of arts graduates competing for 8 million job vacancies traditionally filled by college graduates.

According to the 1979 Surgeon General's report, as many as 40 percent of adolescents between the ages of 11 and 14 years already have risk factors associated with heart disease, and many of these risk factors are precipitated by stress. The Life Event Scale—Adolescents (Fig. 5-2) is a resource for helping adolescents become aware of the stressful life events that require readjustments in their life. To use the scale, the individual enters the weights of the life events that have occurred in the past 12 months in the appropriate column. The weights in each column are added to give 3-month scores. Life events not listed on the scale can be added in the appropriate column, and the weight assigned to a similar event on the scale can be used. Events in the most recent 3-month period are the most stressful, and therefore these scores are not adjusted. Because the passage of time tends to reduce the amount of stress from a life event, the score from the next most recent 3-month period is reduced by 25 percent, the next by 50 percent, and the most distant by 75 percent (see example on p. 119). A high stress score is not indicative of maladaptive behavior but only that the individual is dealing with major adjustments that could cause emotional disorders.[4] What one adolescent finds stimulating may destroy another.

The life-style of many parents contributes to their children's stress. Parents get so caught up with doing and going in their own lives that they have little time to spend with their children and little time to make their children feel valued for who they are rather than for what they accomplish. Some parents place such a strong emphasis on sports that they hold their children back a year in school so that they have a greater advantage on the football field or the basketball court. There is little consideration about the pressure that this creates for the child who may have little interest in sports or little athletic ability. One junior high school student commented that his parents wanted him to participate in everything:

■ They say that they want me to be a well-rounded person. If I get any more rounded, I'll be a ball. Sometimes I would like some time to just do nothing. To my dad I'm just a piece of property that he owns—like stock that he's invested money in, and to my mom I'm something she brags about to her friends. My grades are dropping but the coach tells me that if I drop out of football, he'll make sure that I'm blackballed from other school sports. I don't even know who I am or what I want to do with my life, and I wish people would quit telling me what to do long enough for me to make some decisions on my own. _____

Parents who make unreasonable demands on their children may have been unable to please their parents when they were youngsters. Unless this stressful cycle is broken, another generation of stress may result. Adolescents learn how to handle stress from their parents, and if they see their parents resorting to alcohol or drugs, they are likely to do accordingly. Drug problems are appearing at an increasingly earlier age, and it is estimated that 1.3 million American teenagers have serious drinking problems. Teenagers involved in accidents, homicides, and suicides have increased dramatically, and the National Center for Health Statistics revealed that during 1978 there were 1,686 recorded suicides among 15 to 19 year olds in the United States, and authorities believe that the majority of all suicides and suicide attempts go unreported.

Teenagers can cope effectively with stress in a number of ways. A healthy self-esteem provides a personal resource for coping with change, creating a type of resilience that helps the individual maintain a healthy psychological balance. Describing this inner stability, a 15-year-old adolescent said, "It's a kind of trust in myself or a feeling that I can see the bad times through. Sometimes I don't know how, but I just know that I can." Religion, meditation, and creative outlets such as music and art help some teenagers relieve tensions. "A good game of football with my friends—without the coach—really gets rid of the pressure," commented one 16-year-old boy. "But when we're playing for real, the tension really builds." Teenagers find support in social organizations and in extrafamilial relationships with peers, friends, teachers, or other caring adults such as ministers or school counselors. The most obvious source of psychological support is the family; however, many families are more like a grouping of people who live separate lives with paths that seldom cross long enough to say "hi" and "good-bye." It is the responsibility of parents to provide their children with the love, security, and freedom to discover that life is worth living, and each person has a purpose and a place. In a healthy family love and self-esteem are validated when parents take the time to listen without judging and respond without criticism.

Stage after stage, generation after generation, the cycle predictably repeats itself. It is the older third generation that is not bewildered or frustrated by all of the "Nos," "I will do it myself," "Mom, you don't understand," and teenagers who retreat behind closed doors. Parents make the rules and grandparents recognize the need to make exceptions. With age comes marvelous insight, objectivity, and an appreciation of the value of listening. Grandparents just smile when they hear the ageless questions that they themselves have asked, "How do you communicate with kids?" They offer simple solutions, "Love them and spend time with them because they're only young once," to which parents sometimes respond, "Thank God!" As the years smooth out the rough edges and memory makes adjustments, parents look back on the years when their children were growing up, "Those were the good years, but I didn't take the time to notice."

CHILDREN AND THEIR ART

The idea that children's drawings somehow reflect their precise mental capacity has been widely held among educators and psychologists for many years. Koppitz, Goodenough, Harris, Bender, Lantz, and others say that children's art represents their observation of the world around them and therefore indicates degrees of intelligence.

Kellogg,[8] an internationally known authority on children's art, has collected, analyzed, and interpreted more than 1 million paintings and drawings made by children from all over the world. She contends that many theories about child art come from individuals who have little experience in directly studying large quantities of children's art. Kellogg conducted a study of sets of drawings from some 2,500 public school children who were asked to draw a man each day for 5 days in 1 week. About one third of the children's drawings varied so much in a week's time that ratings done by an expert according to the Goodenough scale changed as much as 50 percent. Kellogg concluded that only a series of drawings should be used as a basis for a reliable intelligence test—even then the child might not do his or her "best" in any given short period of time.

Psychiatrists and psychoanalysts also interpret children's art. They use a qualitative rather than a quantitative or statistical approach and are interested in the individual's emotional condition rather than in mental development.

Freudian writers on art consider art to represent wishes and conflicts that are basically sexual. Jung-ians hold that art expresses emotions arising from the collective unconscious on one level and personal emotions on another level. That art is communication between the artist's id and ego is a theory held by Kris, whereas Rank treats art activity as the full assertion of one's creativity.

For many years, children's art has been used to support diverse and conflicting theories. When conformity, defensiveness, and sophistication overshadow the openness and freshness of children's art, it is then that their message is lost. With openness and acceptance, children tell us through their drawings about themselves and the human condition.

Developmental indicators

The developmental level, perceptual ability, and fine motor skills of children are evidenced in their drawings. Before attempting to analyze or interpret a youngster's drawings, one should know some basic age-specific developmental indicators, which are summarized by McLeavey.[13]

About the earliest the child has the coordination to mark on a paper is 18 months, using vertical or horizontal lines that flare in all directions and often extend off the paper. The 2-year-old child demonstrates definite neuromuscular maturation by being able to hold a pencil and contain the more circular or angular scribbles to the paper. Although the scribbles of the young child appear to be completely without pattern or form, there are close to two dozen basic scribbles composed of vertical, horizontal, diagonal, circular, curving, waving or zigzag lines and dots. These basic scribbles are not learned from adults but are spontaneous and become the building blocks out of which all graphic art is constructed. The child explores this first phase of scribbling before progressing to a more controlled form of drawing.

Preschoolers have progressed in fine-motor and visual-motor coordination and have therefore gained more control in their drawings. This advanced skill in manipulation makes it possible for the child to hold the pencil in a more skillful manner and produce smaller, more controlled, creative shapes distinct from the scribbles of the 2-year-old child.

An average 3-year-old child begins to draw what adults refer to as a sun. This is an important point from which the child proceeds to draw human figures. The drawing progresses to center marks identified as a face, and by the age of 3 to 4 years the child draws a human figure that is recognizable, with arms attached to the head. A 4-year-old child is usually able to draw a three-part person consisting of a head, eyes, and arms or legs or a head, mouth, and eyes or any combination totaling three parts. Within a year the child progresses to drawing a six-part person, usually consisting of a head, eyes, nose, mouth, body, and arms or legs. After children learn to make the human figure with arms, they begin to create the armless figure perhaps because they believe it looks better.

The preschematic stage encompasses the ages 4 to 7 years, when children's drawings represent their mental images. Characteristic at this stage is the lack of spatial relationships in drawings. The chair may be drawn below the table, or the person is drawn at the top of the picture and the table at the bottom. As children develop, the drawings contain more detail, and they progress from drawing a six-part person to a nine-part person. Breasts and phalluses are rarely drawn before the age of 6 years simply because the child is not interested in drawing realistic anatomy. Human figure drawings are followed by drawings of animals that begin around the age of 4 or 5 years, with the child drawing ears on the top of the human head and later drawing the human figure in a horizontal position. Around this same age the first tree is drawn, similar to the armless human, but with a head containing extra markings not needed for a face. Buildings and then transportation details are drawn as children become more aware of the world around them. Contrary to popular belief, the stick-person drawing is not a spontaneous drawing but rather learned at age 5 or 6 years from adults or children who have learned it from adults.

Between the ages of 7 and 9 years the child begins to draw schematically with fine-motor control, logical thinking, and perceptual skills developed to the point that the child can now produce pictures that are recognizable and have order in space relationships. The child begins to draw a "base line," identified as the ground or the floor on which to draw people, animals, flowers, and trees.

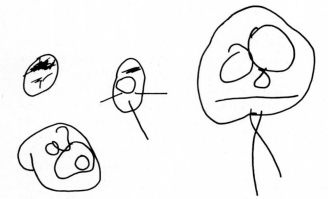

From scribbles to creative shapes.
© *1979 A. Jann Davis.*

The 7- and 8-year-old child draws a 9- to 11-part person and may overemphasize a body part or object that is important or omit something that is insignificant. An x-ray or transparency technique may be used, depicting both the inside and outside of what is being drawn.

The 9- to 10-year-old child draws more detailed human figure drawings, including hair, neck, elbow, and shoulders, and the child 10 to 12 years differentiates male figures from female by the use of clothing and hair styles. At age 12 years the child makes use of stripes, plaids, and dots, shows a midline in figure drawings with belt buckles and buttons, and is generally able to produce a 14-part person. The young adolescent has matured to the point of creating realistic pictures.

A child's early art abstractions are the products of innate patterns of neurological growth and human development. The professional aware of the age-specific developmental indicators will be in the position to identify developmental lag, problems of neuromuscular coordination, or delayed perceptual-motor skills that may be attributed to decreased environmental stimuli. Children not demonstrating the expected skills are good candidates for further evaluation with such screening tools as the Denver Developmental Screening Test. Exercises to improve motor coordination include block stacking or cutting strips of paper with scissors. Many times adults do not realize the importance of a child's scribbling and fail to provide the place, supplies, and supervision for young children to produce their art. This is unfortunate because scribbling and drawing help to develop perceptual abilities that are necessary for learning to read.

Newspaper end rolls, available from most newspapers at a nominal cost, produce yards and yards of continuous paper on which the child may scribble and draw without confinement of an 8½ by 11 inch sheet of paper. Rather than filling in the lines that adults created, children need to spontaneously and innately produce art according to their own esthetic visions. Such encouragement might reduce the number of children in the school systems who have reading problems.

Interpretation of children's drawings

A child's drawing is a statement and a drawing, and like verbal statements it can be analyzed for structure and content. Young children express their feelings and attitudes in graphic images and symbols long before they can convey them in verbal concepts. Once children are able to communicate their thoughts and feelings in verbal or written form, they usually give up drawing as a way of expressing themselves. However, older children may again revert to the language of drawing and graphic imagery when they cannot put into words their anxieties and conflicts.

Children from the age of 2 to 12 years are usually willing to draw a picture of themselves or their family. A pencil and paper attached to a clipboard are all the materials necessary for this assessment tool, and the information achieved can provide information about the developmental and emotional status of the child.

Koppitz[10] identifies three basic principles for analyzing the meaning of a child's human figure drawing. These principles are outlined below[10]:

1. How a child draws a figure, regardless of whom he draws, reflects his own self-concept.
2. The person whom the child draws is the person who is of greatest concern and importance to the child at the time he is making the drawing.
3. What a child is saying in his HFD [human figure drawing] may be twofold; it may be an expression of his attitudes and conflicts, or it may be a wish-dream or both.

Children often draw themselves, for obviously, no one is of greater importance to the child than the self. The signs and symbols employed in a drawing reveal the inner self-portrait of the child and the attitude toward the self. These portraits of the self may be fairly realistic, or they may be distorted until they bear little resemblance to the child's actual appearance. Quite frequently, youngsters identify with their heroes, for example, Luke Skywalker from "Star Wars," or Superman, and may draw their ideal image in the form of these heroes.

Sometimes the child will draw a parent or a sibling who is the child's primary preoccupation, concern, or conflict at that given time, and the way this person is drawn reflects the child's attitude. Occasionally a child will indicate that the figure drawn is a picture of the helping professional. Although this may be flattering for the professional, it is a very poor sign for the child. Such drawings are usually made by children who are social isolates, starved for attention and affection, and therefore overresponsive to the acceptance and friendliness of the professional who is a complete stranger.

Some therapists contend that children should not be asked questions about their drawings and that comments from the adult should be restricted to statements about the art: ''I like the colors,'' ''Very interesting,'' or, ''I like that.'' If children are trying to communicate through drawings, they may want to talk about what they have drawn and are apt to offer spontaneous cues and comments if given the opportunity. Certainly there is no place for an interrogation type of questioning that could result with the child giving answers that will please the questioner. Comments from the child about the human figure drawing can be stimulated by general, open-ended questions such as, ''What kind of person is this?'' and, ''What is he doing?'' The child may also be asked, ''What were you thinking as you were drawing the picture?''

Although emotional features and indicators may have been identified, interpretation without validating meaning with the child may be erroneous. Drawings can be used primarily to open pathways of communication, with the child describing verbally what has been drawn symbolically. Cues can be taken from the child. Some art is simply a statement, not a question or a story, and no amount of questioning can produce what is not there in the first place. There are also times when children's drawings reveal subconscious feelings that they are unable to recognize or verbalize. Each child expresses anxieties, conflicts, or attitudes in different ways, so it is impossible to make an evaluation of a child's behavior on the basis of a single sign on a human figure drawing. The total drawing with various features and indicators must be analyzed, considering the child's age, maturation, and emotional, social, and cultural background as well as other available data about the child.

Features. Burns and Kaufman[1] have listed features in individual human figure drawings that are relevant in clinical interpretation. The following are features from their listing:

Disproportionately small body parts indicate feelings of inadequacy in the specific areas.

Exaggeration of body parts reveals preoccupation with the function of these parts.

Omission of body parts suggests denial of function of these parts.

Facial expressions depicting various emotions are considered to be very reliable indicators of the child's feelings.

Precision, orderliness, and neatness may be viewed as the child's attempt to control a threatening environment. Erasures coincide with conflict or denial.

Pressure applied when the child produces a drawing suggests outward or inward direction of impulse: excessive pressure is associated with aggression or acting out, and the lightly drawn picture is more significant of depression.

Emotional indicators. Koppitz[10] lists various emotional indicators that she has found in human figure drawings:

Poor integration of the parts of a figure, such as parts not joined, connected by a single line, or barely touching, tends to indicate immaturity caused by developmental lag, neurological impairment, regression, or all of these.

Shading of any part of figure except the face is considered normal for the young child but is a manifestation of anxiety for the older child, with the degree of shading related to the amount of anxiety. Shading of the face is significant at any age, with the exception of shading to indicate skin color or such things as freckles or measles, which are not considered emotional indicators.

Figure slanting by 15 degrees or more suggests general instability and that the child lacks secure footing.

Tiny figure drawings of less than 2 inches high are usually drawn by children who are timid, withdrawn, and probably depressed.

Big figures of 9 inches or more in height become significant for the older child and appear to be associated with aggression, immaturity, and poor inner controls.

Teeth are a sign of aggressiveness, which is normal in children. They only become diagnostically meaningful if they appear with other emotional indicators on a drawing.

Arms that are long are associated with reaching toward others, in contrast to short arms, which indicate a tendency to withdraw. Omission of arms is associated with socially unaccepted behavior.

Clouds or any presentation of clouds, rain, snow, or flying birds are often drawn by anxious children who feel threatened by the adult world, especially by the parents.

Children's drawings

When children are asked to draw a person, they usually draw themselves. When children draw themselves and a playmate, it is interesting to note that they usually draw themselves taller than their playmates even though in reality they may be shorter. When children draw their family, the largest person is the most significant or most powerful family member. Children will draw themselves in position and height the way they see themselves within their family relationship.

Fig. 5-3 is a drawing by a 6-year-old girl who was instructed to draw a picture of her family. The family consisted of the mother, an older brother, and the little girl. The parents had been divorced for several years, and the children did not see their father. When asked to identify the figures in the drawing, the little girl stated that the large figure was her mother and the figure next to the mother was her teenaged brother. The almost transparent figure was identified as being a picture of herself.

Without any instruction in interpretive drawing, it is apparent that at the time of the drawing, the little girl had a poor self-image, felt insignificant to the family, and felt distant from her mother.

Fig. 5-4 was drawn by Marjorie, who was 5½ years old when she went to the hospital for a tonsillectomy. Her feelings about this event are illustrated more eloquently than words can describe. She has drawn herself so tiny and helpless in a bed that looks like a cage on tall stilts. The nurse is the size of a fullback, with a hypodermic needle in one hand, a bedpan in the other, and full attention directed on the little girl's suitcase. The drawing of a 5-year-old child often contains poor integration of parts; however, Marjorie's failure to connect one side of the suitcase handle looks almost deliberate rather than accidental. A suitcase with a broken handle is of little use and may be an unconscious expression of her fear that she might not be going home. Even if Marjorie is able to leave the bed without injury, she must get past the big, powerful nurse who stands between the little girl and her suitcase.[10]

Young children hear a great deal about a tonsillectomy from their peers; unfortunately, much of this information is inaccurate. Add child fantasy to the anxiety of being separated from parents and home, and hospitalization can result in a traumatic experience for the young child. One little boy hospitalized for a tonsillectomy was terrified of having surgery. Finally he shared what he thought was going to happen to him. "They're going to cut off my head, cut out my tonsils, and if I'm lucky, they'll sew my head back on right."

Health professionals can do a great deal in responding to the needs of youngsters, who often equate hospitals with separation, pain, and death. Many youngsters have never been in a hospital, and they conjure up their own image of what happens in hospitals. Teachers in Head Start programs, day-care centers, and nursery and elementary schools need special play materials in the classrooms so that youngsters can have the opportunity to play with stethoscopes, play syringes, surgical gloves, mirrors, dolls, cotton, white coats, nurses'

Fig. 5-3. A child's drawing of her family.

© 1979 A. Jann Davis.

caps, adhesive bandages, and surgical masks and gowns. In some schools regular hospital parties are planned in which youngsters are allowed to tour the pediatric department and talk to hospitalized children. They learn about the nurse-call button and play with controls that make the beds go up and down. The children are shown films about what to expect in a hospital. They are encouraged to dress up in surgical gowns, give injections to dolls, and look at old x-ray films to learn about bones. Coloring books and dot-to-dot pictures show pic-

tures of children coming into the hospital, going to surgery, playing in the playroom, and going home. The more children know what to expect, the less they are afraid when they actually face hospitalization.

Many hospitals have special parties for youngsters before their operations. Puppets and movies help explain rectal temperatures, anesthetics, and other procedures with which children are not usually familiar. The children are given information about what to expect in surgery and the recovery

Fig. 5-4. Marjorie.

From Koppitz, E.: *Psychological evaluation of children's human figure drawings,* New York, 1968, Grune & Stratton, Inc.

room, and they are shown where their parents will be during their surgery. They even learn that a syringe makes a good squirt gun.

During the party parents also receive information about what to expect from their child during and following hospitalization. Books such as those listed at the end of this chapter are available for parents to take home and read to their child before hospital admission. Nurses list items that children should and should not bring to the hospital, and parents are encouraged to spend as much time as possible with their child during the hospital stay. Some hospitals permit parents to be with their child through the induction of anesthesia because most small children are more afraid of leaving their parents than they are of surgery. Following hospitalization the child may display what is often regarded as regressive behavior, whereas in fact, the behavior may be more adaptive, serving to reestablish a continuity of safety and caretaking that has been interrupted.

Much is learned at the hospital party, including that there are a lot of nice people who work in hospitals and they help other people get better.

Once children are hospitalized, the importance of explaining things to them in terms that they can understand cannot be emphasized enough. The use of play equipment to demonstrate procedures is very helpful. If the child brings in a favorite toy, the toy can be used to show the child what to expect. Drawings are a valuable tool in externalizing a child's concerns and emotions, and some-

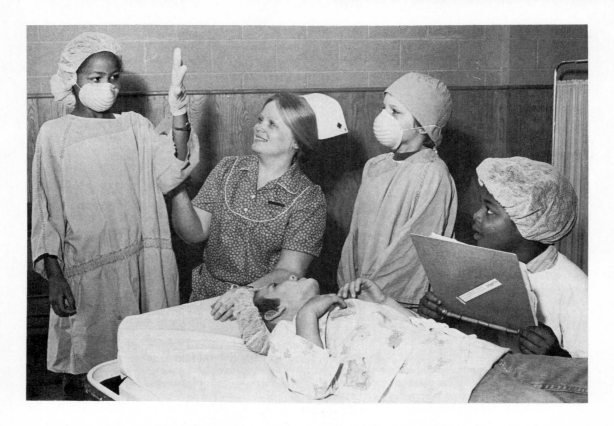

Learning about hospitals.

From Waterloo Courier, May 25, 1980, Waterloo, Iowa.

times children will draw what they cannot talk about. A 4-year-old girl was brought to the hospital with vaginal bleeding. She would not talk about what had happened. Later she drew a large figure with oversized male genitals. Through her drawings, she could reveal that she had been sexually abused. Once others knew the secret she had been warned to keep, she was free to talk about what had happened.

A little boy was hospitalized with leukemia. Although everyone was optimistic about his recovery, the little boy was considering what might happen to him. He drew a picture of a dog in heaven with a ghostlike God and another dog on the ground with what the child described as the devil (Fig. 5-5). When asked what he was thinking about, the little boy responded, ''I hope I get to go home.'' The child needed to talk about what would happen to him if the leukemia was not arrested.

An excellent hospital technique for monitoring the emotional state of children is to have them fill in a drawing of the outline of their body. To obtain the outline, children stretch out on a large sheet of paper, and friends draw around their body. For the bedfast child a nurse can draw a small outline of the child, taking directions from the child. The

Fig. 5-5. A child illustrates his fears.
© 1979 A. Jann Davis.

important thing is that the child is able to identify with the outline. Most children fill in their body outline by drawing favorite clothing, and often they draw themselves holding some special possession. There is more concern for children who draw themselves wearing hospital clothing because they are no longer thinking of themselves as part of the outside world.

Children may not be able to put words to their questions or feelings. The astute care giver must be alert for the child's concerns that may surface nonverbally. Drawings are not a replacement for but rather an adjunct to verbalization of thoughts and feelings. Art produces the intangible, changing feelings into form, allowing thoughts to be seen. For the child the act of drawing is an enjoyable means of expression. For the helping professional it becomes a valuable assessment tool.

• • •

Communication between parents and their child begins before birth, and this special parent-child attachment is enhanced following birth with early and extended contact. For some this early message creates a bond that helps to form a healthy family. For others it is necessary for professionals to facilitate the building of this relationship.

Children receive both verbal and nonverbal messages from their parents, and during the formative years these messages help contribute to a child's self-esteem. Feelings about the self are reflected in the way children interact with others and ultimately with their own children. Therefore the time and effort spent in nurturing a healthy family may be reflected in many generations yet to come.

As youngsters are exposed to stressful situations earlier in life, parental love, understanding, and support may make the difference between coping and succumbing. It is hoped that the family can be the place where individuals are "recharged" and where they can find acceptance and value. Too many families go and do in separate directions without much togetherness or time to communicate with each other. One youngster whose insight is better than his grammar concluded, "You don't get close to nobody by goin' and doin'. You get close by talkin'. If you can't talk together, goin' and doin' don't help. And if you can, you don't need to go."[12]

REFERENCES

1. Burns, R., and Kaufman, S.: Actions, styles and symbols in kinetic family drawings (K-F-D), New York, 1972, Brunner/Mazel, Inc.
2. Carter-Jessop, L.: Promoting maternal attachment through prenatal intervention, Maternal and Child Nursing **6:**106, March/April 1981.
3. Coddington, R.: Life event scale—children, 1981, R. Dean Coddington, M.D.
4. Coddington, R.: Life event scale—adolescents, 1981, R. Dean Coddington, M.D.
5. Condon, W., and Sander, L.: Neonate movement is synchronized with adult speech: interactional participation and language acquisition, Science **183:**99, January 1974.
6. Evans, S., Reinhart, J., and Succop, R.: Failure to thrive: a study of 45 children and their families, Journal of the American Academy of Child Psychiatry **11:**440, 1972.
7. Furman, E.: In Klaus, M., and Kennell, J.: Maternal-infant bonding, St. Louis, 1976, The C.V. Mosby Co, p. 52.
8. Kellogg, R.: Analyzing children's art, Palo Alto, California, 1969, Mayfield Publishing Co.
9. Kempe, H.: Child abuse: the pediatrician's role in child advocacy and preventive pediatrics, American Journal of Disabled Children **132:**255, 1978.
10. Koppitz, E.: Psychological evaluation of children's human figure drawings, New York, 1968, Grune & Stratton, pp. 75-77.
11. Lieberman, P.: Intonation, perception, and language, Cambridge, Massachusetts, 1967, The MIT Press.
12. McCarroll, A., Young people value one-to-one time with parents, Christian Science Monitor, p. 18, Nov. 11, 1980.
13. McLeavey, K.: Children's art as an assessment tool, Pediatric Nursing **5**(2):9, 1979.
14. Rubin, R.: Maternal touch, Nursing Outlook **11:**828, 1963.

BIBLIOGRAPHY

Harris, D.: Children's drawings as measures of intellectual maturity, New York, 1963, Harcourt Brace Jovanovich, Inc.
Holinger, P.: Violent deaths among the young: recent trends in suicide, homicide, and accidents, American Journal Psychiatry **136:**1114, 1979.
Klaus, M., and Kennell, J.: Parent-infant bonding, ed. 2, St. Louis, 1982, The C.V. Mosby Co.
O'Connor, S., and others: Reduced incidence of parenting inadequacy following rooming-in, Pediatrics **66**(2):176, 1980.
Piaget, J.: Play, dreams, and imitation in childhood, New York, 1962, W.W. Norton & Co., Inc. (Translated by C. Gattegno and F. Hodgson.)
Sumner, P., and Phillips, C.: Birthing rooms: concept and reality, St. Louis, 1981, The C.V. Mosby Co.

CHILDREN'S BOOKS
ABOUT HOSPITALIZATION

Rey, M., and Rey, H.: Curious George goes to the hospital, Boston, 1966, Houghton Mifflin Co.
Rockwell, H.: My doctor, New York, 1973, Macmillan Publishing Co., Inc.
Shay, A.: What happens when you go to the hospital, Chicago, 1969, The Reilly & Lee Co.
Sobol, H.: Jeff's hospital book, New York, 1975, Henry Z. Walck, Inc.
Stein, S.: A hospital story: an open family book for parents and children together, New York, 1974, Walker & Co.
Tamburine, J.: I think I will go to the hospital, Nashville, 1965, Abingdon Press.

CHILDREN'S BOOKS ABOUT FEELINGS

Berger, T.: I have feelings, New York, 1971, Human Sciences Press, Inc.
Carlson, N.: Harriet's recital, Minneapolis, Minnesota, 1982, Carolrhoda Books, Inc.
Oram, H.: Angry Arthur, New York, 1982, Harcourt Brace Jovanovich, Inc.
Viorst, J.: Alexander and the terrible, horrible, no good, very bad day, New York, 1972, Atheneum Publishers.
Wells, R.: A lion for Lewis, New York, 1982, The Dial Press.
Wittels, H., and Griesman, J.: Things I hate! New York, 1973, Behavioral Publications, Inc.

6 · Growing old

"Old" is in the eye of the beholder.

An older woman went to a new dentist who had the same name as an old classmate's. When the woman saw the man's bald head, his paunch, and his stooped posture, she concluded that they could not have gone to school together. Out of curiosity, she decided to check anyway. "I think we were at Greene High School together," she said. The dentist looked at her for a few seconds and then responded, "Really, what class did you teach?" (Author unknown.)

Illustration by Tom Weinman.

"Age to me means nothing," quipped comedian George Burns on his eighty-fifth birthday. "I can't get old; I'm working. I was old when I was 21 and out of work. As long as you're working, you stay young."

When playwright Thornton Wilder turned 75 years old, his feelings about the occasion went something like, "Free! Now I can be as arbitrary, eccentric, as wayward as I like. It will all be put down to senility."

America is the land where early retirement is envisioned as being a part of the good life. The goal is to quit while one is still ahead—young enough and healthy enough to enjoy what time is left. Numerous benefits of early retirement are proclaimed by insurance companies, unions, and government agencies. If the tax, medical, recreational, and psychological benefits are not encouragement enough, advocates of early retirement argue, "Consider the young folks, Give them a chance."

Reality for many is not the good life. When the elderly are forced into retirement or cannot find work, they frequently find they are emotionally, financially, and intellectually unprepared. "My doctor tells me I'm in good shape. My mind is filled with ideas, but no one wants them. I don't want to fill in the time before I die with busy work. I want to work at a real job where I can make some money, but everyone says I'm too old."

Bernard[1] describes retirement as "an immediate, usually irrevocable, descent into second-class citizenship . . . . It is the first giant step to the cemetery. . . . In America, activities for old people are manufactured. People get degrees in how to occupy old people with busy work."

Not everyone who retires experiences a retirement syndrome or other such generalizations; however, there are those for whom retirement is pathogenic. Candidates are individuals who feel fine during the workweek but experience the 'blahs' and just generally feel lousy on weekends, holidays, or vacations. Headaches, depression, and gastrointestinal symptoms appear at the time of retirement, and these symptoms contribute to further inactivity rather than being considered symptoms of inactivity: "Looks like I quit working just in time. I could never go to work the way I feel. I don't have the energy to get out of bed. All I want to do is sleep." It is also more socially acceptable to complain of physical ailments than it is to talk about loneliness, which may in actuality be the pathogen of the retirement syndrome. These problems may become everyday occurrences unless fulfilling substitutes for work and the social life that surrounded work can be found. Advocates for the older generation advise, "You worked hard to get what you have. Keep it and enjoy it. The younger generation are strong; let them struggle."

AGING

The industrial revolution in the eighteenth and nineteenth centuries brought up the question of what to do with workers too old to continue working in the factories and mills. These concerns prompted the Social Security Act in 1935. After World War II, medical advances had extended the life span to the point that it became necessary to learn more about the older population. An interdisciplinary science, gerontology, began to seriously study, conduct research, and train others to work with and provide services to older people. Today 11 percent of the people in the United States are age 65 years or older, and this number is predicted to dramatically increase in the future. A thorough understanding of the aging process is a practical necessity, and listening and responding to the needs of the older generation is a moral and ethical responsibility.

The normal process of aging is known as senescence, but many symptoms, such as senility, are often erroneously associated with aging. Aging is not a disease but a stage of development that involves three parts: biological, psychological, and sociological.

Biological aging

Although some researchers contend that aging begins at birth, most agree that it begins when physical maturity has been reached at approximately age 18 to 22 years. Scientists still do not know what causes aging; the only thing that is fully understood is that if death doesn't intervene, aging will occur.

There are numerous theories to explain biological aging *(right),* and many of these theories are tested experimentally in an effort to identify ways to promote health and reduce illness in the older adult. Perhaps in the future the mystery of aging will be solved, making it possible to alter the course of this predictable occurrence.

Some aspects of biological aging may be delayed by exercise, proper nutrition, and good mental health. People who exercise regularly outlive their sedentary peers; however, it is not known if those who exercise are healthy because they exercise or exercise because they are healthy. The results of body abuse, poor nutrition, and inadequate rest in younger years begin to appear with advancing age and contribute to the fact that the majority of the elderly population experience chronic health problems. Researchers have found that people with chronic anxiety, depression, and emotional maladjustment are more inclined to experience early aging, whereas the ability to cope with stress significantly retards midlife decline in physical health.

During the biological process of aging cells reduce, tissues stiffen, and chemical reactions within the body slow down. As the skin loses tissue elasticity, years of smiling and frowning are etched on

---

BIOLOGICAL THEORIES OF AGING

L. Hayflick
Programmed aging theory: organism dies after a specific number of cell divisions have occurred

D. Harman
Free radical theory: end products attach themselves to other cells, causing structure damage or cell disruption.

B. Strehler
Immunologic theory: an autoaggressive phenomenon occurs in the cells of the immune system.

D. Hershey
Cross-link theory: chemical reactions create abnormal bonds between molecular structures that are normally separate.

L. Orgel
Somatic mutation and error theory: faulty syntheses of proteins lead to ''error catastrophe'' and death of the cell.

H. Selye
Stress-adaptation theory: lifelong stress produces cumulative, irreversible wear and tear on the body.

---

the face. A man's skin ages about 10 years slower than a woman's, but while men may display younger looking skin, they also have a greater tendency than women to become bald. As men grow older, they find hair growing in places where it once did not, and in places where it used to grow, it does not. Neither sex is immune to extra cartilage accumulation that makes noses longer and ears bigger.

Many elderly people talk about being cold, and this is caused by reduction of the fatty tissue layer under the skin. The loss of the natural insulation from this subcutaneous fat contributes to a decline in the body's ability to adjust to temperature change.

Slowly the human body shrinks in height as the muscles weaken and spinal disks deteriorate. Unless caloric intake decreases, the body expands in width, particularly around the middle region.

Muscle mass decreases with age as muscle cells stop reproducing and die. Connective tissue slowly replaces muscle fiber, which becomes frayed and filled with deposits of waste material. The remaining muscles grow weaker and stiffer.

Inside the body the circulatory and respiratory system lose elasticity, causing an uneven flow of blood to various organs and a decrease in oxygen capacity. Endocrine functions are altered but do not lead to sexual inactivity. Most people have both the capability and the desire for sexual activity throughout their life.

Psychological aging

Psychological age refers to "adaptive capacities," involving intelligence, learning, problem-solving abilities, memory, motivation, and emotion. The relationship between age and intelligence is relatively insignificant, and what differences do occur involve memory and speed of response rather than overall intelligence. It is difficult to separate memory and learning, and standard intelligence tests are basically memory tests. Another problem with assessing intellect in old age is that the results are compared with young adults who are in the habit of being tested. Many older people are not used to being tested, which may produce anxiety that lowers the test scores.

The old adage "use it or you'll lose it" is true for memory retention, with studies proving that people who exercise their memories maintain past and recent memory well into old age.

Clinicians have discovered that some people demonstrate a marked and sudden decline in cognitive function before death. This decline in function, called "terminal drop," is likely to be the result of physiological deterioration, which makes it more difficult for the person to cope with environmental demands.

Social aging

The third process of aging is the person's performance or behavior in relationship to the standards established by the society of which the person is a member. Prejudice accounts for a large percent of the aging process in Americans, with society in general considering its senior citizens unemployable, unintelligent, and asexual. This creates pressure on the elderly to become what younger people think they are. Some of the negative stereotypes are often supported by the elderly who watch for symptoms of senility in others as a form of self-protection and as evidence of their own soundness of mind. If the victims are identified enough times as senile, they become so.

An interesting phenomenon occurs in later years, with a kind of sex-role reversal. Older men tend to become more passive, nurturant, dependent, and sentimental, whereas older women tend to exhibit more aggressive, instrumental, and independent behavior. The younger sector may observe that Granddad is becoming an old softie, while Grandma has become a women's libber. The reason behind these changes is not known, although it is theorized that when the woman's nurturing role is over and the man's occupation is no longer priority, repressed feelings are able to surface.

A 1980 study based on a survey of older Americans described one fifth of the population aged 60 years and older as unable to cope with everyday life, with predominant factors affecting coping abilities being finances and health. Six people in 10 in the study said they were under a lot of economic stress. The research divided the elderly into three groups: enjoyers, survivors, and casualties. The enjoyers represented 27 percent of the group and described themselves as being able to cope with the difficulties that come with aging. They were found to be healthy, had an income of at least 8,000 dollars a year and a minimum of 26,000 dollars in assets, and had a spouse who was also healthy. The survivors, 53 percent, could cope but were not able to plan on good health for themselves or their spouses. Half of this group reported an annual income of under 8,000 dollars. The 20 percent listed as casualties had fair or poor health, with 70 percent of them having an income of less than 8,000 dollars a year. Although the casualities are only a minority, that minority represents approximately 6 million people.[7]

The government report "Money, Income and Poverty Status of Families and Persons in the U.S.: 1979" reveals that 3.6 million persons—one in seven—age 65 years and older were considered poor, with an annual income falling below 3,472 dollars for a single person and 4,364 dollars for two persons. Although many elderly people have financial difficulties, few are willing to apply for food stamps, disability money, or other government funds. For many, asking for assistance is a last resort for survival because outside help is considered a handout. Elderly people have strong feelings of self-sufficiency, and they need encouragement before they will take advantage of the social services available to them. One man qualified for food stamps long before he was able to accept them. When he was hospitalized with pneumonia, it became evident that his nutrition was inadequate. When it was suggested that he receive help from community or government programs, he was adamantly against what he called "welfare." A social worker was able to point out to him that the funding for food stamps and other community and government programs came from taxes that he himself had paid for many years. It was only after he understood that he would be getting back part of what he had paid earlier in life that he was able to accept the social worker's help.

Chronological aging

In certain small communities existing in such places as Mexico, Ecuador, and the Soviet Union virtually everyone lives beyond 100 years of age. These people expect to live long, useful lives. "May you live to be 300" is a toast in the Ecu-adorian community, whereas in the United States such a toast might be met with, "What for?" Members of these communities are involved in farming, and their work is mostly physical. Without the "benefit" of television or radio, exertion is part of recreation. These people maintain a sense of control over their lives, and it is believed that this sense of control and regular physical exercise helps contribute to their health and longevity.

Chronological age is the poorest predictor of behavior in older people. One can predict what a child will be expected to do at an approximate age, but such predictions are not reliable with older people. Some feel and act old at a young age, whereas others feel and act young at an old age. When groups of elderly people are asked if they feel physically younger or older than their chronological age, most respond that they feel physically younger than their years, and usually the older the group, the greater the number of years they feel younger.

Expectations surrounding age-appropriate behaviors are changing in the United States. Rather than fitting into the stereotype of old age, many older citizens are seeking exceptions to the rule that at a fixed age they become different, impaired, or "nonpeople."

Mandatory retirement has been moved to age 70 years with speculation that it will be abolished nationwide within the next 5 years. Some advocate that whenever possible, the elderly should not retire. If and when other interests become more important than working, then part-time work is recommended. Going from full-time work into retirement produces too many changes all at once and is about as traumatic as being dismissed from a job.

The image of the grandparents as babysitters is no longer realized, with about half of all grandparents living a great distance from their grandchildren. Many people are starting new careers or going back to college at a time once considered retirement age.

Older people are banding together and gaining organized political clout. Organizations such as the

Maggie Kuhn and other Gray Panthers picketing the National Chamber of Commerce in Washington, D.C.

Photograph by Julie A. Jensen.

Gray Panthers are creating powerful political groups for change. This organization started with a group of professional people about to retire but determined not to be "put on the shelf." Joined by people of all ages, these elderly people set out to make reforms in Social Security, housing, health care delivery, income maintenance, and peace and disarmament. In about 12 years the Gray Panthers have grown into an organization of over 50,000 people, and their voices are being heard.

Society is beginning to realize that older people are physically, mentally, socially, and sexually active much longer than was thought. Senescence does bring about change, but decline evidenced in some areas can be balanced by growth and improvement in others. Gerontology researchers work to identify varying aspects of successful aging. Researchers measured the self-image of elderly people by asking a group of senior citizens to compare themselves with the average person their age. Of this group, 83 percent showed a positive self-image by rating themselves as better than average.[7] Ultimately the interpretation of successful aging is unique to each person, and the challenge in life is to die young as late in life as possible.

SENSORY CHANGES

As a person grows older, certain sensory losses take place that require a maximizing of sensory strengths. The normal changes in the aging nervous system require a longer length of time for the impulse to reach the brain, a stronger impulse to produce a response, and increased time to integrate sensory and motor function before a reaction can occur. Rather than accepting sensory losses at any age, care givers must identify the underlying pathological causes and a determination must be made concerning the possibility of prevention or treatment. The sensory losses that will be discussed in this section are listed in the column at right.

Hearing

Verbal communication is such an important element in human interaction that hearing loss can

---

SENSORY CHANGES

Hearing
Of people 65 years and older, 26% have hearing trouble.*

Vision
Of people 65 years and older, 93% use corrective lenses.*

Smell
Up to 30% of people 80 years and older have difficulty identifying common substances by smell.†

Taste
By the time a person is 70 years old, one half to two thirds of the taste buds no longer function.†

Touch
After a person is 60 years old, the threshold for tactile perception rises.†

*Unpublished data from National Center for Health Statistics: National health interview survey, 1977. Data from noninstitutionalized population.
†Generalizations from numerous studies.

---

cause more social isolation than does blindness. Hearing loss is potentially the most problematical of the perceptual impairments, contributing to suspiciousness, paranoia, and a reduction in reality testing. The elderly person who is deaf may be mistakenly labeled as senile and excluded from social activities. A resulting lack of contact with others may contribute to a loss in reality orientation.

The loss of hearing is the result of a breakdown of cells in the cochlea, an organ located in the inner ear that transforms vibrations from the outer ear into nerve impulses. At age 30 years an individual can hear high sounds measured at 15,000 hertz, such as those produced by a cricket chirp. By age 60 years individuals cannot hear sounds above

10,000 hertz, and by age 70 years individuals cannot hear sounds above 6,000 hertz. Fortunately, most conversation is below 4,000 hertz, but many older people still have problems understanding people who have high-pitched voices. Whereas the National Center for Health Statistics estimates that 26 percent of the noninstitutionalized population have hearing deficits, it is estimated that 54 percent of institutionalized elderly have hearing loss.

The elderly person experiences a delay in receiving and sending nerve impulses associated with hearing, in addition to requiring a stronger impulse before sound is perceived. Therefore it is necessary that others speak slower and in lower tones and allow adequate time for response. Although this sounds reasonable and simple in theory, a change in communication pattern takes conscious effort that removes some of the spontaneity from the conversation. It is similar to making a long distance telephone call to someone overseas and experiencing a few seconds delay before the other person's words are relayed. One person is likely to repeat a question at the same time the other person is answering, and confusion is created.

This same frustration is experienced by the elderly person for whom hearing becomes a conscious effort and for those whose messages are not heard. There are times when it is necessary to supplement verbal messages by writing down part of what is said. Sometimes just jotting down a few words from the sentence is enough for the older person to make some sense out of the conversation.

Older people may appear more deaf than they really are. Listening requires concentration that is fatiguing for people who are hard-of-hearing, and rather than wasting limited energy on something of little interest, they choose instead to ignore what they consider unimportant.

Being able to read lips and observe nonverbal cues helps the person with a hearing impairment understand what is being said. Most people augment verbal conversation with nonverbal messages but frequently are unaware of the importance of these messages until they cannot be seen. This is one of the reasons why those who wear glasses understand verbal messages better when they are wearing their glasses than when they are not. The request, ''I need to get my glasses, I can't understand what you are saying,'' points out the relationship between seeing and hearing.

An individual is also able to hear better if he or she is not overly tired or nervous and is not distracted by irrelevant noise. Although people are encouraged to speak slowly and articulate clearly, a normal sentence rhythm is also necessary. Rather than repeating verbatim what is not understood, one may restate in a different way to make comprehension possible. Another suggestion for relating to those with impaired hearing is to direct conversation toward the person's better ear since many people have more acute hearing in one ear.

Too often hearing loss is compensated with shouting, which serves only to frustrate the talker as well as the listener. Tension causes the voice to raise, making it increasingly difficult for the hard-of-hearing person to understand.

A certain amount of knowledge about hearing aids is mandatory for those who work with elderly people in any setting. Common areas for hearing aid problems include a detached or run-down battery, plugged ear mold, receiver turned off or on the wrong setting, and frayed or twisted wires between the earpiece and the hearing aid. There are numerous types of hearing aids that range from the larger body hearing aid to those small enough to fit into the ear, behind the ear, or within the frames of eyeglasses. The improvement in appearance of hearing aids helps to remove some of the stigma of wearing such a device.

Unfortunately, it may be decided that including the hard-of-hearing person in the conversation is too much effort. The individual who is unable to hear or understand may suspect that he or she is the topic of conversation. For people with normal hearing this is not understood until they are amidst others speaking a foreign language. If the language is not understood, people tend to wonder, ''Are they talking about me?''

Helping others hear and understand the sounds of the world keeps them in touch with human existence. Any effort necessary to preserve human contact is reflected in the satisfaction people receive from being able to hear and share life's experiences.

Vision

Of all the medical problems that people experience, the loss of vision is one of the greatest fears. The lens of the eye hardens and becomes less elastic throughout life, making focusing more difficult. The older person's eyes take more time to adjust to light changes, depth perception begins to get worse, and peripheral vision diminishes. As the lens becomes yellower and less elastic, shorter wavelengths of light are filtered out, making it harder to distinguish between blues and greens. With age the cornea becomes less translucent, requiring more external light and more color contrasts for visual perceptions. "Floaters" or black spots are worrisome and distracting and may be an early symptom of a detached retina. Changes in the interior and exterior of the eye produce altered vision that can cause decreasing mobility, poor orientation, and frightening visual impressions that might be interpreted as hallucinations. The possibility of glaucoma and cataracts also causes concern. Most older people experience a loss in visual acuity that requires corrective lenses, and it is estimated that 25 percent of the elderly in extended care facilities are legally blind.

Corrective lenses, material in large print, and "talking books" are available to compensate for visual losses. With encouragement people are able to compensate for failing vision by maximizing other senses. Television may still be enjoyed even though the picture cannot be clearly seen. One older lady commented, "I may not be able to see exactly what's going on, but I've got a pretty good imagination. It's not much different from listening to the radio." Room arrangements should not be changed without explanation, and areas such as door frames, steps close to the floor, and baseboards are easier for the older person to identify when they are painted a more vivid color than the surrounding areas.

Older people value their independence and resent being treated like an object just because they have failing eyesight. Many elderly individuals who are blind are still able to live independently in surroundings that they are familiar with. When the older adult moves about in unfamiliar areas, being able to take hold of another's arm provides security and guidance. The presence of stairs, curbs, and other obstacles should be announced far enough in advance so that abrupt changes do not prompt disorientation.

Vision and speech are so closely related that people have a tendency to raise their voices when talking to someone who has obvious visual impairment. Those entering the room of a blind person should announce their presence and make their positions and their intentions known. Likewise when individuals leave the room, this information should also be given. When people who are unable to see are taken into new surroundings, they are better able to develop a mental image of the area if it is described in detail. Being able to touch items of importance also helps in orientation. When the person is to be seated, it is helpful to place his or her hand on the back of the chair and describe the relationship of the chair to other objects in the immediate area. At meal times the location of foods can be identified in relation to clock positions. Being blind is not synomous with dependency. By training the other senses to compensate for the loss of vision, people are still able to locate and appreciate their places in life.

Bedfast clients may experience visual deprivation even though their vision is not impaired. The view of surroundings from a bed is distorted and limited, and the individual may experience visual deprivation unless others make certain that visual stimuli is provided. The bed can be moved so the client can benefit from the view of the hall or a window, or the entire bed can be moved out of the room into an area of more activity.

Some elderly individuals experience visual overload. They need more time to respond to new experiences and people and may perceive normal activity as rushing or running. Fast movements create alarm, frustration, and feelings of impending danger. It is necessary for care givers to slow down and respond to the needs of the individual client, allowing the person the time necessary to verbalize thoughts.

In a nursing home many people are in and out of a client's room during the course of the day. The following is an older client's comment.

■ When you can't see so well, they all look alike. Makes me feel like a dummy when someone comes in and starts talking to me like I should know them. Who knows, maybe I do know them, but it would sure help if I could see them better. I hate the guessing games, 'You remember me, don't you?' Whatever I answer will make me look like a fool, so I don't say anything and then I feel like a fool. I sure appreciate it when someone tells me their name and connects the name with where I knew the person. Like today, a lady stopped by that I hadn't visited with for months. She came in and told me her name and then added, 'We used to go to church together.' That was nice. _____

The sense of sight is a complex one that is often taken for granted. When this complex sense is impaired, perceptions of the world must be drawn from the other senses. People experience sensory deprivation when isolated from others, and so great is their need for visual stimuli that they may hallucinate the world that they need.

Smell

Odors play a poignant and powerful role in life. From the smell of baked bread from the oven to the freshness of clothes off the line, memories are locked into fragrance. Human sexual odors have been identified in the laboratory, and during research people respond to these musky odors on a subconscious level even when they consciously are not aware of their presence.

Theoretically, the olfactory impulses travel a shorter, more direct route to the cerebral hemispheres than do visual and auditory messages and therefore leave a more lasting impression than the other senses. Olfactory nerves tire easily, and awareness of odors is also hampered by smoking or by simply becoming accustomed to a certain smell. As people become older, they have a lowered capacity for enjoying scents and fragrances and they learn to rely more on texture, temperature, and visual cues.

Olfactory senses decline with age and approximately 30 percent of those aged 80 years and older have difficulty identifying common substances by smell. Clearly there are many causes for anosmia that have nothing to do with the aging process; however, nerve defects, polyps, and a long history of smoking are likely to be factors in anosmia in the elderly. This decreased sensitivity to odors may be a danger for the older person who may be unable to smell smoke or a gas leak. Sometimes elderly people believe that they can rely on their sense of smell to warn them of smoke in the house, and this false security may lead to death.

The olfactory senses can be stimulated by having people practice identifying substances by smell. Items with distinct olfactory characteristics are baby powder, chocolate, coconut, crayons, mothballs, bar soap, bubble gum, coffee, and caramel.

The sense of smell is often dismissed as one of the less important senses. It is more complex than originally believed, and it provides more pleasures than people are aware of until these perceptions are gone. An older man sat in his kitchen in front of a fresh pot of coffee. "I used to awaken in the morning to the wonderful aroma of coffee. For awhile I thought my coffee was old and that was why I couldn't smell it. Then I realized it wasn't the coffee. It was me."

Taste

Taste is usually considered to be subordinate to the sense of smell because two thirds of taste sensations are dependent on smell. The infant has taste buds throughout the mouth, and by adulthood, there are approximately 245 taste buds located chiefly on the back third of the tongue. By the time a person is 70, there may be as few as 80 taste buds left. With the reduction of taste buds there is taste preference change from sweet toward tart, and because of reduced taste perception, elderly persons tend to use more seasoning and spices.

Taste is stronger when a larger area of taste buds are stimulated, so a mouthful offers more sensation than a nibble. Also associated with taste is the texture of the food, such as crunchy, or smooth, and this is linked with past information that enters into the sense of taste. Refrigerated items will have more flavor if they are allowed to come to room temperature before eating. In contrast, the nasty taste of some medicine can be masked by preceding the medication with ice or ice water, reducing the effectiveness of the taste buds.

Molecules of food must dissolve in saliva before they can enter the taste pore and stimulate the sensory cell's nerve fiber. An elderly person's mouth gets drier as the mucous membranes secrete less, and this loss of moisture affects taste.

Taste can be stimulated by having a group of elderly people put pieces of candy with the same flavor into their mouths and see who can identify the flavor first. Wine and cheese tasting parties are not only fun but also stimulate both taste and smell that fade as one ages. Care must be taken that reformed alcoholics or dependent elderly are not involved at these parties, as alcohol is a hidden problem among the elderly.

Many elderly people suffer impairment of taste or smell. For these individuals, the texture of food may add enjoyment even though the flavor is not as acute. The loss of simple pleasures associated with eating may contribute to weight loss as the person's appetite for food diminishes and their joy in eating changes to an effort.

Touch

Minnie Remembers*

God!
My hands are old.
I've never said that out loud before,
   but they are.

*By Donna Swanson, from *Mind Song*, published by Upper Room, 1908 Grand Ave., Nashville, TN. Copyright 1978. Used by permission. All rights reserved.

I was so proud of them once,
   they were soft
   like the velvet smoothness of a firm ripe peach.
Now the softness is like worn out sheets or
   withered leaves.
When did these slender, graceful hands
   become gnarled and shrunken?
When, God?
They lie here in my lap;
   naked reminders of the rest of this old body
   that has served me too well.

How long has it been since someone touched me?
   Twenty years?
Twenty years I've been a widow.
   Respected.
   Smiled at—
   but never touched.
Never held close to another body.
Never held so close and warm that loneliness
   was blotted out.
I remember how my mother used to hold me, God.
When I was hurt in spirit or flesh
   she would gather me close,
   stroke my silky hair and caress
   my back with her warm hands.
Oh, God, I'm so lonely.

I remember the first boy who ever kissed me.
We were both so new at that.
   The taste of young lips and popcorn,
   the feelings deep inside of mysteries to come.
I remember Hank and the babies.
How can I remember them but together?
Out of the fumbling, awkward attempts of new lovers
   came the babies.
And, as they grew, so did our love.
And, God, Hank didn't seem to care if my body
   thickened and faded a little.
He still loved it,
   and touched it.
And we didn't mind if we were no longer "beautiful."
And the children hugged me a lot.

Oh, God, I'm lonely.

Why didn't we raise the kids to be silly and
   affectionate, as well as dignified and proper?
You see, they do their duty.
   They drive up in their fine cars.
   They come to my room to pay their respects.
   They chatter brightly and reminisce
   But—they don't touch me.

They call me "Mom" or "Mother" or "Grandma"
   never Minnie.
My mother called me Minnie
   and my friends.
Hank called me Minnie, too.
But they're gone.
   And so is Minnie.
Only Grandma is here.

And, God, she's lonely.

Touch is the greatest sense in the human body because it is a means of communication established early in life through which most human feelings can be conveyed. Children use tactile communication and stimulation to learn about their world of people and things. By the time the child is in school, touch is replaced with verbal communication. Adults communicate verbally, except under certain circumscribed conditions when tactile communication is accepted. Throughout the rest of life the appropriate use of touch is determined by culture. Touching in the United States is reserved for close friends and significant others. Although the need to be held is quite different from the need for sexual fulfillment, many adults equate touch with sexual contact. As a result "skin hunger" is experienced by children, adolescents, and adults in the American culture.

Affection toward elderly persons is generally not demonstrated by hugging, stroking, and kissing; therefore there is less opportunity for older people to be touched. People who in the past provided touch input for the elderly person are lost through death, and as a result the very old person may be virtually untouched.

The need for touch does not diminish as the person grows older and usually increases during times of stress and illness. As the environment becomes more stressful, human contact becomes more important.

Elderly, institutionalized persons relinquish some of their responsibilities and decision making to someone else. This promotes regression and a kind of therapeutic childishness, creating an intense need for human contact that is not met.

Whether touch is interpreted positively or negatively depends on the meaning intended by the initiator and the meaning inferred by the recipient. Touch is usually experienced as positive if it is appropriate to the situation, does not impose more intimacy than the recipient desires, or does not communicate a negative message. Usually touch to the hand or shoulder by another person of the same or opposite sex is interpreted as nonsexual in nature. A short pat or hand grasp is better tolerated than having someone hold a hand for a longer time. Having an arm placed around the shoulders may be considered condescending unless the contact is between close friends or relatives or at a time when the individual is seeking emotional support.

Certain people are simply "nontouchers." They comment, "I dislike being touched." "See no reason for it." "Touching is unnecessary." An individual who in normal circumstances might enjoy touch may experience sensory overload from pain or rough handling or memories of such and move away from physical contact with others. Some people experience anxiety about two members of the same sex touching, or they may feel aversion to being touched by higher status people who do not want to be touched in return. Individuals signal their desire for distance by pulling away when others get too close, or they may tighten muscles and become tense when they are touched. Touching is a learned behavior that can physically and psychologically benefit those who are comfortable touching and being touched. Touch is not therapeutic when it is forced.

Although many elderly people experience a decline in most sensory modalities, touch is one sensory pathway that does not depreciate dramatically. Until an individual is 60 to 65 years of age, touch sensitivity remains the same as for the young adult, and thereafter the threshold for tactile perception rises somewhat. The need for touch seems to increase in older age, perhaps to compensate for other sensory losses. When institutionalized elderly are encouraged to use affective touch with each other, spontaneous behavior such as laughing, clapping, and smiling also increases. Clients also show in-

The need for touch does not grow old.
Photograph by A. Jann Davis.

creased interest in their surroundings and their interactions. Each nursing interaction with an older individual can be planned to include touch. The following is both an exchange of touch and a nursing assessment.

■ The nurse knocks before walking into Mrs. Adam's room. She waits a few seconds and then greets the client, "Hello, Mrs. Adams." As she walks toward the woman, she extends her hand and waits until the client has had the time to reach toward and grasp her hand. Extending her hand first enables the care giver to determine whether Mrs. Adams is able to reach for and make contact with the care giver. It also helps her assess consciousness, consistency of behavior, control of movement, skin condition, and temperature while at the same time providing much-needed touch for the client. The nurse gives the lady's hand a warm squeeze, which is reciprocated, enabling the care giver to evaluate sensory-motor function and degree of hand grasp. In just a few seconds baseline information has been gained, the care giver has communicated personal and warm interest in Mrs. Adams, and the client has been touched. _____

When touching or holding is not received when it is desired, various substitutes may be used. Rocking in a chair can provide a form of self-stimulus. By actively pushing against the chair, the chair then pushes against the person, accomplishing the goal of not feeling completely alone. Rocking or swaying is a form of self-caressing or self-comforting that is often observed in grief and mourning.

The client who holds and strokes an inanimate object is nonverbally asking to be touched. A lonely person may reach for a pillow, hug it close, and momentarily satisfy a need to hold onto someone. Snuggling in bed and pulling the covers up tight or tucking them against the body simulates the feeling of being embraced, and even on a hot night a light cover may be necessary to provide a sense of well-being. Many people go to sleep holding a handkerchief, which may serve as a substitute for the security blanket from the past.

Older people use many strategies to be touched. Some efforts to reach out to touch another human are misunderstood as sexual approaches. There are times when the motive is sexual, but more often it is the desire for skin contact with another human. Clients may covertly ask for physical contact,

"Would you check my back?" or, "Could you help me with my dress?" One older lady asked that a staff member wind her watch each day. "I'm sure she can wind it herself," the staff member commented, "but this gives her an extra visit and it also provides her with touch."

When all else fails, people hug, embrace, clasp, and touch their own body in a great variety of ways to help soothe away their fears. Bodily contact provides feelings of being loved, protected, and comforted, which are a necessary part of life.

The need for touch begins at birth and does not stop until death. Touch indicates caring, protection, and comfort. It decreases isolation, strengthens interactions, and validates one's existence. Because it is the only shared sense, it is invested with the most emotion. For the care giver touch is one of the most valuable of the helping tools and one of the most effective ways of communicating caring and concern.

A personal understanding of the sensory losses that accompany aging will help the care giver gain insight into the problems faced by the elderly. To develop insight into sensory losses, aging simulation can be created by wearing coated lenses, ear plugs, gloves, and inserting cotton wadding into the anterior nasal passages. With loss of all the senses the person may be overwhelmed by lack of sensory stimulation. With the loss of one or two of the senses, the body adapts and the other senses compensate so that the person can still function. It is through the senses that the world is perceived, and by using this information, people are able to exist in their environment.

Sensory stimulation through "pet therapy"

Few people can resist a kitten or a cute little puppy. Add a kitten to the care plan of an elderly person and something magical happens. Lethargic clients become alert, depressed clients liven up. Even Mr. Nelson in room 207, who has not responded to anyone in weeks, responds to the gentle purr of a kitten or the warm lick of a puppy.

The Colorado Humane Society in Denver, Colorado, is an animal pound and a community service. Not only do they investigate injustice to animals and provide shelter for homeless animals but they also guarantee each and every animal life, love, medical care, rehabilitation if necessary, and placement in a new home. The Colorado Humane Society receives no government support but is funded through donations from caring citizens. Part of their community service is to visit schools and teach the youth the rights of animals and the responsibility of pet ownership. Twice a month the Pet-Mobile arrives at area nursing homes, where dogs, cats, and an assortment of other animals fill the normally quiet room with excitement and affection as they run from person to person. The excited clients reach for a pet to love and spend the next hour touching and snuggling their chosen animals. It is all within the rules of the Health Department, and it has the blessing of the nursing homes.

The Humane Society provides animals of all types and sizes that are carefully selected for their gentle nature. An animal has a sort of perpetual infantile innocent dependence that stimulates a natural protective tendency of the elderly, making it easier for some to relate to a friendly, furry animal than to a professional. There is an animal to match the personality of each client. The terriers are known for their aggressive friendliness, good humor, and playfulness, and have a strong appeal to love-hungry alienated individuals. Other pets are the friendly shy type that are appealing to the more withdrawn person.

A Saint Bernard, a goat, and a rooster are some of the more unique members of the pet therapy group. Clients have difficulty concentrating on television, bingo, or their aches and pains when they notice a Saint Bernard is making eye contact with them in the distance.

Pets do soil, and because of germs they are kept out of the dining area. However, the benefits of pet therapy outweigh cleaning up a puddle or brushing off a little dog hair. There is a special rapport of unconditional acceptance between animals and the

Pet therapy.
Photograph by A. Jann Davis.

elderly. Both are in need of physical contact, and both are willing to respond to each other's need for love.

Sensory stimulation is at its peak with a soft kitten against the cheek. The animals serve as a catalyst to socializing, with clients talking to each other about their pets, which in turn creates adaptive and satisfying social interactions. A person who is able to relate positively to an animal in verbal, nonverbal, and tactile interactions is rewarded with tail wags, licks, and a warm nuzzle. More important, the animal offers love and tactile reassurance without criticism.

CONFUSION

■ The nurse finds Mrs. D. sitting naked on her bed, happily tearing the sheets into long strips. The nurse quietly sits down next to the bed, and slowly the expression on Mrs. D.'s face changes from delight to puzzlement. She looks from the nurse to the strips of sheeting and then to her naked body. Tears began to flow as she leaves the world of her memories and joins the world of reality.

The nurse gently helps Mrs. D. into a robe. The sheets are not important. The nurse cradles the sobbing woman in her arm. "I can't live in two worlds," Mrs. D. cries. "It's like waking from a dream and not knowing who I am. I know I can't live in the past, but the present hurts too much."

When the tears subside, the nurse asks Mrs. D. to share the memories she was living.

"It was almost Halloween time, and the kids decided they wanted to wear mummy costumes. So we took all the old sheets and tore them into strips. We had such fun wrapping the kids up like mummies. They even won first prize at the costume party! I remember being warm, so I took off my sweater . . . only I guess it wasn't a sweater." ___

A scene from a nursing home? An elderly client? Signs of senility? Mrs. D. was a 32-year-old woman in an acute care setting. She had experienced multiple major surgeries within a few weeks and at the time of the above interaction was being treated for acute peritonitis. It is not just the elderly who lose contact with reality. But sometimes it is the elderly who do not receive adequate help in finding their way back.

Confusion can be defined as inappropriate behavior at a certain place and time. It cannot be viewed as a disease but rather as a response secondary to an abnormal condition. A few of these conditions include infections, metabolic disorders, cardiovascular disorders, drugs, cerebral dysfunction, and sensory deprivation. Confusion can also be prompted by a strange environment or when the individual is overly stressed with physical or psychological problems, such as the death of a spouse or the loss of a home and life's sentimental belongings.

It is estimated that about half of the older clients in extended care facilities are there because of confusion or will develop confusion following their admission. There are many reversible causes of confusion in the elderly, and a thorough evaluation is necessary to determine if the confusion is a symptom of an underlying mental or physical pathology that can be treated. There are cases of organic brain syndrome that will not respond to treatment and will continue to deteriorate. However, the quickest way to ensure senility is to treat a reversible syndrome as chronic brain disease, which will undoubtedly contribute to its outcome.

Much confusion in the elderly is predictable and therefore preventable. Individuals 80 years old or older are most vulnerable, with men more prone to confusion than women. Living alone and lacking social support or contact with caring people are causative factors, as are relocation, confinement, and disruptions of sleep and patterns of daily living. Pain or discomfort, drugs, sensory deficits, loss of control over body functions, the use of restraints, and symptoms of amnesia are stressful precipitators.[9] Emotional trauma such as the loss of a spouse or the loss of home and belongings or physical trauma experienced during illness, injury, or treatment are also predictors of confusion. When

these conditions exist, care givers must make special effort to reduce the severity of these manifestations through symptomatic or supportive therapy. This can be accomplished by treating physical and emotional ailments; repeatedly orienting the person to time, place, and person; structuring the environment to maximize the person's strengths; and reducing changes to a minimum.

Reality orientation

As mental function declines, an awareness of time, place, and recognition—in that order—are the first things to be forgotten. As the mental impairment becomes worse, the person loses the ability to count and may ultimately forget his or her own name.

Reality orientation is a basic technique used in the rehabilitation of those having memory loss, confusion, and disorientation as to time-place-person. It is a 24-hour orientation process that is of more benefit to the confused elderly person if it is initiated when the first signs of confusion are noted. Information concerning time-place-person is communicated to the individual naturally and consistently in an informal, nonthreatening, noncritical way. Although it may seem boring, repetitious, and unnecessary to the alert person, it is information important to the one who is confused.

Care givers working with confused clients must have an expectant, patient attitude that conveys understanding, support, and reassurance. The rationale of reality orientation is that people behave the way they are expected to behave, and senility is not expected and therefore not accepted. If people are treated as though they are not responsible for themselves, they become more and more dependent. For example, one study pointed out that 85 percent of the incontinent clients were age 65 years or older and only 5 percent had a pathological basis for their incontinence. The clients took incontinence for granted, and nursing personnel accepted incontinence as a routine part of geriatric care. The study pointed out that the nurses may have unknowingly encouraged these individuals to become incontinent through their accepting behavior.[5]

Symptoms of senility in young adults can also be created by simply having others in the experimental group behave toward them as if they were "old." The "oldsters" are unaware of the instructions but respond to being treated with disdain by rambling, presenting nonrelevant material for discussion, and ultimately becoming inattentive. This experiment has been repeated many times by numerous researchers, always producing the same fact that people act the way they are treated.

Reality orientation encourages people to participate in ongoing life activities, to sustain their hobbies, and most important, to accept responsibility for their own behavior rather than having allowances made because of age.

Structured environment

Environments without planned activities other than daily chores promote symptoms of senility, and clients soon become introspective and speak only when spoken to. Intervention consists of involving the clients in mental exercise, forced concentration, and attempts at remembering without overwhelming them with structure. Environmental clues about person, place, and time should be located in each client's room, and each person's bed should be identified with his or her name. Clocks and calendars large enough to be seen by those with failing vision help older people maintain orientation to time and date. Personal items provide familiarity and should be allowed according to available space.

Some elderly clients may become agitated by an excess of stimulation, such as from a roommate who is active or requires multiple treatments. The constant coming and going of people and equipment overload these clients, who may be less confused in a private room or one with less activity.

Helping a confused, disoriented person find the way back to reality is a tremendous gift care givers can give. Reality orientation does not require additional time and has the potential of replacing agitation with cooperation. People who have given up on life can be helped to have an interest in living again.

Memory orientation

In any shopping mall parking lot there are people wandering among cars, trying to look intelligent and directed, who in all honesty are lost. They haven't the faintest idea of where they parked their car, except that it is somewhere in the parking lot. Some stop and try to remember. Because of the stimulus of people coming and going, cars honking, people staring, kids fighting, and spouses nagging, remembering their parking space becomes a real effort. It is easier to just go back into the mall, shop awhile longer until the cars thin out, and then resume the hunt.

Everyone has experienced this version of hide-and-go-seek at least once, and many people are familiar enough with the accompanying frustration that they attach a pom-pom to the car antenna to make location easier. It is easy to lose a car in a parking lot, especially when one does not pay attention to the large colored letters that identify parking sections. When young people cannot find their cars, they simply tell themselves, "I should have paid attention to the parking lot signs." But when this happens to older people, the silent thought of the person involved—as well as the onlookers—is "Senility!"

When a person is 75 years old, has cataracts and a hearing problem, and is surrounded by a great deal of muddling stimuli, it is not easy to remember where the newspaper is or where the eyeglasses were placed. The individual may wonder if it is worth the effort of remembering or if it would be easier to let someone else locate these items. Older people who practice relying on others become very good at dependency. Remembering becomes a chore because forgetting receives more practice. What could be an independent person, capable of relying on his or her own resources, learns instead to depend on others.

An elderly person is more apt to experience memory loss for recent events than happenings from the distant past, which are retold in perfect detail. It used to be that an elderly person's nostalgic review of the past was discouraged for fear that thinking about the past would make one less aware of or interested in the present. It has now been found

Senile or forgetful—a conclusion often based on age.
Illustration by Tom Weinman.

that reminiscence in the aged is healthy. Memories provide a source of security, helping people cope with the present and serving as an anchor to the past.

There are individuals who decide to live in the past and relive a time when they were vital, needed, and wanted. The past is a link to the present. Reality orientation combined with memories creates a type of memory orientation that bridges the past and the present.

Memory orientation is not a foreign process. In the parking lot situation the person had difficulty remembering where the car was located, but by recalling more distant memories, such as which

parking lot entrance was used and which shopping mall door was entered, the individual was able to bridge the gap to the present and remember where the car was parked. An older person who misplaces the newspaper and eyeglasses can use the same process to locate these items. Forced concentration, mental exercise, and attempts at remembering help elderly people use their mental capabilities to the fullest. Remembering requires patience, practice, and encouragement particularly for those who are used to having others do the remembering for them. In the following example entitled ''Mable and Sylvester'' memories of the past were used to help orient an elderly man to the present:

Memory orientation uses the past as a link to the present.
Photograph by Darrell A. Davis.

■ Sylvester, an 87-year-old man, had lived on a farm most of his life. After moving to town with his wife he continued to keep busy with a large garden and was competent and rational until suffering a series of strokes. Slowly the mists of his mind covered the present, and he began to slip into the past. He wife of 65 years was unable to call him back, and she could no longer care for her spouse. The sad day came when Sylvester was admitted to a nursing home.

Sylvester hardly noticed the change. Routinely he awakened at 5 A.M. and went out to take care of the animals. Sometimes he forgot to dress and would be found wandering around oblivious to the cold. Not wanting to restrain this gentle man, care givers tried reality orientation and made a special effort to keep an eye on Sylvester. Sylvester was alert and agile enough to know when he could slip out the door, and after several escapes restraints were considered. Instead an older nurses' aid, Mable, asked to be assigned to Sylvester. Many years after Sylvester's death, Mable told Sylvester's family how she had helped him find his way back to reality.

"Well," Mable began, "I'd come in early so I could be there when he got up. I could set my watch by him, and exactly at 5 A.M. he would be up ready to head out to the farm. I would greet him with, 'Ves, you're in the nursing home, but if you plan to go outside, get yourself dressed warm. It's cold out there.' ''

She laughed, ''I figured if he got past me, at least he wouldn't freeze. I'd wait until he headed for the door and then holler for him to have a cup of coffee with me. He was always ready for a cup of coffee, and we'd talk about the farm. I asked him so many questions, I knew those animals as well as he did. He talked about sheep, ducks, chickens, hogs, but the horses were his favorite. We'd talk for 15 to 20 minutes, and he'd get tired. I'd just say, 'Ves, you go take a nap. I'll take care of everything outside,' and he would. Once we got through the morning, he seemed to realize he was in the nursing home. Once in awhile he'd start out the door, and I'd ask, 'Ves, where're you going?' Usually it had something to do with taking the hogs to market. I'd tell him he was in the nursing home, 'and anyway, the market's closed.' ''

Mable continued, ''The nurses insisted that everyone use reality orientation with Sylvester, and I insisted that after the reality routine everyone had to ask Sylvester about the farm and the animals. This way he got the best of both worlds. We did this for a month or more. Then one morning he just talked about the horses, no mention of the other animals at all. I never asked him what happened to the animals, but I knew he was ready to give them up. So I learned about the horses, which one to watch out for—you know—which one would nip or kick, how much they ate, the price of the feed, everything. Sometimes I think I bored Sylvester with all my questions. He quit trying to go outside and instead gave me the instructions on how to take care of the horses. I guess I became his hired man.''

''Then for one whole week he slept in until after 6 o'clock. I knew he was ready to give up the horses, so at our morning coffee I asked, 'Ves, do you suppose we could sell the horses? They really are a lot of work.' ''

''Well,'' she said, ''He thought for a moment and responded, 'Might be a good idea. Don't think you could find a buyer though.'

''I persisted, 'How much would you want for them—in case I can find a buyer?' ''

''Sylvester thought for awhile and answered, 'I suppose $350 would be a fair price.' ''

''The next morning he came out of his room at 6 o'clock, and I told him, 'Ves, you can go back to bed if you want. I sold the horses.' ''

''I was scared,'' Mable admitted, ''but his face brightened, 'That's great! How much did you get?' ''

''I told him $375. Thank goodness he was tickled with the price and never did ask me what I did with the money!''

Mable continued using memory orientation to help Sylvester move from the past to the present. She helped him relive selling the farm and moving to town. Day by day, little by little, she allowed an old man his memories that slowly became the link to the present. Before he died Sylvester was oriented to person, place, and time by a sensitive lady who knew how to listen and respond to the needs of the elderly. (© 1980 A. Jann Davis.)

Families can participate in helping older people practice the skill of remembering and at the same time record their own history. This sharing of the past serves as a link between generations that makes history fun for everyone involved. Somewhere in each elderly person's possessions is likely to be a box of pictures and mementos that has been tucked away and forgotten. Some of the most memorable visits when families gather is going through that special box, looking through pictures, reading letters from years ago, and remembering when.

Cassette tapes make it possible to take a trip down memory lane and relive the days when radio was king. Sports, drama, comedy, and commercials have all been recorded from the original broadcasts at a time when the family gathered to listen to old-time radio. The older generation enjoys listening once again to radio personalities such as W.C. Fields, Jack Benny, Amos 'N' Andy, Edgar Bergen and Charlie McCarthy, Abbott and Costello, George Burns and Gracie Allen, Bing

Crosby, Eddie Cantor, Fibber McGee and Molly, Fred Allen, Lum and Abner, The Aldrich Family, The Marx Brothers, Ozzie and Harriet, Laurel and Hardy, Red Skelton, and Groucho Marx. The older generation may be encouraged to share what it was like when they used to gather around the radio. When these memories are brought to the present, the history and the anecdotes from another generation are learned. Diaries are going out of style and so will the sharing of memories unless people care enough to listen.

The greatest waste of time would be to go through life and have no one notice. Reminiscing is a way of making certain that life has had meaning and purpose and that indeed existence was noticed. Through memories the past becomes a bridge to the present, and this link is a necessary component of reality.

ALTERNATIVES TO INSTITUTIONAL CARE

The prevailing stereotype of the elderly as fragile, helpless, and senile is simply not true. According to 1979 figures from the U.S. Department of Health and Human Services, only 5 percent of people aged 65 years and older live in institutions, with the other 95 percent able to live alone or with family or friends. It is estimated that 80 percent of the elderly in the United States are active, mobile, and able to carry on normal activities. It would be inappropriate to refer to these elderly people as fragile, helpless, and senile. Another 10 percent are limited in what they are able to do, but only about 10 percent of the elderly are fragile enough to require assistance with activities of daily living.

The Shepherd's Center

Some of the 25 million people aged 65 and older are banding together to form a tight network, helping each other so that they can remain in their own homes. One such cooperative effort is The Shepherd's Center that exists in 37 cities across the country. It is not a building but rather a concept of linking older people together so that their needs

can be met and their lives can be sustained with meaning and dignity.

Sponsored by churches and synagogues, the program began in 1972 in Kansas City with five people helping seven people, and it has grown to become hundreds helping thousands. The Shepherd's Center does not use any government funding but depends totally on small individual fees and contributions. One full-time staff person oversees and coordinates the program, and volunteers keep the costs down. The unique feature of the centers is that they are operated and controlled by older people themselves. Some of the home services provided through The Shepherd's Center are also available in communities without such a center.

Meals on Wheels makes it possible for elderly people to have meals delivered to their homes. The meals are planned by a dietitian to meet special dietary needs, prepared at a restaurant or health center in the community, and provided at cost to elderly people unable to prepare their own food. The number of meals delivered to an individual each week varies in different communities, and sometimes the noon delivery includes a packaged meal that can be eaten for the evening meal.

In addition to delivering the meals, volunteers are able to check on the older person and report concerns or needs to the center. Sometimes this in itself is a life-saving measure. While meeting nutritional needs, volunteers provide social interaction that is very important to elderly people.

Shoppers Service assists older individuals who are able to cook for themselves but have a difficult time shopping because they do not drive, cannot take advantage of public transportation, or simply do not see well enough to purchase what they need. The shoppers either do the shopping for the person or take older persons on a weekly shopping trip. The enjoyment, companionship, and stimulation of a weekly outing is an important aspect of this service.

The Handyperson Service is one of the most called for, with retired carpenters, painters, electricians, and plumbers working for small fees, taking care of the minor home situations that become major when income is small and people are unable to do the repairs themselves. Requests for services are received by the center, which then makes the assignment to the appropriate handyperson. The program has the approval of trade union leaders as long as the handypersons do not do new work or major remodeling.

The Night Team is a team of volunteers who operate a 24-hour answering service, responding to emergencies involving older people. These volunteers have a listing of people who are prepared to respond immediately. Although this service is seldom used, it provides security and reassurance for elderly people.

The Care XX Program helps low-income elderly receive some of the services provided through provisions of Title 20 of the Social Security program. Those who qualify for these services are referred to the authorized public agency, and the center coordinator does a follow-up to see that their needs are met.

The Friendly Visitors are volunteers from community organizations who make regular visits to isolated or homebound elderly people.

Companion Aids are persons who provide company for older people in need of extra attention for as little as an hour or two or for as long as a day. The aids are not expected to do housework but prepare light meals and assist with activities of daily living. Often the aids are older women who enjoy looking after others while earning the hourly fee set by the center.

The Security and Protection Program deals with preventing crimes against the elderly. Trained aids aged 65 years and older work to resolve anxiety, establish prevention measures, and provide safety instructions for older people.

One of the purposes of The Shepherd's Center is to serve as an information and referral source, maximizing existing services rather than duplicating those that already exist. One example is Home Health Care under the direction of a health care agency within the community. Through this service nurses and home health aids provide physician-ordered health care services within the home. This home care service is covered under the Medicare program.

The center also acts as a liaison between older people and a multitude of other community services that are available to them without cost. A few of these include income tax assistance; legal aid providing information about legal rights, legal procedures, and referrals; employment services for those who prefer part-time paid employment to volunteer work; counseling on a short-term basis; home sharing and housing services for those who want to share housing for companionship and to save expenses. Without the benefit of the center many elderly people would not be aware that these community services are available to them.

In addition to coordinating home and community services, The Shepherd Centers also addresses the question "Why survive?" Older people are constantly having to adjust and reconstruct their lives, and life enrichment and reconstruction programs help those with drained physical, emotional, and spiritual resources to find new beginnings in their lives. Adventures in Learning is the largest of these programs, offering as many as 40 courses that provide over 1,000 elderly people with meaningful experiences rather than activities that simply fill time. These classes are taught by retired teachers or professors whose topics range from creative writing, Social Security, and Medicare to how to cope with the death of a spouse. Other classes include yoga, defensive driving, speed reading, how to stretch your dollars, how to cook for one, estate planning, health lectures, and exercise programs. One participant commented, "Here I feel alive. Where I live there are a bunch of old women who sit around and rock themselves to death. I figure I've a lot of good years left and I'm going to make the best of them."

The Shepherd's Center responds to the needs of elderly persons 24 hours a day, 7 days a week. Through these services many older people are able to live independently with dignity and security in their own homes and apartments within the community.

Minneapolis Age and Opportunity Center

Other communities rely on both private and public funding, as is the case of the Minneapolis Age and Opportunity Center in Minnesota. Founded and governed by senior citizens, the center provides an alternative system for persons not needing 24-hour care. Based on a medical-supportive concept including both medical intervention and social services, the Minneapolis Age and Opportunity Center in partnership with Abbott-Northwestern Hospital provides free health care to eligible older persons. The network of care includes a clinic in which older persons receive medical attention 6 days a week and are able to have prescriptions filled at cost. They have the benefit of legal services, home-delivered meals, homemaking services, handy-person/chore services, grief therapy, alcohol and drug dependency support groups, counseling, emergency food closet and crisis fund, personal home care, employment service, transportation program, plus still more. These supportive efforts have kept many of the elderly out of institutions. The program has been proven both cost effective as well as humanly effective.

Nursing homes without walls

New York State and its concept of nursing homes without walls has kept many potential nursing home clients out of institutions and in their own homes. Before Medicaid would reimburse the cost of the services, the cost had to be 75 percent or less of what the services would cost in an institution. The concept not only pleases the elderly but also saves more than 25 percent over institutional costs. Under a federal waiver, Medicaid pays for 10 services: respite care, moving assistance, social day-care, transportation to day-care, home maintenance, heavy chore services, medical-social services, nutrition counseling, and respiratory therapy. Those not eligible for Medicaid pay their own bills directly or through third-party coverage such as private insurance or Medicare.

The concept of nursing homes without walls is an alternative to nursing home care that usually results in increased dependence, loss of possessions, and isolation from friends and family. Not only has the concept of nursing homes without walls been able to curb the costs of nursing home care, it also provides meaningful and appropriate care for the elderly.

Mutual-support system

The elderly are also gathering together to form a mutual-support system. Communes and collective houses that in the past were considered "hip" or cheap are becoming more of a necessity for the elderly, who are finding that a collective life-style is protection against the stress of living alone. "We look after each other," commented one of the tenants in apartments for the elderly. "If a shade isn't up by 9 in the morning, someone is sure to be checking to see if the person's okay. If someone gets sick, we do everything possible to keep them out of the hospital or nursing home. Our home means everything to us. All our memories are there."

Too often helping professionals are not aware of community services available to the elderly. Many of the clients in nursing homes would not be there if they could receive supportive services in their own homes. One elderly lady commented, "I know that I'm going to die, but I don't want to die every day." Resources within the community make it possible for people to remain in their own homes as long as possible. It is the responsibility of the helping professional to be aware of these resources so that they can be of greater help to those who are no longer in a position to fend for themselves. It is also the responsibility of helping professionals to respond with advocacy and organization to help develop community resources to benefit elderly citizens.

PROTECTING THE ELDERLY

Although the greatest majority of elderly Americans are living independent, fulfilling, happy lives, there are some who do not. Congressional panels have heard reports from elderly people who have been robbed and beaten not only by strangers but by close family and friends. It is estimated that of the elderly living with and dependent on their children, from 500,000 to 2.5 million are being abused. The term abuse is used to describe physical, mental, emotional, and material harm. There are obvious signs of abuse: unexplained bruises, lacerations, malnutrition, dehydration, soiled clothing, and physical uncleanliness. The less obvious are isolation, neglect, and psychological abuse.

Abuse of the elderly

Four specific areas of abuse have been identified: physical abuse, psychological abuse, material abuse, and violation of rights. Physical abuse includes not only actual beating but withholding of personal care, medical care, or food. Psychological abuse includes verbal assaults and threats, provocation of fear, and physical or emotional isolation. Material abuse involves theft or misuse of money or property. Violation of basic rights is more encompassing; these rights include basic necessities, feelings of self-worth, medical care, employment based on merit, and sharing in recreational and educational resources within the community.

The majority of incidents of abused elderly involve individuals 65 years and older, with the typical victim being a frail woman, 75 years old, who is functionally dependent on others because of inadequate resources or physical limitations. The victims frequently refuse to report the abuse because they fear reprisals or lack somewhere else to live. There is also loyalty to relatives and a certain amount of shame and stigma in having to admit that they have been abused by their children. In some instances the abusing children were once abused children and in later years release a lifetime of bitterness toward their parents.

The emotional and economic responsibility involved in the care of one's elderly parents over a prolonged period has been given little attention. The elderly are often left without a role in the family and may be considered a burden or in some cases a threat to the parenting roles. A family may be caught in a dual role of caring for elderly parents and teenaged children, and when this stress is combined with inflation and rising unemployment, overwhelming tensions may result.

The most important method for preventing abuse of older persons is through community and government supportive services, and many people are not aware that a wide range of services are available for the elderly. Health professionals play a vital role in making these services known to those who are caring for older persons. They also play a pivotal role in fostering changes that can result in the development of alternative care facilities. More day-care centers for elderly need to be established so that the family can receive a needed rest and the elderly person can take part in meaningful activities that entertain as well as stimulate and use the elderly person's capabilities.

Many states have adult protection laws that require citizens—lay or professional—to report suspected cases of abuse to a public agency such as the social service authorities. The case is investigated and when justified is reported to legal authorities. Most states grant immunity from prosecution for those who make a good faith report of abuse or neglect. Penalties for not reporting may be a fine or a jail sentence. Some laws contain a provision that on request the person filing the report can be notified of the findings. Helping professionals must become the advocate of the elderly when abuse is suspected. It is important to remember that the elderly person is not all good and the relative all bad. Both must receive treatment.

Adult protective services

There is a delicate balance between the need of society to protect its elderly citizens and the need to respect their individual rights. Protection is often justified; however, there is growing evidence that many of the elderly are stripped of their rights without just cause. The following scenario is such an example.

■ Relatives of Mrs. B. say she is senile and incompetent. "She's highly forgetful and needs help. She can't handle her bills or her checkbook anymore. She forgets where she puts things and then accuses others of stealing them.'' The relatives ask Mrs. B to sign a paper. She trustingly signs what she has not read. What she did not know was that she signed a voluntary conservatorship petition, giving up her right to her property, her money, and her freedom. ———————————————

Elderly individuals who voluntarily sign conservatorship petitions frequently do not understand their legal rights or the fact that they will no longer be their own boss. Others report that they were pressured into signing by family members. Once the document is signed, the person's fate ends up in the hands of a guardian or a conservator, who in some cases is court appointed. The individual is notified of a hearing, but if he or she does not appear, the court can go ahead and appoint a guardian or conservator. The person may lose the right to buy or sell property, to sue or be sued, to write checks, or to generally engage in financial transactions of any kind. He or she can also lose the right to marry, drive a car, consent to or refuse medical treatment, or decide where to live. In the eyes of the law the person or ward is reduced to the status of a child.

■ Mrs. B. 'voluntarily' signed the petition, and later a relative took her on what she thought was a ride to see a friend. She was dropped off at a nursing home. Mrs. B. was frantic. She had been widowed 10 years earlier and had no children to turn to for help. ''One day I was living in my home, where I've lived for 40 years, and the next day I'm in a nursing home. All I see of the money my husband and I worked hard for all our lives is a few dollars each week. They've even sold some of my property.''

Mrs. B ran away from the nursing home and returned to her home. Authorities learned about her plight and a restraining order was obtained to prevent relatives from removing her from her home again. A new conservator was established to oversee her finances, and community services made it possible for her to remain in her own home. ———

There are countless stories similar to Mrs. B.'s, but unfortunately, most do not have happy endings. Their narrations are credited to senility or simply ignored. The irony is that once elderly people lose control of their finances, they lack the funds to pay for a lawyer to reestablish their rights.

The elderly are growing older and living longer, with the number of persons living to age 75 years and beyond increasing dramatically. This group often has health, social, economic, or environmental problems requiring supportive services. Such weaknesses can lead to abuse or exploitation by others or self-neglect. To resolve these problems, many states have enacted adult protective services legislation. With a system of social and health services coordinated by a caseworker, these services are available to those who voluntarily accept or through the use of guardianship, conservatorship, or special court proceedings for involuntary intervention.

Weaknesses in the law

There are special proceedings to establish protective service orders; however, most make little reference to procedures designed to protect the client.

1. Adequate notice to the client of the filing of the petition. In some states no mention is made of this requirement, and in others notice requirements vary from ''some notice'' to 5 or 10 days. Some who do receive the notice fail to understand the terms, the importance of the document, or that they can protest the action at the hearing.
2. Client's right to be present at the hearing. Rarely is a physician required to certify in writing that the client is unable to attend the hearing.
3. High standard of evidentiary proof of incompetency. Many states fail to prescribe any evidentiary standards.
4. Right to free counsel. In the states providing special proceedings that bypass guardianship, counsel is appointed for indigents.

However, the legislature's failure to define the duties of appointed counsel often results in their functioning as guardians rather than contesting the petition as an adversary. In the case of guardianship and conservatorships some states do not provide free counsel.

5. Guardian or agency given only limited powers. Rather than being granted authority only in the areas the person needs, a guardian or agency is usually given unnecessary and dangerously broad grants of authority that encompass virtually any kind of social or health service, including property management, medical care, and the power to institutionalize the person.

6. Accountability of the guardian or agency. Once an order for protective services is issued, the agency is granted the responsibility for the client and is not required to file reports or to seek renewal of the court order. In many cases the courts fail to monitor annual financial reports required of conservator or guardians.

The Uniform Probate Code defines an incapacitated person as one ''who is impaired by reason of mental illness, mental deficiency, physical illness or disability, advanced age, chronic use of drugs, chronic intoxication, or other cause (except minority) to the extent that he lacks sufficient understanding or capacity to make or communicate responsible decisions concerning his person.'' This formulation makes it quite possible for a mentally competent, yet physically incapacitated person to be the victim of a court-sanctioned involuntary guardianship. An individual's constitutional right to privacy includes the right of self-determination as long as the person is competent. Although some states require only findings of functional limitations, some findings of mental incompetence must be a necessary part of protective service acts and guardianship laws.

Legal safegards for protection of the elderly are sadly lacking. It is not enough to assume that guardians, conservators, or agencies mean well and then completely ignore the impact of depriving people of their rights. Health care providers must become advocates for the elderly, recognizing those who need a little help and those who are truly incompetent.

Drugs and the elderly

According to the National Institute on Drug Abuse, older adults consume at least 25 percent of all the prescription drugs used in the United States although they make up only 11 percent of the population. The elderly have a higher incidence of health problems that require medication; however, their inability to tolerate increased drug therapy causes problems.

A study of the drug-taking habits and drug knowledge of 61 elderly people, living independently and responsible for their health care, revealed that fewer than 5 percent of those taking prescription drugs actually knew enough about their drugs to ensure safe use. They were confused about the purpose, the dosage, and the schedule and hesitated to ask their physicians about their courses of medication because they considered the physician too busy or uninterested. One woman alternated her new prescription with drugs she had taken in the past so that none would be ''wasted.'' Sometimes the dosage was decreased to save money. It was not uncommon for the elderly person to have more than one physician, each treating different conditions, with some of the prescribed medications actually working against each other. When over-the-counter preparations were added, a potential life-threatening situation was created.[6]

Medication instructions for the elderly must be written down and explained verbally, and then as an added safety measure the client should be asked to repeat the instructions. It is important to find out what other drugs clients are taking, but rather than asking *if* they are taking other drugs, the care giver can obtain more information by asking *what* over-the-counter drugs or other prescription drugs they are taking. Unfortunately, those who take nonprescription drugs assume that these drugs are relatively innocuous, and it is up to medical personnel to caution clients that over-the-counter drugs contain potent ingredients with potential for harm. Clients also need to be warned about medical crises brought on from drug interactions.

Polypharmacy is dangerous, particularly for the elderly. The therapeutic and toxic effects of drugs change with age, and taking drugs concurrently increases the chance of adverse effects from drug interactions. Individuals who are over 60 years of age experience twice the number of adverse drug reactions as younger people, and those taking six or more drugs have a 25 percent chance of altered drug reactions.[9]

On June 25, 1980, a Select Committee on Aging reported to the U.S. House of Representatives that older Americans living in nursing homes were taking an average of 7 to 10 different drugs each day. This compared with 4 to 7 different medications taken by the noninstitutionalized elderly person. The 1980 study sponsored by Congress showed that a great majority of nursing home clients were not tested for potential side effects from combinations of medications, despite federal law that mandates a monthly medication review. The House Committee on Aging reported that many elderly nursing home clients were receiving dangerous, unnecessary, or ineffective drugs that too often were administered by unlicensed, untrained personnel.[3]

The widespread use of neuroleptics or tranquilizers to treat confused, agitated, and depressed elderly individuals has created a drug-induced problem called "tardive dyskinesia." Symptoms vary from mild to severe and resemble Huntington's chorea or parkinsonism. The syndrome is characterized by involuntary twitching of arms and legs and sometimes neck and arm stiffness. Facial movements include cheek puffing, lip smacking or pursing, chewing movements, and undulating and repeated tongue thrusts, and there is difficulty in swallowing and speaking. The drug should be discontinued whenever there is detection of tremor or movement of the mouth. There are times, however, when the physician considers neuroleptic therapy more important than preventing tardive dyskinesia, and an antispasmodic is added rather than with-

drawing the drug. The nurse administering neuroleptics to the elderly client should be aware of the implications of administering drugs with such potentially permanent hazards.

Night time is quiet time, and this philosophy is reflected in the number of hypnotics given on the evening shifts in hospitals and nursing homes. Deep sleep almost disappears in old age, and the person normally awakens easily and more frequently. This natural occurrence is treated as a widespread insomnia problem among the elderly, with sleeping pills routinely administered rather than providing a place for those who cannot sleep and something quiet for them to do. Sleep laboratories have proven that sedatives are only effective for short-term use, with a loss of sleep-promoting properties within 3 to 14 days of continuous use. Although the drug becomes ineffective for sleep-promoting, it continues to circulate in the system for some time. The plasma half-life of flurazepam (Dalmane) is between 50 and 100 hours in adults.[8] This buildup of medications becomes even more obvious in people aged 61 years and older who frequently require twice the amount of time to excrete drugs than do young adults. For example, the plasma half-life of diazepam (Valium) is 38.7 to 44 hours for young adults and 86.3 to 93.8 hours for people aged 61 years and older.[4] This carryover produces drowsiness, poor coordination, and poor mentation, which unfortunately may be credited to advanced age rather than the increased time for the drug to lose effect.

Ritualization may lead to continuation of drugs for months or years for persons who do not respond or are asymptomatic. Digitalis is one such example. Approximately half of all nursing home clients have congestive heart failure, with the treatment of choice being digitalis. A recent study published in the *New England Journal of Medicine* reports that as many as half the people who take digitalis for congestive heart failure are not helped by the medicine.[2] Although digitalis has been used since the eighteenth century and is now the drug of choice in treating heart failure, it has never been subjected to controlled study to find out whether it really works. Any person taking digitalis preparations is a candidate for toxicity, with signs and symptoms including confusion, agitation, depression, headache, dizziness, visual disturbances, disorientation, hallucinations, apathy, fatigue, and weakness, to name just a few. The study points out that health professionals have exposed people to the risks of digitalis without adequately assessing if the person is receiving any benefits from the drug.

Nurses cannot blindly follow medication orders of physicians without determining the effects on the individual for whom the medication is prescribed. Such unquestioned obedience risks the life of the person who is receiving the medication and may place the nurse in legal jeopardy.

Depressive illness is prevalent among the elderly and may be recognized by more physical complaints, the client spending more time in bed that is physically necessary, diminished ability to concentrate, and a change in adaptive behavior. The Division on the Elderly of the National Institutes of Health estimates that 20 percent of the elderly have a significant alcohol problem. Helping professionals may hesitate to interfere when the elderly use alcohol as a method of coping, even though the elderly have the same right to treatment for physical or psychological problems as the younger person. Alcoholism is only the visible problem; the cause may be located by a comprehensive assessment, including the person's physical, psychological, social, financial, cognitive, and self-care status.

Elderly people sometimes withdraw and become less involved so that they do not feel the bad things in life. Too many problems in their lives have been credited to old age, and they just quit trying to change what they feel is inevitable. When an elderly person withdraws, others respond by being more distant. Ultimately the person is left without any source of affection, interest, or caring. The first step for the care giver is to reach through the barrier and dare enough to care. Often the elderly person is surprised to find that some of their problems can be solved.

Drug abuse and misuse is on the rise in the United States, and the elderly are not excluded. The American society wants quick relief from discomfort, be it physical or psychological. Unfortunately, drug therapy is not without side effects. It is the knowledge base of drug effects, side effects, and the ability to evaluate the individual's response to the drug that is paramount. In some cases the side effects are more damaging than the original problem, which might have been resolved if someone had taken the time to listen. Drug therapy must never replace the human interaction. It is time nurses refuse to be part of ritualized drug treatment and rely instead on the tender loving care that is synonymous with their profession.

• • •

Aging is both a cultural and a biological process. In the American society the elderly grow old and unneeded in a throwaway, disposable culture. In the past the older person used the years between work and death to groom successors and to share knowledge, but in a highly technical era their information is outdated and their services are not needed. Families live at a distance, and many older people find that they are alone and lonely. The years between work and death are without responsibility, and the majority of America's aged do not have the resources for a life of leisure. With time on their hands and not enough money in their pockets, some of the elderly lack a reason to live and simply exist until they die.

The American culture is beginning to recognize the rights of the elderly and the need for significant functions for American aged. By the year 2000 it is estimated that nearly 32 million persons will be aged 65 years or older. A generation of adults has watched the older generation unsuspectingly grow old and unneeded. If people do not start listening and responding to the needs of the elderly today, who will care for the elderly of tomorrow?

REFERENCES

1. Bernard, K.: The first step to the cemetery, Newsweek, p. 15, Feb. 22, 1982.
2. Chia-Sen, D., and others: Heart failure in outpatients: a randomized trial of digoxin versus placebo, The New England Journal of Medicine 302:699, 1982.
3. Drug Abuse in Nursing Homes, Hearing before the Select Committee on Aging, House of Representatives, June 25, 1980, Washington, D.C., 1980, U.S. Government Printing Office.
4. Greenblatt, D., and others: Age, sex diazepam kinetics (abstract), Clinical Pharmacology and Therapeutics 25:227, 1979.
5. Lowenthal, M., Metz, D., and Patton, A.: Nobody wants the incontinent, RN 21:82, January 1958.
6. Lundin, D., and others: Education of independent elderly in the responsible use of prescription medications, Drug Intelligence and Clinical Pharmacy 14:335, 1980.
7. Pollock, J.: Aging in America: trials and triumphs, Survey conducted by Research & Forecasts, Inc., Monticello, Illinois, 1980, Americana Healthcare Corp.
8. Update on sedative hypnotics: IOM report on use of sleeping pills, FDA Bulletin 9(3):17, 1979.
9. Wolanin, M., and Phillips, L.: Confusion: prevention and care, St. Louis, 1981, The C.V. Mosby Co.

BIBLIOGRAPHY

Beck, C., and Ferguson, D.: Aged abuse, Journal of Gerontological Nursing 7:333, 1981.
Birren, J., and Schaie, K., editors: Handbook of the psychology of aging, New York, 1977, Van Nostrand Reinhold Co., Inc.
Butler, R., and Lewis, M.: Aging and mental health, ed. 3, St. Louis, 1982, The C.V. Mosby Co.
Caranasos, G., Stewart, R., and Cluff, L.: Drug-induced illness leading to hospitalization, JAMA 228:713, 1974.
Domestic violence against the elderly, Hearing before the Subcommittee on Human Services of the House Select Committee on Aging, April 21, 1980, New York, Washington, D.C., 1980, U.S. Government Printing Office.
Ebersole, P., and Hess, P.: Toward healthy aging: human needs and nursing response, St. Louis, 1981, The C.V. Mosby Co.
Hendricks, J., and Hendricks, C.: Aging in mass society: myths and realities, Cambridge, Massachusetts, 1977, Winthrop Publishers, Inc.
Mitchell, A.: Involuntary guardianship for incompetents: a strategy for legal services advocates. Clearinghouse Review 12:451, 1978.
Plawecki, H., and Plawecki, J.: Act your age, Geriatric Nursing, 1:179, 1980.
Regan, J.: Protecting the elderly: the new paternalism, The Hastings Law Journal 32:1112, 1981.
Rottenburg, R.: Prescribing for the elderly—safely, Patient Care 16:14, 1982.

7 · Stress and disease

The widespread use of tranquilizers, especially among women, has led to a growing problem of dependency on legal drugs. Solutions to stress do not come from bottles.

Illustration by Tom Weinman.

Stress is a popular topic anytime people gather, with discussion centering around the cause of stress and how to cope with it. Whereas one person talks about the stress of raising preschoolers, another contends, "Preschoolers are no problem at all. Wait until they become teenagers." Stress, like happiness and success, means different things to different people.

How to cope with stress is met with equal contrast. Yoga, meditation, and relaxation techniques are found by some to be effective means of alleviating tension. For others, regular physical exercise such as jogging, tennis, or golf helps to induce a sense of relaxation. "Working in my garden helps me when I'm uptight," one woman commented. Talking about a problem is also a method of stress reduction, as is the emotional release achieved by crying. Since emotional tears have been found to be chemically different from tears produced in response to eye irritation, it is theorized that crying helps to eliminate body chemicals that build up in response to stress.

Unfortunately, too many people decide that messages of stress communicated by the body are outside of their control and elect to cover these feelings with drugs or alcohol. According to the Food and Drug Administration, approximately 45 million prescriptions were written for diazepam (Valium) during 1978, and it was estimated that between 10 and 15 percent of all Americans would take the drug during 1980. A 1981 report from the Department of Health and Human Services stated that two thirds of the adult population drink alcoholic beverages, and the National Safety Council maintains that drunk driving kills far more Americans than other accidents. Solutions to stress do not come from bottles. When people cover anxiety rather than doing something to relieve the anxiety, their "remedies" add to the problem.

FACTS ABOUT STRESS
Stress response

Stress adaption includes physiologic responses from the neurologic, endocrine, and immunologic systems. The neurologic "fight or flight" response helps prepare the body for action that protects it from danger. The endocrine system releases surges of hormones, including epinephrine from the adrenal glands, which prompts the heart and lungs to work more quickly. The immune system also responds to situations of high tension, and there is increasing evidence that stress generally reduces an individual's resistance to microorganisms.

Stress can be measured. Biofeedback makes it possible to transfer neurologic or biologic function into visible and audible signals so that evidence of physiologic changes prompted by stress can be seen and heard. Brain waves manifest high-frequency beta activity in response to the fight or flight stimulus, and by-products of stress can be measured in both urine and blood. People frequently become so inured to the myriad of adaptation responses going on within their body that they no longer sense the presence of a causative agent. Rather than serving as a warning, stress becomes instead a silent threat. Before stress can be dealt with in a healthful manner, it must be recognized. Unfortunately, it takes a health crisis, such as a heart attack, before many people become aware of stress overload.

Researchers estimate that stress produces between 50 and 80 percent of all diseases, and a conservative list of such diseases includes ulcers, colitis, asthma, dermatitis, allergies, fever, arthritis, Raynaud's disease, hypertension, hyperthyroidism, amenorrhea, enuresis, paroxysmal tachycardia, headache, sexual dysfunction, insomnia, alcoholism, and a whole range of neurotic and psychotic disorders.

Selye,[6] a pioneer in stress research, describes the body's response to stress as a general adaptation syndrome comprised of three stages: alarm, resistance, and exhaustion. The initial response is the "alarm reaction" during which chemical and organic changes necessary for the body's defense are stimulated. As the reserve of adaptive hormones is used, the organism's ability to adapt is reduced. No organism is capable of living in a continuous state of alarm; therefore if the organism survives and is capable of adaptation, the "stage of resistance" follows.

The resistance stage is characterized by a mobilization of resources, a rise in adaptation energy, and normalization of the body's chemical and organic functions. Most stresses are short term and quickly dealt with, and equilibrium is restored. Severe or prolonged stress can cause irreversible organ changes.

After prolonged exposure to a noxious agent, the body is unable to resist and enters the "stage of exhaustion," which is evidenced by grave illness or death. After a lifetime of the cumulative, irreversible effects of stress, exhaustion is an apt description for growing old.

Researchers have found that this adaptation syndrome is initiated by injuries to a conscious animal or human, but not to an unconscious one. This raises the possibility that the critical factor may be the psychological significance of the injury rather than the physical injury itself.

Not all stress is damaging; in fact, to live without stress is to be dead. Essentially different things such as cold and heat, drugs and hormones, and sorrow and joy are all stressors that require the body to readjust or adapt. Stress becomes distress only when it occurs too frequently, lasts too long, deteriorates performance, or results in a stress-related disorder. Stress-related disorders are prompted by failure to adapt in combination with a biological weak link or predisposition. This predisposition contributes to one person having a migraine headache whereas another may develop ulcers.

The most important thing that needs to be understood about stress is that stress is the response to the stimulus or stressor and is not the stimulus or stressor itself. Therefore stress is not dumped onto the person but rather is a response created by the person. The task then is to help individuals understand that they are responsible for what they do with stress. If people learn to pay attention to their body and respond to their own physical and psychological needs, there will be less illness and more people in control of their own health.

Sources of stress

At the turn of the century, Adolf Meyer, a professor of psychiatry at Johns Hopkins University, kept "life charts" on his clients and began to find a relationship between certain life events and the onset of illness. Subsequent research indicated that stressful life events—both good and bad—evoked neurophysiological reactions that played an important causative role in disease onset.

Holmes and Rahe[3] of the University of Washington School of Medicine developed a systematized method of correlating life events with illness. They investigated the relationship between social readjustment, stress, and susceptibility to illness and observed in retrospective studies that life events tended to increase before disease onset. Their next step was to establish a scale of life events that could be used to predict the probability of disease onset (Table 7-1). These life events included occasions for joy as well as sadness, ranging from minor violations of the law to the death of a spouse. Marriage was established as an arbitrary standard, with other items scored according to the amount of readjustment required as compared with marriage.

Holmes and Rahe tested their hypothesis with more than 5,000 clients and found a statistically significant positive relationship between the life experiences and the total number of illnesses reported within a certain amount of time. They found high agreement with the rating of items made by men and women and people of different ages, educational backgrounds, and religious groups. Studies among populations in other countries have also shown that the life events listed in the Social Readjustment Rating Scale tend to be universal in significance.

To use the scale individuals check off events that they have experienced within the previous 12 months and add the assigned values of each event. The higher the score, the more likely that illness or health change will occur. A score of 150 indicates a 50 percent chance of experiencing a health change, and scores greater than 300 points increase the chance of experiencing a health change to almost 90 percent.[3]

The intent of the scale is not to alert the person to the probability of becoming ill, but rather to encourage preventive measures to reduce the probability. When people make decisions concerning future changes, they often fail to take into account the impact of stress from the past and the inevitable readjustments that are forthcoming in the future. Too many adjustments in too short a time lower resistance and deplete the adaptive capabilities of the human body. People may unknowingly push themselves into stress overload, experience illness, and not be aware that the situation might have been prevented by postponing or eliminating some of the changes over which they had control. Change must be considered in relationship to the past as well as

Table 7-1. The social readjustment rating scale

Life event	Mean value	Life event	Mean value
1. Death of spouse	100	23. Son or daughter leaving home	29
2. Divorce	73	24. Trouble with in-laws	29
3. Marital separation	65	25. Outstanding personal achievement	28
4. Jail term	63		
5. Death of close family member	63	26. Wife begins or stops work	26
6. Personal injury or illness	53	27. Begin or end school	26
7. Marriage	50	28. Change in living conditions	25
8. Fired at work	47	29. Revision of personal habits	24
9. Marital reconciliation	45	30. Trouble with boss	23
10. Retirement	45	31. Change in work hours or conditions	20
11. Change in health of family member	44	32. Change in residence	20
12. Pregnancy	40	33. Change in schools	20
13. Sex difficulties	39	34. Change in recreation	19
14. Gain of new family member	39	35. Change in church activities	19
15. Business readjustment	39	36. Change in social activities	18
16. Change in financial state	38	37. Morgage or loan less than $10,000	17
17. Death of close friend	37		
18. Change to different line of work	36	38. Change in sleeping habits	16
19. Change in number of arguments with spouse	35	39. Change in number of family get-togethers	15
20. Mortgage over $10,000	31	40. Change in eating habits	15
21. Foreclosure of mortgage or loan	30	41. Vacation	13
22. Change in responsibilities at work	29	42. Christmas	12
		43. Minor violations of the law	11

the future, with the benefits weighed against the costs of readjustment.

One source of stress that most people can identify with is not having enough money to meet increased living costs. As financial pressures bring about a lowered standard of living for many people, they become more limited in their ability to reduce the effect of stressors by eating out, hiring baby-sitters, or going on vacations. Other people find that some necessities must go. The most dangerous effect of economic recession is when people begin to feel trapped and out of touch with their own destinies. Feeling that they are victims of a situation that they cannot see an end to or a way out of, individuals develop a feeling of helplessness, loss of control, and a loss of hope and ambition. Being out of control economically is very frightening, and the results of this stress are seen in increased crimes, suicide, and child abuse and neglect. When the effects of financial loss are considered within the context of the stress scale, it becomes easier to understand why illness and accident rates strongly reflect economic changes.

For Susie, a 26-year-old licensed practical nurse, the stress scale helped her take control of her life at a time when she felt completely out of control.

■ Susie appeared at a university counseling center, requesting information about returning to school to become a registered nurse. When asked about major changes in her life within the past year, she said that her mother had recently died and that 6 months ago her husband had filed for a divorce. She went on to explain that he had left several times during the last year but always came back. "This time, I'm afraid he's gone for good."

Susie said that she was currently working 2 days a week in a nursing home but would be changing jobs to get full-time work. "I'd rather work part-time in the nursing home, but right now the money for school is more important."

Susie added up the values of the events that had happened to her in the past 12 months: divorce (73), marital separation (65), death of a close family member (63), marital reconciliation (45), sex difficulties (39), change in financial state (38), change in number of arguments with spouse (35), mortgage over $10,000 (31), trouble with in-laws (29), revision of personal habits (24), change in recreation (19), change in social activities (18), change in sleeping habits (16), change in number of family get-togethers (15), change in eating habits (15), vacation (13), and Christmas (12). Her total score was 550 points without considering the stress of her three preschoolers. When she added the score of changing to a different line of work (36), change in responsibilities at work (29), and change in working hours or conditions (20), her score became an ominous 635 points—without considering 26 points for going back to school.

Susie was surprised to learn how many stressors she had experienced in such a brief time. She commented, "I knew things were bad, but not that bad." She talked about the death of her mother—whom she described as her best friend—without any display of emotion. In fact, her entire conversation was without affect. Susie was apparently experiencing such a stress overload that she was unable, at that time, to acknowledge the impact of her losses.

She agreed that no major decisions had to be made for several weeks and was advised to study the stress scale before making any additional changes in her life.

Several weeks later, Susie returned to the counseling center. "I'm going to stay at my part-time job at the nursing home. Maybe in a year, I'll go back to school. Right now, I really need to take care of myself, or I won't be of any help to anyone." _____

Many people are unable to balance their stress budget, and some have paid the price with their health. Hospitalized clients in one study were asked to score their life experience scale retrospectively for the 2 years preceding their health change. There was a significant positive relationship between the seriousness of that illness and the severity of the life stressors the person had experienced in the 2 years before the illness onset.[10]

Individuals with chronic illnesses find that keeping an accurate accounting of their life-change scores often points out a relationship between their health and the stress in their life. Retrospective scores before the onset of their illness and each time they experience a health change make this correlation even clearer. As soon as a relationship between stress and illness is recognized, an element of control has been returned to the person.

Reducing stress

Stressors can be actual physical threats or perceived threats, and even when the danger is not real, the feeling of anxiety can be a producer of stress. It is almost impossible to separate psychological and physical stress since most anxiety-producing situations have both components. Because people are unique, the same stressor will have quite a different effect with different people. Health care providers are acutely aware that no two people react in an identical way to the same illness or injury, just as there is a wide variance in the response of family members whose loved ones have experienced a health change.

Past experience. Previous experience with similar kinds of stressors helps to determine the significance of the current situation. When individuals are anticipating new experiences, such as treatments, tests, and procedures, they have little to help them interpret what is going to happen. Consequently their actions may be inhibited, hesitant, or inappropriate. If, however, clients are given preparatory information about the aspects of procedures that are noted by the majority of clients, they can form an idea of what to expect. This information reduces the impact of the stressor when it occurs and helps to restore control to the client during the new experience.

Personal resources. The individual's personal resources also influence the way a stressor is perceived. If there have been a number of health changes within a short time, it may be necessary for others to assume many of the person's activities until adaptive energy is replenished. There are times when energies are so depleted that the client

is unable to cope with such simple decisions as filling out a menu.

Although it is harmful to expect too much from a client, it is just as harmful to perform services for a client that he or she is capable of doing without help. Sometimes it is a difficult decision for nurses to know when to support clients in their efforts toward self-care and when to assume responsibility for the client's care. According to Orem,[4] candidates for nursing care are those clients who are unable to provide necessary qualitative and quantitative self-care or dependent care or who are expected to lose this capability to provide care. It may be necessary for the nurse to completely compensate for the client's inability for engaging in self-care, or the client may only need partial compensation while performing some but not all self-care actions. In the event that the client can assume all self-care actions, the nursing role becomes one of support and education. These necessary variations help the client recover from or cope with the effects of a health change.

Support from significant others. Family members of clients with chronic illness often relate that they feel so helpless. They need to be told that their presence—just being there listening and offering support—helps their loved one cope with the stress of illness. During hospitalization, the family is usually the most important thing in a client's life. The more clients can see their loved ones, the less frightening and stressful the hospital situation is for them, and the same is true for family members.

Amount and duration of stress. Other important variables in perceiving and managing stress are the magnitude of the stressor and the amount of time it is present. Whenever a person faces a sudden, dramatic event, all the adaptive energies are summoned for the fight or flight response. When the threat has passed, the stress-alarm reaction is followed by a "sigh of relief" as the person experiences a letdown or energy depletion before returning to a normal level of funtion. This normal adaptive stress reaction occurs when the stressor is identifiable and clear, but when the stressor is more ambiguous and prolonged, the person may come to accept it as a normal part of life. This potentially damaging stress reaction is maintained rather than recognized as a condition that should be alleviated. Prolonged stress without relief contributes to the development of stress-related disorders.

Perceived control. One of the most important resources for coping with stressors is preceiving some control over the situation. People want to maintain an element of control over their being as well as their environment. Sometimes a client simultaneously experiences feelings of depersonalization and powerlessness in a strange, unyielding environment. Such a feeling may prompt the person to assume power in another way, such as by pulling tubes, defying orders, or displays of anger. By allowing clients to participate in the decision-making process of day-to-day care as well as providing them the opportunity to verbalize concerns, needs, or desires, the care giver helps to maintain a client's autonomy. Choices whenever possible provide the client an opportunity to decide and control an outcome, and once the client's wishes are known, these must be carried out.

Many people maintain that they have no control over the stressors in their life or how they respond to these events. When the relationship between stress and health is not recognized, there is also a tendency to consider illness and health beyond control. With the help of medical personnel, people can be taught to listen to their own body more intently, and relate behavior to what goes on in illness and health. Once individuals become responsible participants in their own health care, they learn to value their bodies more and realize the risk of living highly stressful lives. This change in focus comes about when individuals believe that they *can* develop life-styles that reduce major health risks. When this active participation becomes prevalent, preventive medicine will become a reality and health care will see horizons that are not yet visible.

THE STRESS OF HOSPITALIZATION

A high percentage of hospitalized clients have an underlying chronic illness that either contributed to their hospitalization or is the cause for the hospitalization. A chronic illness depletes an individual's resistance, making the person more susceptible to acute illness. Psychosocial stress affects not only the illness process but also the speed of recovery. Since hospitalized clients must deal with many factors, including strange surroundings, fear of diagnosis and prognosis, and loss of contact with significant others, the need to measure the general psychological stress induced by hospitalization is important.

The Social Readjustment Rating Scale developed by Holmes and Rahe provided methodology for the construction of a scale to measure stress experienced by hospitalized clients. Initially clients, lay people, nurses, and physicians were asked about their experiences with stress related to the experience of hospitalization, and from these interviews, a list of events that might happen to a hospitalized client were compiled. The event "emergency admission" was used as the arbitrary standard and respondents then arranged other events experienced during hospitalization relative to an emergency admission to the hospital. A score was assigned to each of the events to indicate the level of stress produced or the readjustment required.

Ultimately 49 events were selected that satisfied at least three of the four following criteria: the event would (1) be experienced fairly commonly by general hospital clients, (2) be experienced within 1 or 2 days after admission to the hospital, (3) not be too dependent on the seriousness of illness, and (4) be specific enough that the client could easily determine whether it had been experienced. When 261 hospitalized medical and surgical clients were asked to rank the 49 experiences related to hospitalization, there was a high degree of consensus among different groups as to how the events should be rated. The Hospital Stress Rating Scale in Table 7-2 provides a valuable tool that can be used to quantify the measurement of psychosocial stress experienced by short-term hospitalized medical and surgical clients.

The scale ranges from the least stressful event

Table 7-2. Hospital stress rating scale

Rank/event	Mean rank score
1. Having strangers sleep in the same room with you	13.9
2. Having to eat at different times than you usually do	15.4
3. Having to sleep in a strange bed	15.9
4. Having to wear a hospital gown	16.0
5. Having strange machines around	16.8
6. Being awakened in the night by the nurse	16.9
7. Having to be assisted with bathing	17.0
8. Not being able to get newspapers, radio, or TV when you want them	17.7
9. Having a roommate who has too many visitors	18.1
10. Having to stay in bed or the same room all day	19.1
11. Being aware of unusual smells around you	19.4
12. Having a roommate who is seriously ill or cannot talk with you	21.2
13. Having to be assisted with a bedpan	21.5
14. Having a roommate who is unfriendly	21.6
15. Not having friends visit you	21.7
16. Being in a room that is too cold or too hot	21.7
17. Thinking your appearance might be changed after your hospitalization	22.1
18. Being in the hospital during holidays or special family occasions	22.3
19. Thinking you might have pain because of surgery or test procedures	22.4
20. Worrying about your spouse being away from you	22.7
21. Having to eat cold or tasteless food	23.2
22. Not being able to call family or friends on the phone	23.3
23. Being cared for by an unfamiliar doctor	23.4
24. Being put in the hospital because of an accident	23.6
25. Not knowing when to expect things will be done to you	24.2
26. Having the staff be in too much of a hurry	24.5
27. Thinking about losing income because of your illness	25.9
28. Having medications cause you discomfort	26.0
29. Having nurses or doctors talk too fast or use words you can't understand	26.4
30. Feeling you are getting dependent on medications	26.4
31. Not having family visit you	26.5
32. Knowing you have to have an operation	26.9
33. Being hospitalized far away from home	27.1
34. Having a sudden hospitalization you weren't planning to have	27.2
35. Not having your call light answered	27.3
36. Not having enough insurance to pay for your hospitalization	27.4
37. Not having your questions answered by the staff	27.6
38. Missing your spouse	28.4
39. Being fed through tubes	29.2
40. Not getting relief from pain medications	31.2
41. Not knowing the results or reasons for your treatments	31.9
42. Not getting pain medication when you need it	32.4
43. Not knowing for sure what illness you have	34.0
44. Not being told what your diagnosis is	34.1
45. Thinking you might lose your hearing	34.5
46. Knowing you have a serious illness	34.6
47. Thinking you might lose a kidney or some other organ	35.6
48. Thinking you might have cancer	39.2
49. Thinking you might lose your sight	40.6

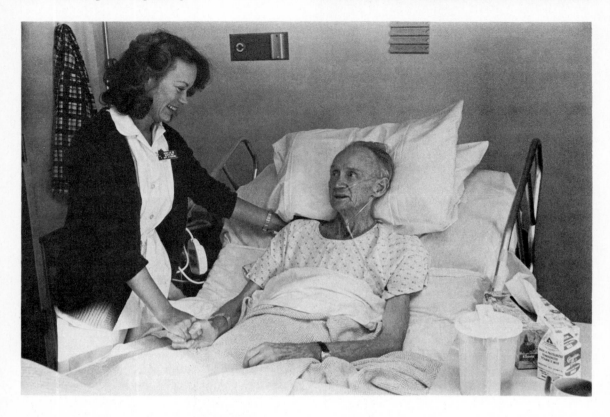

A small amount of caring can go a long way to help reduce the stress of hospitalization.
Courtesy of Providence Medical Center, Portland, Oregon.

of "having strangers sleep in the same room with you" to the most stressful of the 49 hospital experiences, "thinking you might lose your sight." Inconveniences associated with hospital stay, such as eating at times different than usual, sleeping in a strange bed, wearing a hospital gown, or having to stay in bed or the room, were considered far less stressful than being hospitalized away from home, missing spouse, and not having family visits. Financial concerns, including not having enough insurance to pay for hospitalization and losing income because of illness, were moderately stressful events. Several highly rated items included what

clients perceived as lack of information about their condition: not being told a diagnosis, not knowing the illness, not knowing results or reasons for treatments, and not having questions answered by the staff. According to the Hospital Stress Rating Scale, some of the most stressful aspects of hospitalization were related to a lack of effective communication on the part of the hospital staff.[9]

Sometimes care givers fail to explain things so that the client can understand, and the individual may not be assertive enough to ask for a clearer explanation. Whereas mild anxiety may be conductive to learning, anything beyond mild stress prevents learning from taking place. When the stress of illness and hospitalization are considered, one can understand why clients do not remember everything that has been explained. The flight response to stress does not merely take place on the physical level but also on a psychological level. The mind can deal with only so many matters at once, and the rest are lost. People sometimes reach their maximum capacity to handle more information, and additional information is not retained, regardless if this information is good or bad.

Clients may respond as though they understand instructions and information from care givers. They may even go through the body motions of nodding, offering "uh-hmms," and verbally saying that they understand, while the words they remember are "heart attack," "malignancy," "bed rest," and little more. Sometimes care givers do not evaluate at a later time what the client really has heard or understood. Unless this is done, questions may be left unanswered and concerns not expressed.

In one situation the nurse and the client's husband were present when the physician told the woman that she had a malignancy, and the treatment and prognosis were described in detail. The woman later told her family how relieved she was to know that she did not have cancer. The family promptly notified the physician, who repeated the information to the client. She remained adamant that she did not have a malignancy, and it became apparent that she was using denial to relieve her anxiety associated with cancer. It was necessary for care givers to find out what the diagnosis meant to the client. She talked about pain, isolation, and "treatments that left people bald and violently ill. Thank God I won't have to go through that hell."

Factual information concerning treatment was presented to the client. She was told about medications that eliminate or greatly reduce the nausea and vomiting of chemotherapy. She was shown a special cooling cap that reduces hair loss by decreasing the amount of chemotherapy that reaches hair follicles. She was also given factual information concerning cure, remission, pain, and pain

control. Her family provided additional support. Slowly as her anxiety was reduced, the woman's denial began to disappear.

Another example involved a client unable to "hear" good news. The young woman awakened from emergency surgery to find that she had an unplanned colostomy. Each time the doctor talked about the colostomy, he told her that the colostomy was temporary and that he planned to close it in several months. Three days after the surgery the client overheard nurses talking about the colostomy closure. She asked the nurses, "Why didn't someone tell me it was going to be closed. What else have you kept from me?" It was several days before the client accepted the fact that her physician, the nurses, and her husband had all told her that the colostomy was temporary. She said that all she remembered was the word "colostomy," and after that she did not hear anything else.

Most individuals do want to know what is going on with their bodies and how changes in their health affect their lives. Before any person can be an active partner in health care, this information is mandatory. Written instructions and facts help to clarify. Clients who do not want to know about their health are often the ones most in need of this information. Therefore anxieties must be dealt with before factual information can be assimilated.

Discharge planning should include an evaluation of what the person knows concerning his or her health and what questions remain. Questions from the nurse should be open ended or phrased so that they cannot be answered with "yes" or "no." "How will your illness affect your life?" "What questions do you have about your health?" "What concerns you the most?" Written instructions will also need to be carefully reviewed. An interested care giver generates questions from the client and provides an opportunity for the person to express feelings.

Because a client's illness is unique to that person, it is quite easy for the individual to magnify anxiety out of proportion to the reality of the situation. With the help of the care team, clients are able to move beyond psychological immobility to achieve some degree of acceptance of their illness and control over their being.

PERSONALITY AND CHRONIC ILLNESS

As early as the second century medicine was ruled by the theory that one's disposition was related to disease. The anatomist Galen claimed that all human beings belonged to one of four "humors," with each group developing a different kind of illness. In the 1930s Franz Alexander also postulated that a group of specific diseases had their origin in emotional conflicts. Today psychosomatic experts are convinced that personality factors are involved in disease. In addition to the emotional factors of illness, they also maintain that other factors, such as genetics and nutrition, also help to determine whether or not a person develops a disease.

There are several hundred articles written on the topic of emotions and stress and their relationship to serious diseases. In these articles there is a general agreement that a prolonged and unabated stress level produces alterations in the body's neurophysiological function that create the preconditions for illness development. Although it is difficult to demonstrate a link between personality factors and disease, it has been noted that when a prolonged stress response is combined with a particular personality, a specific disorder often results.

In 1948 Betz analyzed the psychological profiles of 45 medical students at Johns Hopkins University in Baltimore. Despite superficial similarities, three temperament types were identified: alpha—steady and self-reliant, beta—lively and light hearted, and gamma—moody and insecure. Betz maintains that a person's basic temperament does not change from birth to death, and this inborn temperament combines with life experiences to produce a person's personality. She further theorizes that this temperament contributes to everything that happens to that person, including the diseases that are eventually developed. Over the course of 30 years Betz[1] found that many of the Johns Hopkins Medical School graduates suffered major illness, and 77 percent of the moody, irritable persons with gamma personalities had experienced a heart attack, cancer, or other disorders as compared with only 25 percent of the calm, stable persons with alpha personalities or 27 percent of the lively, flexible persons with beta personalities. From this study it could be concluded that a person's temperament and approach to life are variables that affect resistance to disease.[5]

Type A behavior

The leading cause of death in the United States is heart disease, and it has been determined that a behavior pattern called type A contributes heavily to the risk of coronary disease. This correlation between behavior and cardiovascular disease has gained credibility through the work of Friedman and Rosenman.[2] Through the years they have developed a detailed profile of the high-stress type A personality, which is characterized by competition, achievement, and the acquisition of material wealth.

The two traits that make up the type A personality include an excessive, competitive drive and a chronic, unrelenting sense of time urgency. The person walks, talks, eats, and does everything as quickly as possible and is highly frustrated when anyone or anything slows the pace. These two characteristics are accompanied by an easily aroused hostility that is well rationalized and displayed at unexpected times. A fundamental aspect of the competitive ambition is aggression, which is contained and properly channeled, projecting self-confidence, achievement, and efficiency. Underneath, however, are constant feelings of inferiority and failure, prompting individuals with type A personalities to incessantly try to increase the quantity of their achievements within less time. These characteristics carry over into leisure time, which is taken over by the need to be accomplishing something constructive so as not to waste previous time. Accomplishments are measured in terms of numbers of dollars earned, with no idea when enough is enough. Typically the person is aggressive and extroverted, with a strong "social" personality that

Type A behavior.

Illustration by Tom Weinman.

conceals a deep-seated insecurity about self-worth.

When an individual's security is measured by the quantity of achievements gained through competitive struggle, great stress and insecurity result. Relationships with others become secondary to achievement, unless an individual is perceived as being able to contribute to achievement.

Although the relationship between type A behavior and coronary heart disease was initially viewed with skepticism, research over the years has produced convincing evidence that type A behavior is a major risk factor in coronary heart disease. Laboratory data indicate that the blood abnormalities typical of the person with coronary heart disease are present in the individual with the type A behavior pattern. Although the theory is not

universally accepted and certainly does not make a heart attack inevitable, type A behavior is indeed a serious risk factor for coronary heart disease that operates in addition to and in conjunction with the classical risk factors.

The components of irritation, impatience, aggravation, and anger comprise the pathogenic core of the type A behavior pattern. Because this consistent pattern of behavior frequently exists among coronary clients, many physicians give advice on behavior modifications to their clients, with the hope of modifying or avoiding this destructive behavior before physiological symptoms appear. Unfortunately, there is little success in the modification of type A behavior in individuals who have not suffered myocardial infarction. The routine associated with the type A behavior provides security for individuals who attribute their success to this behavior pattern. As with other illnesses, people tell themselves, ''These things always happen to someone else.'' Changing a behavior pattern is stressful, and such an endeavor requires a great deal of time from both the individual and the physician. Unless the person is convinced that a behavior change is paramount to survival, any attempt is likely to be discontinued with the rationalization that there is no real proof of any prophylactic effectiveness.

Following a myocardial infarction individuals have the opportunity to reflect on the past and see their behavior pattern as being counterproductive. They have the proof that type A behavior can lead to ischemic heart disease, and if they begin to slip back into their old pattern of doing too much in too little time, symptoms of ischemic heart disease may be experienced. Once clients are motivated to change, they must consciously begin the process of slowing their pace and substituting affection and tolerance for hostility. Without the support and encouragement from the physician and significant others, few people with type A personalities are able to change their personalities.

Too many individuals with type A personalities love things and use people. A longer, more healthful life may come from loving people and using things. For many this change cannot be accomplished unless they resign or retire from their previous vocations.

Sometimes characteristics of type A personality are seen because of situations that an individual cannot avoid. Nurses, particularly those working in a tension-filled arena such as intensive care, develop on-the-job type A traits. They frequently have too many clients and not enough time to attend to the total needs of each person, and it becomes mandatory that they do everything as quickly as possible throughout their shift. They compete with the clock, creating a hurry syndrome that continues throughout the day as lunch is gulped and coffee breaks are skipped or taken at the back of the unit. This syndrome is many times not by choice but

out of necessity to maintain the lives of those under their care. On the outside nurses project self-confidence and efficiency, but inside there is always the reminder that they hold life and death in their hands and that only minutes separate the two. Anxiety and irritation emerge from too much stress. The work is never completed. There is always a client who needs special attention and another on the way from the emergency room.

The human body adjusts to short-term activation, but when the demand is generalized and the effects diffuse, the prolonged stress in this type of situation contributes to ''burn-out.'' The stress from the workday carries over into home life, and the person may be unable to ''let down'' and replenish adaptive energies.

There must be care for the care givers working in high-stress areas. They need time out of the unit for lunch and breaks when they are not required to be a moment's notice away from responding to a cardiac arrest. Adequate trained staffing is mandatory. Research supports the fact that it is far cheaper to provide these necessities for nurses than it is to retrain the constant turnover of professionals prompted by those who decide that their own physical and mental health must take priority over a stressful work situation.

Type B behavior

Friedman and Rosenman[2] have identified the counterpart of the competitive type A behavior as the noncompetitive type B behavior. Although there is a wide range of variation possible and instances when the person with a type A personality may exhibit the traits of a type B personality, essentially people tend to match with one category or the other.

It is important to identify characteristic type B traits because people often have the misconception that the type B person will be less successful than the type A person. There is no special pattern to the type of occupation that attracts either personality type. Individuals with type B behavior patterns are just as likely as persons with type A personalities to be nurses, physicians, lawyers, or ac-

countants. Type B persons may also be just as ambitious and have just as much drive as their type A counterparts; however, this drive gives confidence and security rather than causing irritation and frustration.

Individuals with type B personalities are usually free of time urgency, except when it is truly warranted on the job. Unlike their type A counterparts, they value leisure time for relaxation. Personal goals and self-satisfaction are more important than material or social success. Because they take more time to contemplate and consider options as well as implications, they are often more successful in their vocations than are individuals with type A personalities.

People with type B personalities are more thoughtful, and less abrasive personally, and lead life-styles far more likely to approach genuine happiness. Individuals with a type A personality, based on achievement and insecurity, would do well to learn as much as possible about their counterparts, whose lives are based on inner stability and a low-stress mode of behavior that is far more conducive to health maintenance. Learning more about the type B approach to life may help to modify type A behavior.

Cancer and personality

The second leading cause of death in the United States is cancer, and theories linking cancer and personality remain both fascinating and highly controversial. In 180 A.D. the ancient physician Galen observed that melancholy women were more apt to develop cancer than the cheerful, hopeful, sanguine women. In the nineteenth century a cancer surgeon by the name of Parker proposed that grief was a predispositional or an exacerbating cause for cancer. Only recently have cancer and personality been studied, and numerous researchers have concluded that individuals with cancer psychologically resemble each other. Factors that have been found to predispose an individual to the development of cancer include prolonged depression, difficulty expressing emotions, and the loss of a significant role or relationship.

Investigators have found that individuals with cancer frequently report an unhappy childhood, that they were raised by emotionally distant parents, or that early in life they experienced the death of a parent or a sibling. Because early attempts to form warm and satisfying relationships failed, in adult life these individuals overcompensate by trying to please others and win their affection. This behavior sometimes masks a chronic low-key depression and feelings of unworthiness and self-dislike. Feelings of hostility are likely to be bottled up or suppressed rather than being worked through. During adult life a healthy central relationship is usually achieved through marriage, a career, or parenthood, and within 6 months to a year following the loss of this crucial central relationship the first symptoms of cancer appear.

Because some cancers are very slow-growing, with up to 20 years before symptoms are present, the question arises, does the personality prompt the disease, or is it the other way around? Scientists agree that there is a relationship between emotions and cancer, but they also point out that cancer is influenced by genetic predisposition and environmental factors. Research continues to determine how important the role between emotions and stress is to cancer and how this role can be influenced.

Hopelessness and cancer

In the eighteenth and nineteenth centuries, physicians recognized that reactions of despair and hopelessness prompted by a major frustration or loss in a person's life frequently occurred before the development of cancer. Current research points out that feelings of hopelessness, helplessness, and despair may predispose the individual toward organic pathology. The diagnosis of cancer often deepens this "helpless-hopeless" cycle, and as psychological defenses fail, the disease aggravates the depression. Unless this cycle is altered, the individual is left totally defenseless as the disease runs its course. Schmale and Ikler[5] have conducted a series of studies to investigate the relationship between the trait "hopelessness" and cervical cancer. One study involved women between the ages of 20 and 50 admitted to a hospital for cervical cone biopsies following atypical Pap tests. None of the women had gross evidence of cervical disease, and aside from the cervical dysplasia, all were considered healthy. Before the biopsy the women were given specific tests and interviews and, on the basis of this information, it was determined whether or not they had a hopelessness-prone personality. Hopelessness was interpreted as being a sense of frustration for which the individual believed there was no resolution. Personality traits included low self-esteem, perfectionist attitude, preoccupation with pleasing others, and feelings of guilt and shame when they were unable to meet their own high expectations. These classifications were then used to predict whether the woman had cancer. When predictions were matched with pathology reports after biopsy, 73 percent of those predicted to have cancer because of their hopelessness-prone personality actually had cervical cancer. Similar prospective studies by others have correlated emotional factors of hopelessness with cancer of the cervix.

Many researchers have found a consistent relationship between coping mechanisms and the survival rate of individuals with cancer. Cancer clients described as being quiet, polite, apologetic people who accept their disease are more likely to be short-term survivors. In contrast, long-term survivors are less well adjusted to their illness and have a coping style more expressive of psychological distress and negative emotions and reactions.

The research between coping mechanisms and survival time has strong implications for nursing and other health professionals. For a number of years it was considered therapeutic to help clients progress in their coping from their initial denial of their illness to the ultimate stage of acceptance. Health professionals believed that they had done a good job when clients accepted their cancer, and those clients who made a poorer adjustment to cancer represented failure. A large body of research indicates that just the opposite might be true. If one considers the short-term survival of individuals who are accepting of their cancer, acceptance could result in a letdown in the body's defense mechanism that may permit the cancer to develop and grow. Members of the medical team may be able to lengthen survival time by helping clients consciously express their negative emotions and psychological distress, rather than helping them suppress or deny their distress through acceptance of their illness.

Simonton and Matthews-Simonton[7] are among the first researchers to evaluate the results of psychological intervention in the treatment of cancer. Recognizing that a psychological component may have a direct relationship to the development and course of cancer, the Simontons mandate that their clients receive counseling in addition to appropriate medical treatment. Clients undergo a battery of psychological tests that facilitate the identification of strengths and weaknesses, and they are also helped to deal with hopelessness that prevents the process of self-healing to take place. Relaxation and mental imagery is a central psychological process used to assist clients in becoming more active participants in their own health. After 10 years of work the Simontons report that their clients survive up to twice as long as the national average. Although they readily acknowledge that client expectancy and the placebo effect may have influenced these outcomes, they also maintain that addressing the emotional issues plays a role in lengthening survival time.

The optimism from research that points out a relationship between personality and illness is that psychosocial and personality factors can be changed to promote self-healing. Because people

are resistant to change, it is going to take time, money, and research to learn how to help people alter their maladaptive behaviors. The Health Care Financing Review for September 1982 reports that national health expenditures from 1965 to 1981 increased by almost 700 percent. Because the dramatic health improvements anticipated were not realized, it would seem more prudent to concentrate resources toward the prevention of chronic disease rather than toward the treatment of disease. However, there is a reluctance to allot money for something that may not show cost-effectiveness for many years. If psychosocial and personality factors are as vital as they appear to be in the development of illness, the potential benefits of health education outweigh the costs. The most important gain will be in reduced human suffering and improved quality of life.

BEHAVIORAL MEDICINE

At several medical centers across the country a new branch of psychosomatics is being pursued. As the links between mind and disease are being discovered, behavioral medicine is attempting to form effective solutions to prevent pathology. In 500 BC. Socrates recognized the relationship between the mind and the body when he stated, "There is no illness of the body apart from the mind." In behavioral medicine the healing powers of the mind are used for preventive care and the establishment and maintenance of optimum levels of health.

Progressive relaxation

Progressive relaxation is a stress reduction technique that involves systematic tensing and relaxing of various muscle groups. Since anxiety and muscular relaxation are opposite states, the philosophy of progressive relaxation is that is is impossible to be nervous in any part of the body that is relaxed. This technique does not require special equipment or a physician's orders, and it can be done in a variety of settings with both children and adults. Frequently used in treatment of headaches, insomnia, anxiety, and pain, techniques that teach people how to relax and cope with stressors have far-reaching implications in health care.

Progressive relaxation was originated in 1929; however, it evokes a relaxation response similar to meditative techniques that date back over 2,000 years. The relaxation response is described as a response that brings about decreased heart rate, lowered metabolism, and decreased respiratory rate. Whether the technique is old or new, the same physiological and psychological results are produced if they incorporate a quiet environment, a passive attitude, a comfortable position, and an object to dwell on, such as a word, sound, or a visualization. Counting sheep is an effective method of resolving insomnia because the verbal activity of the left hemisphere is blocked while the visual capacity of the right hemisphere is busy with sheep.

The progressive relaxation technique consists of tensing and relaxing groups of muscles in a logical progression throughout the body. Attention is directed to the contrasting states of tension and relaxation and the feelings associated with each. Because many people have learned to overlook the sensations of tension, they need to be re-taught to recognize and pinpoint tension before they are able to substitute relaxation.

Before the session begins the client should be offered the chance to use the rest room, and any constraining items such as eyeglasses, contact lenses, watches, and shoes should be removed to promote comfort. Ideally the technique takes place in a quiet, darkened room with the client in a comfortable position with eyes closed. Usually 20 minutes should be allowed, although the length of time necessary to complete the relaxation technique depends on the number of muscle groups used. For example, each hand can be tensed and relaxed separately, together, or in combination with other muscle groups. Initially muscles are usually divided into 16 groups and later combined according to the needs of the client.

Relaxation is unlikely to occur unless there is a shift in conceptual processes to a nonvoluntary, free-flowing, drifting, mental activity that lets go of both past and future. Sometimes an individual will need to dwell on a word or sound before being able to achieve this "here and now" state. The normal rhythm of breathing can help also enhance the repetition of the sound or word.

Following each session the client is encouraged to comment on things that were or were not helpful in achieving relaxation. Usually an open-ended question similar to "How do you feel?" or "What areas did you have the most trouble relaxing?" will encourage a sharing of problems or concerns that came up during the session. Sometimes there is concern over strange or unfamiliar feelings during relaxation. Sensations often experienced are the feeling of warmth in the hands and feet, which is prompted by vasodilation in the peripheral arteries, and the sensation of heaviness, which is a perception of muscular relaxation. If the person is encouraged to enjoy these sensations and understand that they are characteristic of deep relaxation, they are less likely to cause concern.

As most health care providers realize, it is sometimes impossible to have the ideal situation of a quiet environment, a comfortable client, and 20 minutes to spend teaching progressive relaxation. Distraction from environmental noise can be reduced with sound-conditioning devices such as "white sound" that produces a smooth sound of rushing air that masks otherwise disturbing noise. The sound from a fan, a vaporizer, or an air conditioner is similar to those produced by a sound conditioner and may be particularly effective during relaxation techniques. Another method of overcoming unpleasant environmental noise is with cassette recordings of environmental sounds: the ultimate thunderstorm, a meadow with the sounds of birds and crickets, a slow ocean with sea gulls, or a sailboat complete with creaking mast, the cries of circling gulls, and splashing spray. It is advisable to let clients select the environmental sound they find most pleasant; otherwise, seasickness may follow instead of relaxation.

A person who is uncomfortable or very anxious is usually less willing to participate in progressive relaxation but may welcome a back rub as an effective adjunct to progressive relaxation. While the client is asked to tense his or her muscles, the care giver rubs the back in a shorter, more brisk fashion and then smooths out into long soothing strokes during muscle relaxation. The person may also be more receptive to tensing muscles all at once rather than concentrating on individual muscle groups.

Cassette recordings of progressive relaxation techniques can help instruct and guide clients when the care giver is not able to spend the uninterrupted time. The recording also provides additional practice that is necessary before an individual is able to initiate the relaxation response without guidance.

Youngsters can also benefit from relaxation techniques, but they may not understand terms like "stress" and "tension" and their attention span is too short to progress through separate muscle groups. Children love make-believe stories, especially if they are a character in the story, and relaxation techniques can be built around stories that are interesting and brief enough to hold the child's attention. A fantasy situation can be created in which the child must be as small as possible such as a ballerina who dances a flower dance, first with all the petals tucked in tight and then as a beautiful blooming flower. If the child responds better to excitement and adventure, have the child become small enough to fit through the door of a spaceship or a fairy princess's carriage or to sneak the football through a whole bunch of football players to make a touchdown. The nurse encourages the child to be smaller and smaller, and after a few seconds announces, "You made it through. Doesn't it feel great to be big again!" Needless to say, other tight situations routinely develop so that the child has several opportunities to tense and relax muscles. Children love to tell part of the story and may even give the nurse a part in the make-believe story.

People need help in learning to recognize the feelings of tension before they are able to achieve relaxation. By drawing attention to these feelings during progressive relaxation, clients learn to differentiate tension from relaxation. A helpful relaxation technique that does not require extended time or a quiet atmosphere is taking several deep breaths and, during exhalation, making a conscious effort to relax. By learning to use relaxation techniques, people are able to cope more effectively with difficult situations. The ultimate goal is to achieve a more balanced physiological and psychological state of being.

Meditation

Whenever the topic of meditation is brought up, people imagine gurus sitting cross-legged on the floor, eyes closed, repeating in unison a word or sound in long, drawn-out monotones. Beyond the mystery and the mystique are results that could benefit those who take the time to understand and experience this method of deep relaxation. Although researchers have demonstrated that meditation is psychologically and physiologically more refreshing than deep sleep, some maintain that benefits from meditation result from the individual's high expectations rather than from the technique itself. Meditative techniques, including Transcendental Meditation, Shavasana, and Zazen, are helping people adjust to stress on a number of different levels. For these techniques to be more effective it is necessary to have the guidance of someone trained in the particular area of interest.

During Transcendental Meditation the meditator strives to achieve a psychological state of transcendental awareness, which is achieved by two basic methods. First, the meditator restricts or focuses attention on an object of meditation or on a physiological process such as internal sensations. The meditator sits in a comfortable, upright position with eyes closed and repeats the sound, or mantra, for 15 to 20 minutes each day. This concentration on the mantra absorbs attention and quiets the mind. The second step involves opening up of attention, in which the meditator enters a state of undistracted receptivity with thoughts and images allowed to flow through the mind without distracting from meditation. With the mind stilled the meditator perceives new levels of experience until finally achieving the ultimate goal of transcendental awareness.

Shavasana is an ancient yogic technique that has been demonstrated to achieve general stress reduction. The individual lies supine with feet apart and relaxed and arms lying at a natural distance alongside the body with palms up. The person is instructed to keep eyes closed and to focus on breathing without controlling it. Each breath is monitored by feeling the ingoing and outgoing flow of air at the tip of the nostrils. Breathing becomes the object of meditation to focus attention, prevent sleepiness, and stop intrusion of unsettling thoughts. Many experiments in managing hypertension are conducted during this yogic exercise. The entire meditative practice consists of assuming this posture and concentrating on breathing for 15 minutes three times a day.

Zazen, or "sitting meditation," is another simple and straightforward stress reduction technique. Although the classical Zen posture is sitting in a lotus position on a cushion on the floor, a chair can also be used. A primary requirement is correct back posture, which is straight but relaxed with a concavity in the small of the back. A great deal of emphasis is placed on comfortable body positioning so that the meditator is not distracted from the object of meditation. A type of swaying helps in determining each person's position of comfort. Eyes are kept lowered but open, breathing is through the nose and not the mouth, and thoughts are permitted to come and go without being entertained or pushed away. At the end of the meditation period, the person begins to sway back and forth and finally gets up and walks away.

Biofeedback

Clinical biofeedback emphasizes the attainment of a state of relaxed internal awareness, enabling the individual to identify and develop a harmony between mind and body. There are those who feel biofeedback is a panacea and others who dismiss biofeedback as quackery. Neither is accurate. Reliable research is lending increased legitimacy to biofeedback, prompting many health professionals to consider both its applications and limitations in clinical application.

Biofeedback is a process in which an individual's biological information is fed back in the form of visual or auditory information. Through electrodes attached to the skin, electronic sensors in the equipment pick up the minute signals produced by the physiological processes of the body. These signals are then amplified and converted into information that can be seen or heard, letting individuals know precisely how they are functioning. This process of using devices to detect signs of inner physiological activity is not new to health care, and some more common devices include the thermometer for determining temperature, the sphygmomanometer for reading blood pressure, and the electrocardiograph for monitoring heart activity. Biofeedback provides a communication link between the mental self and the physical self, making it possible to regulate and control a wide variety of physiological functions.

Biofeedback did not achieve significant clinical application until 1974, and since then, rapid innovations in biomedical technology have created an extensive potential for clinical biofeedback. There are numerous biofeedback instruments that are applied to specific disorders, such as temperature training for treatment of vascular migraine, or the galvanic skin response (GSR) for helping clients become sensitive to the interaction of emotions and physiological responses. More often a general approach involves an overall state of relaxation that can be manifested in many physiological systems simultaneously. Therefore it may be possible to use different instruments to produce the same response.

During a typical biofeedback training session small electrodes are attached to the skin over the frontal muscle of the client's forehead. Some people fear that they will be shocked by the electrodes or that the machine will do something to them; therefore explanation and reassurance should be repeated until the person is comfortable. The electrodes are connected to the machine, and the client is made comfortable in a quiet room. The following general instructions are given to each client.

Learning to reduce stress through biofeedback.
Photograph by Charles D. Davis.

The electrodes that are attached to your forehead measure the exact amount of muscle tension you are producing in your forehead muscles. Usually this tension reflects the tenseness throughout your body. The higher the pitch of the tone that you hear, the more tense your muscles are. You will need to determine what helps you relax and thereby lower the tone.

Initially the client may not be convinced that the tone is associated with tension; however, a relationship between movement and tone is soon recognized. Once this connection is made, the first step has been achieved in establishing the link between mind and body. With the help of the therapist the individual begins the next step of exploring the interaction between psychological events and physiological changes, which is a fascinating and rewarding process that should be explored thoroughly. At first the person limits this interaction to tightening and relaxing muscles or breathing exercises.

With encouragement from the therapist a more sophisticated understanding of the relationship between the mind and body is reached with the realization that thoughts affect tension. The person may discover that feelings of heaviness and warmth or visualizing pleasant scenes produce a greater depth of relaxation.

Biofeedback involves individual explorations of the subjective and physiological self. Part of the process is intuitive, and people can regulate certain biological functions without being able to verbally explain this control. Some people concentrate on rhythmic biological function such as breathing or heart rate, others flex and relax muscles, and a few engage in spontaneous visualization. Biofeedback is largely dependent on internal processes involving attention and attitudes, and what helps one person achieve relaxation may not benefit another.

As a more sophisticated understanding of mind

and body interaction is achieved, the person is able to remember and duplicate these sensations at any time throughout the day. The fundamental process of clinical biofeedback is realized when the person progresses from an unconscious to a conscious awareness of psychosomatic interaction and to being able to integrate this information into daily life.

Biofeedback works in conjunction with the person's physical, psychological, spiritual, and environmental needs. It is integrated into other therapeutic techniques when indicated by the physical and psychological factors of a disorder. Meditative or deep relaxation techniques help reinforce the specific skills learned through biofeedback and also encourage individuals to become reliant on their own biological systems rather than laboratory equipment. Although meditation and biofeedback achieve many of the same results, one major advantage of using biofeedback during initial treatment is that the specific biological function that needs to be corrected can be monitored. Through this instantaneous feedback, the process of alleviating the dysfunction is speeded.

Although the principles of biofeedback can be applied to any function that can be monitored, research has concentrated on areas such as electroencephalography (EEG), electrocardiography (ECG), electromyography (EMG), and thermal-sensor biofeedback. New biomedical technology continues to challenge the ingenuity and creativity of the client and the therapist with many more experimental applications in progress.

During EEG feedback brainwaves are monitored, and it has been shown that the occipital alpha wave associated with relaxation can be changed reliably. Although a relationship is made between relaxation and increased alpha levels, the question remains whether the alpha levels produce relaxation or simply accompany it. Alpha feedback has been used in pain control, with an abundance of alpha activity apparently helping an individual detach somewhat from the pain. Theta activity appears to exist between conscious and unconscious awareness and is thought to be important in imagery,

creativity, and integrative experiences. Personal growth becomes a new dimension of biofeedback.

With ECG, or heart-activity feedback, clients are surprised to learn that minor movements or breathing changes have a profound effect on the heart. Attempts to modify cardiovascular functions through ECG biofeedback continue although there is no evidence that clinical cardiovascular problems can be modified to any significant degree through biofeedback alone. Research with hypertension shows that individuals are able to obtain significant decreases in blood pressure in the laboratory; however, it is difficult to show persistence of lowered pressure outside the laboratory. Cardiovascular disorders remain a promising area of biofeedback research and investigation.

Perhaps the most extensive work has been done with EMG biofeedback, or muscle activity measurement. Muscle feedback is a potent tool in rehabilitating clients with paralysis or spasticity and is usually used in conjunction with other physical therapies. Training of muscle responses is accomplished by inserting needle electrodes into affected muscles, and by monitoring the electrical activity the individual is able to locate and improve control of these muscles. Even a minute change in a muscle can be registered on the EMG instrument, providing encouragement for further effort.

The use of EMG biofeedback for treatment of tension headache has been well demonstrated. Over 100 million people in the United States suffer from tension headaches, which they describe as a steady, dull, "bandlike" pain located in the occiput, or posterior region, often extending around to the forehead region. Tension headaches are believed to develop as a result of excessive activity in the muscles about the scalp, forehead, and neck. EMG feedback makes it possible for the individual to monitor and reduce the high EMG levels that are typically found among tension headache suffers. The use of feedback procedures for problems involving abnormal muscular tension has provided some of the most consistent results in the field of clinical biofeedback.

Encouraging results have also been found in applying thermal-sensor biofeedback for vascular disorders such as Raynaud's disease. Vasoconstriction is reduced if the person is able to raise the skin temperature in the affected extremity. Once this is achieved, circulation improves and symptoms diminish.

Approximately 20 million people in the United States suffer from migraine headaches, characterized by periodic localized or general vasodilation, which may be associated with nausea and vomiting. Whereas the tension headache is likely to occur early in the stress cycle, the vascular or migraine headache appears to be a rebound phenomenon occurring after the stressful period. It is theorized that as the stress diminishes, the extracranial arteries "rebound" into an exaggerated vasodilative state. When migraine subjects are trained to voluntarily "warm their hands" or raise the temperature of their hands through peripheral vasodilation, their headaches are often decreased or even eliminated. Individuals learn the technique while being monitored with thermal-sensor biofeedback, and following the initial laboratory training the client practices daily using a portable home unit until the same results can be achieved without feedback.

Typically clients with stress disorders are overresponders, and sometimes they tense up when they begin receiving feedback. Sometimes it helps to encourage clients to "let go" or "not try" and allow an internal quieting to gradually occur instead of striving so hard. It may be necessary to turn the feedback off from time to time until the client learns to maintain a low level of EMG activity with the feedback on. Once this is possible, the person can begin to use the feedback as a guide for reaching even lower levels of relaxation.

With deep relaxation the client may notice sensations of heaviness, warmth, tingling, drowsiness, floating, spinning, sinking, and changes in limb position or length. With gentle encouragement from the therapist, the client can learn to regard these sensations as indications of deep relaxation and use these same sensations as a guide in achieving this relaxed state without the use of biofeedback. Sometimes these sensations will trigger

memories from a past traumatic experience in which consciousness was forcefully changed in the body because of such happenings as a near-drowning experience, gas anesthesia, a fall, or accident. Clients may need to deal with the feelings associated with these memories before they can progress with deep relaxation. When this is done, the person is usually able to accept that these body sensations do not lead to traumatic past events but are signals of deep relaxation. If concern continues, clients can be instructed to eliminate these sensations by deep breathing, opening their eyes, or tensing muscles. Although relaxation will be less pronounced, this element of control may take away the frightening aspect of these sensations.

Biofeedback is a new medium of communication between the mind and the body. Through visual or auditory signals, the human body expresses emotional and mental messages that people can learn to respond to and control. Unless clients are properly motivated, they are not usually willing to spend the time to practice the technique until their learned response becomes habit. The effectiveness of biofeedback in treating chronic illness depends on the willingness of individuals to meet their physical and mental needs.

Visualization

Visualization is the process of forming and holding a mental image in the mind and is a central element in virtually all Eastern meditative techniques. Although spontaneous imageries occur frequently, they are seldom deliberately induced or even acknowledged. Under the guidance of a therapist an individual can learn to achieve focused awareness while remaining detached from thoughts and emotions characteristic of ordinary consciousness. Although the method is termed visualization, the individual does not have to have an actual visual image with which to work. Some people are able to visualize in color with a definite form and shape, whereas others see only a hint of a form. It is not necessary that there be a total visual image; in fact, some individuals use tactile, olfactory, or auditory senses. Deliberate visualization can be a technique for exploring psychosomatic interaction and inducing change in patterns of behavior. One theory for the success of visualization practices is that psychological energy follows patterns of thought, and it is hypothesized that this energy can be used for the purpose of self-healing.

The vanguards in the area of visualization and psychosomatic medicine are undoubtedly Simonton, a radiation oncologist and his wife, Matthews-Simonton.[8] Their application of meditative and visualization medical techniques is used in addition to intensive psychotherapy and traditional treatment. They emphasize the treatment of the whole person, including the psychological factors involved in the development of the disease. The Simontons theorize that illness is prompted by emotional needs that are not being met in an individual's life. They maintain that people have a personal responsibility for the development of disease and the capabilities of affecting the cure. By involving the client, the family, and the physician, the Simontons help clients meet their emotional needs other than through the secondary gains from illness.

During relaxation and imagery clients are taught to visualize their disease, their treatment, and their white blood cells. Once they are able to make changes in their lives to get in touch with what caused life to lose its meaning, the clients are able to visualize their treatment and their immunological system destroying the cancer cells. A positive attitude about the outcome of treatment and the fact that clients can visualize themselves as healthy is a greater determination of positive disease outcome than is the severity of the illness.

The Simontons' integration of traditional and psychosomatic approach has shown a dramatic effect on the disease process. Because of the controversial nature of their approaches, they are confronted with issues of scientific proof for their theories. They do not maintain that psychotherapy and stress reduction cure cancer but rather that they are invaluable adjuncts to standard treatment. Research continues, although a large number of variables, including the subtle processes of imagery and emotion, are involved.

Therapeutic touch

Therapeutic touch is an act of healing or helping that is gaining more recognition in nursing through the efforts of Krieger and others. Used in addition to standard medical and nursing practices, touch has been proven to be a powerful therapeutic tool. The basis for the interaction between the client and the healer is the concept that the healthy person has an excess of energy and the ill person has a deficit. During therapeutic touch a transfer of excess energy takes place.

Before therapeutic touch can be effective, the healer must have an intent to help or heal and must also have a fairly healthy body. Although clients do not need to believe in therapeutic touch, they do need to have an open mind about the procedure and a genuine desire to be well.

At the onset of the technique the healer enters a meditative state and slowly moves his or her hands over the client's body, keeping a distance of a few inches from the skin. A different sensation is noted over areas that are not healthy, and the healer then redirects energy in these areas.

Studies demonstrate that clients who received therapeutic touch produce significantly higher hemoglobin levels than control groups who receive routine nursing care without therapeutic touch. However, the most renowned healers do not claim a cure rate above 30 percent, which is consistent with placebo effect.

Whatever the reason for client improvement, therapeutic touch has been proven effective in lowering temperatures, speeding healing, and reducing pain. Whether it is the transfer of energy or the reduction in anxiety, therapeutic touch maximizes a client's natural recuperative powers. Learning to potentiate an energy for self-healing is in itself a significant contribution to medicine.

•   •   •

The mind, emotions, and the body act as a unit, and when the physical and psychological needs of the individual are not met, illness results. Anxiety states are accompanied by incessant sympathetic arousal, which is likely to produce stress-related disorders. Stressors do not cause illness, but rather the person's response to stressors permits an illness to take place. People have a choice as to how they respond to stress, and some have learned that when warning signals of stress are observed, it is time to back off, ease up, and put off today what can be done tomorrow.

There is substantial evidence that stress and feelings of hopelessness can tip the balance of life toward death. Many techniques are available to help individuals listen to and respond to their body's needs and to maximize personal resources in promoting and maintaining health. Many people believe they have no control over their health, leaving this responsibility in the hands of medical personnel. The emphasis is then placed on technology rather than the resources within the person, and illness is viewed as a technical problem rather than a personal challenge. Techniques viewed with awe and skepticism today may be understood through the research of tomorrow. Unfortunately, people often criticize what they do not understand, and what is criticized is difficult to accept. Years ago it was recognized that teachers with high expectations produced a sharp rise in student IQs. Perhaps it is time to also recognize the potential of the client in the health care system.

REFERENCES

1. Betz, B., and Thomas, C.: Individual temperament as a predictor of health or premature disease, The Johns Hopkins Medical Journal **114**(3):81, 1979.
2. Friedman, M., and Rosenman, R.: Type A behavior and your heart, New York, 1974, Alfred A. Knopf, Inc.
3. Holmes, T., and Rahe, R.: The social readjustment rating scale, Journal of Psychosomatic Research **11**:213, 1967.
4. Orem, D.: Nursing: concepts of practice, ed. 2, New York, 1980, McGraw-Hill Book Co.
5. Schmale, A., and Iker, H.: Hopelessness as a predictor of cervical cancer, Social Science and Medicine **5**:95, 1971.
6. Selye, H.: Stress without distress, Philadelphia, 1974, J.B. Lippincott Co.
7. Simonton, O., and Matthews-Simonton, S.: Cancer and stress counselling the cancer patient, The Medical Journal of Australia **1**:679, 1981.
8. Simonton, O., and Mathews-Simonton, S.: Belief systems and management of the emotional aspects of malignancy, Journal of Transpersonal Psychology **7**(1):29, 1975.
9. Volicer, B., and Bohannon, M.: A hospital stress rating scale, Nursing Research **24**:352, 1975.
10. Wyler, A., Masuda, M., and Holmes, T.: Magnitude of life events and seriousness of illness, Psychosomatic Medicine **33**:115, 1971.

BIBLIOGRAPHY

Bahnson, M., and Bahnson, C.: Ego defenses in cancer patients, Annals of the New York Academy of Sciences **164**:546, 1969.
Derogatis, L., Abeloff, M., and Melisaratos, N.: Psychological coping mechanisms and survival time in metastatic breast cancer, JAMA **242**:1504, 1979.
Friedman, M.: The modification of type A behavior in post-infarction patients, American Heart Journal **97**:551, 1979.
Garant, C.: Stalls in the therapeutic process, American Journal of Nursing, **80**:2166, 1980.
Goldfarb, C., Driesen, J., and Cole, D.: Psychophysiologic aspects of malignancy, American Journal of Psychiatry **123**:1545, 1967.
Greene, W.: The psychosocial setting of the development of leukemia and lymphoma. In Weyer, E., and Hutchins, H., editors: Psychophysiological aspects of cancer, New York, 1966, New York Academy of Sciences.
Kissen, D.: Personality characteristics in males conducive to lung cancer, British Journal of Medical Psychology **36**:27, 1963.
Krieger, D.: Therapeutic touch: searching for evidence of psychological change, American Journal of Nursing **79**:660, 1979.
Lazarus, R.: A cognitively oriented psychologist looks at biofeedback, American Psychologist, **30**:553, 1975.
LeShan, L.: An emotional life history pattern associated with neoplastic disease, Annals of the New York Academy of Sciences **125**:780, 1966.
Pelletier, K.: Mind as healer, mind as slayer: a holistic approach to preventing stress disorders, New York, 1977, Dell Publishing Co., Inc.
Simonton, O., Matthews-Simonton, S., and Sparks, T.: Psychological intervention in the treatment of cancer, Psychosomatics **21**:226, 1980.
Solomon, G., Amkraut, A., and Kasper, P.: Immunity, emotions, and stress: with special reference to the mechanisms of stress effects on the immune system, Annals of Clinical Research **6**:313, 1974.
Thomas, C., and Duszynski, K.: Closeness to parents and the family constellation in a prospective study of five disease states: suicide, mental illness, malignant tumor, hypertension and coronary heart disease, The Johns Hopkins Medical Journal **134**:251, 1974.

8 · The pain experience

People react differently to the pain experienced by others.

Illustration by Tom Weinman.

ated, and integrated within the cortex, and this interpretation is then modified and influenced by cultural, psychological, and social factors. The total process determines if a stimulus will be perceived as painful and how much discomfort will be associated with the stimulus.

Laboratories are able to measure some components of pain; however, laboratory conclusions are not always applicable in a clinical setting. Different situations bring about different reactions, and controlled experimental conditions with artificially produced pain may prompt responses unlike those experienced when the condition is pathological and without parameters.

Because care givers are unable to feel, see, or touch another's pain, they must rely on subjective interpretation rather than having an objective evaluation from which to work. While one care giver is able to accept a client's interpretation, another may decide that the client is malingering. The most therapeutic attitude toward anyone with pain is also an operational definition of pain: "Pain is whatever the experiencing person says it is, existing whenever he says it does."[9]

> It is the client who teaches the health professional about pain.
> These lessons are taught while the pain is alive.
> Once it is gone,
> The process of denying and forgetting alters the memory.
> This compromise occurs with the care giver as well as with the client,
> For pain is a reality that begs to be remembered as less.

THE CONCEPT OF PAIN

Pain is a complex phenomenon that is one of the most difficult problems to deal with in health care. Because the experience of pain is unique to each person, it eludes definition. Pain can be described as a warning to actual or impending tissue damage; however, the reaction is not necessarily proportional to the stimulus, and pain may continue after the danger is gone or damaged tissue has healed. Messages surrounding pain communicate far more than danger or damage to tissue and may include such messages as "I'm afraid," "It's all my fault," and "Now I don't have to go to work." Some of the pain reported by those who are lonely, elderly, or terminally ill may be an attempt to establish a valid reason for continued contact with health professionals.

Many events take place in the brain between the reception of a sensory impulse and the response to this stimulus. The sensation is compared, evalu-

Responding to pain

Just as the experience of pain is unique to each individual, the word "pain" has different interpretations. Some clients deny having pain, but they say that there is pressure, discomfort, or even an ache. Nausea or being unable to rest may be the presenting complaint although the underlying problem is pain. A more accurate appraisal may be obtained if the person is questioned about the presence of discomfort rather than pain.

Although some people are able or willing to tolerate more pain than others, studies do demonstrate that the point at which pain is perceived—the pain threshold level—is relatively uniform among people. The tolerance or reaction level varies with individuals, and the same person will have different tolerances at different times. Sociocultural and psychological factors contribute to pain tolerance and response to the pain experience.

Some people withdraw and want to be alone

when pain becomes severe. They may have their own methods of handling pain that require being alone, or perhaps aloneness protects them from showing an emotional response. Privacy allows the individual to release emotions that they are uncomfortable expressing in the company of another. One man commented that about the only thing in his life that he had any control over were his emotions. "I've never bawled in front of anyone yet, and I'm not going to start now." When the client does cry in front of medical personnel, it is necessary to determine if the tears are an emotional release or a request for pain relief, reassurance, or attention.

Many men in the United States have been taught since childhood to be brave and not cry, and therefore they do not have the freedom that women do to express pain or the accompanying feelings. There is also a certain amount of social stigma attached to complaining about pain—particularly chronic pain. As one client said, "People have their own problems and are not interested in someone else's pain. Besides, I don't want others to think that I'm a hypochondriac or a complainer." Sincere interest, genuine sensitivity, and emotional support are necessary before the client has the security to share anxieties and perceived losses associated with pain.

Although it is assumed that the hospitalized client will report any pain, this is not necessarily so. Some clients believe that the nurse will automatically bring around pain medication whenever the physician orders it. The person may have been told to report any pain, but the only thing remembered may be phrases such as, "After surgery, we'll be giving you something to keep you comfortable," or "I'll leave orders for pain medication." This type of misunderstanding can be prevented by frequently checking with the client regarding discomfort and restating the importance of reporting any discomfort before it becomes severe.

Pain medications are more effective when they are administered with information regarding the action, timing, and a positive suggestion that the medication will work. Too often the client waits until the pain is severe before asking for pain relief,

and because the person is in misery, it seems like an eternity before the nurse arrives on the spot with the medication. By then the client is not receptive to anything but "Give it to me!" The anxiety and the pain have interacted until it is unlikely that one dose of analgesic will take away the pain.

If the client is having a great deal of pain or is overly anxious, it is necessary that the nurse stay with the person for awhile. Pain is an all-encompassing experience, and sometimes just having someone to be with helps to mitigate the isolation of pain. A backrub helps to facilitate relaxation while providing the therapeutic benefits of touch itself. Perhaps the most important message the nurse can convey is that the client is significant enough to warrant both time and concern.

Acute versus chronic pain

Acute pain is identified as pain that lasts less than 6 months and is usually caused by injury or organic disease. The pain serves as a warning that something is wrong and action should be taken, and once healing has taken place, the pain subsides and ultimately disappears. When acute pain is of low to moderate intensity and superficial in origin, the sympathetic nervous system temporarily produces increased blood pressure, heart rate, respiratory rate, and muscle tension, which may return to normal in minutes without change in pain intensity. Pain more severe in intensity or visceral in origin affects the parasympathetic system, depressing vital functions such as blood pressure and heart rate. This parasympathetic response is often accompanied by nausea, vomiting, weakness, and fainting.

The physical signs of acute pain may be reflected in the client's appearance, behavior, posture, and gestures. The face may be anxious, tense, and distressed. Fists may be clenched. The person may be writhing and restless or may lie very still and rigid. The absence of visible signs of pain does not, however, negate the presence of pain.

It is not difficult to accept that an individual is experiencing pain if behavior associated with acute pain is observed and if there is a known physical

Chronic pain diminishes both the quality and quantity of meaningful living.

Illustration by Tom Weinman.

stimulus such as trauma or a malignancy. Almost invariably, acute pain is used as the model for all pain, and the difficulty then arises when there are no observable symptoms and no diagnosed causality.

Chronic pain lasts for 6 months or longer. It may be pain that will end following a lengthy healing process or with death. The pain may be intermittent or continual and with or without a known pathology. Some practitioners delineate chronic pain into the categories of limited, intermittent, and persistent. Limited pain is identified as pain caused by a known pathology that will end with healing or with death. Intermittent pain leaves the individual free of discomfort at times, and the cause may or may not be known. Persistent pain is almost continual, and although the pathology—if it is known—does not threaten life, the pain is persistent despite treatment. Sometimes persistent pain is also called intractable pain, prolonged pain, or chronic benign pain.

With chronic pain the body adapts physiologically to the painful stimuli and will probably not produce any changes in vital signs. Fatigue, distractions, and other factors may make it possible for the individual to control or minimize voluntary expressions of pain. Although there are indications of physiological tolerance, the person psychologically builds an intolerance to pain, creating a vicious cycle of pain and depression. Chronic pain robs from both functional and cognitive abilities. Eating, resting, and sleeping become more problematic, and the quality and quantity of meaningful life diminish. Depression and irritability circumvent existence. Socialization diminishes, and the person becomes virtually isolated in a prison of pain that frequently dictates life. The two wishes of the person in chronic pain are "Please believe that I have pain. Please make the pain go away." Too frequently what is not understood is negated. Unfortunately, this premise does not benefit the person with chronic pain.

Psychological factors

All pain has psychological components, but it is very rare to have psychological pain without accompanying organic changes. There are cases in which psychological factors are not secondary to pain but the cause of the pain. Sometimes depression, anxiety, guilt, or fear masquerades as a pain syndrome. Unable to attend to these feelings, the person subconsciously projects them onto pain that can elicit sympathy, provide control over others, allow dependence, relieve responsibilities, or protect against criticism. Unlike the malingerer who feigns pain, the individual with psychogenic pain hurts as much as the person whose pain has an organic basis. Unfortunately, it is only after repeated patterns of emotional upheavals followed by vague medical problems that the possibility of psychogenic pain is considered. Realistically, a psychiatric evaluation should be included in any chronic pain evaluation, even those with documented organic basis. In pain centers a psychiatrist is part of the team and sees each client routinely, and there is no stigma associated with the visit. Chronic pain causes any number of changes in a person's life, and psychiatric help may be one of the most important services made available to the person. Too frequently the psychiatrist is a last resort, and by then the client is unreasonably defensive and the maladaptive behavior has been repeated enough times that he or she is resistant to change.

■ Jane was in her last semester of college when she began to have headaches severe enough to impair her vision. She was a good student who placed a lot of emphasis on a high grade point, but because of her headaches, she was having trouble keeping up in her classes. A complete diagnostic evaluation failed to reveal an organic cause for her pain. Jane's physician suggested that she drop two of her courses to lighten her study load, and although this would make it necessary for Jane to attend another semester of college, she reluctantly agreed. Within a few weeks the headaches were virtually gone. Jane continued to feel well, until once again she was in her last semester of college and the headaches returned. When a second diagnostic evaluation failed to reveal organic causality, she was sent to see a psychiatrist. After two visits it was determined that the headaches were not related to class work but rather to her graduating and leaving the protected life-style of college for one of self-support. It was necessary for Jane to deal with her displaced fears before she was able to be free of pain and finish the requirements necessary for her degree. _____

Psychological factors can influence expectations, responses, and actual sensations of pain. For some people pain becomes a way of coping with emotionally traumatic situations in life. Before the pain can be eliminated, it is necessary for the person to unmask the pain and deal with the underlying emotional problems.

Sociocultural factors

There are many sociocultural factors that influence the expression of pain. Some people respond to pain by remaining calm or trying not to let their discomfort show, and others moan and cry out for pain relief. Age, sex, occupation, religion, and body parts involved may prompt different reaction patterns. Cultural conditioning will also affect whether curative or palliative treatment is sought and how long the pain is endured before this treatment is requested.

A member of a minority group that has been deprived educationally, economically, and occupationally is usually hesitant to ask for pain relief and will usually delay seeking medical help until an emergency state exists. Once in the hospital, there is conflict between wanting and distrusting help, and the person may submit to care without asking for information. This client is characteristically present-oriented out of necessity and may not comply with lengthy treatment.

Members of almost every culture will respond differently when pain involves the genitalia or rectum. Factors that influence the client's confidence include the care giver's age, sex, and perceived competency. Because the physician is seen as the one capable of cure, usually clients will hide any embarrassment and tell their physician about pain involving ''private'' parts of their body. However, since people are more comfortable sharing personal information with someone of the same age group and sex, this information may be presented to the nurse rather than the physician. A care giver of the opposite sex, particularly one who is young, may inhibit a client from communicating concerns involving either genitalia or rectum. Therefore an older female client is unlikely to tell a young male nurse that she is having ''female problems.'' Instead, if the physician is not available, this information may be given to an older nurse.

To members of each culture, their ways, behavior, and attitudes are the correct ones. Medical personnel are more receptive to clients when they understand that people respond in a certain way because their behavior has been reinforced by their culture. For the client the behavior is right, and acceptance of this behavior is a prerequisite in providing helpful care.

MEANING OF PAIN

The way people react to pain depends on how they perceive it as being a threat in their lives. The three categories of psychological stressors include injury or threat of injury, loss or threat of loss, and frustration of drives.[7] These experiences are easier to assimilate into a person's life if they can be dealt with intellectually and emotionally. Therefore being able to find some meaning in pain enables a

person to deal with the experience consciously and rationally. Unfortunately, this meaning cannot be ascribed by another. It is sometimes a slow and frustrating process that professionals can facilitate by listening as clients attempt to incorporate psychological stressors into their lives.

Injury or threat of injury

Pain often serves as a warning of injury or threatened injury, and when pain results from an unknown cause, it may be more threatening than when the cause is known. Perhaps this is the result of a tendency to believe that if the cause is known and labeled, a cure can be achieved. It is not unlike hearing a strange noise in the middle of the night, and until the source of the noise is located and attended to, all sorts of causes are imagined.

Chronic pain is sometimes without known parameters, such as cause, implications, or expected duration. This ambiguity procedures fear and anxiety that can be every bit as painful as physical pain. ''The hurt begins long before I feel the pain,'' one client commented. ''It's the fear of unbearable pain that causes infinite suffering.''

Prior to impending pain experiences, information helps to remove the threat of the unknown. An honest discussion on what to anticipate and what can be done to alleviate any discomfort helps in reducing anxiety. A client should be instructed on the ''whys'' and ''hows'' of activities that may be painful but necessary, such as coughing to clear the lungs following surgery. If practice precedes the actual event, clients are more willing to carry out these activities when pain is involved.

Professional judgment is necessary in determining how early and how much information should be presented to the client. Too much too soon will increase rather than reduce anxiety. A client who turns away when information is presented or refuses to attend preoperative classes or view teaching films may benefit more from a brief forewarning and minimal detail. The client may comment, ''Everybody is trying to scare me to death.'' Rather than overwhelming the individual with information, the care giver may provide a brief explanation, followed by questions such as ''What concerns you the most?'' and ''What questions do you have?'' which help focus information in the areas of concern.

Loss or threat of loss

A loss or threatened loss prompts a grief response with feelings of despair, helplessness, hopelessness, and powerlessness. This reactive depression can be in response to the loss of a body part or the failure of a body part to function, and grief responses are also experienced when a person is no longer able to function in his or her accustomed role. Energy depletion from dealing with persistent pain makes it difficult to deal with problems of everyday life. Losses extend into the future as medical expenses rob savings, and dreams once shared are no longer realistic. It is understandable that pain can be intensified by the knowledge that the diseases producing the pain could ultimately cause death. Chronic debilitating pain may also threaten the desire to remain alive. Such were the feelings of a young woman with chronic pain who questioned the reason for her existence. She shared these thoughts.

■ I wanted to live, but because there was so much love, I wanted to relieve my family of a sick, hurting, dependent mother. A soft-spoken psychiatrist stood at my bedside and listened to me talk about my family and the wonderful times we had shared together. I cried for the good times I believed we would never share again. People often refer to psychiatrists as shrinks. Maybe this is an accurate name, for sometimes they are able to shrink problems into a manageable size. He made me realize that my death would create far more psychological problems for my family than my ill health could cause. By being alive, I was able to listen to my family, share their good and their bad, and contribute the love of a wife and mother.

The quiet depression slowly changed into a rage of anger. This alien, worn-out, hurting, sick body was now mine. Worse yet was the isolation of a serious illness as it slowly reduces the world to a blank ceiling and four empty walls. I needed to find a reason—a meaning—something to help me find the exit out of this nightmare. _____

With psychiatric help, this woman was able to move beyond her depression toward the task of ascribing meaning to the pain that had so drastically changed her life.

Frustration of drives

All the basic drives are affected by pain. Clients suffer from fatigue because their sleep is interrupted. Anorexia, nausea, and vomiting are often side effects of pain, treatments, or medications. Sexual needs and the need to be held close by another human being are often not satisfied. Depression and decreased self-esteem contribute to further isolation. Without help from caring people, many of these manageable side effects of pain are left to exaggerate the pain out of proportion.

Pain treatment for acute or chronic pain needs to be initiated before the pain reaches a high intensity. Many times it is indicated that analgesics be administered on a scheduled basis to prevent pain rather than being administered when necessary in response to pain. A change in position, back rubs, warm baths, and relaxation techniques can help potentiate the pain medication. Analgesics, hypnotics, and sedatives may be critical in ensuring proper rest. Antiemetics given with analgesics help reduce nausea, and when they are administered so that the client is comfortable during meals, eating becomes more enjoyable. Smaller servings are more appealing to the small appetite, and when permitted, special food from home helps to pique an interest in eating.

In adults pain may prompt childhood memories of punishment, rejection, and the need to be held, comforted, and reassured by a loved one. Physical contact fosters a feeling of self-worth, something that is often lacking in a person with chronic pain. When a person is hospitalized, close physical contact with a loved one is seldom realized. Privacy is not assured, and people feel conspicuous holding each other in front of others. Children are more willing to assert their needs and it is not uncommon to find a hospitalized child sleeping soundly next to a parent on a roll-away bed rather than in the hospital bed. One older man who was hospitalized asked if his wife could sleep beside him in his bed. "I know I could rest better if she were here. We've slept together for 50 years." The nurse responded, "I'll have a roll-away brought in so if the bed gets too small, you wife will have someplace else to sleep."

The meaning an individual attributes to pain is influenced by the way the psychological stressors associated with the pain are perceived. Beecher[1] compared badly wounded solders with civilian clients and found that the pain perception threshold of the wartime casualities was dramatically higher than the civilians. He determined that the intensity of suffering was determined by what the pain meant to the individual, and whereas the civilians perceived their wounds as a threat, the solders saw their injuries as a reprieve from threat. The civilian group required several times more pain medication than did the military group.

Copp[4] interviewed 148 hospitalized persons who were experiencing pain and asked what their pain meant to them. Their responses are categorized in Table 8-1. Over one fourth of those interviewed were able to report value in their pain experience. Some looked at their pain as a challenge to overcome; others considered pain an expression of their weakness. Pain was also interpreted as punishment with some redeeming aspects.

The intensity of discomfort an individual percieves is affected by the meaning of the pain. Fear magnifies pain, and through factual information much of the fear and fantasy surrounding pain can be reduced or eliminated. When primary, palliative, and symptomatic treatments are combined with thoughtful care and perceptive attentiveness, caring professionals can help clients find meaning in a meaningless situation and hope in the midst of hopelessness.

Table 8-1. Meaning of pain

Percentage of respondents	Description of pain
26%	Reported value in the pain experience, with strong religious connotations expressed by many.
22%	Described pain as a struggle, fight, and something to overcome.
13%	Described pain as a punishment with some redeeming aspects.
11%	Described pain and suffering as a challenge with positive effects on their future health
10%	Described pain as a personal weakness.

Modified from Copp, L.: The spectrum of suffering, American Journal of Nursing **74:**491, 1974.

POWER OF THE PLACEBO

The faith healer lit a candle and moved it slowly over the woman's body, up and down, and then across from hand to hand. While brushing the woman's body with a branch to sweep out the illness, she prayed and called for the woman to be whole again. The woman suddenly sensed a feeling of calmness and knew that she was well.

A young Congo native was warned by a wizard not to eat wild hen or death would follow. As a joke a friend gave him wild hen, telling him it was a different fowl. The young man ate it and enjoyed it. Two years later the friend laughingly revealed his secret. Overcome with fear, the young man died 24 hours later.[2]

Lizard's blood, crocodile dung, flesh of vipers, bat wings, and a variety of foul-smelling potions are among the formularies that have been prompting curative powers since ancient Egyptian times. For thousands of years physicians prescribed useless medications that helped many of their clients. The benefits had to come from the placebo effect, for it is now known that many of these medications were not only useless but often dangerous. The "miraculous" cures of faith healers and quack physicians are believed to be credited to the physiological mechanisms involved in the placebo effect. It is an effect that has been documented to improve such conditions as rheumatoid arthritis, depression, vertigo, gastrointestinal disorders, angina, hypertension, bronchitis, and allergies and can be prompted by something as simple as a sympathetic bedside manner.

Defining the placebo

Placebo is a Latin word meaning "I will please." The fascinating phenomenon of the placebo effect is brought about by implicit or explicit intent and is a response to a substance that is inert or a procedure that is without intrinsic therapeutic value. The effectiveness of a placebo depends on the person's belief that the substance or procedure will be beneficial. Various drug studies have demonstrated that although a placebo is an inactive substance, it is between 30 and 60 percent as effective as the active medication with which it is compared.

Although placebos are usually thought of as substances given as medications, procedures can also bring about a placebo response. Perhaps one of the most dramatic examples that can be given involving procedure as a placebo deals with a surgical treatment for angina pectoris that was popular during the early 1940s. The procedure consisted of ligation of internal mammary arteries to increase the blood flow to the heart, and spectacular results showed that the majority of the clients experienced marked symptomatic relief. A skeptical surgeon decided to perform a sham operation, and after the client was anesthetized the incision was made but the arteries were not tied. The results were equally as good as when the arteries were ligated. Several studies followed in which subjects agreed to evaluate a surgical procedure for relief of angina, and both the ligated and the nonligated subjects reported significant improvement. Ultimately it was determined that benefits from internal mammary artery ligation were not caused by the ligation but

by a placebo response, and the surgical procedure was discontinued.

Placebo response is prompted by something other than physical or pharmacodynamic effect, and an important element in the production of the placebo response is the relationship between the care giver and the client. For example, many studies have pointed out that nurses can significantly reduce the number of clients who vomit postoperatively by simply giving clients more reassurance before surgery. This is a placebo response not prompted by substance or procedure but by a relationship with the nurse that increased the psychological well-being of the client. Studies have also proven that the therapeutic results of surgery can be influenced by the enthusiasm or skepticism of the surgeon.

Unfortunately, the placebo response is often not understood, and the person who responds to a placebo is considered to have feigned the problem. Because of the negative attitudes surrounding placebos, this self-healing capability within each person has not received the attention or the enhancement that it deserves. This potential needs to be understood and nurtured and it is within this frame of reference that placebo actions will be pursued further.

Behind the placebo response

Research during the past 50 years has begun to document some of the mechanisms of mind over matter. At one time it was believed that there was a relationship between the amount of tissue damage and the intensity of pain. However, as Beecher pointed out, only 25 percent of the badly wounded men in his study complained of pain or requested pain medication. Apparently these men were so euphoric at simply having survived, their joy apparently blocked out their pain. Beecher[1] compared these statistics with a group of civilian men undergoing surgery and found that 80 percent wanted pain medication although they had far less tissue damage than the soldiers.

In 1965 Melzack and Wall hypothesized that the body's interpretation of and response to painful stimuli were dependent on a gatelike mechanism that opened to admit pain impulses or closed to block them. According to their theory, many factors were involved in deciding whether the gate stays open or shut. For example, positive emotions such as excitement or pleasure tend to close the gate, whereas negative emotions such as anxiety and apprehension are more likely to open it.

The next major discovery occurred in 1970, when opiate receptor sites were discovered on the cell membrane in the human brain. These sites were considered analogous to the ''gate'' theorized by Melzack and Wall because these receptors regulated what entered and exited from the cell. It was not until 1975 that natural opiate painkillers were discovered and found to be more potent than morphine in binding to the receptors in the brain. The discovery of endorphin, or endogenous morphine, supplied the missing link in the puzzle of pain.

The research done with endorphins sheds more light on the biochemical phenomena of the placebo. In 1975 Levine and others[8] postulated that placebos reduce pain by causing the body to release its own natural morphine, endorphins. Their study to test this hypothesis involved 51 individuals who had undergone dental surgery for extraction of molars. Each person received a placebo, morphine, or the morphine antagonist, naloxone. Those receiving naloxone reported significantly more pain than those who had received a placebo. Next, those who had received a placebo were given naloxone. Persons who had reported pain relief from the placebo reported increased pain following naloxone administration. It was concluded that the placebo responders had released endorphins—their own natural morphine—and the action of the endorphins was blocked by the naloxone.

It is theorized that the placebo motivation or suggestion is received by the temporal lobe of the brain in which memories of past experiences interact and influence the hypothalamus. From the hypothalamus the message travels to the pituitary gland, causing the release of hormones, and one of these hormones may be the substance called endorphin. It is also proposed that endorphins exert a wide-range effect by stimulating any of a number of natural healing mechanisms in the body, such as interferon, which fights viral infections, and steroids, which counter inflammation. Perhaps future research will reveal an endogenous chemical similar to naloxone that props the ''gate'' open to pain or prevents individuals from healing themselves. The effectiveness of placebos provides dramatic support for the holistic view that the mind and body are too closely interwoven to be treated as independent entities.

Placebo phenomena

Many health professionals know little about placebos and tend to use them for the wrong reasons. Too often the administration of a placebo is considered a test to see if the client's pain is real or imagined, and supposedly if the placebo works, the pain was imagined. First of all, pain still hurts whether the cause is organic or psychogenic. People who gain relief from placebos are those who believe the prescribed medicine will benefit them. It is only after continuous use that the placebo may lose its effectiveness for pain control.

Some care givers believe that it is the malingerer or the whiner who is most susceptible to placebos; however, investigators point out that placebo responders are not unique since anywhere from 30 to 90 percent of all clients will respond to placebos. Responders are not typically men or women, young or old, or persons with a specific personality profile but all kinds of people with different illnesses in a variety of settings.

Not only have placebos been proven effective in helping clients feel better psychologically but they have also been proven to help the clients improve physically by enhancing the curative mechanisms of the body. This points out the tremendous need to educate the public about the powers within the body. If the client or the care giver believes that a drug will work, clients are apt to respond to the drug plus the additional benefit from the placebo effect. The converse is also true. If clients are given sleeping pills but are told that the medication will make them jittery and keep them awake, it is likely that the individuals will counteract the pharmacological effect of the medication and respond the way they were told the drug would affect them.

Medical personnel may also underestimate the power of the placebo, maintaining that it cannot harm the client. Toxic reactions can occur with the administration of the placebo, and many of the complaints clients share about side effects of a drug may be caused by the placebo effect rather than the drug. Researchers are very familiar with participants who complain of dry mouth, nausea, drowsiness, and rashes only to discover that the person was taking a placebo and not an active drug. In some cases anaphylactic reactions have been reported. Physiological changes brought about by a placebo must be taken into account whenever drug studies are designed. This is why a drug being studied is compared with a placebo that appears similar and is administered in the same way, rather than comparing it with no drug at all.

Rather than thinking of a placebo as a sugar pill or an injection of saline, it is more accurate to consider a placebo as a potential for self-healing that is within each person. Members of the medical team act as a catalyst in encouraging this response, which then potentiates the therapeutic action of medications or procedures. Once placebo response is fully understood, the dispensing of medications or the completion of procedures changes from being a ritual or a technique to a therapeutic interaction affecting the effectiveness of all medications and all procedures.

STEPS TOWARD COMFORT

Many clients report that one of the most difficult aspects of hospitalization is depending on someone else for pain control and waiting until it is time before the medication can be administered. Unfortunately, pain does not delay for either. Clients who have had previous hospitalizations often sneak medications into the hospital to help them through the times when pain medications are inadequate or the interval between dosages is too long. An un-

forgettable case from years ago is still vivid today. A dying man was in pain, and on the back of his tissue box he kept track of the hours until it was time for his pain medication. Four marks equaled four hours, and a line drawn through marks indicated an injection. He kept his records carefully dated and painfully accurate. He left behind a legacy of endless pain that had been created out of fear of narcotic addiction.

Today it is known that pain medication scheduled to prevent pain is more effective than administering pain medication to relieve pain, and fear of addiction is never justification for leaving a dying person in pain.

Analgesia at the bedside

Clients hospitalized with chronic pain associated with malignant disease were probably the first to be permitted analgesics at the hospital bedside. Many of these clients have handled their own medications at home, and since there was a great deal of anxiety associated with depending on others for pain relief, it seemed reasonable that self-medication should be considered. In 1979 a pilot program was initiated on a 32-bed neurooncology unit at a cancer center in New York. To be included in such a program the individuals are evaluated according to their alertness, judgment, physical capability of administering their own medications, and willingness to participate in the program. When accepted, the client and the client's family receive information concerning the purpose and goals of the program. The goals for the client include (1) active participation in pain control, (2) demonstration of basic understanding of the principles of analgesic use, and (3) implementation of a self-medication routine that can be continued after the client is discharged from the hospital.

To understand the principles of pain control the clients and family members learn about effects and side effects of analgesics and the rationale for combination drug use. They also learn about therapeutic plasma levels, tolerance, and physical dependency. Before individuals are given the responsibility of administering their own medications, they must demonstrate ability and confidence in taking and recording medications.

Once this competency has been determined, the nurse and client fill out a standard medication Kardex, which is kept at the bedside, and it is the responsibility of the client to keep this recording sheet up to date. The nurse leaves a 24-hour supply of analgesics in a container at the client's bedside, and clients on the around-the-clock regimen are given the choice of using an alarm clock or being awakened by the night nurse to take medications. Any narcotics are signed out on the narcotic record, noting that the client is on a self-medication program. At the end of each shift the medication nurse reviews the client's recording sheet and compares the number of pills recorded as taken with the number remaining in the container. This information is then transcribed into the official Medex. New medications, their actions, and side effects are also discussed with the client as well as reasons for change. When clients are no longer able to administer their own medications, they are removed from the program. Included in this group are those who have had surgery, require injections, or are too debilitated to be responsible for analgesics at the bedside.

Clients who have participated in a program of self-medication report decreased anxiety and pain and an increased feeling of self-esteem and control. They comment that they feel less dependent and more like participants in pain control.[5]

Continuous drip narcotics

Continuous drip narcotics were first introduced for clients who failed to respond to conventional methods of pain treatment. Clients receiving continuous intravenous narcotics are evaluated as being more alert and coherent, less short of breath, and less anxious than clients who receive conventional administration of narcotics. The rationale behind this pain treatment is that lower doses of drug are necessary to provide uniform and better pain control and these lowered dosages also result in fewer side effects for the client. Continuous drip narcotics are indicated when adequate relief cannot be obtained by oral, intramuscular, subcutaneous, or rectal analgesia.

A number of institutions have performed trials of intravenous narcotics, and in most studies this pain treatment has been limited to clients who cannot take medications orally and when intramuscular or subcutaneous injections are contraindicated because of prolonged pain. In 1980 a hospital in London initiated a study comparing different methods of administrating morphine and the effectiveness of each method in alleviating postoperative pain. Forty-five clients received a slow intravenous injection of morphine until their pain was relieved, and then they were divided into three groups to receive either continuous intravenous morphine, regularly scheduled intramuscular injections, or intramuscular injections when necessary. Clients administered continuous intravenous morphine received between 28 and 63 mg of morphine during 72 hours to maintain analgesia. This amount is compared with 72-hour dosages of 90 to 160 mg of morphine administered intramuscularly on a regularly scheduled basis and 80 to 280 mg of morphine administered whenever necessary. Clients receiving continuous intravenous morphine required considerably less drug than the other regimens and also achieved better pain relief.[10]

Client-controlled narcotics

Past studies have pointed out that conventional narcotic dosing strategies provide poor control for some clients and excessive sedation in others. Although the average dose of narcotic administered intramuscularly is tailored to the average requirement for pain relief, it does not take into account individual variations. Therefore some clients are left in distressing pain, whereas others experience excessive sedation.

Perhaps the most revolutionary study of client-controlled analgesia involves postoperative clients who are allowed to control their own intravenous narcotic doses. With two pushes of a button, the client activates an infusion pump at the bedside that administers a preset dose of narcotic intravenously. A "lock-out" feature prevents delivery of a further dose for a preset time.

In a study conducted by Bennett and colleagues individuals all underwent similar surgical procedures and received the same premedication and operative anesthesia.[3] Immediately after surgery clients using client-controlled morphine gave themselves higher doses of morphine than the usual intramuscular dose, which may have contributed substantially to their overall higher satisfaction with this method of pain control. These individuals tapered their doses with time and used significantly less drug than those receiving intramuscular morphine. After the third postoperative day all clients went on an intramuscular schedule, and those who had controlled their own analgesia continued to require less pain medication.

A unique aspect of this study is that demand analgesia helped to normalize the person's sleep-wake cycle. It is theorized that clients who are awake during normal waking hours and asleep during normal sleeping hours may recover faster. Of those using the client-controlled morphine, only 17 percent reported being drowsy during the daytime, in contrast to half of those receiving intramuscular morphine. When individuals anticipated increased activity, they administered an extra dose of morphine but lessened the amount when they anticipated going to sleep.

The client-controlled morphine has been proven both effective and safe. Based on experience with several thousand persons, the addiction potential has been determined as small. People are willing to accept a small amount of residual pain that they know they can control, and most clients do not want complete sedation, much less euphoria. In the past the choice was either accepting or refusing pain medication. Client-controlled morphine also allows the client to control the dosage.

When clients receive prompt and adequate pain relief, an overall reduction in pain medication is frequently noted. According to researchers, the use of analgesic medication is not higher for individuals who attribute control in their life to external factors rather than internal factors. A factor that does attribute to increased analgesic use is anxiety, and when the client is assured of prompt and adequate pain relief, anxiety is reduced and less pain may be experienced. It is also known that the effectiveness of an analgesic is far greater if it can be administered before pain becomes severe, and with continuous or client-controlled analgesia, early administration may contribute to an overall reduction in the amount of analgesia needed. When an element of control concerning pain relief is returned to the client, the individual no longer has to worry about waiting in pain for pain relief. Continuous and client-controlled analgesia take the fear out of pain, and this in itself may be the most important factor in pain reduction.

COMPLEXITIES OF CHRONIC PAIN

Chronic persistent pain is pain that continues despite treatment or exists in the absence of demonstrable disease. Many chronic pain sufferers have unsuccessfully run the gamut of traditional medical and surgical treatments. They have exhausted surgical options and dependence on medication is a problem for many. In the past these individuals were often left behind as health professionals moved on to more salvageable cases. Some chose suicide rather than live a life wracked with pain. New modalities in pain control are now offering hope to those whose lives have been governed by pain.

Assessing chronic pain

It is difficult to accurately assess pain, particularly prolonged or chronic pain. The client is likely to assume that health professionals know about the pain or that it really is not of interest or of importance, and health professionals may believe that the client will tell them about any discomfort. In frustration the person becomes discouraged and the pain picture presented may be inadequate or inaccurate.

Some clients report that answering a myriad of

questions about their pain or filling out questionnaires actually makes them feel worse. It is also difficult for individuals who are experiencing pain to remain objective in their answers. As one client commented, "When I am hurting, I remember everything being worse than it really was. But when I am feeling good, I wonder if the pain was really that bad."

Because research and clinical practice suggests that many clients minimize their pain experience, numerous indexes have been developed that are effective in measurement of pain and in the evaluation of different treatments. Sometimes only portions of a tool or guide are appropriate for an individual client, and there may also be instances when an assessment tool can be formulated to meet specific needs.

No one knows more about a client's pain than the individual with the pain. That person has a wealth of information that may provide a solution to the cause of pain or a method of pain relief. The health team needs the expertise of the client in the management of his or her own pain, and therefore the more personalized a pain assessment tool, the more useful information may be made available for evaluation.

Pain assessment tools often use numbers or a scale of descriptive terms for use in identifying the intensity of pain. The numbers may range from 1 to 10 and words from "none" to "excruciating." Words have different meanings for different people, and although some people will agree that the worst pain is indeed "excruciating," others may not even understand the term. Most individuals with chronic pain know words that describe their pain. Terms such as "hell," "terrible," "fire," "very bad," "horrible pressure," and "like a knife" may describe what they feel, whereas terms such as "severe" or "excruciating" do not apply.

Fig. 8-1 is a sample of an assessment tool without preestablished response sets or other factors that might influence a client's reporting. The scale contains only four categories of pain intensity, with descriptive terms that range from no pain to worst pain and numbers that range from 0 to 3. The scale can be increased to allow for more sensitivity, depending on the needs of those using this assessment tool.

Clients are encouraged to use their own words to describe their pain and to identify how different levels of pain affect their daily activities. Whatever the client routinely does or takes to reduce pain is also listed, and this listing should include not only prescription drugs but over-the-counter drugs, alcohol consumption, application of heat or cold, or anything else the client usually does to reduce the pain. An example of a completed form is illustrated in Fig. 8-2.

Once this basic information is filled out, it is used as a reference for completing the daily graph as shown in Fig. 8-3. Whenever the client feels pain, the intensity of pain is identified, comparing both the word description and the activity level, and this intensity is plotted on the graph at the appropriate time, along with any pain intervention. If the location of the client's pain changes, a notation of the painful area can be written on the vertical line. Clients are also encouraged to keep a daily journal of activities, stressful events, social interactions, sexual relations, sleep pattern, food intake, and anything at all that might directly or indirectly affect their pain. The care giver and clients may look back over this information to assess pain levels, evaluate pain intervention, and examine information to locate precipitating factors that may have been unnoticed in the past. The client is the vital link in this assessment tool, and the tool is only as good as the client's willingness to be a part of the team that is working toward pain relief through palliative or curative measures.

Pain clinics

Pain clinics are treating persistent chronic pain with neurosurgery, nerve blocks, transcutaneous electrical nerve stimulation, psychotropic drugs, and occasionally narcotic analgesics. Centers for pain management are helping individuals for whom no specific medication or surgical procedure is feasible. Through a multidisciplinary team, including psychiatrists, psychologists, sociologists, nurses,

Name_____ Date_____

```
3 ─────────────────────────────────────────
2 ─────────────────────────────────────────
1 ─────────────────────────────────────────
0 ─────────────────────────────────────────
  12  1  2  3  4  5  6  7  8  9  10 11  12  1  2  3  4  5  6  7  8  9  10 11
  a.m.                                noon
```

Words to describe your pain
3 = Worst pain
2 = Moderate pain
1 = Least pain
0 = No pain

```
3 _____
2 _____
1 _____
0  No pain _____
```

How much does pain limit your daily activities
3 = Worst pain
2 = Moderate pain
1 = Least pain

```
3 _____
2 _____
1 _____
```

Things you take or do to reduce your pain
A _____
B _____
C _____
D _____
E _____
F _____
G _____

Fig. 8-1. Pain assessment tool.

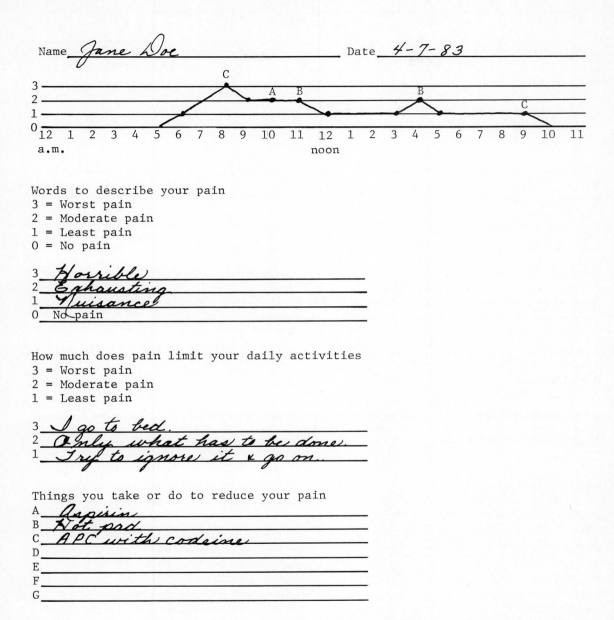

Name *Jane Doe*   Date *4-7-83*

Words to describe your pain
3 = Worst pain
2 = Moderate pain
1 = Least pain
0 = No pain

3 *Horrible*
2 *Exhausting*
1 *Nuisance*
0   No pain

How much does pain limit your daily activities
3 = Worst pain
2 = Moderate pain
1 = Least pain

3 *I go to bed.*
2 *Only what has to be done.*
1 *Try to ignore it & go on.*

Things you take or do to reduce your pain
A *Aspirin*
B *Hot pad*
C *APC with codeine*
D
E
F
G

Fig. 8-2. Completed pain assessment tool.

Name _____   Date _____

3 ──
2 ──
1 ──
0 └──┬──
  12 1 2 3 4 5 6 7 8 9 10 11 12 1 2 3 4 5 6 7 8 9 10 11
a.m.   noon

Daily journal

───

───

───

───

───

───

───

───

Fig. 8-3. Daily pain assessment tool.

occupational therapists, physical therapists, internists, social workers, and other consulting professionals, the total person is treated. Because the burden of suffering is shared by those close to the client, some centers require a family member or a significant other to be included in part of the treatment program. The goal for pain management is to help the person cope with pain, to teach self-treatment methods, and whenever possible, to reduce pain.

The treatment for prolonged, treatment-resistant pain involves a combination of techniques, including acupuncture, rehabilitation medicine, biofeedback, meditation, and behavior modification.

Clients may be admitted to a center following a complete diagnostic evaluation that indicates no specific medication or surgical procedure is feasible. An important aspect of the treatment emphasizes techniques that reduce the use of medications and complaints of pain while increasing physical activity and independent function. This involves behavior modification that is based on the premise that behavior is influenced by its consequences. For example, if care givers, family, and friends show concern when the client lies in bed and refuses to walk because of pain, this attention encourages some people to become inactive. However, if lying in bed is ignored and walking is praised, activity is encouraged. Excessive complaining and reliance on others, in addition to unnecessary physical restrictions, produce needless disability. Not all persons with intractable pain are candidates for behavior modification; therefore careful screening is of utmost importance. Before such a pain management program can be effective, the individual must understand and accept the treatment program, and full cooperation is also required of the staff, the client's family, and visiting friends before favorable results can be expected.

Increased exercise is usually a part of pain clinics since a relationship has been found between exercise and the secretion of endorphins, or the body's own endogenous analgesic. Activity diverts attention away from pain and helps to relieve the depression that usually accompanies chronic pain.

Chronic pain becomes a way of life for many people, and before this adaptive life-style can be changed, a great deal of cooperation and effort is required. People prefer miracles, not treatment that requires 2 to 3 hours of effort every day that must continue for months or a lifetime. Despite the fact that many chronic pain sufferers have already experienced a number of operations, they may still believe that surgery will cure them. Understandably, those who benefit from a pain management program are individuals with chronic pain who have a great deal of faith in their physician and agree with the prognosis that no specific medication or surgical procedure is feasible.

Living with prolonged pain

The following narration entitled "The Picture of Pain" depicts the fears, feelings, and frustrations surrounding pain. It points out how pain distorts reality by exaggerating the negative, negating the positive. A blending of denial and hope prevented acceptance of the diagnosis of chronic persistent pain, and the search for health became an obsession. Unlike many with chronic pain, the author found the missing piece from the puzzle of pain. The author later commented, "What happens to people who are too old or too sick to satisfy their search for health? Do they eventually accept the

pain, or do they just exist in a state of despair?" It is hoped that her narration will help others understand that people in pain need someone to care and to help them find their way out of the maze of pain, either through curative or palliative measures.

Pain*

Pain . . . Pain . . . go away.
If you must come, then another day.
Today give me rest, let me be.
One day to be me. One day to be free.

You've clawed and gnawed at my flesh and my soul.
Not happy with part, you strive to take whole.
You chip at my patience; you've corroded my life.
You strip me of dignity; you've left only strife.

Oh Pain, to awaken and find you not here.
What joy it would be not having your fear.
Free of the gloom. Alive in the sun.
Oh Pain, go away. Let your work be done.

■ The pain has been so long, it has turned me into something I am not. It governs my activities as well as my family's, and I long to be free. The doctor had said there was no organic cause for my pain. Pain so very real with such a hidden cause. I desperately want and need a diagnosis. The word neurotic goes through my mind, but the doctor was very tactful and did not use this word. Instead he had talked of intractable pain: pain that could not be alleviated with specific medication or surgical procedure.

There have been so many surgeries in such a short time. A relatively routine operation mushroomed into complications, more surgeries, and now this gnawing, relentless pain. Many doctors have been involved in my repetitious fight for life. With bright, pain-free faces they tell me how lucky I am to be alive, "Be thankful for what you have." What I have is not enough.

The past 8 months flash through my mind. Days, weeks, months have mingled into a steadfast vigil

*From Davis, A.: Please see my need, Charles City, Iowa, 1981, Satellite Continuing Education, Inc. © 1981 A. Jann Davis

awaiting the day when I would awaken pain free. At one time there was concern that I could become addicted to pain medications, and in a weakened condition I had also become allergic to many drugs. Despite the diagnosis of peritonitis, all pain medication orders were canceled. When the severe pain had come, I received nothing for pain. Alone in my hospital room in the dark and loneliness of night I had cried out for relief. The long hours had changed night into day and exhaustion had finally left me to sleep. I had watched many, many sunrises following sleepless, pain-filled nights.

Unable to accept disability, I had challenged my health and returned to work—a quiet desk job. Other people's problems would give me less time to dwell on myself. I would improve! I ignored the increased symptoms and pushed on. When the pain became unbearable, I hid in the rest room and cried. I worked until I could no longer move, and my weight dropped until I was a shadow of my former self. Secretly I hoped to swell the mysterious pain so that it would burst forth with the truth and I would once more be free. Slowly I was being transformed into the impatient, irritable, debilitated person that was once my father. I wondered if I was destined to live in pain as he had lived. I had loved him, felt sorry for him, and learned to hate his impatience and irritability. As a child I used to long for all the things we could never do together, and now I cried for all the things I could no longer do, for the hate my young family would learn. When one is young, it is devastating to be ill. I wonder, is it any easier at 50 or 70? Once again, I wrote to my doctor and begged for an appointment. When it arrived, I cried for joy, for new hope.

The doctor talked of a pain center, acupuncture, nerve blocks. I grasp at anything that promises relief and agreed to be admitted to the hospital for control of the pain. I have learned to hate hospitals, the cheerful chatter of those so full of health, small talk, so free with advice. I long ago stopped engaging in idle conversation about the weather and the pretty flowers. I wonder if people expect a reply or do they chatter to hide their own fears?

My hope is now in the pain center and the methods of pain elimination the doctor had mentioned. I hold to the promise, "You will not be left with the pain." When there is nothing tangible, one holds onto hope.

In a year I have experienced many forms of medical hell. I have learned much about myself and have gained much empathy for others, many of whom have suffered far more than I can ever imagine. The vanguard of pain control is moving ahead, offering much to those who have no more doors to open, I am young and full of life to live. My stamina pushes me on, searching for what I have lost. One cannot close a door of hope without opening another. My hope now rests behind the door marked "Pain Center."

Four months have passed since this writing. The chronic pain became acute and revealed its secret. Emergency surgery relieved life-threatening obstructions caused by adhesions secondary to peritonitis. _____

Free of the gloom. Alive in the sun.
Oh Pain, thank God, your work is done.

CHILDREN AND PAIN

A group of 119 hospitalized children between the ages of 4 and 10 years were asked, "Of all the things that have ever happened to you, what hurt you the worst?" Sixty-five of the children replied "a shot" or "a needle." This is particularly significant since six of the children had each undergone 25 or more operations and they still considered the shot worse.[6]

There are researchers who have questioned whether infants have the neurological capacity to receive painful stimuli at birth, and yet an infant's response to being circumcised or to having a heel pricked for a blood sample leaves little question to an ability to perceive pain. Some investigators theorize that the younger the child, the lower the pain threshold; therefore it may be possible that children experience more pain than an adult under

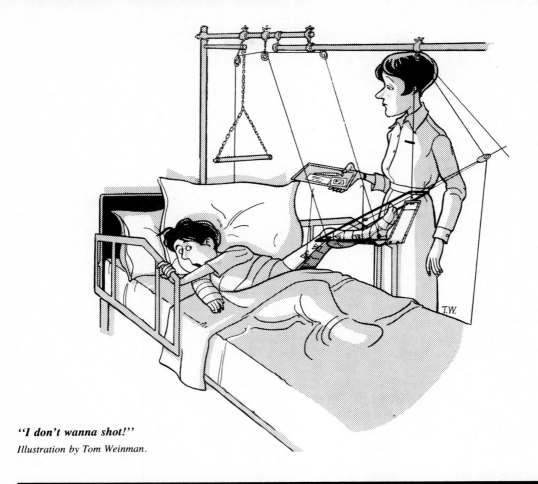

"I don't wanna shot!"
Illustration by Tom Weinman.

similar circumstances. However, in one study, when hospitalized adults and children were matched according to diagnosis, the adults received approximately 27 times the number of doses of analgesics as the children, and many of the adults and children had the same nursing and medical staffs.[6]

Children do feel pain, and the fact that many do not receive pain medication may be in part caused by a child's difficulty in interpreting and communicating pain, and in part caused by a health professional's lack of information about dealing with children in pain. Among the factors that affect a child's response to pain are prior pain experiences and the youngster's cognitive ability. These factors will be covered here in an effort to understand a child's unwillingness to report pain and a care giver's reluctance to intervene in a child's denial of pain.

Prior pain experience

A child does not attach meaning to a situation because of its seriousness but to the feelings aroused by the situation, and most children have had the opportunity to nurture feelings about injections. Early inoculation experiences can be recalled well enough that youngsters are likely to respond with fear to a needle, a white uniform, or to being restrained. Shots hurt. This is a fact that most children know from experience. The hospitalized youngster also learns that there is a relationship between complaining about pain and the nurse with the needle. The shot adds to the child's discomfort, and for the young client it is difficult to relate the injection with pain relief that does not happen for awhile.

Sometimes nurses think they are in a no-win situation. They do not want the child to hurt, but they also do not want to restrain the child and administer a shot that the child adamantly does not want. So rather than initiating what often ends with cries of "I hate you; you're mean," the nurse sees the child as restless, upset, or wanting a parent and is not likely to intervene in a child's denial of pain. Children cry for their parents and use techniques such as activity, aggression, or denial to cope with their pain. The last thing that either the child or the nurse wants is interaction with a needle. Through an understanding of the child's cognitive development, the nurse can help the child gain mastery over what is considered a threatening situation.

Cognitive development

Although children are just as capable of perceiving pain as adults, they are not miniature adults in their thought process or understanding. Explanations and teaching plans for children must be adapted to their level of understanding, and it must be remembered that children are likely to regress when they are stressed or sick.

Infant and toddler. A child up to about 3 years of age learns about the world through the senses, and because thought and reasoning are not yet developed, verbal explanations are difficult to fully comprehend. The child does understand love and security and is often more frightened by being separated from a parent than from a painful experience. Whenever parents can remain with a child during a procedure, they need information about what to expect so that they do not convey fear or anxiety to the child. A father brought his 18-month-old son to the emergency room after the child fell and cut his head on a table. After being told what to expect, the man helped hold his son while the laceration was sutured. Several days later when the sutures were removed, the father shared that he and his son had been the best of friends since the emergency room visit. "I thought the kid would hate me for holding him down, but instead I'm his pal."

Preschool child. Children from 3 to 5 years see the world from their own viewpoint and believe that everyone else sees things the way they do. Adult language is often mimicked but is not completely understood. "Fix" is a word that may prompt fear for preschoolers because to them the work means broken or torn. They are familiar with Dad or Mom "fixing" toys and clothes, and they also know that sometimes these items cannot be fixed and are thrown away. When the care giver explains, "We are going to fix your leg," the child may be afraid that it will have to be thrown away. "Take" is another word that causes concern to the preschool child. In their frame of reference "take" means "to remove." Therefore statements such as, "I'm going to take your blood pressure," cause anxiety that could be prevented by saying, "I'm going to measure your blood pressure."

It is difficult for a youngster in this age group to understand that a pill will make a hurt leg feel better since the pill goes into the stomach and not the leg. Also, having a shot that hurts now to make another hurt go away is almost impossible to comprehend. Since youngsters in this age group are usually unable to tell time, a timer set when the child receives the injection so it will ring when the medication is taking effect helps the child associate pain relief with the shot. Providing distraction during the interval between the injection and pain relief is important for the child. A parent can be encouraged to read to the child or involve the youngster in other interests. If a parent is not available, it is important that the nurse giving the injection stay with the child for awhile. Although there may not be enough time to stay until pain relief is achieved, the nurse may be able to provide the special treat of letting the child listen to a record or cassette, such as from the popular Sesame Street series. By the time the recording is finished, the medication will have started to take effect.

The preschool child views the nurse who gives a shot as bad because the child believes the nurse's intent was to cause pain. If the nurse returns when the youngster is comfortable and relates the pain relief to the shot, the next injection may not be as frightening for the child. This also provides an opportunity for the nurse to be seen as a caring person instead of the "meanie with the needle."

Children between the ages of 3 and 5 years have a difficult time understanding something they cannot see, touch, hear, and relate to concretely. By using teddy bears, dolls, and other stuffed toys caregivers can show the child how equipment, including oxygen masks and anesthesia equipment, work and how such procedures as intravenous fluids and dressings are done. It the child is to have a cast, one can also be applied to a doll. It is ideal when this is done before applying the child's cast; however, the child's condition may necessitate that the doll's cast be applied later. When it comes time for cast removal, the doll is first. Children are not so frightened by the dust, vibrations, warmth, and loud noise from the cast cutter when they have the opportunity to see, hear, and feel these sensations when the doll's cast is removed. One little girl held her doll and innocently looked up at the doctor and asked, "Are you sure you're not sawing up her bones?" The child was reassured that the cast cutter would not hurt the doll or the little girl when it was her turn to have her cast removed.

School-aged child. The 6 to 12 year old views the world more objectively and realistically, with the ability to consider the past, the present, and the future into his or her thinking. By this age most youngsters understand a comparison made between something that they have already experienced and something yet to happen. Before a 9-year-old boy received a preoperative injection, the nurse asked if he had ever had a shot before. He replied that when his throat was sore, he had had a shot and it really hurt. The nurse was able to reassure the child that this shot would not hurt as much because the medicine was different.

School-aged children judge actions by their logical effect and are usually more cooperative about taking medication if they understand how the medication will help them. For instance, a child reports that a shot hurts for a little while, but since it makes her head feel better, it is worth it. Pictures, drawings, and models help children understand what is going on with their bodies. School-aged children want to know why they cannot take pills or drink medicine instead of having injections. They want to know what to expect during procedures and why they have to have something done to them. Before starting an intravenous infusion on a 9-year-old, the nurse took the time to explain about the procedure and why the physician had ordered it. "Your stomach needs a rest, so we are going to have to give your body water and food another way." She used a small piece of intravenous tubing to illustrate the vein and inserted an intravenous needle into the tubing. "Water and a special liquid food will drip into your vein. It will travel with your blood to every part of your body so that you won't get hungry or thirsty." The nurse also explained that the intravenous treatment would hurt only when the needle went through the skin, and then it would not hurt at all. She told the youngster that it was okay to cry when the needle went in, but since the vein was so small, it was important to hold still until everything was taped securely in place.

The school-aged child with a broken bone can be helped to understand the injury by seeing pictures of the body with transparency overlays that show the relationship between the bones and muscles. Once a basic understanding is achieved, it may be appropriate to let the child look at x-rays, pointing out the broken bone and explaining how the bone will heal.

Play is important to all children, especially the hospitalized child. Spontaneous play is for fun, diversional play helps keep their mind off their discomfort, and therapeutic play reflects feelings that the child frequently is unable to put into words.

Helping children understand about procedures.
Courtesy of the University of Oklahoma College of Nursing, Oklahoma City.

Sometimes children will role play with a family of dolls, and other times they distance themselves by using a family of animals. A variety of stuffed animals can fit any child's feelings. A little boy hospitalized for second degree burns on his legs frequently selected a crocodile puppet and had it bite a white toy kitten. He repeated this over and over until the nurse responded, "It looks like the crocodile is very angry with the kitten." The little boy responded, "Yes, and if she doesn't quit hurt-ing him, she's going to get her head eaten off." The nurse interpreted his actions to mean that he was angry with someone—probably a female nurse wearing white—who was hurting him. Although the child always denied having pain, his play activity indicated otherwise. The nurse discovered that the child had only received one dose of pain medication since his admission 2 weeks ago, and that was an injection. The physician had since changed the analgesic order to a pill, but the child had not been told of the change. The nurse asked the little boy if he would like to take a pill before his next treatment so that he would not hurt so much. He agreed but commented, "I'll take a pill, but I won't take a shot."

Children also like to dress up in surgical garb and play with toy equipment similar to that used in their care. They enjoy giving shots and starting intravenous infusions on dolls. Uniform catalogues provide a good supply of pictures of physicians and nurses. One child cut out a picture of a physician and flushed it down the toilet. Toys for aggressive play include punching bags, large stuffed animals, and trucks. Crayons, soap bubbles, and finger paints provide for both expression and creative play.

Adolescent. Young adolescents are a blending of child and adult. On the outside they can appear cool, calm, and in control, while in reality they may be lost in a world of unknowns. In their quest to leave their youth they physically and psychologically distance themselves from adults. Adolescents may hesitate to report pain for fear of being considered a baby. A nurse who had a good rapport with adolescents commented, "If I think a teenager is trying to hide pain, I don't ask about pain. Instead I ask if I can bring them something for the pain. Somehow that makes it easier for them— kind of like it was my idea, not theirs. Sometimes these big kids are just as afraid of shots as the little ones, and it takes a bit of encouragement to convince them that the shot is worth it."

Rather than depending on adults to make decisions for them, adolescents want to have a say about what is going on with their health care. Although young teenagers may not ask for information, they are usually anxious to know what is going on with their bodies. They do not want to appear stupid by asking questions that others might consider dumb. Questions such as, "Do you understand about . . . ?" put the adolescent on the spot. Pictures, charts, models, and demonstrations help to answer the unasked questions, and written material reinforces verbal information. Young teens with chronic illnesses are very concerned about any

effect their illness will have on their physical appearance, and reassurance from the care giver may have to come in different forms before it is believed. The adolescent needs the freedom of independence and the security of dependence, which is sometimes difficult for the adult to understand.

Communicating pain

Although children may verbally deny pain because they do not want an injection, they will identify the location of their pain on body outline draw-

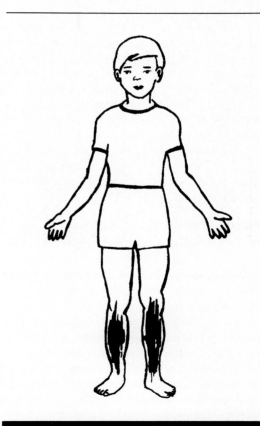

A child illustrated the pain in his legs that he verbally denied because he did not want a shot.
Courtesy of Dr. Joann Eland.

ings. In Eland's studies[6] children were given crayons and drawings of body outlines and were instructed to color where they hurt on the outline. The word "hurt" was used instead of "pain" or "discomfort" because many times younger children do not comprehend these words. After coloring the hurt, children were asked if the area hurts now or earlier in the day and why they hurt. The research indicates that children can tell when something hurts, exactly where it hurts, and when there are multiple hurts, which is the worst. They also say what causes the hurt, such as from venipuncture, surgery, or shots. In one case a child placed a deep red X over the abdomen. The child could not explain why he had drawn the X, and there were no clinical signs or symptoms to explain the coloring. Fifteen hours later the child was taken to the operating room with a small bowel obstruction. After surgery he colored both legs, saying the left one hurt because of a splint he was required to wear at night. He was unable to explain why he had colored the right leg. Once again, there were no signs or symptoms of the cause, but 3 days later his right leg developed a cellulitis and began draining. Despite the intense pain this little boy experienced, he denied pain because he did not want an injection.

Intravenous narcotics in pediatrics

Several institutions have performed trials of intravenous narcotics with children who have not received adequate relief with other narcotic routes. In some pediatric units giving intravenous pain medication is standard because of the rapid onset of action and the greater degree of dosage control. Narcotics given intravenously reach a maximum effectiveness within 20 minutes as compared with 50 to 90 minutes given subcutaneously. When an infusion pump is used, an accurate and steady rate of administration can provide a dosage high enough to achieve complete relief of pain and low enough to minimize drowsiness.

Liquid methadone

For the child with chronic pain from cancer, home care has proven to be a feasible alternative to hospitalization as long as there is effective control of symptoms. Oral methadone provides good pain control with numerous advantages over other commonly used narcotics. The most important advantage is that methadone achieves analgesic effectiveness lasting 6 to 8 hours, whereas oral meperidine (Demerol) or morphine must be given every 3 to 4 hours. The widely spaced doses of methadone allow for a full night's sleep, an essential component for effective home care. Within 24 hours after the initial dose of methadone, parents often report that their child's behavior begins to return to normal and that the child is able to move around without pain. A frequent comment is, "Thank you for giving us back our child."

For the child of all ages honesty and truthfulness are important. The little girl who is told that she is going on a ride and ends up in surgery will have difficulty trusting others. As a child's cognitive ability changes, so does the care giver's approach in explaining techniques and procedures. Words used to explain or teach must be appropriate, simple, and truthful. For without these essential elements, care is incomplete, unhelpful, and in some cases even harmful.

• • •

Pain is a complex total experience unique to each person. It is a psychophysiological phenomenon dependent on an interplay of information from the past and present for interpretation. The basic nature of pain eluded researchers until recently, but with the discovery of endorphin new clues are being offered to solve the mystery of pain. Through the understanding of endorphin, placebo response may ultimately be recognized as a healthy potential within each person that deserves encouragement rather than criticism. This self-healing response potentiates the effects of medications and procedures and can be stimulated with something as simple as tender loving care.

Acute or chronic pain, with or without a known pathology, involving child or adult deserves the attention of the health care professional. The overwhelming experience of unmanaged pain must be remedied before it immobilizes its victim in a prison of pain.

REFERENCES

1. Beecher, H.: Relationship of significance of wound to pain experienced, JAMA **161**:1609, 1956.
2. Cannon, W.: Voodoo death, American Anthropologist **44**:169, 1942.
3. Check, W.: Results are better when patients control their own analgesia, JAMA **247**:945, 1982.
4. Copp, L.: The spectrum of suffering, American Journal of Nursing **74**:491, 1974.
5. Coyle, N.: Analgesics at the bedside, American Journal of Nursing **79**:1554, 1979.
6. Eland, J., and Anderson, J.: The experience of pain in children. In Jacox, A., editor: Pain: a source book for nurses and other health professionals, Boston, 1977, Little, Brown & Co.
7. Engel, G.: Psychological development in health and disease, Philadelphia, 1962, W.B. Saunders Co.
8. Levine, J., Gordon, N., and Fields, H.: The mechanism of placebo analgesia, Lancet **2**:654, 1978.
9. McCaffery, M.: Nursing management of the patient with pain, ed. 2, Philadelphia, 1979, J.B. Lippincott Co., p. 11.
10. Rutter, P., Murphy, F., and Dudley, H.: Morphine: controlled trial of different methods of administration for postoperative pain relief, British Medical Journal **280**:12, 1980.

BIBLIOGRAPHY

Almay, B., and others: Endorphins in chronic pain. I. Differences in CSF endorphin levels between organic and psychogenic pain syndromes, Pain **5**:153, 1978.

Beecher, H.: Surgery as placebo, JAMA **176**:1102, 1961.

Boyer, M.: Continuous drip morphine, American Journal of Nursing, **82**:602, 1982.

Cobb, L., and others: An evaluation of internal-mammary-artery ligation by double-blind technic, New England Journal of Medicine **260**:1115, 1959.

Diamond, E., Kittle, C., and Crockett, J.: Evaluation of internal mammary artery ligation and sham procedure in angina pectoris, Circulation **18**:712, 1958.

Evans, F.: The placebo response in pain reduction. In Advances in neurology, vol. 4, New York, 1974, Raven Press, pp. 284-296.

Haslam, D.: Age and the perception of pain, Psychonomic Science **15**(2):86, 1969.

Hiller, J., Pearson, J., and Simon, E.: Distribution of stereospecific binding of the potent narcotic analgesic etorphine in the human brain: predominance in the limbic system, Research Communications in Chemical Pathology and Pharmacology **6**:1052, 1973.

Hughes, J.: Isolation of an endogenous compound from the brain with pharmacological properties similar to morphine, Brain Research **88**:295, 1975.

Jacox, A., editor: Pain: a source book for nurses and other health professionals, Boston, 1977, Little, Brown, and Co.

Levy, D.: The infant's earliest memory of inoculation: a contribution to public health procedures, Journal of Genetic Psychology **96**:3, 1960.

Lyerly, S., and others: Drugs and placebos: the effects of instructions upon performance and mood under amphetamine sulfate and chloral hydrate, Journal of Abnormal and Social Psychology **68**:321, 1964.

Martinson, I.: Nursing care in childhood cancer: methadone, American Journal of Nursing **82**:432, 1982.

Melzack, R., and Wall, P.: Pain mechanisms: a new theory, Science **150**:971, 1965.

Miser, A., Miser, J., and Clark, B.: Continuous intravenous infusion of morphine sulfate for control of severe pain in children with terminal malignancy, Journal of Pediatrics **96**:930, 1980.

Perry, S., and Heidrich, G.: Placebo response: myth and matter, American Journal of Nursing, **81**:720, 1981.

Pontious, S.: Practical Piaget: helping children understand, American Journal of Nursing, **82**:114, 1982.

Sternbach, R.: Pain: psychophysiological analysis, New York, 1968, Academic Press, Inc.

Swafford, L., and Allen, D.: Pain relief in the pediatric patient, Medical Clinics of North America **52**:131, 1968.

Wise, T., Hall, W., and Wong, O.: The relationship of cognitive styles and affective status to post-operative analgesic utilization, Journal of Psychosomatic Research **22**:513, 1978.

9 · Until death

The American dream: to live healthy, happy, alert, independent, and competent until a quick death do us part at a ripe old age.

Illustration by Tom Weinman.

■ Down the hall in hospital room 207 is a 75-year-old woman with a fractured hip. The woman is alert, comfortable, and as she says, "Anxious to have the thing pinned so that I can get back to living." The woman's husband sits by her bed and is quick to fluff her pillow or hold her hand. They live alone together "except when the kids and the grands and great-grands come," and they appear to be totally devoted to each other. When asked how the fracture occurred, they both laugh and the white-haired woman with a sparkle in her eyes responds, "It's my great-grandson's fault. He dribbled past me for a bank shot, and I slipped."

The woman healed and returned to her home and her husband. For 2 more years they enjoyed life together before the man died quietly in his sleep. Shortly thereafter the woman experienced a brief illness and died. _____

The American dream is to live healthy, happy, alert, independent, and competent until a quick death do us part at a ripe old age. Is it a reality? Not always.

Technology and social change have made a tremendous impact on the experience of dying. Death has become the dragon to be slayed at any cost. Health professionals are spurred into action by an increase in the number of malpractice suits, and many clients unable to convince the system to leave them alone exist in a vegetative state while lawyers battle out the issues in court. What are the rights and realities of dying a good death?

At one time organ transplants, hemodialyzers, respirators, and pacemakers were all considered medical miracles. They are now common medical procedures. Medical technology has advanced to the point that human life can be sustained almost indefinitely, but even though this technology is available, people question if it must be used. They wonder if knowledge has advanced more rapidly than the ability to use it wisely.

Such complexities are part of ethical dilemmas that arise when there is a need to determine right and wrong from equally unfavorable alternatives. Because bioethical dilemmas involve health care situations that seem to be without satisfactory solutions, professionals need to develop a philosophy in dealing with these issues. By understanding some of the ramifications surrounding the legal and ethical issues of death, health care providers may be better able to assist, support, and otherwise be of service to clients, families, and other members of the health care team. Many bioethical dilemmas could be prevented if people were encouraged to talk about death and to prepare for it. Instead, reassurances from health care workers prevent clients from making their wishes known at a time when they are capable of making decisions about what they want or do not want done to maintain their life.

The mortality for life is 100 percent. The American dream of a peaceful death after 75 healthy years will come true for some. For others the line between life and death will become nebulous as medical technology replaces a peaceful death with a life in limbo.

THE UNWRITTEN CONTRACT

Once the physician-client relationship is established, an unwritten contract exists between them. The physician has the responsibility to exercise the best medical judgment to make a diagnosis. In the process of establishing therapy and minimizing suffering the physician gives as much information as possible to the mentally competent client, including options available, outcomes of these options, and what he or she considers to be the proper option. As a partner in the decision-making process the mentally competent client has the right to decline available medical procedures and have this refusal honored.

In the case of the incompetent client the contract is between the physician and the client's immediate family or guardian. If the client made his or her wishes known to the physician before becoming incompetent, the physician must abide by these prior wishes even if they are in opposition with those of the client's family. This does not prevent the physician from discussing the client's treatment with the family, but it does prevent the family from making any medical decisions.

In August 1981 a 76-year-old woman in West Virginia told her family that she wanted to leave the hospital where she was a client and go home. Mrs. Yoder's condition was deteriorating following surgery, and aware of this change, she requested that all treatment be stopped. Six of Mrs. Yoder's seven children initiated court proceedings to prevent the physician and the hospital from halting her treatment. On August 29, 1981, a bedside hearing was held, and it was concluded that Mrs. Yoder was fully competent and understood that she would die if treatment was stopped. Two days later during a formal court hearing the hospital called to say that Mrs. Yoder had stopped breathing but had been resuscitated and placed on a respirator. At this point Mrs. Yoder's children agreed to abide by their mother's wish to have her treatment discontinued. They instructed the physician to disconnect the respirator, and their mother died minutes later. After the court session the judge issued a statement that if he had been required to rule, he would have followed the client's wishes and ordered life support stopped.[1]

The converse of the previous situation is the family who wants treatment withheld in the quest for what they describe as "a dignified death" for their loved one. Intravenous infusions, nasogastric feedings, and other unfamiliar procedures and apparatus often cause more discomfort to the family than they do to the client. Time spent with family members answering questions, explaining procedures, and listening will help remove part of the unknown that looms as loved ones sit and wait. When relatives advocate removal of life support equipment because of impatience or ignorance, this dramatically signals the need for more information and time from health professionals. Having a loved one close to death is an extremely difficult period for the family, and they so desperately need compassion at a time when they are overwhelmed by technology.

When the decision from a competent person is lacking and it is necessary for the physician to consult the next of kin concerning a code or no-code decision, that is, whether or not to initiate life support, there is understandably a lack of objectivity in decisions involving other family members. Families fear both the responsibility and the guilt that may be connected with such decisions. When family members are asked their opinion without being presented the facts, they almost always respond, "Do everything possible." When the physician presents facts along with options and outcomes of choices and his or her opinion of the proper choice, the burden of the decision is lightened and the next of kin is more apt to agree with the physician. When family members have different opinions, an ethics committee should be consulted, and if the family remains divided in their decision, a judicial ruling may be necessary.

CONSTITUTIONAL RIGHT OF PRIVACY

According to the courts, the constitutional right of privacy includes the right of a competent adult to refuse treatment that may prolong his or her life, and under certain circumstances this right may be exercised by others. In the case of a person who has become incompetent a decision to withhold treatment may be made by the physician, sometimes assisted by the family, on the basis of the client's best interests. At other times this decision is made in the form of a "substituted judgment" exercised on behalf of the person by the guardian or court, who is asked to make the decision the incompetent person would make if he or she were able. The following court cases are presented to further explain substituted judgment.

Substituted judgment

Ethics committee decision. The concept of substituted judgment was a factor in the decision of the New Jersey Supreme Court in the case of Karen Ann Quinlan. On April 15, 1975, 21-year-old Karen Ann Quinlan was found unconscious and not breathing. Exactly how long she was without oxygen is not known and neither is the exact cause for the comatose condition that followed. The respirator stood between her and death. Physicians determined that she had suffered irreversible brain damage. Karen's parents believed that all the respirator was keeping alive was a vegetable, and they requested that Karen be removed from the respirator. Permission was denied by the lower court. The Quinlans filed suit in superior court, requesting that Karen be declared incompetent and that as her parents they be appointed as guardians with the right to disconnect the machine that sustained her life.

In March 1976 the Supreme Court ruled that if the hospital ethics committee agreed that there was no chance that Karen would emerge from her present comatose condition to a cognitive, sapient state, her father as her legal guardian could have his daughter removed from the respirator, and all parties involved would be immune from liability. In this case, the New Jersey Supreme Court entrusted the issue and legal liability of discontinuing life-support to a hospital ethics committee, ending a year-long battle to have Karen removed from the respirator.[14]

This famous right to refuse treatment ruling was based on the existence of the client's right of privacy, entitling the person the right to refuse life-sustaining medical decisions. Since Karen was determined incompetent, the final decision belonged to her family and guardian.

Karen Quinlan was disconnected from the respirator in 1976 and was able to breathe unassisted. She was 29 years old in May 1983 and has spent the last 8 years of her life in limbo between life and death.

Judicial decision. Joseph Saikewicz was 67 years old, incompetent, and seriously ill with leukemia. Treatment for his form of leukemia was described as painful and would extend his life by approximately 2 to 13 months. Without treatment, he could expect a painless death within a few months. Mr. Saikewicz was considered terminally ill, which in a legal sense is the expectation that the person will be dead within 1 year from an identified disease or condition. Authorities at the institution where he lived wanted him to undergo chemotherapy. Because Mr. Saikewicz was determined incompetent, a guardian was appointed who protested the treatment. The guardian's proxy judgment, along with medical evidence involving cure or relief of the illness that brought the person to the threshold of death, was weighed by the court. The probate court judge ordered treatment withheld, and Joseph Saikewicz died shortly thereafter. In November 1977 the Supreme Judicial Court of Massachusetts upheld the ruling of the lower court.[15]

Many lawyers, physicians, and institutions interpreted the Saikewicz decision to mean that final court sanction was required before treatment could be withheld from incompetent, terminally ill clients. This interpretation would mean that such decisions could not legally be made by a physician, the family, a guardian, or even an ethics committee. This understanding led to numerous incidents of gross overtreatment of terminally ill clients who were not viable. Some of this confusion was clarified by the following case.

Medical decision. Mrs. Shirley Dinnerstein, a 67-year-old widow, had suffered from Alzheimer's disease for 6 years. She had experienced a massive stroke, leaving her totally paralyzed on her left side and confining her to a hospital bed in a vegatative state. Her condition was complicated by high blood pressure and serious coronary artery disease. Because Alzheimer's diseases runs its course over an average of 5 to 7 years, her condition was considered terminal.

The family of Mrs. Dinnerstein joined with her physician and the hospital in seeking permission from the probate court to enter a no-code order on the client's chart without judicial approval, or if this prior approval was necessary, then the granting of that approval. The probate court did not decide the legal questions but reported them to the appeals court for answers.

On June 30, 1978, the Massachusetts Appeals Court determined that successful attempts to resuscitate Mrs. Dinnerstein would do nothing to cure or relieve the illness that brought the client to the threshold of death. Since the question related to the process of death itself, the court placed responsibility for decision on the physician. The court also noted that in the course of a terminal illness when cardiac or respiratory arrest is unrelated to rather than a natural consequence of the terminal illness, the decision not to authorize a code status is a medical question.[4] This was the first decision in the nation to uphold the validity of no-code orders.

Question of competency

Before the mature adult can refuse medical recommendations that may prolong life, the adult must be competent. The legal issue in establishing competency is whether the client understands the relevant risks and alternatives and whether the resulting decision is a deliberate choice of the client.

Ms. Candura was a 77-year-old client with diabetes who refused to have her gangrenous leg amputated after signing a consent form 1 day earlier. She had already had a toe and then a part of a foot amputated and told a number of people that she would rather die than live incapacitated in a nursing home because of additional amputations. Mrs. Candura's daughter petitioned the court to have her mother declared incompetent. She requested that she be appointed guardian for her mother for the purpose of consenting to the operation.

Mrs. Candura was senile, depressed, and occasionally confused, and the lower court found that she was unable to make a rational decision. In 1978 the appellate court found that although she was unable to make a rational *medical* decision, she had made the decision when she was lucid and fully aware that the physicians thought the alternative was death. The lower court's decision was reversed on the grounds that Mrs. Candura had the constitutional right to refuse treatment no matter how irrational that refusal might appear to others.[9] If Mrs. Candura had either a dependent spouse or minor children, the state might have interfered on the grounds of protecting the interests of the spouse or minor children.

Informed consent

Before a physician can proceed with treatment or surgery, the client's consent is required. Informed consent contains the basic elements of voluntariness, competency, and knowledge.

Voluntary. The individual must feel that he or she has a real choice, without any physical or psychological coercion, whether or not to agree to the treatment.

Competency. The individual must be an adult, of sound mind, and legally and mentally capable of making a decision that will affect the person's well-being. An individual who is drugged or drunk or a child is usually considered incompetent to consent to a medical procedure that carries risk of serious bodily harm or death.

Knowledge. The person must have adequate knowledge concerning the disease or infirmity and the treatment prescribed. The U.S. Department of Health and Human Services stipulates that the following information must be given to the individual[2]:

1. A fair explanation of the procedures to be followed and their purposes, including an identification of those that are experimental
2. A description of any expected discomforts and risks
3. A description of the benefits
4. A disclosure of appropriate alternative procedures

The two exceptions to disclosing inherent risks to the client are in certain emergency conditions and when risk disclosure poses a threat to the person. When the individual is unconscious or incapable of consenting, failure to treat would cause risk of death or serious bodily harm that would outweigh any harm threatened by the treatment. In this case a relative may consent for the person or a court order may be obtained, and in situations in which time does not permit, the law in emergencies is to treat first and ask legal questions later.

When disclosing risks poses a threat to the client, the courts have given the physician the privilege of keeping the information from the person. This would only be applicable in the case in which past experience with the individual enables the physician to predict that disclosure of the risks would cause the person to become so emotionally distraught that he or she would be unable to make a rational decision about a medical procedure.

Many states have passed what is called the "Good Samaritan" law to protect physicians, nurses, and other medical personnel from liability for ordinary negligence when they give emergency aid outside their normal work setting to accident victims or similarly injured people. These statutes vary greatly from state to state, but regardless of these laws, medical professionals have the moral and legal obligation to give emergency care to highway accident victims or persons injured in similar emergency situations.

When the client is a minor

Emancipated minors can consent to their own medical treatment and that of their children. Emancipation is recognized by law when a child leaves home and becomes economically independent from his or her parents. In some cases minors may still be considered emancipated even if they live at home and pay room and board.

The most common way emancipation is fulfilled is through marriage, with or without consent of parents. States differ in their definition of emancipation; for example, in one state a girl who has given birth to a child is considered emancipated, whereas in another a girl qualifies if she is pregnant or believes she is pregnant. Emancipation can also be realized by consent or agreement between parent and child and is effected when the child is abandoned or forced to leave home. In some states the law restricts the definition of emancipation for purposes of consenting to medical and health care, which may be recognized at age 15 or 16 years or in some states not until graduating from high school.

Perhaps the most difficult cases involve newborn infants who are born so premature or with birth defects so serious as to preclude normal existence. As smaller and smaller neonates are kept alive, there is an increase in both serious physical and mental handicaps, with an alarming incidence of blindness. The basic room rate in some facilities approaches $1,000, and total bills can amount to hundreds of thousands of dollars.

Infanticide is being brought out in the open by cases such as Infant Doe, as he was called by the courts who debated for 6 days on whether or not he should be fed. Infant Doe was born in April 1982 with Down's syndrome and a deformed esophagus. His parents refused surgery to save his life, and while the case was being debated in the Supreme Court, Infant Doe starved to death.

Such cases have prompted enough national attention that the U.S. Department of Health and Human Services has stated that hospitals receiving federal money that fail to treat infants with birth defects risk loss of federal funds.

LIFE AND DEATH DECISIONS

Many hospitals are establishing their own ethical advisory panels or prognosis committees, partly to resolve bioethical disputes outside the courts. A typical ethics panel or committee consists of physicians, nurses, social workers, and lay persons. Although the decisions of the committee are not binding, the decisions are described as being a definite help. Other hospitals are forming guidelines concerning the initiation or termination of advanced life-support measures and for identifying circumstances appropriate for issuing "do not resuscitate" orders. Different legal interpretations and ethical positions provide various ways of looking at health care dilemmas and different outcomes to these situations.

Ethical theories

There are three traditional ethical theories that serve to structure and clarify ways of looking at bioethical dilemmas. Although these theories do not solve the problems, they do enable those involved in the decision-making process to clarify their thinking.

Egoism. The egoistic position is based on the decisions that what is right is what is best for oneself. In the case of a health care provider this decision does not take into account the needs of the client or the client's family but only the personal needs of the health care provider. An example is the physician who sees death as the enemy to be prevented at any cost and without regard to the quality of life saved.

Utilitarianism. This teleological theory focuses on the outcome or consequences of actions. That which is right results in the greatest good or the least amount of harm for the greatest number of people. Neonates with birth defects left to die or who die because medical treatment is withheld are an example of utilitarianism thinking. Supposedly these deaths benefit more people than they harm.

Deontology. In the formalist position the nature of the act itself is considered rather than one's own personal position or the consequences of actions. This position requires that the same decision be applicable in all cases regardless of time, place, age, or persons involved. Such an example is the American ethic that declares that everything medically possible must be done for every human being in this country.

These different theories offer perspectives from which judgments can be made. The outcome is determined by legal, ethical, moral, and medical considerations that take into account those involved, the setting, the time element, proposed action, intent of action, alternatives, and consequences of the proposed action. Bioethics is concerned with the deliberate and reflective thinking process that precedes decisions and actions rather than justifying these decisions and actions after they have occurred.

Reasons to resuscitate

The widespread familiarity with cardiopulmonary resuscitation (CPR) techniques and the accessibility of "crash carts" in hospitals have made it possible to attempt resuscitation in virtually all hospital deaths. Initially CPR training courses were established for coronary care unit (CCU) nurses and ultimately for all nurses. In many hospitals supervisory personnel outside of nursing service are also required to pass basic CPR courses. To implement these lifesaving programs many hospitals established policies stating that CPR would be instituted on all clients experiencing sudden and unexpected cardiopulmonary arrest. The use of standing orders protected qualified personnel to do CPR and defibrillation before the physician's arrival.

With these policies came the need to write no-code orders to protect those clients with a disease process in which the natural course was expected to be death. There is general agreement that people should be resuscitated when they experience cardiopulmonary arrest in the setting of good health or a reversible medical condition and that their charts should contain "no code" when the underlying condition is one of rapid and inevitable progression to death. It is the condition between these two extremes that requires both wisdom and judgment.

Many times other health team members begin resuscitative effort, and it is up to the physician to determine if these efforts should be continued. In Petty's article "Don't Just Do Something—Stand There!" four basic questions provide major assistance to the physician in justifying respiratory and cardiac support[13]:

1. Do I know the patient's underlying disease process and its course and prognosis?

2. Do I know the patient's quality of life within the context of his disease process?
3. Do I have anything more to offer the patient by resuscitative efforts designed to gain more time?
4. Do I wish to gain more time through resuscitative efforts to resolve these other questions?

If the answers to the first two questions are not known, it is highly likely that support should be offered until the answers are known. If the answers to the first two questions are clearly ''yes'' and the last two are definitely ''no,'' then resuscitative efforts may need to be questioned.

What is right for one client may be entirely wrong for another, and a decision reached today may need to be reversed tomorrow. This is pointed out by the following example. A 45-year-old woman with metastatic cancer had a short time to live. To the outsider her quality of life in the context of her disease process appeared bleak. Those who took care of this woman knew that life was more valuable to her than perhaps it had ever been. She made her physician promise that everything humanly possible would be done so that she could see her first grandchild. Once the grandchild was born, her quality of life in the context of the disease process deteriorated dramatically, and she quietly told her physician, ''Now I'm ready to die.'' A no-code order was written on her chart, and 2 days later she died.

Standards for brain death

The common legal definition of death is defined in *Black's Law Dictionary* as ''the cessation of life, the ceasing to exist, defined by physicians as a total stoppage of the circulation of blood, and a cessation of the animal and vital functions consequent thereupon such as respiration, pulsation . . . .'' Cerebral death means total and irreversible destruction of cortex, white matter, basal ganglia, and thalamus bilaterally. Brain death is cerebral death plus irreversible destruction of the brain stem, even though respiration and circulation can be artificially maintained. The standards for irreversible coma that indicate brain death identified by the

Harvard Medical School include the following criteria[8]:

- No response to pain or other stimuli.
- Absence of reflex action.
- No spontaneous respiration during a three-minute period without assisted ventilation or muscular movement for at least one hour.
- A flat electroencephalogram.
- The above tests are to be repeated in 24 hours, in the absence of intoxicants or hypothermia, with a finding of no change.

After 13 years it was thought that these standards needed revision. Although there is no record of anyone recovering who met the criteria, some points are considered too strict and others too lax. Although some debate continues between Black's definition involving breathing and heartbeat and Harvard's criteria centering around brain activity, in 1981 a presidential commission joined the American Bar Association and the American Medical Association and recommended that all states recognize cessation of brain function—including the brain stem—as a definition of death.

This conservative definition would consider people with working brain stems, such as Karen Quinlan, as alive. At the time of the Quinlan trial Karen responded to painful stimuli, yawned occasionally in a spasmlike fashion, and at times breathed on her own, and her pupils dilated in response to light. She fluctuated between sleeping-comatose and sleep-awake-comatose. It is thought that the sapient functions enabling a human being to talk, see, feel, and think are absent in Karen. The vegetative-regulative functions of the brain, including control of body temperature, breathing, blood pressure, heart rate, swallowing, and sleeping, are intact. There is much supposition in these statements. Some experts said Karen could not breathe without the respirator, but she did. Karen's parents question, how expert are the experts who say there is no hope?

A person with brain stem damage or swelling is more able to be maintained on a respirator than the person whose brain stem has been destroyed. When the brain stem no longer functions, a comatose person cannot usually be sustained on a respirator for long.

Wrongful death

Some litigation-conscious physicians have become reluctant not to try everything possible to prevent death. As one physician put it, ''I have to try everything. If I don't, next week the wife will read in the newspaper that there is some miraculous cure made out of snake oil and bat wings and I'll be sued for not extending her husband's life.'' In some hospitals CPR is a mandatory activity before people are allowed to die. For clients who are not viable, the procedure is justified with, ''It's good experience for the team.'' CPR is a violent intrusion that is certainly justified in many cases, but in other cases it serves only to disrupt what would have been a peaceful final stage of life.

There have not been any malpractice actions in natural death cases; therefore the fear of malpractice does not justify the use of heroics that serve merely as suspension of the natural dying process. When one considers wrongful death actions, it is unlikely that substantial damages could be claimed if such court action were to be initiated in natural death cases. The following are the three elements of damages in a wrongful death action[3]:

1. Loss of earnings; as a terminally ill, incompetent person cannot be earning anything, his death cannot cause a loss of earnings.
2. Pain and suffering; a natural death shortens the patient's pain and suffering.
3. Out-of-pocket medical expenses; after a natural death there are no such expenses.

Of more concern is the likelihood of being sued for failing to discontinue treatment when requested by an informed, competent client. The health professional could then be liable for pain, suffering, and expense caused by unauthorized treatment.

Prior wishes honored

Brother Joseph Fox, an 83-year-old member of a religious order, had expressed the wish to priests close to him that his life not be prolonged if he ever became incompetent like Karen Quinlan. Following minor surgery Brother Fox suffered cardiac arrest, lapsed into a vegetative state, and was maintained by a respirator. The hospital refused to turn off his respirator as requested by his religious superior. Brother Joseph Fox was kept alive in a vegetative coma for 114 days while lawyers argued whether the respirator would be withdrawn. He was on the respirator when he died of congestive heart failure.

Despite his death, the appellate court completed its review of Brother Fox's case. In the absence of a written statement of intent the substitute judgment was made by a court-appointed guardian. The guardian, a member of Brother Fox's religious order, was able to relay that Brother Fox had made it clear that he personally would not want extraordinary measures taken to keep him alive. This recommendation and the relevant medical evidence were weighed by the appellate court, which on March 27, 1980, upheld the lower court order to terminate respirator treatment.[5] This was the first case in which a court has given conclusive weight to previously stated wishes of a comatose person.

Most recently in federal district court in California, a decision was reached in the case of William J. Foster, a 67-year-old retired mechanic with amyotrophic lateral sclerosis, a disease resulting in death within 2 to 5 years. Mr. Foster had been hospitalized for over a year, was paralyzed from the neck down, had pain, experienced great difficulty speaking, and was kept alive by a respirator. As a competent person, Mr. Foster asked to have the hospital discontinue his respirator. The hospital and its physicians feared civil and criminal liability and refused to discontinue the respirator without a prior court order. Because California law was not clear, the legal counsel for the hospital requested a federal court order. While pending this court decision, William Foster suffered a cardiac arrest, was resuscitated, but lapsed into a coma.

On November 16, 1981, the federal court judge in California ruled that Mr. Foster was competent at the time he made the decision to have the respirator discontinued, and not following his expressed wish violated his constitutional rights. The judge ordered removal of the respirator and stated that if death followed, it would be the result of William Foster's neurological disease and not caused by any form of suicide or euthanasia.[6] This was the first time that a client's right to refuse treatment has been the issue before a federal bench.

Unwarranted prolongation of dying

In fear of civil and criminal liability, some physicians and hospitals have violated the constitutional rights of competent and informed adults who have refused treatment. Depending on the outcome of a lawsuit initially filed in December 1981 in the U.S. District Court in Cleveland, Ohio, and refiled in 1983 at the state level, there may be more danger from litigation by not honoring these constitutional rights.

The husband of a woman who was kept alive for 22 months despite her expressed wish not to be placed on a respirator has filed a lawsuit to seek damages for unwarranted prolongation of dying. In the fall of 1979 Mrs. Leach was hospitalized suffering from amyotrophic lateral sclerosis. She gave instructions to her family and her family physician that she not be placed on a respirator should the need arise. Later she suffered a heart attack, became comatose, and was placed on a respirator. The hospital and her physician would not remove the respirator without a court order but subsequent to this order still refused to remove the respirator. Ultimately a physician from another community turned off the machine, and Mrs. Leach died. The hospital and Mrs. Leach's attending physician are being sued for 2.3 million dollars. This is the first lawsuit in the United States to seek damages for unwarranted prolongation of dying.[10]

LIVING WILL, NATURAL DEATH, AND RIGHT-TO-DIE ACTS

The fact that a person is incompetent should not deprive the person the right to die a natural death. The substituted judgment used by guardians and courts when the individual is determined incompetent is the decision they feel the person would make if he or she were competent to do so. Essentially, documents such as the "Living Will" allow individuals to put their wishes in writing while they are still competent rather than leaving the decision to a substitute judgment.

The document is drawn up while the person is competent and expresses the person's desire to die a natural death without intervention of extraordinary medical procedures to prolong life. It must be executed using the same formalities as an estate will, with the person signing the directive in the presence of two witnesses who are unrelated to the person and are not in the position to benefit financially from the person's death. The contents must be discussed with family members and with any physicians who may be involved in the person's care. Unlike an estate will, the document should not be locked away but should be kept in an accessible place such as the purse or billfold. Copies should be given to the physician to be placed with the individual's medical records. Additional copies should be given to family members, the person's attorney, clergy, and anyone else who is most likely to be concerned in the event the individual becomes comatose or incompetent. It should be checked, dated, and initialed each year to make it clear that the person's wishes are unchanged.

One Living Will reads, in part, as follows*:

To My Family, My Physician, My Lawyer and All Others Whom It May Concern

Death is as much a reality as birth, growth, maturity and old age—it is the one certainty of life. If the time comes when I can no longer take part in decisions for my own future, let this statement stand as an expression of my wishes and directions, while I am still of sound mind.

If at such a time the situation should arise in which there is no reasonable expectation of my recovery from extreme physical or mental disability, I direct that I be allowed to die and not be kept alive by medications, artificial means or "heroic measures." I do, however, ask that medications be mercifully administered to me to alleviate suffering even though this may shorten my remaining life.

This statement is made after careful consideration and

*Reprinted with permission from Concern For Dying, 250 West 57th Street, New York, NY 10107.

is in accordance with my strong convictions and beliefs. I want the wishes and directions here expressed carried out to the extent permitted by law. Insofar as they are not legally enforceable, I hope that those to whom this Will is addressed will regard themselves as morally bound by these provisions.

Fourteen states have passed right-to-die laws that recognize a written directive as assertion of the individual's right to self-determination over his or her own body. The states having passed right-to-die laws are: Alabama, Arkansas, California, Delaware, District of Columbia, Idaho, Kansas, Nevada, New Mexico, North Carolina, Oregon, Texas, Vermont, and Washington. Each state stipulates various requirements in their directives, and the following are key features that may or may not be applicable in each state[7]:

1. Time after which directive must be reexecuted
2. Form provided
3. Hospital and physician legally protected unless negligent
4. Binding on physician
5. Can be executed by adult in good health
6. In order to be binding, must be re-executed after patient becomes terminal
7. Void while patient is pregnant
8. Provides for an agent to act on behalf of a minor
9. Provides for "ombudsman" for a patient in a skilled nursing facility
10. Provisions for revocation
11. Penalities for hiding, destroying, or falsifying directive or revocation

Although it is paramount that people make their wishes known in writing while they are competent, some authorities in jurisprudence warn that right-to-die legislation may prove counterproductive. Such laws do provide legal shelter for hospitals, physicians, nurses, and other health care personnel who comply with the directive, but they may limit or inhibit the wishes of the individual. These bills pertain to a diagnosed terminal illness, and only the bill passed by the District of Columbia makes any provision for other conditions, such as severe trauma, stroke, or dealing with a comatose person with severe brain damage. The need for such legislation is also questioned in view of the fact that precedents from federal and state courts have upheld the rights of clients to refuse treatment even when death may result.

There are many questions that are brought up by right-to-die legislation. For instance, what happens if the individual has signed the document of his or her state but is in another state when life-support systems are necessary? If legislation is considered a must by the American Medical Association and the American Bar Association, then a universal directive covering extreme physical or mental disability, whatever the cause of the disability, would clear up some of the confusion that centers around different directives in different states. Still the question remains, does *not* signing such a directive mean that individuals want everything possible done to maintain their life?

Many people are allowed to die a peaceful death without gaining prior "permission" from the courts, but more frequently than not this is only when the client, physician, family, and the institution are all in agreement. Decisions that are made out of guilt or fear of litigation may not be the same decision that the client would have wanted. The very existence of such court cases as have been presented in this section demonstrate that both physicians and prosecutors are not certain that the law prevents liability in the termination of life-prolonging treatment.

If a person is comatose or unable to communicate with the physician, a document such as the Living Will would eliminate the necessity of a substitute judgment. Although the courts have not been asked to judge the legality of such a document, it is believed that it would be upheld in court.

The public needs to know that opting for hospitalization automatically subjects individuals to some treatments that are essentially routine in such a setting. Routine can mean anything from catheters to respirators, depending on the situation. Within a hospital setting there is always the possibility of mechanical maintenance of life, and turning on a respirator is easier than turning it off.

Pneumonia is no longer the friend of the aged;

neither is advanced technology. Health professionals become the victims of their own success, as good nursing care and medical technology can keep a human body alive almost indefinitely.

Although death should be a personal event, it will continue to be governed by law, procedure, directive, or policy unless people plan ahead and share their wishes with their loved ones and their physicians while they are able. This last decision in a person's life should reflect that person's wishes, and not those of anyone else.

Dying In Academe*

His name was Eli Kahn. He was 78 years old. He was admitted to the hospital because of abdominal pain and vomiting. X-rays taken on admission suggested a small bowel obstruction. Having reviewed his films, I walked over to the division to work Mr. Kahn up.

He was a thin, frail old man with a weathered face and marvelously bright eyes. When I entered the room, his attention was fixed on Mr. Kovanich in the next bed, an old man recently operated on for colonic cancer. Mr. Kovanich had not done well, and now he lay entwined in a tangle of drains and tubes, breathing laborously.

I introduced myself.

Mr. Kahn wrenched his gaze from his neighbor and looked up at me. "I'm dying," he said.

"Don't be silly."

"What's silly about dying?"

"Nothing. But it's not allowed. You are in a hospital, a university hospital, equipped with all the latest technology. Here you must get well."

"My time has come."

"Time is measured differently here."

"What do you understand about time? Wait until you have lived 78 years. Wait until you are 78 years old and tired and alone and have a pain in your belly."

There was no arguing with him.

Physical examination revealed an erratic heart beat, a few crackles in the lungs, a tender, distended abdomen, an enlarged prostate, and arthritic changes in the joints.

"You see," said Mr. Kahn, "the engine is broken down; it is time for the engineer to abandon it."

We discussed the case with our attending and elected to decompress the bowel for a few days before attempting

*From Caroline, N.L.: Dying in academe, The New Physician, **21**:655, 1972.

surgery. When I went into Mr. Kahn's room to pass a Miller-Abbott tube, I found him again staring at the patient in the next bed. Mr. Kovanich was comatose.

"We have to pass a tube down into your stomach, Mr. Kahn."

"Like that?" He gestured toward the tube protruding from Mr. Kovanish's nose.

"Something like that."

"Listen, doctor. I don't want to die with tubes sticking out all over me. I don't want that my children should remember their father that way. All my life I tried to be a *mensch,* you understand? All my life, I tried to live so I could hold my head up. Rich I wasn't, but I managed. I put my sons through college. I wanted to be able to hold my head up, to have dignity, even though I didn't have much money and didn't speak good English.

"Now I'm dying. O.K. I'm not complaining. I'm old and tired and have seen enough of life, believe me. But still I want to be a man, not a vegetable that someone comes and waters every day—not like him." He looked over at Kovanich. "Not like him."

"The tube will only be down for a few days, Mr. Kahn. Then we'll take you to surgery and fix you up."

"What, are you going to make me 25 years old again with your surgery?"

"No, we can't accomplish that."

"So what are you trying to do?"

"We're trying to make you feel well again."

He seemed suddenly tired of the conversation. "You don't understand," he said more to himself than to me. "You don't understand."

That evening, I stopped by to start an I.V.

"Another tube?" Mr. Kahn asked.

"You've become dehydrated. We have to get some fluids into you."

He nodded, but said nothing. He watched silently as I started the I.V. and secured the line with tape. Every so often he glanced across at Kovanich. Still he said nothing.

Early the next morning, I heard the hospital page issuing the code for a cardiac arrest. I raced up to the division to find nurses dashing in and out of Mr. Kahn's room. Inside, I saw Mr. Kovanich lying naked on his bed in a pool of excretions with the house officers laboring over him—pounding on his chest, squeezing air into his lungs, injecting one medication after another, trying to thread a pacemaker down his jugular vein. The whole thing lasted about an hour. Mr. Kovanich would not come back, and finally all labors ceased.

The nurses began clearing the resuscitation equipment out of the room, while we filed out to begin the round of postmortem debates.

"Doctor, wait a minute." Mr. Kahn was signalling me. I went over to his bed.

"What is it, Mr. Kahn?"

His eyes were frantic. "Don't ever do that to me. I want you should promise you'll never do that to me."

"Mr. Kahn, I know this has been very upsetting . . ."

"Promise!" He was leaning forward in bed and his eyes were boring through me. There was an interminable silence.

"All right, Mr. Kahn, I promise."

Satisfied, he leaned back against the pillow and closed his eyes. I was dismissed. I wandered out into the hall, where my colleagues were discussing Kovanich's defection.

"It looked like a pulmonary embolism. I knew we should have anticoagulated him."

"Did you get permission for an autopsy?"

"Don't lose his last EKG; we'll need it for the conference."

I walked away. I had other things to think about.

On the fourth hospital day, Mr. Kahn went into congestive heart failure. I found him cyanotic and wheezing on morning rounds. Swiftly the house staff swung into the practiced and coordinated action of acute care: morphine, oxygen, IPPB, tourniquets, digitalis, diuretics. But despite our skilled efforts, Mr. Kahn responded poorly. His blood gases continued to show a dangerous degree of hypoxia, and our attending wondered whether he might not have sustained a pulmonary embolism. "He's exhausting himself trying to breathe, and he's still hypoxic," our attending said. "I think he ought to be intubated; it will give him a rest and will help us oxygenate him and get at his secretions."

When the anesthesiologist arrived to intubate him, Mr. Kahn was gasping. I explained to him about the endotracheal tube. His breathing became more labored as he struggled for words. "You promised . . ." was all he could say.

"But this is different, Mr. Kahn. This tube is just for a short while—maybe just a day. It's to help you breathe."

He stared off in another direction. The anesthesiologist intubated him without difficulty, and we hooked him up to the ventilator.

"I think he ought to be monitored also," our attending said. "We don't know what sent him into heart failure, but it may have been an arrhythmia, and if so it could recur."

So we brought in the cardiac monitor and pasted the leads onto Mr. Kahn's chest while he looked on, not stirring, his face expressionless, his eyes dull.

Mr. Kahn was asleep that night when I stopped in for an evening check. The room was still save for the beep-beep of the monitor, the rhythmic whoosh of the ventilator and the hum of the nasogastric suction apparatus. And Mr. Kahn looked suddenly so very old and frail, lost among tubes and wires and enormous, imposing machines. I could not help thinking of the physiology laboratories in medical school where we used to put dogs to sleep and hook them up to all kinds of intricate recording devices. I checked the settings on the ventilator and slipped out of the room. There were a lot of other patients to see.

Sometime late that night, Mr. Kahn woke up, reached over and switched off his ventilator. The nurses didn't find him for several hours. They called me to pronounce him dead. The room was silent when I entered. The ventilator issued no rush of air, the monitor tracked a straight line, the suction machine was shut off. Mr. Kahn lay absolutely still. I mechanically reached for the pulseless wrist, then flashed my light into the widened, unmoving pupils, and nodded to the nurses to begin their ritual over the body.

On the bedside table, I found a note, scrawled in Mr. Kahn's uneven hand: "Death is not the enemy, doctor. Inhumanity is."

EUTHANASIA

Whenever there is a discussion of withholding or withdrawing treatment from a dying person, the topic of euthanasia usually follows. The word "euthanasia" is a Greek word with the derivative "eu" meaning good and "thanatos" meaning death—hence a "good death." When the goal of a "good death" is discussed, questions center around the interpretation of extraordinary measures and the precise meaning of such phrases as "extreme physical or mental disability" found in the Living Will. The old adage, "One person's ceiling is another's floor," is true. What one person considers an acceptable life, another might find deplorable; what was interpreted yesterday as extraordinary is considered ordinary today. Therefore the paramount issue to consider is, For whom is the death good?

Passive euthanasia

Passive euthanasia refers to situations in which lifesaving measures are withheld from a person who is already dying or who would be left in a deplorable condition if lifesaving techniques were used. Passive euthanasia is becoming more common, especially when a competent individual requests that no extraordinary measures be taken. As can be anticipated, the difficulty lies in differentiating between ordinary and extraordinary. Resuscitation and dialysis are two examples of techniques that may be considered ordinary by health professionals and extraordinary by the public.

An example of passive euthanasia involved Infant Doe, born with Down's syndrome and a deformed esophagus that prevented him from taking food, except intravenously. Because of the Down's syndrome, the parents decided against having the esophagus corrected and the infant was placed in the nursery until he died of dehydration and starvation. Although the baby died by passive means, proponents of active euthanasia maintain it would have been more merciful if the baby had died by active rather than passive means.

Active euthanasia

Active euthanasia is the direct performance of an act to hasten the death of a person who is already dying or who would otherwise live in a deplorable condition.

According to the nationwide Harris Poll, 1981 is the first year that a majority of persons surveyed believed that a terminally ill person had the right to active euthanasia. Of the 1,253 people included in this survey, 56 percent supported active euthanasia and 78 percent supported passive euthanasia.

Active euthanasia is far more controversial than passive euthanasia because it is much easier to accept doing nothing to maintain the life of a person who is already dying or who would live in a deplorable condition than it is to actively take steps

to end the life. Active euthanasia is often called mercy killing. Some cases have created strong public sentiment leading to jury acquittals or commuted sentences, usually on the grounds of temporary insanity.

Voluntary euthanasia

In an attempt to further qualify euthanasia, the terms "voluntary" and "involuntary" have been added. Voluntary euthanasia refers to situations in which the individual requests either active or passive euthanasia.

A particularly strong case of voluntary euthanasia was demonstrated in 1978. Mr. Perlmutter, a 73-year-old man, had an incurable disease, amyotrophic lateral sclerosis. After failing in several attempts to turn off his respirator himself, he retained an attorney and filed suit against the medical center to have the extraordinary, expensive, and painful mechanical means of prolonging his life discontinued. Five months and several court hearings later, Mr. Perlmutter was found mentally competent, and the respirator was ordered disconnected. His death was defined as from natural causes and not suicide.[12]

Involuntary euthanasia

Involuntary euthansia involves clients such as infants or comatose clients, who are unable to participate in making a decision.

For a comatose adult the substituted judgment is reached after weighing all the evidence, and the decision is one the court or guardian believes the person would make if the person were able. When the client is a minor, the state is far more likely to favor life and oppose what in essence would be involuntary euthanasia.

The pros and cons of euthanasia continue. Some contend that pulling the plug on a respirator is active euthanasia because the intent is to kill the person. Others say that it is passive because it allows the dying process to continue.

This same debate prompts issues such as quality of life and sanctity of life. Is the intent to maintain a person or a living body? Moral and ethical questions center around the imposition of another's values to determine quality of life. Opponents of active euthanasia maintain that to justify killing one group of clients may eventually lead to infanticide and genocide or that the ultimate criterion for euthanasia may simply become whether or not a person is productive to society.

The need to die has become a valid issue both to the general public and to health care providers. The jury will not continue to nullify active euthanasia, and ultimately the choice may be to create new laws that legally permit self-chosen death or to enforce the current law of criminal homicide, which some maintain includes active euthanasia.

SUICIDE

The negative connotations associated with certain words such as euthanasia may deter objective discussion of the topic. Other terminology within the euthanasia controversy, such as abetting suicide, has even greater inherent limitations than the word euthanasia. Numerous organizations in the world advocate suicide as the legal and human right of the individual, and some make available to their members how-to books on suicide. The history and legal framework of suicide precede discussion of organizations abetting suicide.

History of suicide

In the Old and New Testament a number of suicides are recorded without any implied moral judgment. Early Christians considered dying for their faith as a way of guaranteeing a life in heaven after death, and many committed suicide in the name of Christianity. It was an early church father, Augustine, who denounced suicide, stating that it violated the Sixth Commandment, "Thou shalt not kill." Later in medieval times a person attempting suicide received heavy penalties, and in some cases the person was actually hanged.

According to the Stoic philosophy in Greece, it was believed that suicide was a resolution of certain kinds of problems, including terminal illness, grief, and dishonor. The Stoics believed that the physi-

cian's function was to identify untreatable individuals, for whom the physician provided a lethal potion to put them out of their misery.

The Christian in medieval and modern times emphasized that suffering was a means of achieving salvation, and intervention of this suffering through suicide was not condoned.

With the present emphasis on self-determination, some advocate the development of social mechanisms for sorting out acceptable and unacceptable suicide. For example, suicide in the case of irreversible, painful terminal illness would be acceptable, whereas the suicide of a lovesick teenager would be unacceptable. Proponents of voluntary euthanasia maintain that guidelines should be established by the disciplines of religion, medicine, and law, for without total acceptance from all representatives, such guidelines would be without value.

Legal framework of suicide

The dual concerns of society are to safeguard individual autonomy and liberty while protecting the disturbed and depressed from impulsively killing themselves. The courts are recognizing the moral and legal rights of a dying person to refuse life-sustaining treatment. Although the law does not punish suicide, people who seek to kill themselves are not protected from intervention by others.

Issues involved in assisted suicide include validity of the dying person's consent, the possibility of abuse, and the possibility of erroneous assessment of diagnosis. The law on assisting suicide is complicated. In general a person who intentionally aids another to kill him or herself can be prosecuted for homicide, although some states have passed statutes treating such actions as a felony or in some cases only a misdemeanor.

A case of assisted suicide was brought before the Connecticut superior court in 1981. The victim, Kenneth Wright, had been paralyzed in a wrestling accident and was confined to a wheelchair. He was in constant pain and was refused pain medication on the ground that he might become addicted. His mother said that he talked openly about suicide. On September 27, 1980, two of Kenneth's friends sawed off the barrel of a shotgun and wheeled him into the woods, where they left him with the gun. They later notified the police.

Although the defendants were considered to have limited involvement in the actual suicide of their friend, they knowingly helped their friend kill himself. The judge convicted the defendants of second-degree murder for their role in the suicide; however, he imposed unconditional suspended sentences on both defendants, sparing them legal penalties. The judge stated that "the memory of leaving their friend in the woods with a gun was punishment enough."[16]

Organizations abetting suicide

There are approximately 23 countries that have some form of right-to-die or euthanasia society, with goals that differ greatly. In some countries "death with dignity" is a relatively new concept, and issues are centered around medical technology. Some countries do not have laws that address suicide or pertain to assisting suicide, and many of the societies have not taken a position on any aspect of suicide. The International Federation of Right-to-Die-Societies has been formed for the purpose of sharing information and assisting other countries in establishing right-to-die societies.

Currently there are several countries that have organizations that advocate assisted suicide or active euthanasia for the terminally ill. Perhaps the one that has made the most headlines is Exit, based in England. The principal object of Exit is to promote legislation allowing an adult person suffering from an incurable severe illness to receive an immediate painless death if that is his or her wish. The Exit group refers to this immediate painless death as voluntary euthanasia and adds that the terminally ill person may need the aid of a physician to obtain this painless death.

The 1961 Suicide Act of Britain declares that it is no longer a criminal offense to commit suicide or to attempt to do so. However, the Suicide Act does make aiding suicide an offense punishable by 14 years imprisonment. The British Medical Association condemns euthanasia and affirms the fundamental objects of the medical profession as the relief of suffering and the preservation of life.

In 1979 Exit announced plans to publish *A Guide to Self-Deliverance,* containing all the information necessary to commit suicide. Membership jumped from 2,000 to 10,000 in 1 year. Over 10,000 inquiries about the booklet were received during this same time. Just before the scheduled publication date the Exit executive committee announced that they would not publish the booklet. Legal counsel could not eliminate the possibility that publication might result in prosecution for abetting suicide. Although a new executive committee was formed that was willing to publish the booklet and be imprisoned if necessary, a court injunction temporarily prevented the distribution of *A Guide To Self-Deliverance.*

Much publicity and controversy surrounded Exit's activities, and ultimately the police were involved. Nicholas Reed, the general secretary of Exit, and an aid, Mark Lyons, were indicted on charges involving the death of six persons who had requested information or help. These individuals had contacted police after changing their mind about suicide. In several cases, the methods of death were sophisticated enough to deceive physicians into issuing standard death certificates. In April 1981 Nicholas Reed was found guilty of two charges of assisting and abetting suicide and two charges of conspiracy to assist and abet suicide and was sentenced to 2½ years in prison. Later a court of appeals reduced the sentence to 18 months. Mark Lyons was convicted of five counts of assisting and abetting suicide and two counts of conspiracy to assist and abet suicide. He received a 2-year suspended sentence because of his age—he was 70—and the fact that he was in custody for many months pending trial while Nicholas Reed had been free on bail.

In 1982 the Exit group changed its name to the Voluntary Euthanasia Society. Their guidebook on suicide has been published, and they have sold more than 10,000 copies.

Exit—the Voluntary Euthanasia Society in London.
Photograph by A. Jann Davis.

In April 1980 a Scottish branch of Exit was formed. Scottish law does not consider it a crime or offense to advise a person on how to terminate life, although assisting a person with suicide is a serious offense. Just months after the Scottish Exit was organized, it published *How to Die with Dignity,* a book offering how-to advice on suicide methods. In describing the book the secretary-treasurer of the Scottish Exit states that the book contains a list of drugs that has been checked by leading toxicologists in Scotland to make certain that the dose is lethal.

The Scottish Exit is making its booklet available to members who are Scottish residents or residents of countries other than England or Wales, where the booklet might be in breach of the law. Persons must be members of the Scottish Exit for 3 months before they can apply for a copy of the booklet. All members are warned that crucial contents are to be kept confidential and not divulged to anyone, and each booklet has a number printed on it that corresponds with the purchaser's address. The booklet suggests that the purchaser store the booklet in a secure place until further reference is required and that persons using self-deliverance should destroy the booklet before doing so. The purchaser bears total responsibility for abuse and is liable to arrest if the booklet finds its way into anyone else's hands.

In August 1980 an organization called Hemlock began in Los Angeles. This organization is led by Derek Humphry, who in his book *Jean's Way* tells about helping his cancer-stricken wife commit suicide. One of the goals of Hemlock is law reform that would eliminate legal and ethical problems associated with active voluntary euthanasia.

Less than a year after Hemlock began, the organization published and began distributing *Let Me Die Before I Wake*. Described as being informational material to help members decide the manner and means of their death, the book contains the names of lethal drugs, instructions on administering the drugs, and ways to facilitate their effect. As a safeguard against impulsive decisions, a 3-month membership was originally required before the book could be purchased from Hemlock. Currently, *Let Me Die Before I Wake* is available to the general public in bookstores.

There is much controversy over the publication of material advising persons considering suicide about methods for carrying out their intent. A how-to book offering advice on suicide methods may be misused, and rather than being a manual on ways to commit suicide, it may be used instead as a manual on ways to commit murder. The advice within such a booklet is standardized and makes no adjustments for individual differences. Instead of producing the painless death the manual advocates, it may instead produce paralysis or massive brain damage without killing.

Most health care professionals can recount numerous cases in which the client makes a remarkable recovery after months of extreme physical or emotional distress. The following is one such account given by a man whose wife had been hospitalized and bedfast with severe pain for several months. He described what he called the "ruff times."

■ Doctors said there wasn't much they could do for her. Said she'd die if she had surgery . . . and she'd be dead within 6 months without it. She couldn't eat, and just getting out of bed to go to the bathroom made her really sick. One day she asked if the pain got too bad . . . if she couldn't get out of bed at all . . . would I bring her enough sleeping pills to stop the pain forever? I told her that I would. But when the pain got bad, she would always say that she could handle it then, but not if it continued until tomorrow. Well, I guess that we just took today and kept tomorrow out of our thoughts. It was so hard watching her and not being able to do anything. We finally went for the surgery. Figured we didn't have much to lose. Today she's leading a normal life. Looking back though, I don't know how we made it. I really don't know what I would have done if she had asked for the pills. ───────────────────────

The fact that the organization Hemlock exists in the United States and has a membership exceeding 7,000 points out the need for professionals to look at the issues surrounding death in this country. Such organizations may lead people to believe that pain is an inevitable part of death and that dependency on others is degrading. If enough social pressure is exerted, the right to die may become a duty. There are also people who join such organizations out of curiosity, and they may read how-to material for the same reason. The risk is that satisfying curiosity today may lead to satisfying an impulse at a later time.

The constitutional rights of an individual include the right to refuse treatment. Few professionals believe that this includes the right to ask nurses and physicians to take active measures to end a life. The emotional burden of aiding or abetting suicide is ominous, and few people want to carry this burden for the rest of their life.

HOSPICE CARE

Ultimately life and death decisions may be solved not by the client, family, physician, or courts but by finances. The 1981 report of the Health Care Financing Administration states that in the United States Americans spend about 10 percent of the total gross national product on health care. Looking at this expense in another light, nearly 1 of every 10 dollars Americans earn is spent on health care. The majority of people in the United States pay only a fraction of their health care bills. Medicaid, medicare, and private insurance such as Blue Cross–Blue Shield pay 89.2 percent of the cost of hospital care services and 62.1 percent of the cost of physician services.

People are less willing to suffer minor ailments, and those with private insurance are anxious to get something for their insurance money. "Free" medical programs are often used wastefully and thoughtlessly. Every wasted Medicaid dollar curtails government spending in the areas of education, research, and aid to the poor.

Essentially, health care costs are increasing drastically without a corresponding rise in general health or even in consumer satisfaction. Technology is being used ineffectively and resources wasted when the dying person is subjected to everything medically possible, particularly if the person does not want to be the recipient of such technology and care. A more humane alternative is hospice care. Rather than being robbed of life while death is postponed, the client receiving hospice care is relieved of symptoms so that life can be lived to the fullest until death. The result is an appealing increase in quality of care with a corresponding decrease in costs. Studies in the United States support the premise that hospice care is less costly than traitional terminal care, with the potential of saving over 2 billion dollars per year nationally. The 97th Congress approved the hospice reimbursement legislation, and November 1, 1983, marked the onset of Medicare coverage for hospice care for the dying. Hospice care may solve some of the moral and ethical problems created by unlimited technology and finite resources. The hospice that has been the original model for the growing hospice movement in the United States is St. Christopher's Hospice in England. A firsthand view of this hospice reflects the care, compassion, and hope that signify hospice care throughout the world.

St. Christopher's Hospice

Dame Cicely Saunders, an English nurse and physician, is recognized around the world for her accomplishments in the humane care of the dying. In 1967 she founded St. Christopher's Hospice in Sydenham, England, a suburb of London. Serving a population of approximately 2 million, the Hospice maintains 85 percent occupancy of its 62 beds, with the median length of stay 14 days. Despite a large number of medical personnel, the full cost of care for a week is about half that in a local teaching hospital. Most of those who receive care at St. Chiristopher's die in the hospice and not in their homes.

St. Christopher's Hospice stands majestic among tall trees, lush greenery, and beautiful gardens. The outside walls are almost entirely of glass, creating a unification with nature. Nestled behind the main building is a beautiful private garden, complete with sculpture, a lily pond, and an array of flowering plants. Whether the garden is a place to walk, to sit, or to admire through a window, its tranquility is shared by everyone at St. Christopher's.

Inside St. Christopher's are beautiful paintings, sculpture, and lovely plants. Noticeably absent are intravenous set-ups, respirators, crash carts, or other equipment designed to prolong lives. Those arriving at St. Christopher's have frequently been given up on by hospitals or overprotected by families. Treatment of symptoms is now priority, and relief of pain without dulling awareness enables these individuals to live the last part of their lives rather than just existing. They are not bothered with routine temperature, pulse, respiration, or blood pressure checks because the disease process is no longer the center of interest. The focus of interest shifts to symptom control and family relationships.

Rooms are bright and cheerful, personalized with plants, flowers, pictures, mementoes, and special items. The sounds of television, music, and people talking and laughing are in the background. A dog bounds into the ward and scampers up on his master's bed. Families—including children—frequently visit and sometimes spend the night. There are no tasteless diets, for everyone is per-

St. Christopher's Hospice in Sydenham, England.
Photograph by A. Jann Davis.

mitted to eat what they want and food from home is allowed.

Favorite gathering places are the cozy fireplace room or the activity room, where art materials and crafts are available. An adjacent balcony becomes an open greenhouse for those who want to care for plants. There is tea in the afternoon and a favorite drink can also be purchased at the weekly open bar.

Mondays are known as "family day off," and outside visitors are not expected, except for special reasons. This allows the family to rest and catch up on things at home. The staff and volunteers plan special Monday events, including beauty salon activities, group sings, records, and slides. Special entertainment is occasionally presented by the children of St. Christopher's day nursery. These children belong to staff members and volunteers and continually brighten the lives of those associated with the hospice.

The bereavement program for the family begins before death occurs. Doctors, nurses, and social workers spend a great deal of time helping individual family members prepare for their loved one's death and for living without this person. Care givers also attempt to identify the person at risk during the bereavement period and provide extra help to minimize this risk. Approximately 2 weeks after the death the family is called by telephone to see how they are coping. Sometimes this call points out someone who is having a lot of problems that were not anticipated by the hospice staff. Bereavement visits are made by volunteers who are very skilled at listening. Sometimes they visit only once, and other times, depending on each family's needs, they visit frequently. Occasionally an individual needs more than listening skills, and he or she will be seen by a social worker or referred to a psychiatrist.

Hospice care: helping people live until they die.
Hospice of York. (Photograph by Bill Schintz, York, Pa.)

the client is expected to experience pain before treatment is given. There are various modalities of pain control that range from position change to nerve blocks. Frequently liquid morphine is given around the clock, thereby preventing pain. Dosages are adjusted until the pain is controlled without sedating the client.

Physical dependence on narcotics is not a practical problem for the client who may require relief from pain until death. When more pain medication is required, it is usually caused by the disease process rather than drug tolerance. During the last days of life the client may require less pain medication because of decreased circulation, excretion, and increased toxicity. With less medication the person may be just as comfortable and remain alert to spend meaningful moments with loved ones.

Interdisciplinary team. The hospice interdisciplinary team provides a holistic approach to care that ensures the availability of training, support, and presence of care givers whenever necessary to provide a continuity of care and comfort for the client. This team includes a physician, registered nurse, social worker, pastoral or other counselor, and volunteers, with a variety of consultant services available as needed. The hospice concept of the interdisciplinary team arose because many people reported feelings of abandonment when curative care was no longer possible. A man in his early 50s described the following scene between himself and his physician, who believed that nothing more could be done for him:

■ I'll remember as long as I live sitting in that chair in Doc's office. I've known Doc for years. He delivered both my boys.

About a year ago Doc sent me to the city to see the cancer specialist, and after I'd had the surgery and finished all the treatments, they turned me back over to Doc. Things went pretty well for awhile and then I started having problems again. I saw Doc several times. Figured it was the flu. One time, he asked me to wait for him in his office.

I'd never been in Doc's office before, not even when he first told me I had cancer. When he came in the office, he didn't look at me much. Looked at my chart a lot. I think it was as hard for him as it was for me. It was so formal. "There's nothing more the specialists or I can do for you." He went on talking but I didn't hear any of it. I just kept looking at all those degrees on the wall. Not worth a damn in my case. I guess I just sat there. Pretty soon Doc went to the door and opened it. He said, "I'm sorry," and then he shook my hand and told me good-bye.

All I remember about leaving was hearing my own footsteps. Seemed like I was the only person in the whole world. I've never been more alone and more frightened in my whole life. ⎯⎯⎯⎯⎯⎯

Without an interdisciplinary team, the disease process may make office or clinic visits more difficult or even impossible, and the person becomes virtually cut off from medical care unless the physician is willing to make a home visit. The following comments are from an elderly lady.

■ I called my doctor about checking my blood pressure on account of the headaches. Anyway, he couldn't come to the house but said I could check into the hospital or nursing home for a few days. He really wants me in a nursing home because I fall a lot and then have trouble getting up. I guess

it's my business if I want to spend time on the floor. No one's getting me into a hospital or nursing home until it's time, and I don't figure that's now. ⎯⎯⎯⎯⎯⎯⎯⎯⎯⎯⎯⎯⎯⎯⎯⎯

Symptom control is a medical concern, making it essential that hospice programs be physician directed. Routinely the primary or community physician admits the person into a hospice program on approval of the hospice medical director. The primary physician is considered a member of the interdisciplinary hospice team, which includes the client, family, clergyman, nurses, social workers, volunteers, and other health workers. Whenever the client needs a physician, the medical director is available, regardless if the person is at home or in a health facility.

Autonomous administration is important to prevent diluting the care given to the dying person. In a hospital-based hospice, there is always the temptation to transfer one of the hospice nurses to another area that is short staffed. Continuity of care helps care givers recognize client and family needs and provides a quality of care that cannot be possible with inadequate staff or with care givers who are not familiar with the client or the client's family.

Volunteers are an integral component of the interdisciplinary hospice team, and they assist the professional staff in continuity of care. A wide variety of services are provided by volunteers, such as companionship, shopping, recreational activities, or assisting with household duties while the client is at home. Although volunteers are carefully screened and receive an intensive training program, they are not trained to be counselors for the dying. Quite frequently they are described by clients as "a friend" or "an ordinary person like me." In many instances clients feel more comfortable relating to volunteers and are able to share things with them that they are unable to discuss with a member of the professional staff.

Staff communication and support. During weekly staff meetings, the concerns of the staff are presented on a one-to-one basis, and each client's situation is discussed and reevaluated. Changes in physical, emotional, social, and spiritual needs are an ongoing process brought about by a changing situation, and the more that is known and shared about a client, the more effective is that person's therapeutic regimen. Hospice care givers know the people they care for: their likes and dislikes, what makes them happy, what increases their pain. They develop a close relationship with their clients and experience grief when the individual dies. Just as clients and families receive psychological support from the hospice team, the hospice care givers receive support from other members of the team. Dr. Magno, former executive director of the National Hospice Organization, talked about a concept she called "burning in," which refers to the feeling of replenishment and satisfaction enhanced by the support system within the hospice. Dr. Saunders refers to the central unity of religion and to working as a team rather than giving primary care as effective elements in helping hospice workers receive the emotional support that they need. Hospice work demands an emotional commitment that must be replenished, and care for the hospice care giver helps to prevent emotional and mental calluses from developing.

Bereavement support. The hospice concept is based on the needs of both the client and the family, and family needs continue after the death of the client. Before the client dies, the family begins the process of saying "good-bye" and making adjustments to living without the person, and at the same time, the dying person begins the difficult process of "letting go."

When the client dies, the hospice team assists with funeral arrangements, and several from the team attend the funeral. After the funeral, hospice team members continue to offer support, assisting with such matters as insurance, attorneys, or finding a job. There is no specific time for mourning. Some studies indicate that it takes a minimum of 2 years following the death of a loved one before a fairly normal emotional equilibrium is achieved.

To prevent the morbidity and mortality of grief described by numerous researchers, bereavement follow-up continues with the number of visits and the length of time for this care based on the needs of the individual family. This follow-up provides for mutual support for the hospice staff, who have also lost someone that they cared about.

Through hospice, a comprehensive program of care is realized that addresses the combined physical, psychological, sociological, emotional, and spiritual needs of hospice clients and their families. It provides a humanistic approach to the final stage of life that helps individuals live their lives to the fullest until their death.

• • •

Medicine is both art and science, and because it contains human data, it can never be truly objective. For this reason it is imperative that health professionals be alert at all times so that their own social and religious values do not interfere with the wishes of those they are caring for. The job of the health professional is to serve the client. When resuscitation affords the necessary time to resolve acute, reversible, life-threatening processes affecting the circulatory and respiratory systems or when it provides additional time requested by the client, it serves the client. But when resuscitation is in response to an irreversibly failing organ system that precludes physiological life, resuscitation only prolongs the inevitable.

Hospice recognizes the limits of modern medical intervention with all its technical sophistication and acknowledges that there is a time to set aside curative attempts and turn instead to the physical, social, spiritual, and psychological needs of the dying. Health care professionals have the responsibility to listen and respond to the needs of their clients so that they do not become desperate enough to seek the help of organizations such as Hemlock to solve their problems. Supportive, palliative care enables people to live their life until the end without having to leave the burden of suicide for the survivors to bear.

REFERENCES

1. Action in the courts, Concern for Dying Newsletter **7**(4):3, 1981.
2. Brown, B.: Behavior modification—in the right hands, Trial Magazine, p. 33, November-December 1975.
3. Concern for Dying Council: A legal guide to the living will, New York, 1979, The Council, p. 7.
4. *In the matter of Shirley Dinnerstein,* 6 Mass. App. Ct. 466, 380 N.E. 2d 134, 1978.
5. *Eichner v. Dillon,* 73 A.D. 2d 431, 426 N.Y.S. 2d 517, 1980.
6. *Foster v. Veteran's Administration,* Federal case 81-5046, 1981.
7. Friedman, E.: 'Natural death' laws cause hospitals few problems, Hospitals **52**:124, May 16, 1978.
8. Harvard Medical School: Report of the Ad Hoc Committee to Examine the Definition of Brain Death: a definition of irreversible coma, JAMA, **205**:85, 1968.
9. *Lane v. Candura,* 6 Mass App. Ct. 377, 376 N.E. 2d 1232, 93 A.L.R. 3d 59, 1978.
10. *Leach v. Akron General Medical Center,* 68 Ohio Misc. 1, 22 Ohio Op. 3d 49, 426 N.E. 2d 809, 1980.
11. National Hospice Organization: President's letter, McLean, Va., 1982, The Organization.
12. *Perlmutter v. Florida Medical Center,* Broward County, Floria, 78-1486, 1978.
13. Petty, T.: Don't just do something—stand there!, Archives of Internal Medicine **139**:920, 1979.
14. *In re Quinlan,* 70 NJ 10, 355 A 2d, 647, 1976.
15. *Superintendent of Belchertown State School v. Saikewicz,* 373 Mass. 728, 370 N.E. 2d 417, 1977.
16. Taylor and King decisions (friends), Taylor: CR 10 114-752, King: CR 10 114-751, 1981.

BIBLIOGRAPHY

Annas, G.: Reconciling Quinlan and Saikewicz: decision making for the terminally ill incompetent, American Journal of Law and Medicine **4**:367, 1979.

Aroskar, M.: Anatomy of an ethical dilemma: the theory, American Journal of Nursing, **80**:658, 1980.

Battin, M., and Mayo, D., editors: Suicide: the philosophical issues, New York, 1980, St. Martin's Press, Inc.

Creighton, H.: Terminating life support, Supervisor Nurse **9**(9):68, 1978.

Davis, A., and Aroskar, M.: Ethical dilemmas and nursing practice, New York, 1978, Appleton-Century-Crofts.

DeRuvo-Keegan, L., editor: Information bulletin: special topic—hospice care, Kensington, Maryland, 1981, National Health Standards and Quality Information Clearinghouse.

Detsky, A., and others: Prognosis, survival, and the expenditure of hospital resources for patients in an intensive-care unit, New England Journal of Medicine **305**:667, 1981.

Freebairn, J., and Gwinup, K.: Ethics, values & health care, Irvine, California, 1980, Concept Media.

Glick, I., Weiss, R., and Parkes, C.: The first year of bereavement, New York, 1974, John Wiley & Sons, Inc.

Health Care Financing Administration: National health expenditures: 1981, Health Care Financing Review **4**(1):1, 1982.

Homan, R.: Ethical, legal, and medical aspects of brain death: a review and proposal, Texas Medicine **75**:36, June 1979.

Lampton, L., and Winship, D.: The "no code blue" issue: Missouri is not Massachusetts, Missouri Medicine **76**:259, 1979.

Mappes, T., and Zembaty, J.: Biomedical ethics, New York, 1981, McGraw-Hill Book Co.

Pavalon, E.: Human rights and health care law, New York, 1980, American Journal of Nursing Co.

President's Commission for the Study of Ethical Problems in Medicine and Biomedical and Behavioral Research: Defining death, Washington, D.C., 1981, U.S. Government Printing Office.

Rabkin, M., Gillerman, G., and Rice, N.: Orders not to resuscitate, The New England Journal of Medicine **295**:364, 1976.

Saunders, C.: Caring to the end, Nursing Mirror, **151**:52, 1980.

Schram, R., Kane, J., and Roble, D.: "No code" orders: clarification in the aftermath of Saikewicz, The New England Journal of Medicine **299**:875, 1978.

Spencer, S.: "Code" or "no code": a nonlegal option, The New England Journal of Medicine **300**:138, 1979.

Turnbull, A., and others: The inverse relationship between cost and survival in the critically ill cancer patient, Critical Care Medicine **7**(1):20, 1979.

Waring, R.: Massachusetts approves no-code orders, Legal Aspects of Medical Practice **7**(2):34, 1979.

10 · Children and death

I feel bad for you I have a baddbad feeling but I hope you come home Soon!

Illustration by Tom Weinman

© 1979 A. Jann Davis.

The topic of death is now being discussed throughout society in the United States. Courses on death and dying are taught at more than 1,000 U.S. colleges, universities, and nursing schools, and more emphasis is being placed on death education in the secondary schools. But how often are preschool and elementary level youngsters excluded from discussions on death because "they're too young to understand?"

Because of their own emotional inability to confront death-related issues, parents are sometimes reluctant to discuss the topic of death with their children. One parent commented, "Before I can teach my child about death, I've got to get some things straight for myself." Other parents are uncertain about what to say and do not know when or where to begin. "I figure the schools will teach my kid about death," one father rationalized. "When I finally got enough nerve to talk to him about sex, he told me things I didn't know. I figure he'll learn about death the same way."

Unfortunately, a child's exposure to death does not wait until he or she has received proper death education. Too often a crisis such as the death of a parent or grandparent finds the emotionally overwrought adult trying to explain to the frightened child what has happened. Some parents do not know what else to say, so they tell their child things that they themselves do not believe. Other adults may try to "protect" their children by not talking

about "it." No one can be separated from the awareness of death. Children are astute behaviorists and are able to detect the gap between what adults say and do. They sense the underlying feelings that cause more confusion and distress than if the truth were told. In reality the youngster is not protected at all. Left with "a bad, bad feeling," the child is deprived of the opportunity to share and learn and the chance to receive support and information when it is desperately needed.

DEVELOPING AN UNDERSTANDING OF DEATH

Many years ago high mortality made death a very real and frequent part of life. Early literature had a prevalent death theme, and in the New England Primer, published in 1788, are these words:

In the burying place you may see
Graves shorter there than I
From death's arrest, no age is free
Young children too may die.

Anguish and suffering were predominant topics in the diaries of the early settlers. Living under the constant threat of death from disease, childbirth, war, or accidents, these pioneers viewed death as a frequent and natural phenomenon.

In 1900 two thirds of those who died were less than 50 years old, and most died in their own beds. Through the help of medical scientists, the life expectancy in the United States is 25 years longer than at the turn of the century. Death has been taken out of the home, with 70 percent of all Americans presently dying in hospitals or other institutions.

With longevity emerged a death-denying society in which death was not talked about or was camouflaged with euphemisms. Such phrases as "passed on," "eternal reward," "gone to heaven," "laid to rest," "gone to sleep forever," "kicked the bucket," "croaked," "the great beyond," "happy hunting ground," "eternal sleep," "giving up the ghost," and "departed" are used instead of the words "died," "dead," or "death." People "visit" the "departed" in the "slumber" room and give "living" memorials. Although the shroud around death is being lifted, the concern about what to tell the children continues.

Through nursery schools and day-care centers, the young child is influenced by external forces much earlier than in previous years. Television exposes children to death at a very young age. Many studies indicate that average American children will spend 15,000 to 16,000 hours in front of television by the time they graduate from high school as opposed to approximately 12,000 hours in formal classroom instruction. During this time the youngster will have witnessed some 18,000 deaths on television that are usually without any sign of remorse or grief. Several times more violence is depicted during programs identified for children as compared with programs for adults. Saturday morning cartoons for children younger than 10 years old depict one violent act every minute. Tom and Jerry are continually scrunched by a wringer or bashed by a mallet. The hapless coyote is forever being tricked into disaster by conniving Roadrunner. Because these and other characters return to face destruction over and over, the young, impressionable mind ponders if death is really final.

When does a child develop a basic concept of death? At what age is the child capable of cognitive reciprocity and therefore able to benefit from learning outside the realm of his or her own experience? At what age is the average youngster able to distinguish animate from inanimate objects, living as opposed to nonliving, and the terms "past," "present," and "future?" When does the secondary-process thinking become sufficient to comprehend

The average American child spends more time in front of a television than in a classroom.
Illustration by Tom Weinman.

that death is irreversible and that because something is dead, it can no longer function?

Table 10-1 shows that the development of a concept of death is a gradual process, influenced by psychosocial and cognitive skills. Children mature at different times and have different coping abilities. Girls are usually more mature than boys, but at any given age, some children will be responsible whereas others are immature. The ability to understand the concept of death—whether it relates to the self or to others—depends on the child's developmental maturity and coping abilities.

Infant and toddler (1 month to 3 years)

Although the concept of death is not possible for the infant and toddler, it is known that at approximately 6 to 7 months infants separated from their mothers or primary care givers experience loss and mourn this loss. It may be that infants younger than 6 months also experience loss when separated from the maternal figure, but they may not be able to express this distress in a way that can be differentiated from their other needs. Failure to thrive without organic cause and prolonged and delayed recuperation from infection are physical results evidenced in some infants who experience prolonged separation from their mothers.

The newborn has the task of differentiating self from the environment, and to develop a sense of being, Maurer[1] maintains that the infant also develops a sense of nonbeing. By three months of age, the healthy infant is secure enough to experiment through games with contrasting states of being and nonbeing. The game peek-a-boo provides a safe opportunity for the child to experience fear and delight, evidenced by the baby's widely staring eyes when the cloth is first removed and delight when eye contact is made with a smiling face. Interestingly, the words "peek-a-boo" stem from Old English words meaning "alive or dead?"

During the high-chair age, babies play games of "disappear and return," which may also be experiments with being and nonbeing. Any adult with the patience to retrieve an item dropped from the tray of the high chair knows that this simple game involves both fretting and ecstasy and will be repeated over and over again. Gradually the child learns that all things do not return and "all gone" becomes a favorite phrase.

"All gone" situations produce curiosity and sometimes fear. Toddlers may consider their feces as part of their bodies, and seeing this being flushed away may prompt children to try and retrieve what is theirs. Flushing the stool after the youngster is out of the room eliminates this concern.

Toddlers are fascinated by the water circling around the bathtub drain after the plug is pulled, but they are quick to scamper out of the tub before they too are "all gone." The toilet is a favorite place to make all sorts of things disappear until the

---

Table 10-1. The development of a child's concept of death

| Researcher | Question | Response | | |
		Preschoolers	Early school-aged children	Middle school-aged children
Piaget	Identify what is alive	Activity in general	Spontaneous movement	Restricted to plants and animals
Nagy	Tell me about death	Asleep in a coffin	Ghost, spirits, skeleton	Death happens from within
Koocher	What causes living things to die?	Eating dirty bugs Swimming alone	Cancer, guns, poison	Illness, old age, accidents

youngster watches in dismay while the plumber retrieves the plastic toy from the overflowing bowl. Blowing out a lighted match, stepping on the pedal of the garbage can, and turning off and on the light switch are all experiments with being and nonbeing and are some of the earliest representations of the child's expression of the self.

Preschooler (3 to 5 years)

Preschoolers view the world from the perspective of their own experiences. Although the child may use the word "die" or "dead," true understanding of the word is absent because young children have difficulty comprehending what they have not experienced. They rely on what they learn from adults, their playmates, and their exposure to media such as television.

When trying to identify what is alive, youngsters at this age depend on the structure and appearance of the object. If something is able to move, is of use, or can do something, then it is alive. Such items include the sun because it gives light, a bicycle when it is going, a watch because it runs, and poison because it can kill people. A tree is not alive unless it has fruit on it and lightning is not good, so it is not alive.

Preschool children do not usually discuss death freely because they do not understand it. They do, however, think about it enough to arouse negative feelings. Death is life but on a reduced level. If prompted, some youngsters report that they feel sorry for people who are dead because living in a grave would be scary, lonely, and boring, Dead people lie down and do not move. Their arms are at their sides. Although the coffin limits movement, nourishment is still possible. Dead people sleep like people at night, and they can feel it if someone is at the grave or talking or placing flowers on the grave.

Most children at this age are not satisfied that the dead disappear. They know about funerals and equate the absence and funerals but want to know where and how the person continues to live. They consider death reversible and a condition from which the person can return or awaken. The most painful aspect of death for these children is separation itself.

Magical thinking and fantasy reasoning are other characteristics of this age group. If the child wishes the mother to go away and she walks out of the room, the child feels responsible. When the youngster is hungry and thinks about something to eat, presto, mother announces dinner is ready. A little girl covers her eyes and asks for her father to find her. The little girl believes that because she cannot see her father, he is unable to see her.

When children under the age of 6 years are asked what causes living things to die, they frequently relate death to not heeding instructions from parents. For example, "crossing the street without looking" and "walking in the water without your boots on" are given as reasons for death. In each case the child considers the act rather than consequences of the act as being the cause of death.

This age group also fails to recognize the irreversibility of death and may say that dead things can be brought back to life by taking them to the doctor or to Grandma's.

Reactions to death. Preschoolers have learned that good is rewarded and bad is punished. Cinderella goes to the ball; the wicked witch dances in red-hot slippers. When the little boy's father dies, he may conclude that Daddy "got dead" because he did not pick up his toys or because he thought bad things about Daddy. His mother is crying and spends little time with him, which further reinforces his belief that he is bad. When the youngster cannot make his father come back by wishing him back, he may then become angry at his father, whom he concludes is staying away to punish him. The child may be afraid to express these hostile feelings, fearing the anger will keep his father away. Fearful of this retaliation, the child directs this misplaced anger onto the self or toward others.

Young children fail to comprehend that death is final, and the use of euphemisms encourages this premise. "Even if Mommy went away to heaven, she will come back like she did when she went away to Chicago. Grandma says its permanent—

it's forever. But I know it's not. Mommy says permanents never last. She will come back.''

Responding to the preschooler. A child fears being unloved and deserted, and for some youngsters, death brings these fears into focus. A 3-year-old girl who is dying in the hospital may not understand about dying, but she knows she misses her parents. A 4-year-old boy with a brain tumor has been told that he is dying. He's too young to understand death, but he understands that his family is sad. He is overheard telling his little sister, ''When I'm dead, I'll make it snow for you.''

Children around the age of 3 years have a short attention span and will therefore need repeated simple explanations about the death of a loved one. They need reassurances that being dead is nothing at all like being alive. Dead people do not need food, and they do not need to go to the bathroom. Grief is recurrent, interspaced with laughter and play. Mourning may be manifested in play or through disturbances in eating and sleeping.

A 5-year-old boy's grandfather dies. His parents tell him he is going to the funeral in 2 days. He does not know what a funeral is. Each time he hears people say the word funeral, they get sad and cry. There are lots of whispers. The little boy concludes that bad, scary things happen at funerals. When it is time to go to the funeral, he screams, ''I'm not going. You can't make me go!'' and runs crying to his room. A 3-year-old girl is sent to relatives when her grandfather dies. When she returns to visit her grandmother, all pictures and items belonging to her grandfather are gone. She is told, ''Grandpa went to heaven.'' The little girl quietly looks through her grandfather's drawers and closet. Finally she tells her mother, ''Grandpa forgot to tell me 'good-bye,' but he 'membered to take his toothbrush.''

Preschoolers may not understand about death, but they do understand about separation. The facts surrounding a death and funeral do not frighten the child nearly as much as the unexplained behavior of their parents. Children need to be told about the death of a loved one as soon as possible and in a way simple enough for them to understand. It is better if this information comes from a person the child loves and trusts. Instead of trying to hide grief, it would be wiser for parents to tell their children the reason they are sad.

Young children are usually interested in attending funerals and weddings even though they may not understand everything about death or marriage. *No* child should be forced to attend a funeral. A great deal of anxiety is already present if the child resists, and the use of force only compounds this anxiety. At a later time the child may want to go to the cemetery and see the grave.

Before children visit the funeral home or attend a funeral, they need to know what to expect. It is better if the child is taken to the funeral home to privately view the body before the funeral. The less a child is able to understand intellectually, the more dependent the child is on the emotional environment, and a supporting adult can answer questions and respond to the needs of the child. Because preschoolers are curious and may touch the body, they need to be told in advance that because the person is dead, the body is cold. A child should never be forced to touch or kiss the body.

Sending children away during mourning periods often creates more problems than it solves. Parents unable to cope with themselves and the preschooler during intense grief may be able to secure the help of a relative or friend so that the child is not left with feelings of being unloved and deserted at a time when ''something bad is happening.''

A child's questions and feelings about a person who has died cannot be eliminated by removing pictures and not talking about the person. The person lived and died. Memories, through sharing, live on.

Death education. Virtually every child will have some contact with death by the age of 5 years. By the time the child reaches kindergarten, as many as 5 percent of the children will have experienced the death of an immediate family member. To avoid dealing with this topic until the death of a family member or friend is to wait too long. Remedial education does help, but it is not as therapeutic as assisting youngsters in developing some understanding of death before they must handle it personally.

Death education for a child should be nonthreatening and contain information that the child will not need to unlearn later. Because attention span is short for preschoolers, they will require multiple and simple explanations. One of the most nonthreatening ways to begin death education is by using nature as a teaching aid. Children can be asked to differentiate between things that are alive and things that are dead. The leaf on the tree is alive. The one on the ground is dead.

The following is an example of a youngster's first exposure to death. The experience was nonthreatening and the child was encouraged to use her own thinking and problem-solving processes.

■ My neighbor Mitzi is a very bright 3-year-old who often comes over to my house to ask questions. We were taking a walk one day and I noticed that about 10 feet ahead and off to the side of our path was a dead bird. Well, Mitzi is a curious child and rather than get involved with a lot of questions about a dead bird, I made a detour and directed her attention in the opposite direction. I learned then that if you don't want a 3-year-old to see something, you step on it. Walking around it only makes it more obvious.

"What's that?" Mitzi asked.

"It's a dead bird," I responded.

As we approached the bird, she questioned further, "What's dead?"

"Dead is when the bird's heart doesn't go thump-thump anymore. The bird doesn't breathe. It can't sing or fly anymore."

"Oh," she acknowledged and started to pick up the bird. The bird had been dead for several days, so I stopped her from touching it, giving her a stick instead to investigate the bird with. Very carefully she turned the bird over. There were worms and bugs on the bird, but this didn't bother Mitzi at all. I made sure she couldn't see my face because it bothered me.

"Can I take it home?" she pleaded. I suggested that instead, we cover it with leaves, and Mitzi agreed.

She gathered a bunch of leaves, and as she placed them on the bird, Mitzi asked, "Do birds go to heaven?"

I thought to myself, here we go. I'd learned a long time ago that Mitzi frequently has her own ideas about what she asks, so I responded, "Do you think birds go to heaven?"

She thought for awhile and decided that they did. She continued to gather leaves and place them on the bird. All at once she started taking leaves off the bird and announced, "It won't work."

I knew things had been going too smoothly. "What won't work, Mitzi?"

"The bird can't be in heaven and still be on the ground." She sat down next to the bird and used the stick to poke at it. I was trying to figure out how to explain things to her without adding to her confusion when her face brightened and she asked, "Can part of a bird go to heaven?"

"What part?" I asked.

"The part that made the bird sing and fly."

I put my arm around her and answered, "Yes." Together we covered the bird and continued on our walk. It's true what they say, from the mouths of babes comes the wisdom of scholars. _____

Children need the experience of being in a funeral home and attending the funeral of someone who is not significant to them before they are faced with the death of a loved one. If prior arrangements are made, most funeral directors permit children to visit, look around, and ask questions. The intent of the visit is not for the child to view a body but rather to have the opportunity to look at a coffin, have it opened, look at the rooms in which families and friends view the body, and have questions answered. Too many children are frightened when they first see a person in a casket because they think the person has been cut in two. At another time an adult should allow the child to view the body of someone the child is not emotionally close to. Once again, the child must know what to expect. The following is an example of an explanation given to a 4 year old before the child attended a visitation at a funeral home.

■ When we get there, we'll sign our names in a book, and you can sign your name too. Then we will go into a room where the dead man is laying in a pretty box called a casket. The lid will be open so we can see him from the waist up. His legs and feet will be covered. He will have his eyes closed and even though he looks like he is asleep, he is not. He is dead.

There will be people there who loved the man and they may cry because he is not alive anymore. When people are sad it helps them to talk to other people, like you and me. We will tell them we are sorry that he died. You'll see pretty flowers and maybe some candles and you may hear soft music. We'll talk to the people for just a little while and then go home. _____

As children grow older, their concept of death changes. Adults sometimes feel frustrated because the same questions that they answered yesterday or last week come up again. This does not mean that the adult did a poor job of responding to the child's questions. It just means that an explanation that was appropriate at that time no longer satisfies. Until the child is around 6 years old, there is rapid development in the concept of death, and repeated questions simply indicate that the child is now ready to learn more.

Early school-aged child (6 to 9 years)

In early school-aged children magical thinking persists although these youngsters are gaining in their ability to test reality. Girls and boys around the age of 7 years no longer believe in Santa Claus and are also beginning to develop their own sense of moral judgment. Girls may be a year or two ahead of boys in both social and intellectual skills, which contributes to the lack of popularity between the two sexes at this age.

Early school-aged children attribute life to anything capable of spontaneous movement. They are able to differentiate animate and inanimate objects but still believe that the clouds, wind, stars, sun, and rivers are alive. Whereas children younger than 6 years old seldom talk freely about death, children between the ages of 6 and 9 years relay countless stories—all without affect—about death. Personification of death as a ghost or bogey-man is more typical of children who rely on their imagination to describe death. In the United States, television takes the imagination out of death, and narrations from school-aged youngsters sound like a television story plot. Death is caused by a gun; car accidents make people die; death happens in the hospital. Early school-aged youngsters are very persistent in trying to get their parents to stop smoking so they will not get cancer and to drive carefully so they will not be in a car accident. The real safety from death for children in this age group rests in their belief that death is not inevitable. They believe that if people are careful they can live forever.

Reactions to death. Magical thinking continues even though the child is adding scientific information. Some children believe if they do not cry, it is not real. An adult shared the fact that his father had died when he was in grade school. "I never cried, not even when I was alone. I felt terrible, but I didn't cry. Ever since Dad died, I have looked for him whenever I'm in a crowd of people. I think it might be easier to go home and cry."

Following the death of a loved one, adults are sometimes so involved in their own guilt that they fail to realize that children too wish that they had treated the person better, done more, or been better individuals while the person was alive. Young people can be spared some of this guilt if they understand that it is a common human experience.

Jimmy's mother had been ill for some time. His parents talked to the 7-year-old boy about the fact that his mother was not going to get well; she was going to die. The mother shared that the little boy had lots of questions.

■ It was certainly harder for me to answer Jimmy's questions than it was for him to ask them. He wanted to know where I would go after I died. I talked about our religious beliefs and also told him about the funeral and the cemetery. I even showed him the dress I was going to be buried in. We tried to prepare him as best we could. His daddy took him to the funeral home and to the cemetery, and he had the chance to look around. Then one day

I heard him ask, "How does Mommy know when she's going to die?" His daddy tried to explain that I didn't know, that no one knew for sure when they were going to die. Jimmy just kept asking the same question over and over. Finally he came running to me crying, "If you don't know when you are going to die, how will you know when to put on your dress?" We had neglected to tell Jimmy that at the funeral home they bathe dead people, fix their hair, and dress them so that they will look nice when people come to see them before they are buried. _____

Almost all youngsters have the experience of having a pet die. Parents are anxious to spare their children grief and may quickly dispose of the dead pet when the child is not around. Children need the opportunity to psychologically say good-bye to their pets. Whenever the child was frightened or punished, the pet was there to offer comfort, and this nonjudgmental acceptance will be missed. Because animals are not identical any more than human beings are, children need to grieve for their dead pet before they can accept another. They may plan elaborate funerals and later unbury the pet to see what has happened to it.

■ Bill and his dog, Blackie, were the best of friends. Shortly after Blackie had puppies, a large malignant growth was discovered on one of her breasts. Although the malignant tumor was removed, the veterinarian predicted that Blackie would live only a short time. The puppies were weaned, and one by one, people began to select a puppy and take it to its new home.

Bill noticed that when people came to look at the puppies, his mother kept the small black puppy apart from the rest. Finally he asked his mother, "Why are you hiding the little black puppy?"

Bill's mother wasn't aware that anyone had noticed what she was doing. "I thought that you might like to keep the little puppy to take the place of Blackie when she dies."

Bill was quiet for awhile and finally responded to his mother. "If I knew for sure that you were going to die, I wouldn't want a new mother until a long time after you were dead."

The next day, a family fell in love with the small black puppy and took it home with them. _____

Responding to the early school-aged child. The child with a life-threatening illness may require special medical treatment that is available only in large centers. Many of these centers are devising cooperative efforts between specialists and hometown physicians. The specialist draws up the treatment plan, which is carried out by the family physician, making it possible for children to remain in their own community and frequently within their own home. One mother commented, "When Susan has to go to the center for treatment, she feels the sickest. When she is in the local hospital for the same treatment, she doesn't feel as sick, and when she receives it at home, she doesn't feel bad at all."

Ronald McDonald Houses become a home away from home for families of pediatric clients who must leave their community to receive treatment for life-threatening diseases. Financed in part by the McDonald's Corporation, there are some 26 houses across the country in which families can avoid costly motel and restaurant bills by doing their own cooking and cleaning. Not only do Ronald McDonald houses prevent families from being separated, they also offer support and understanding during a difficult time.

There are still many hospitals in the United States that do not allow young children to visit loved ones who are hospitalized. Children imagine all sorts of things when reality is withheld, and their fears are compounded when loved ones are dying. A young boy did not have the opportunity to witness the changes brought about by his mother's illness. After her death he was taken to the funeral home to see his mother. He took one look and cried, "That's not my mother!" It was some time before the boy could accept that his mother's appearance had been changed by the illness.

Before visiting the hospital, children will need to know what they will see and what to expect from

A pet may be a child's best friend.
Photograph by Charles D. Davis.

their loved ones and other clients in the same room. A 6-year-old boy went to visit his grandmother in the hospital. He had been told that she would be in bed and that there would be a tube in her arm giving her water so she would not be thirsty. He was also told that his grandmother would look thin and would probably act tired. The youngster walked into the room, looked his grandmother over, and then directed his attention at the client in the other bed. His main concern was, "What's that green stuff coming out of the tube in that lady's nose?"

When children visit, their visits should be supervised and be kept brief. Adults should be encouraged to check at the nurses' station before taking the child into the client's room so that the visit is at an appropriate time and the child can be prepared for whatever is currently going on in the room.

Death education. Frequently parents consult with health professionals about what to tell a child after a loved one has died, and they may even request that a member of the health team be present to help inform the child of the death. When a child's first exposure to death takes place in a tension-filled environment—such as outside the emergency room—and the adults close to the child are having difficulty coping, the information comprehended will be quite different than had prior education taken place.

Whenever death education takes place, the atmosphere must be warm and supportive to prevent any minimal anxiety from being magnified. The adults involved need to have worked through their own taboos and fears regarding death if they are going to help children cope with the topic and reality of finiteness.

As an addendum to death education received from parents, information applicable to the last part of life should be included in the school curriculum. Children will be exposed to death, and they need help in understanding the meaning of these experiences and a variety of ways to cope with them. The teacher must have the skill to deal with young people and the diplomacy and restraint that may also be necessary to prevent personal religious beliefs from being imposed on those who seek help. The following suggestions for death education for the child between the ages of 6 and 9 years apply to a classroom, to a hospital, in the family context, or to any environment where there is a warm, supportive atmosphere.

Around the age of 6 or 7 years children are usually more open and direct and generally very interested in discussing their ideas with an interested, attentive adult. It is almost as though they are able to "master" death by knowing as much as possible about it and about what makes things die.

Many classrooms already contain material that is helpful in teaching grade school children about dying. The class can be divided into groups, with each group planting seeds in a container. Later, the youngsters may want to dig up a seed to see what is happening, so several seeds should be planted, with each location marked. They learn that they must take care of their plant or it will die. When one of these plants does die, it is a good time to discuss the difference between alive and dead and what caused the plant to die.

An aquarium provides a nonthreatening, first-hand experience about life and death. One teacher warned, "Don't buy all cheap fish. They live forever. Buy an expensive fish and you can count on a funeral."

Youngsters enjoy being involved in setting up the aquarium and helping decide what kind of fish to put in the tank. This involvement increases their interest in the aquarium, and frequently the fish are named. The following is a typical exchange between two first graders.

"Something's wrong with the black fish."

"Naw, he's just sleeping."

"No he's not. Let's call the teacher."

"Poke him and he'll wake up."

"You do it. I don't wanna."

The second child pokes the fish, and when it doesn't swim away, the first little boy responds.

"See, I told you he wasn't asleep. He's sick or something. I'm getting the teacher."

What happens next is directed by the questions from the class and the guidance of the teacher. Once the children agree that the fish is dead, the next decision is what to do with it. Although flushing the fish down the toilet is an easy method of disposal, it may cause concern for children who are apt to wonder if this is where dead people go. The teacher can ask the class members what they should do with the fish now that it is dead. One or two class members are usually anxious to volunteer information about funerals and burying people. A flower pot makes an excellent burial spot that is also accessible so that the children can dig up the fish to see what happens to dead things.

It is important that the teacher realize that children who hold defensive positions in regard to their thinking about death may do this out of emotional necessity, and it is therefore inappropriate to try and convince the children otherwise.

If a child's relative or friend dies and this is mentioned aloud in class, the teacher will need to be alert to the needs of the child. To focus attention by asking the child to share feelings about what has happened may increase the emotional strain the child is already feeling. It perhaps would be more appropriate to respond, "When people die, others miss them very much." This gives the child the opportunity if he or she wants to share, while also providing an easy out if the child does not want to talk about it. In private the teacher can spend some extra time with the child evaluating emotional needs.

An aquarium provides a nonthreatening experience about life and death.

Illustration by Tom Weinman.

Middle school-aged child (9 to 12 years)

Somewhere between the ages of 9 and 12 years children change from their thinking that everything that moves is alive to conclude that some things that move are not alive. Finally they understand that the sun, stars, and wind are not alive and that the term ''alive'' is limited to plants and animals. Also, during these years children generally recognize that death is a state of internally caused dysfunction that results in the cessation of life. They understand that death is an inevitable process that ultimately takes place within each person and that the body eventually crumbles to dust. Children between the ages of 9 and 12 years list illness, old age, and accidents as causes of death, or simply that part of the body no longer works right.

Reactions to death. It is also during these preteen years that children begin to talk about affective reactions to death and emotional attachment to the deceased. Sometimes they are able to share more feelings when talking about the death of a pet than the death of a significant other. This does not mean that the pet is more important but that perhaps this experience is more distant and safer to openly explore than is the death of a loved one.

Middle school-aged children are learning to understand both the biological process of death and the emotional aspects of death. Following a death in the family, the school-aged child may be left without support during the grieving process. Parents are depressed, withdrawn, and so involved in their own grieving that they do not recognize the emotional needs of the child. The child does not want to do or say anything that will add to their parents' grief, so they stay as out of the way as much as possible and assume the role of the "brave, understanding child."

Responding to the middle school-aged child. Children between the ages of 9 and 12 years have not developed coping mechanisms that enable them to deal with death and may only be able to deal with the reality of death a little at a time. Denial attenuates what is too painful to accept and allows the child to accept reality in manageable doses rather than being overwhelmed by it. As one 11-year-old child with leukemia commented, "It is nice not knowing all about the bad things."

When a youngster uses denial in dealing with the death of a loved one, a great deal of anxiety is present. Rather than encouraging denial, a supportive adult needs to offer small amounts of reality in addition to large amounts of emotional support. When the child is more secure, he or she will be able to confront reality and deal with it constructively.

One of the first ways in helping preteen children deal with death is to recognize their grief. Adults usually have support from persons outside the family who allow them to talk about their loss, but the school-aged child must depend on family members for this support. For example, very few children ever receive sympathy cards following the death of a sibling or a parent. When people make condolence calls, they avoid talking to children, and if they do say anything to the youngster, it is usually "How's school?" or "My, have you ever grown." An insightful funeral director suggested that a relative or close friend stay with a child during the

ceremonies following death to make certain that the child is included. Too often they stand in the background without anyone to talk to. The child can be given something genuine to do such as greeting people, helping with the guest book, or telling people good-bye at the door. They also need to be told that it is okay to talk about the person who has died—even though the conversation may prompt tears. When it comes time to go through the deceased's personal belongings, the school-aged child should be included. Some belongings may be very special to the youngster that others may not be aware of, and there may be items that the child wants someone special to have. While family members sort through these items, the sharing of memories and the sharing of sadness makes the loss easier for the school-aged child to come to terms with.

Death education. Children between the ages of 9 and 12 years are more able to understand the facts surrounding death than they are the feelings. Many of these youngsters have been shielded from death, and they have fantasies and fears that they try to cover with jokes and giggles. A nonthreatening way to begin discussions on death can start with a field trip to an old cemetery. Youngsters can make rubbings from old tombstones and attempt to establish the age of the cemetery by locating the oldest marker. Old tombstones often state the cause of the person's death, and some even tell a story about the person. All kinds of epitaphs have been reported, and some are very humorous. On a lawyer's tombstone is written, "1867-1946 The defense rests." A man by the name of Johnny Yeast has a tombstone inscribed, "Here lies Johnny Yeast Pardon me for not rising." A Boot Hill cemetery is the final resting place of Lester Moore. His demise is attributed to "Four slugs from a forty-four No Les No More." A favorite epitaph among youngsters reads, "I told you I was sick!"

Following the death of a fifth grader, many of the classmates were left with unanswered questions and feelings not expressed. Only two or three of the children had attended the funeral, so the teacher sent notes to the parents, asking permission to take

Finding the oldest tombstone is part of a field trip to an old cemetry, where epitaphs reveal both history and mystery surrounding death.

Photograph by John Hennessey III.

the children to visit their classmate's grave. Approval was given, and several parents accompanied the class to the cemetery. The tombstone had not been erected, so each student was handed a blank sheet of paper and a pencil with the suggestion that they draw a tombstone and write a message about their friend. The children were given the choice of keeping what they wrote or placing the message in an envelope to be sent to the child's parents. Not only did this give the children a chance to say good-bye to their friend but it also provided a great deal of comfort to the child's par-

ents as they read these special messages from their child's classmates.

Adolescent (12 to 18 years)

The young adolescent shares many of the adult's concepts of death, and they cope with death in a similar fashion. Adolescents are future oriented. This is not to say that they do not review the past or view the present, but emphasis is on previewing the future. Thoughts become philosophical. ''Who am I?'' ''What am I going to do with my life?'' ''What about this thing called death?'' Their own mortality is kept in the distance, superseded by youth, plans, and the future. The death of a classmate bring mortality into focus. The diagnosis of a life-threatening illness brings mortality into view.

Reactions to death. Young adolescents are in the process of tumultuous change, much of which is completely out of their control. A certain amount of autonomy is necessary in each person's life, and when individuals lose this control in one area, they are apt to compensate by asserting control in another. It perhaps may be death denying or death defying that prompts the adolescent to attempt to challenge, master, or control death through such areas as speeding vehicles or experimentation with drugs. Accidents remain the leading cause of deaths among American youth, and they occur at a time when sensory, physical, and psychomotor function is at its peak.

Although adolescents are in the process of freeing themselves from their parents and establishing independence, there is a simultaneous need to be able to depend and rely on their parents. Therefore the death of a parent makes this transition from childhood to adulthood more difficult. Bereavement differs from the feelings surrounding the divorce of parents since death is more mysterious and completely irreversible. The adolescent is left with feelings of guilt and loss that must be worked through in addition to dealing with the surviving parent's grief.

After his father died, a young adolescent spent as little time at home as possible. Ultimately he confided to the school counselor, "Living at home is like living in a morgue. All my mom does is bawl. I miss him too, but I can't stand bawling all the time. So I just don't come home." Once his mother became aware of the home environment she was creating, she sought outside help in dealing with her grief to provide a better home for her son.

Responding to the adolescent. The early part of adolescence is marked by real concern with body image. A life-threatening illness that affects appearance may be more devastating than the illness itself. At a time when the individual is in the process of pulling away and making independent deci-

sions, a life-threatening illness places control once again in the hands of the adult. Health professionals need to realize the adolescent's need not to be manipulated and dominated wholly by others. It is mandatory that the adolescent be included in the decision-making process and not treated like a puppet with the total identity dictated by the string of illness. Adults become frustrated when the teenager will not share thoughts, feelings, and emotions. Perhaps this is the only area in which the teenager has any control, and this control may be more important than sharing with adults.

A mother mentioned that her teenaged son never turned on his stereo again after learning that he had cancer. The music he loved was filled with life that he had felt had been robbed by cancer. Music about death served only as an overwhelming reminder that he was finite. After his death his mother found several new albums that had been given to him by friends, and they were still sealed.

Adults who face death can review the goals they have achieved. Adolescents with life-threatening illnesses preview goals that perhaps will never be achieved. They need the help of those who care for and about them to put some meaning into their lives. There are no formulas. An adult who is there but allows privacy, autonomy, and freedom gives a gift that may help the child understand life and comprehend the meaning of death.

Death education. The giggles of the 9- and 10-year-olds give way to serious questions, as those in early adolescence begin to question for themselves the myths and realities of death. A course on death and dying for this age group can begin with a reality-based, somewhat intellectualized approach, with the students comparing different cultures, funeral practices, and religious beliefs. A multidimensional class involving professionals from various disciplines makes death education more encompassing. In some schools a section on aging is included in the course, with the psychological and social aspects of aging presented by someone in the field of gerontology. Films such as *Peege* by Phoenix Films, Inc., portray both the affect and the reality of aging. Students can be given the choice of writing a term paper on aging or completing 3 hours of volunteer work in a nursing home in recreational activity. Some of the activities students help with are sing-alongs, bingo, or planning a party. Many students are surprised to find the nursing home experience a good one, and they readily admit, "The only reason I went to the nursing home was because I didn't want to write the paper."

It is helpful if an attorney talks about wills, probate court, and estates and answers questions such as "What happens if the person dies and doesn't leave a will?" Religious leaders from the community share different beliefs and funeral practices. Cremation, euthanasia, cryogenics, and immortality are topics that prompt a great deal of discussion and debate. Information concerning organ donation should be presented. During the field trip to a funeral home, students prepare an itemized cost of their own funeral and later write their own obituaries and eulogies and present these to the class.

This type of formal course has proven beneficial to more than those directly involved in the class. Some students found the information of great help when a member of their immediate family died. A 16-year-old girl's baby sister died at birth. Her mother was unable to help with any of the funeral arrangements. After the funeral her father talked to the teacher who had taught the course on death and dying. "I don't know what I would have done without her help. She knew what needed to be done when I didn't have the faintest idea."

Many times adults are ready to jump in with information when all the adolescent really needs is help in clarifying the ideas he or she already has. An adult who is able to respond in a way as to encourage the person to evaluate thinking and behavior succeeds in helping the individual clarify values. Clarifying responses do not criticize, moralize, or give values and do not encourage the person toward a predetermined answer. They are used in situations involving feelings, attitudes, beliefs, or purpose in which there are no right answers.

Examples of such responses that could be used during discussions about death are "Is this some-

thing you believe?" "What do you mean by _____ ?" "Are you saying that _____?" "Have you thought much about that?" "What are some good things about that idea?" "What do you think happens?" and "Can you give me an example?" Rather than teaching or adding to another's ideas, the clarifying response stimulates individuals to clarify the ideas they already have.

Outside the parent-child teaching-learning dyad, the instructor's beliefs and opinions should remain as such. Phrases that begin with "If I were you . . ." "In my opinion . . ." "If it were me . . ." or "I believe . . ." are introductions to the speaker's personal feelings, attitudes, or beliefs. Frequent use of these phrases by the instructor may indicate the person's limitations in being able to work with others on this topic.

Education about death begins at birth. It is the responsibility of those who care for and care about children to teach them about dying and death and support them through their mourning. When children are faced with the reality that relationships are not lasting, they respond according to their own past experiences, their families' religious and cultural heritage, their relationship with the dead person, their developmental level, and what they have been taught about separation, loss, and death. In the midst of the crisis, children need help and support as they try to understand the loss. It is frequently someone in the helping field who reminds, "Don't forget about the children."

SEPARATION AND LOSS ILLUSTRATED

■ Sally was a 5-year-old girl whose mother was hospitalized for severe nausea and vomiting secondary to metastatic leiomyosarcoma. Her mother, Samatha, was trying to gain enough strength so that she could find a home for Sally and her teen-aged brother before she died. Samatha's husband had disappeared 2 years earlier when cancer was diagnosed, and later he divorced her and refused to care for or have anything to do with the children.

Sally and her brother stayed with friends when

their mother was unable to care for them, and during her hospitalization they lived with foster parents who were considering adopting the children.

The little girl had not been told that her mother was dying. Her mother commented, ''I had hoped that it wouldn't be necessary, and now I don't have much time.'' Samatha asked that the nurse-counselor spend some time with Sally. ''I want to tell her, but I feel it's important that she has someone she knows here and can talk to if she needs to.''

During the initial visit between Sally and the nurse-counselor, Sally ignored the play equipment and stayed as close to the nurse as possible. She appeared to be preoccupied with pleasing the nurse and spent time smoothing her dress, fixing her hair, and trying to act like an adult. Sally talked about the ''nice room'' and the ''pretty dress'' the nurse

was wearing and made frequent comments about liking her. Sally was asked to draw a picture of her family, and she quickly drew Fig. 10-1, *A*, which was completely void of people. After she had finished the picture, she laughed and said, ''I forgot the people,'' and then added the people as shown in Fig. 10-1, *B*.

Children may not draw human figures, but their drawing may still contain information about significant people in their lives. Repetitive items in the picture may coincide with the number of family members important to the child. In Sally's initial drawing the three flowers could represent the three members of her family. The largest flower would signify her mother, who is the most important person in her life, and the two smaller flowers may represent Sally and her brother. The large building

Fig. 10-1. A, Sally's initial drawing of her family.
© *1979 A. Jann Davis.*

drawn between the large and smaller flowers denoted separation, whether it be the hospital, the foster home, or death. It is unusual that a child includes two suns in one picture, which further emphasizes that Sally sees her mother and herself being separated. She and her mother will not share their sun, and her mother will therefore need one of her own.

After Sally finished adding human figures, she quickly became involved with items on the nurse's desk and did not offer any comments about the drawing. When asked if she wanted to talk about the drawing, she responded, "It's a picture of my family," and then changed the subject. The topic was not pursued further.

The second part of Sally's drawing—that with human figures—is considered separate from the initial drawing without human figures. The drawing can be evaluated without benefit of Sally's interpretation. The largest figure would be the most significant person in Sally's life and that person would probably be her mother. A second figure is somewhat larger than the rest of the figures and is therefore likely to represent the second most important person in her life at that time. The six figures are more than her immediate family of three and her two foster parents. It was theorized that the sixth figure was her father, whom she had not seen in 3 years. An important point is that one of the figures is armless, which might be accidental, but this is unlikely since the other five figures have arms. If the omission is not accidental, it may reflect socially unacceptable behavior involving arms or hands or denial of function of these parts. The

Fig. 10-1. cont'd. B, Sally later added people to her drawing.

fact that Sally had been physically abused when she was 3 years old makes the omission of arms even more important.

When it came time for Sally to leave the nurse's office, she was openly reluctant to go. At the door she remembered the picture she had drawn and asked, "Do you want me to tell you about my picture?" Needless to say, the nurse made arrangements to extend the visit.

Sally identified the large figure as her mother, the figure standing next to her mother as her brother, and the third in line as her foster mother. The fourth figure was identified by Sally as being her foster father. She made no comment about the fact that he was armless, and made no attempt to add arms. Sometimes children will fill in omissions when they are talking about their picture. The fifth figure Sally said was a picture of herself. At this point she smiled at the nurse and volunteered, "The last picture is of you."

Sally drew herself away from the most significant person in her life and placed herself next to an armless man and a person she had just met. She saw her teenaged brother as being closer to her mother and her foster mother. In reality the teenager was causing a lot of problems for his mother, and he was receiving a great deal of negative attention from her. Sally, on the other hand, was her mother's "little darling," and although she received less time from her mother than did her brother, the attention was positive.

It does not take an expert to see that Sally drew the nurse's arm extended toward the drawing of herself. The nurse held out her arms to the little girl who quickly crawled up on her lap. The two sat quietly holding each other for several minutes.

Later that afternoon the foster mother called the nurse-counselor. She relayed the fact that they were planning to adopt both children in an effort to keep them together. When the foster mother was asked how she felt about adopting the boy, she commented that she was very comfortable with him. "I've had boys, and I understand them." When asked how she felt about adopting the little girl, the foster mother admitted, "I really don't know

how to take care of a girl. I just want to keep the children together."

The nurse-counselor then asked how the foster father felt about the children. "Oh, he thinks the boy's fine, but he's really thrilled to be getting a little girl. Because of her bad experience when she was 3, he has never touched her. He would love to hold her, but he's afraid he will frighten her. Do you think it would be all right for him to touch her or hold her?" At this point the nurse realized that Sally had omitted the arms on her foster father because to her, they did not function.

The nurse responded that Sally needed to be held and loved, but that the foster parents should take their cues from Sally. The nurse also said that Sally was very perceptive and sensed that her foster mother was more comfortable with her brother and that she felt closer to her foster father. What could not be expressed in words was drawn on paper.

Later Sally's mother explained to Sally that she was going to die. Sally was old enough to understand about separation but was not old enough to comprehend the permanence of death. She later reported to the nurse-counselor, "My mommy's going to be dead, but it's okay because then she won't be sick anymore. When she's through being dead, she'll come home." _____

Children sometimes do not know the words or the ways to express feelings they do not understand and do not know what to do with. A child's drawing may be an expression of feelings, and the person who receives the drawing receives a gift. Evaluated on the basis of the child's age, maturation, emotional status, and background, this gift may be a display of creativity or an insight into human feelings.

CHILDREN'S BOOKS ABOUT DEATH

Parents and teachers often ask health professionals for resource material to help teach children about death. Books are an excellent medium from which to learn at a safe distance, as others cope with realities of life. When children look at a picture book or listen to a story, they take with them the information they need and are able to comprehend at that moment. Growth is an innate process for the child, and it is important that books presented are of a quality that will contribute to and encourage vigorous mental, emotional, or spiritual development.

Children's books present death in a multitude of themes. Those that use folk tales, fairy tales, fables, or fantasy should all be viewed carefully so that the child is not confused by inaccurate information. For example, the much loved story *Snow White and the Seven Dwarfs* does not present factual information about death. Fables often present untruth or supernatural happenings in which animals or plants sometimes speak and act like human beings. It is up to the adult to evaluate each fable for its merit, for in some there is a theme of wisdom. One example is *The Story of Ick*, by Gynne, which exaggerates the effects of pollution until the only human alive is one little boy. The use of fantasy in children's literature is a form of allegory, and the child will need to rely on experience and reasoning ability to differentiate reality from fantasy. In DePaola's book *Nana Upstairs and Nana Downstairs* there is reference to a falling star as being a kiss from the grandmother who used to live upstairs in the house before she died.

If books are used to teach young children about death, it is important that the information be nonthreatening and true. A list of books with death themes for children from preschoolers to adolescents is included at the end of this chapter, and a few of these books will be discussed here. Each book should be evaluated before its use so that the information presented to the child will be appropriate and acceptable for the situation, the adult, and the child.

Preschool

Books with nature themes are excellent introductions to the topic of death. *The Apple and the Moth*, by Mari and Mari, is a picture book without words, encouraging children to follow a caterpillar until it develops into a moth and an apple blossom until it becomes an apple. Another book about nature is *Seasons*, by Burningham, which is filled with beautiful pictures that help the child discover the cycle of nature.

Sometimes an author will equate an animal's death with departure or sleep, and in the book *When Violet Died* the author, Kantrowitz, writes that the children "planted" Violet, the dead bird. The use of euphemisms in children's books do nothing to help the child understand death.

A good factual book for young children is *About Dying*, by Stein. Early in the book the children's pet bird dies, and later their grandfather dies. Vivid photographs and a simple text present life, death, burial, and the feelings that accompany these events. The accompanying text for adults provides more specific detail in handling questions and discussion prompted by the child's natural curiosity. Two other books dealing with the death of a grandparent include *Nonna*, by Bartoli, and *My Grandpa Died Today*, by Fassler.

A book that deals more about death than is immediately apparent is the book *Owliver*, by Kraus. In the story Owliver is pressured by parents who each have their own idea about what Owliver should be when he grows up. Owliver feels so pulled that he pretends that he has no parents. The book offers reassurance to children who may not be aware that such wish-dreams are common, acceptable, and normal and that such wishes do not cause death to happen.

School age

In the classroom discussion it is not unusual to hear 8- or 9-year-olds share morbid stories about what happens after death. "You get buried and you rot away. The worms eat you up." Young school-aged children need factual information. "Yes, all dead things will rot or decompose until only bones are left. They smell bad when this happens. That is why they are buried or cremated."

Books that present facts about death will help satisfy the child's need for more information. In the book *A Look at Death*, by Anders, death is described as part of life, sometimes expected for the very old and unexpected for the young. The funeral, burial, religious faith, importance of grief, and customs of mourning are presented through text and photographs on every page. Another outstanding book is *Tell Me About Death: Tell Me About Funerals,* by Corley, which introduces the processes of aging and death through a father-daughter conversation.

Since children up to the age of 10 or 11 years have the tendency to endow events, objects, and animals with psychological attributes, they may be less threatened about the use of fantasy rather than fact in death education. The use of magical thinking and fantasy is used by White in *Charlotte's Web* to teach children about life's realities and feelings. Wilber the pig was to be butchered but is ultimately saved from being butchered by Charlotte's cunning spider webs. Charlotte's death conveys the reality that all life ends in death, and Wilber is able to manage his sadness by caring for the next generation of spiders. The story is full of magic and wonder that teaches about death in a gentle way through the use of fantasy.

Different customs and religions are also presented in children's books on death. Coutant's *First Snow* shares customs and beliefs of a Vietnamese Buddhist family. Lien's grandmother is dying, and although Lien has been taught that life and death are two parts of the same thing, she does not understand until she watches snow melt for the first time. *Scat,* by Dobrin, is about a black boy in the South, where there are jazz funerals. After the little boy's grandmother dies, he pays tribute to his grandmother by playing his harmonica at her grave. In the book *Annie and the Old One* the author, Miles, presents customs and beliefs of a Navaho Indian family. Annie's grandmother tells the family that she will die when the rug is woven, so Annie tries to hold back time by preventing completion of the rug. The grandmother gently tries to help her understand that death cannot be prevented. *The Birthday Visitor,* by Uchida, is a book of Eastern culture and the view that death is a natural event and that the funeral need not be sad.

There are numerous books about the death of a child's pet that have been written to appeal to this age group. Some authors use a new pet to resolve the child's grief or comfort the child with the information that their buried pet will help things grow. Two such books include *The Old Dog,* by Abbott, and *The Tenth Good Thing About Barney,* by Viorst. In reality these solutions may not be too effective in comforting a child whose pet has died. The death of a child's pet can create a great deal of guilt for the child. In the book *Do You Love Me?* the author, Gackenbach, confronts the troubling and all too frequent occurrence of the accidental death of an animal. In this story a youngster accidentally kills a hummingbird he was trying to catch for a pet. Later, when he is given a puppy to take care of, he is afraid he will hurt the puppy the way he did the hummingbird.

Children are frequently warned by parents, "If you don't give your dog food and water, he will die. Keep him out of the street, or he will be killed." *The Accident,* by Carrick, is a poignant story that brings a young boy's feelings of outrage, despair, and grief to the surface after his dog is hit and killed by a car. The father buries the dog while the boy is sleeping, which only compounds the boy's anger.

Another serious yet sensitive book is *A Taste of Blackberries,* by Smith, which portrays the events and feelings of an 8-year-old boy whose best friend dies from anaphylactic shock following a bee sting. This book deals with the questions about death and the feelings that result. The neighbor responds to the probing question of "Why?" by answering that some questions are without answers. To the child this made a lot more sense than something about God needing angels. The book offers children many answers to their questions about death. It provides a repertoire of suggestions for understanding accidental death and the feelings created when a friend dies.

Some contend that death education for children should be limited to a cognitive, factual approach. Others recommend that children's literature should depict death with realism while avoiding dramatic scenes. Children of any age do not need either the continuous weeping of those who have not resolved a death in their lives or the callousness of the unfeeling. However, if death is to be depicted with realism, it is necessary to also deal with the emotional reactions. To treat affect as undesirable behavior is to ignore an important aspect of death education.

Adolescent

Somewhere around the age of 10 years youngsters have reached concrete operations in cognitive skills, and their understanding of death has enlarged. In the process of finding their identities many adolescents tiptoe around death, viewing it from all sides, seeing it as a challenge, a threat, and for too many, a solution for stresses they are unable to handle.

Know Your Feelings, by Hyde and Forsyth, offers a reassuring analysis of feelings that range from happiness to depression. The book has material on death and separation and helpful suggestions on coping with the myriad of changes that adolescents experience.

Klagsbrun has written the extraordinary book *Too Young To Die: Youth and Suicide.* Suicide is increasing among adolescents, and this comprehensive book backed by research analyzes both the causes for suicide and the plight of the survivors.

A poignant story of a drug-related death is revealed in the book *Go Ask Alice,* whose author is anonymous. The drug scene, premarital sex, and aloneness all create an impact not soon forgotten.

The book *Eric,* by Lund, is the story of a 17-year-old with leukemia. Eric's anger and grief are indelible as he celebrates life in the midst of his struggle to free himself from death.

Krementz's *How It Feels When A Parent Dies* is a sharing of experiences and feelings of 18 youngsters who have had either a mother or a father who has died. The feelings of anguish, guilt, confusion, and anger are presented in such a way that the reader will know that these feelings are normal and appropriate.

The classic book for the young adolescent is *Little Women,* by Alcott. This book is interwoven with the events of Beth's life and her sense of impending death. Throughout the entire book great sensitivity to feelings is conveyed, as death is treated as a reality of life.

• • •

Parents, teachers, physicians, nurses, and other helping professionals are able to help children explore their attitudes and anxieties about separation, loss, and death only if they are prepared to confront and explore their own perceptions and feelings on this issue. Children react differently to loss than do adults, and a child's perception of death varies at different ages. Unless adults are perceptive to the specific needs of children, they may be left to deal with unresolved grief the rest of their lives. It is neither possible nor permissible to conceal death from the child. To attempt to do so leaves a child without the love and trust that can greatly diminish the shock and pain of death.

REFERENCE

1. Maurer, A.: Maturation of concepts of death, British Journal of Medical Psychology **39:**35, 1966.

BIBLIOGRAPHY

Blinder, B.: Sibling death in childhood, Child Psychiatry and Human Development **2**(4):169, 1972.

Grollman, E., editor: Explaining death to children, Boston, 1967, Beacon Press.

Koocher, G.: Why isn't the gerbil moving anymore? Children Today, p. 18, January-February 1975.

Menig-Peterson, C., and McCabe, A.: Children talk about death, Omega **8:**305, 1977-1978.

Morris, B.: Young children and books on death, Elementary English **51:**395, 1974.

Nagy, M.: The child's theories concerning death, Journal of Genetic Psychology **73:**3, 1948.

Nelson, R., and Peterson, W.: Challenging the last great taboo: death, The School Counselor, **22:**353, 1975.

Piaget, J.: The child's conception of the world, New York, 1929, Harcourt, Brace & Co.

Romero, C.: Children, death and literature, Language Arts **53:**674, 1976.

CHILDREN'S BOOKS ABOUT DEATH
Preschool (3 to 5 years)
Bartoli, J.: Nonna, New York, 1975, Harvey House, Publishers.

Borak, B.: Someone small, New York, 1969, Harper & Row, Publishers, Inc.

Brown, M.: The dead bird, Reading, Massachusetts, 1958, Addison-Wesley Publishing Co., Inc.

Burningham, J.: Seasons, New York, 1969, The Bobbs-Merrill Co., Inc.

Fassler, J.: My grandpa died today, New York, 1971, Human Sciences Press, New York.

Grimm Brothers: Snow White and the seven dwarfs, New York, 1972, Farrar, Straus & Giroux, Inc.

Harris, A.: Why did he die? Minneapolis, 1965, Lerner Publications Co.

Kantrowitz, M.: When Violet died, New York, 1973, Parents Magazine Press.

Kraus, R.: Owliver, New York, 1974, Windmill Books, Inc.

Mari, I., and Mari, E.: The apple and the moth, New York, 1970. Pantheon Books, Inc.

Stein, S.: About dying, New York, 1974, Walker & Co.

Tresselt, A.: The dead tree, New York, 1972, Parents Magazine Press.

Zolotow, C.: My grandson Lew, New York, 1974, Harper & Row, Publishers, Inc.

School age (6 to 12 years)
Abbott, S.: The old dog, New York, 1972, Coward, McCann, & Geoghegan, Inc.

Anders, R.: A look at death, Minneapolis, 1977, Lerner Publications Co.

DePaola, T.: Nana upstairs and Nana downstairs, New York, 1973, The Putnam Publishing Group.

Carrick, C.: The accident, Boston, 1976, Houghton Mifflin Co.

Corley, E.: Tell me about death: tell me about funerals, Santa Clara, Claifornia, 1973, Grammatical Sciences.

Coutant, H.: First snow, New York, 1974, Alfred A. Knopf, Inc.

Dobrin, A.: Scat, New York, 1971, Four Winds Press.

Gackenbach, D.: Do you love me? New York, 1975, The Seabury Press, Inc.

Gynne, F.: The story of Ick, New York, 1971, Windmill Books, Inc.

Le Shan, E.: Learning to say good-by: when a parent dies. New York, 1976, Macmillan Publishing Co., Inc.

Miles, M.: Annie and the old one, Boston, 1971, Little, Brown & Co.

Smith, D.: A taste of blackberries, New York, 1973, Thomas Y. Crowell Co.

Uchida, Y.: The birthday visitor, New York, 1975, Charles Scribner's Sons.

Viorst, J.: The tenth good thing about Barney, New York, 1971, Atheneum Publishers.

Warburt, S.: Growing time, Boston, 1969, Houghton Mifflin Co.

White, E.: Charlotte's web, New York, 1952, Harper & Row, Publishers, Inc.

Adolescent (12 to 18 years)
Alcott, L.: Little women, New York, 1962, Macmillan Publishing Co., Inc.

Anonymous: Go ask Alice, Englewood Cliffs, New Jersey, 1971, Prentice-Hall, Inc.

Armstrong, W.: Sounder, New York, 1969, Harper & Row, Publishers, Inc.

Beckman, G.: Admission to the feast, New York, 1971, Holt, Rinehart & Winston.

Bernstein, J.: Loss and how to cope with it, New York, 1977, The Seabury Press, Inc.

Green, C.: Beat the turtle drum, New York, 1976, The Viking Press.

Hyde, M., and Forsyth, E.: Know your feelings, New York, 1975, Franklin Watts, Inc.

Klagsbrun, F.: Too young to die: youth and suicide, Boston, 1976, Houghton Mifflin Co.

Klein, N.: Sunshine, New York, 1974, Avon Books.

Klein, S.: The final mystery, New York, 1974, Doubleday Publishing Co.

Krementz, J.: How it feels when a parent dies, New York, 1981, Alfred A. Knopf, Inc.

LeShan, E.: What makes me feel this way? Growing up with human emotions, New York, 1972, Macmillan Publishing Co., Inc.

Lund, D.: Eric, Philadelphia, 1974, J.B. Lippincott Co.

Orgel, D.: The mulberry music, New York, 1971, Harper & Row, Publishers, Inc.

Segerberg, O.: Living with death, New York, 1976, E.P. Dutton, Inc.

Shanks, A.: Old is what you get: dialogues on aging by the old and the young, New York, 1976, The Viking Press.

Stolz, M.: The edge of next year, New York, 1974, Harper & Row, Publishers, Inc.

11 · Bereavement

Illustration by Tom Weinman.

© 1979 A. Jann Davis.

When a loved one dies, the bereaved person must deal with this loss and all the accompanying feelings of grief, anger, guilt, and frustration. Feelings of guilt about what should have been done and what was neglected are common among those who grieve. ''I should have called the doctor sooner.'' ''Did the baby inherit it from me?'' ''Mommy died because I was bad.''''I didn't give you enough attention.''

People learn appropriate behavior for different situations either from being directly involved or from watching others who are involved. Mourning is a culturally patterned response to bereavement, but the resulting feelings of grief come without benefit of vicarious learning. Grief is a personal experience that consumes total attention and supersedes one's usual needs. For many it is overwhelming.

Helping families deal with the emotional crisis surrounding death requires that the care giver become involved with each individual in a unique and totally new way. Sensitive, empathetic care is a fine line between sharing and supporting. The mother whose child is stillborn needs someone who understands her grief and will help her work through the grief she feels from the death of her child as well as the loss of a part of herself. Parents must learn how to say good-bye to what might have been. Sometimes overwhelmingly, children make the transition from two-dimensional artificial television death to the reality of involvement as they grieve for a sibling with whom they have fought or for a parent who has made them angry. Widowed persons often find that with the death of their spouse, old affiliations no longer apply, and they do not know how to deal with loneliness.

This chapter is about life, love, death, and survival. It is about bereavement. Its purpose is to help care givers assist individuals as they learn that grief never completely goes away, it just becomes more bearable.

SOCIETY AND GRIEF

Bereavement is a state that is brought about by the death of a loved one. It prompts the normal emotional response of grief, which includes both an emotional and a behavioral adjustment process. This adjustment is hard work and includes psychological withdrawal from the deceased, readjusting one's life without the deceased, and the formation of new relationships. How something so painful can be normal is difficult to comprehend. Yet those who do not yield to the grief process or accept the discomfort of bereavement are likely to hurt the longest. Bereavement requires painful growth. It is also a process that heals.

Patterns of grief

Death is a frightening, sorrowful, and mystical happening. In primitive societies the feelings surrounding death were openly expressed by wailing, rituals, and pacifying the spirits with gifts and sacrifices. Families in some cultures hired mourners to help them express their overwhelming grief. Up to the turn of this century most societies in the world had certain rules and rituals for mourners to follow and for those interacting with mourners. With the advancement of medicine and the advent of the mobile family, mourning customs in the United States have all but been eliminated. Families who once gathered to share, offer comfort, and help support each other now frequently live too far away to do little more than attend the funeral. Friends and neighbors may resort to the commercialized hallmark of caring and send flowers or cards rather than offering personal help or support. The reality of death that was once brought home to adults and children alike is now shrouded from view, and those who grieve are left alone with feelings they do not understand or know how to handle.

It was not until the 1940s that grief was first defined as a clinical syndrome consisting of psychological and somatic symptoms. As the mental and physical consequences became more apparent, it was suggested that grief be considered a disease with a variety of possible biopsychosocial complications. Clinicians verify that the overall effects of bereavement place the bereaved person at a higher risk for mortality and morbidity. Although this health risk was first considered to be the result of alterations in the bereaved person's life-style, the causative agent has since been determined to be the feelings of despair surrounding grieving itself.[10]

Whereas some today believe that all grief is pathological, others identify pathological reactions as delays, prolongations, or distortions of normal grief. Lindemann[8] cites nine examples of morbid grief reactions indicating pathological grief:

1. Overactivity without a feeling of loss
2. Taking on symptoms similar to those of the last illness of the deceased
3. Psychosomatic conditions, including ulcerative colitis, rheumatoid arthritis, and asthma
4. Progressive isolation toward friends and relatives
5. Furious hostility against specific persons such as the physician, minister, or funeral director
6. Repression of feelings of hostility, resulting in complete absence of emotional expression
7. A lasting loss of social interaction resulting from a lack of decision and initiative
8. Actions detrimental to one's own social and economic existence
9. Agitated depression with needs for self-punishment producing a behavior that is dangerously suicidal

Individuals with these reactions usually respond to immediate and skilled intervention from a psychologist, psychiatrist, or counselor.

Shortly after a death it is difficult to differentiate normal from abnormal bereavement behavior. There will be unusual actions and reactions that are merely isolated occurrences brought about by the crisis of death. It is when the abnormal appears in extremes and persists that there is reason for concern and intervention. For example, one widow notices only the void in her life and frequently starts to share something with her husband before she remembers that he is dead. Another widow carries on imaginary conversations with her dead spouse and continually sets a place for him at mealtimes.

There are also factors in a person's history that may predispose an individual to abnormal reactions to the death of a loved one. These include alcoholism, death of a parent or sibling in childhood or early adolescence, homosexuality, hospitalization resulting from psychiatric problems, history of depressive reactions to relatively minor incidents, lasting conflict with deceased, and excessive dependence on the deceased.[2] By being aware of these factors, physicians, nurses, clergy, counselors, and other helping professionals may be able to provide the extra support necessary to prevent abnormal grief from occurring. If pathological reactions do appear, prompt intervention is provided so that debilitating depressions and mental illnesses can be prevented.

During normal grief, people are able to work their way back from utter despair to a near normal living. In abnormal or pathological grief the psychological or physical symptoms persist for an unreasonable amount of time. Theorists disagree on the length of time involved for normal grief work, with the time span varying from weeks to months or years. Many things must be taken into account when duration of mourning is considered. The maturity and temperament of the bereaved are important considerations as are the quality and duration of the relationship with the deceased. It is usually considered that a year is the minimum duration of mourning, with 1 to 2 years an average duration.

There is much about grief that is not understood. When something is not understood and cannot be prevented, an element of control is established when it can at least be predicted. Although categorizing experiences makes them easier to understand and provides a kind of control, there is always concern that behavior will be directly or indirectly shaped to fit the categories.

Table 11-1 points out some disagreement among theorists; however, clinical experience suggests that the bereaved person experiences initial shock and disbelief, resulting in a general life disruption characterized by dysphoria, which is gradually worked through until an emotional readjustment is made.

Society and the bereaved

Society sets certain standards for dealing with grief and tends to fit all bereaved people into a pattern. This standardization fails to take into account the circumstances of the death, the person who survives, or the amount of emotional investment into the relationship. The extent of grief experienced is always unique, and when all grief is dealt with in a uniform manner, the one who is mourning may be hindered more than helped.

One of the initial mistakes often made with bereaved individuals is not allowing them to grieve in their own way. People give advice according to their own needs, such as "Don't cry," which can be interpreted to mean "I can't handle it," and "Go ahead and cry," which may mean "I'll feel better if you do." Grieving is work that can be accomplished in a number of ways that are dictated by each person's makeup and personality. For children the big loss may hurt too much, so they cry over the little things that are not so painful. Men have often been raised to believe that crying is not manly, and after years of being stoic some find they are unable to cry or are frightened when they do break down and cry. After the death of his wife an Iowa farmer made the funeral arrangements and then climbed on his tractor and plowed for the next 2 days. "I can't cry when I'm really upset. I have to work out part of the pain first."

People are discouraged from grieving the way that they want to or for as long as they need to. Sorrow is uncomfortable for those who are not grieving, and frequently a coordinated effort is made to get the person involved, out of the house, away from the memories. A flurry of too early invitations is often declined without customary graciousness. One widow commented, "My friends gave me several weeks, and then I was supposed to be as usual. I tried to explain that grief wasn't major surgery that healed within a few weeks. I finally quit trying to explain. If you haven't been through it, you don't understand, and even if you have, time helps to erase the pain."

Rather than pushing the sorrowing person out of

Table 11-1. Normal stages of grief

Author	Stage 1	Stage 2	Stage 3	Stage 4	Stage 5
Bowlby	Protest	Despair	Detachment		
Engel	Shock and disbelief	Dysphoria	Restitution and recovery		
Greenblatt	Shock and denial	Depression	Emancipation and readjustment	Identity reconstruction	
Kubler-Ross	Denial	Anger	Bargaining	Depression	Acceptance
Lindemann	Shock	Sadness	Withdrawal	Protest	Resolution
Parkes	Numbness	Yearning and protest	Disorganization	Reorganization	

the house, the real friend can best help by being there to listen as the memories are relived and feelings of loss and aloneness are shared. Although repetition of stories may cause concern or discomfort for the listener, this sharing is excellent therapy that helps make it possible for the bereaved individual to let go of yesterdays. More often than not ''get out and get involved'' may be a remedy for the onlooker rather than the person involved in grief.

Grief that has not been resolved may be indicated by statements such as ''I still cry . . . get upset . . . hide tears,'' ''I cannot . . . am unable to accept . . . feel it's unfair,'' ''It's painful to remember or recall. . . . Things still remind me,'' and ''I am preoccupied . . . can't avoid thinking about.''

Hostility is sometimes a part of bereavement and may contribute to words and acts that are quite out of normal character. If both the mourner and sympathizer could accept any bitterness expressed as a temporary and not a permanent character trait, it would be less difficult for the mourner to resume normal social contacts after the death of a loved one.

After the initial bereavement is over, persons often find it difficult to reenter society. Widows and widowers may suddenly not be welcome among their friends. Their previous relationships were couple oriented, and now as singles, they may be perceived more as a threat than as friends. Many women whose identities were built around their husband's have found widowhood compounded with an identity crisis. ''Who am I now that he's gone?'' Survivors who had activities, work, and friends outside the marriage get through bereavement with less difficulty than those whose lives were totally tied to their spouses.

Helping the bereaved

Bereaved people should be discouraged from making major decisions and changes in their life during the first year. Although they may feel that they are completely in control and are making decisions that are deliberate, careful, and responsible,

hindsight will verify the wisdom of leaving important decisions for a minimum of 6 months and ideally for a full year. Actress Helen Hayes sums up her grief experience this way:

For two years I was just as crazy as you can be and still be at large. I didn't have any really normal minutes during those two years. It wasn't just grief. It was total confusion. I was nutty, and that's the truth. How did I come out of it? I don't know, because I didn't know when I was in it that I was in it.[9]

Many people shy away from those who are grief stricken because they simply do not know what to say or what to do. Specific suggestions may help others feel more confident in their ability to be helpful and therefore more willing to approach those in sorrow.

The most important thing that can be said is to acknowledge the loss. ''I am sorry that John is dead.'' If only one thing is known about the person who has died, one should build on that. ''Jimmy was our paper boy. He used to come in for milk and cookies. We will miss him.'' Helpful statements are those that relate to the general strength of the person who has died. These strengths may be characteristics or things the person has said or done. Some people mention the person's kindness, pleasant personality, warm smile, and friendliness. They may also recognize accomplishments, the person's talents, or time that was volunteered in the community, church, or clubs. Funeral directors may encourage family members to bring a few mementoes to the funeral home before visitation and as friends pay their last respects, these items encourage reflection on the person's attributes. For example, next to the casket of a college track star were several of the medals that she had won. Another example involved an older lady who loved to knit and over the years had made many lap robes for elderly people in nursing homes. Draped at the foot of her casket was one of her lap robes, and many who came to offer condolences commented about her unselfish giving to others. Rather than trying to invent good qualities or a relationship that did not exist, it is better to simply acknowledge the loss and show concern for the needs of the survivors.

As long as comments are positive the exact wording is seldom remembered. What is remembered is the concern and care that the visits and comments signified. Frequently people admit, ''I don't remember anything that anyone said, but I do remember that they were there and that was more important to me than I can ever express with words.'' A minister shared his first experience in making a condolence call:

■ It was my first time to call on a family after the death of one of the family members, and I was really concerned about what to say. On the way to the house I practiced my speech over and over, but when I got to the door, all I could remember was ''I'm sorry.'' That's all I needed to say, and for the next 2 hours I listened. Looking back I realize that I had been so uncomfortable that I wanted to structure the interaction. My needs almost got in the way of my parishioner's. _____

The words ''Let me know if there's anything I can do'' are usually not heeded. People who are grieving are grateful to those who come to the house, notice tasks that need to be done, and then do them. Services such as answering the phone, greeting callers at the door, caring for the children, bringing in food, cooking, helping with cleaning or shopping, and running errands are greatly appreciated.

Following the funeral most families welcome supportive visits, and those who do not will make this wish clear. These visits let the family know that they are remembered and are not alone in their grief. This support is very much needed after the funeral is over and relatives have returned to their homes. Widowed people appreciate being taken out to dinner, especially on holidays and on dates such as the deceased person's birthday, the anniversary of the death, and dates that were meaningful in their married life.

Many helpful and appreciated services for those in grief require little expertise. All that is needed

is a willingness to give time and aid to those in sorrow and to allow them to experience what is necessary before they can begin their lives anew.

STILLBIRTH OR NEONATAL DEATH

Much has changed since the eighteenth century when more than one fourth of the babies born never survived infancy. Even today broken dreams are created by 45,000 infant deaths each year in the United States. Many times the parents have a hard time discussing their loss with each other, let alone with friends and relatives who frequently do not understand the depth of their grief or how to acknowledge it. A stillbirth is an event in which there is guilt and shame and no memories to share.

Not knowing what to say, people make remarks to the bereaved parents that can hurt more than they soothe, such as ''It was for the best,'' ''It probably wouldn't have been normal if it had lived,'' and ''You're young, you can have more.''

More effective responses, such as ''I'm sorry'' and ''We were so sad to hear that your baby died,'' are based on empathy. Empathy differs from sympathy in that it leaves clear the parents' right to react in their own way. It shares in sorrow and loss but allows for the expression of anger, guilt, and grief and is therefore more generous, kind, and therapeutic. Empathy provides the opportunity for the parents to share their thoughts: ''Why our baby?'' or ''It must be my fault.''

Sympathy, on the other hand, becomes judgmental, telling the parent how to handle their grief: ''You'll get over it'' or ''It's God's will.'' Few parents will share their anger, guilt, or grief with such responses.

Facilitating mourning

Bereavement is usually facilitated by sharing memories about the deceased, but when there are no memories—only hopes and dreams—parents have little to share with friends and relatives. There are times when the baby was not named and the parents did not see the infant. It is almost as though the baby never was.

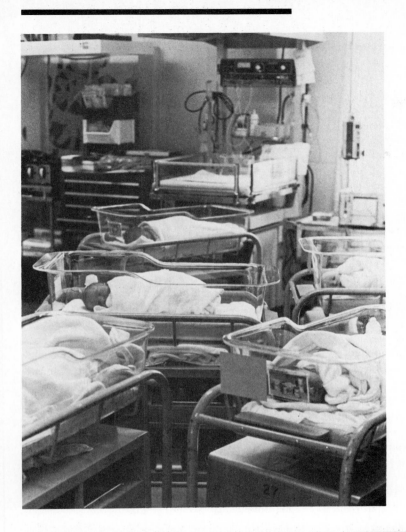

The death of a newborn is the loss of hopes and dreams—with no memories to share.
Photograph by John Hennessey III.

Furman[5] delineates the mourning process into opposing mechanisms. The first is the process of "detachment." Each memory is relived and then painfully loosened, provoking anger, guilt, pain, and sadness. The second process is "identification." The bereaved begins to take on some characteristics of the deceased, soothing the pain of loss. Neither the process of detachment nor iden-tification is possible with a stillbirth or neonatal death because there has not been time to establish strong ties and memories. In essence the newborn remains a part of the parent's self, having never materialized and without a chance to be detached. This creates a very different process of mourning. The parents mourn for the loss of a part of the self with a pain of a different kind that is accompanied by emptiness, loss of self-esteem, and feeling low. They often do not receive the support that is accorded the bereaved.

Parents need to be informed by the physician about the death of their infant as soon as this has been confirmed. If the infant has not already been baptized, the parents should be asked if they would like to have this done. It is best if tranquilizers are withheld—except for occasional bedtime sedation or when medically indicated—since they tend to dull the mourning reaction in such a way that it may never be completed. Bereavement is so foreign to most people that they are totally unprepared for a magnitude of grief that may make them believe that they are losing their minds. Bereaved parents are better able to handle grief if they know that normal grief reactions include several weeks of intense waves of sadness, imagining that they see their baby alive and well, and feelings of both guilt and anger about the death of their infant.

Parents should be provided the opportunity—but not forced—to see and handle their infant after its death. Sometimes parents hesitate because they do not know what to expect, so a brief description of the infant helps to eliminate the fear of the unknown. "Your baby is a little blue. The body is cool but not cold and will feel somewhat firm." Parents are told of any abnormalities, and these can be draped so that the baby appears normal. Although a mother and father may initially refuse to see the baby, they may change their mind, so it is a good idea to keep the infant on the delivery floor for a few hours. There are parents who do not want to see their baby but want to hold the infant as a bundle wrapped securely in a receiving blanket. Although nurses and physicians may find the experience of parents seeing or holding their dead infant upsetting, this contact helps to make the death real for the parents. The mourning process has been found to be prolonged and more difficult to resolve when this is not done. Naming the baby helps the parents to acknowledge the infant's identity, and many parents have later expressed regret when this was not done.

A stillbirth or neonatal death is followed by an extremely difficult time for mothers who are unable to leave the hospital and therefore are without their support systems. The father and mother need to spend as much time as possible together so that they can hold and support each other and share their grief. If the father is unable to stay or the mother is a single parent, she should be permitted to have another significant other share this time of crisis with her.

In some hospitals the bereaved woman is isolated, avoided, and discharged as quickly as possible. She may be deprived of the chance to talk about her loss, which would help her mourn. The death of an infant is a tragedy that can seriously affect the mental health of a bereaved mother and her family. Failure to mourn a stillbirth or neonatal death can cause psychotic breakdowns or severe marital difficulties. Mothers who are unable to mourn the death of their infant may have mothering difficulties with an infant born subsequently.

In one instance a mother was unable to see her infant girl before the baby was transferred to a neonatal center. The baby died and was buried while the mother was still hospitalized. Her husband carefully and patiently described how the baby had looked, her face, her hair, her delicate body, and her tiny hands and feet. Later the mother went to see the nursery where her baby had died. Nurses showed her an infant the same size as her baby, and this helped her form a mental image of her child. Once she was able to accept the reality of her baby, she was able to grieve for her death.

A photograph of a dead baby can help parents who were unable to see their child. Some hospitals take pictures of every stillborn infant or live-born infant who dies. The parents are told about the picture and that they can see the photo whenever they would like. It might not be until months later that a parent will call and ask to see the picture. At this time they are invited back to the hospital and have the opportunity to see the picture in a supportive atmosphere and ask any questions. Many parents ask to have a copy to take home, and this is provided.

Parents are also encouraged to explain to other

children in the family what is happening. It is particularly hard for parents to be responsive to the needs of youngsters when the parents are self-centered with grief. However, children need and deserve an explanation for behavior not characteristic of their parents, and they need help at a time when they may already be harboring guilt feelings over the death of the new baby.

Siblings, grandparents, and other significant others should be encouraged to see the baby so that they can psychologically accept that birth and death did occur. This viewing is also a shared experience on which the detachment aspect of grief work can begin. Years later one grandmother talked about her stillborn granddaughter, "She was just beautiful. Being able to see her was so sad, but when I saw her, I suddenly realized that this was not only my grandchild but my child's child. I knew that the hurt I felt was small compared with hers. They let me go into her room at the hospital. She was alone, and when she saw me, she asked, 'Mom, did you see her?' I nodded and gathered her into my arms, and we cried and talked about how beautiful Jennifer was."

Most parents find that having a simple private funeral or memorial service facilitates the grieving process. This service can be delayed until the mother is able to attend, and there are times when a memorial service is held in the hospital before the mother's dismissal. Some states mandate that a fetus of gestation age of 20 weeks or older requires the services of a mortuary. Some parents are financially unable to afford the cost of a private funeral, and city burial can usually be arranged without cost to the parents. Parents who decide to let the hospital or city handle burial need to know what will happen to their infant. If they are not informed, they may envision that their infant is somewhere in a jar or that the baby was thrown away. One mother accused the staff of lying to her—that her baby was not really dead but instead had been put up for adoption. Hospital personnel are sometimes uncertain as to the actual disposition of an infant's body and therefore need to find out the infant burial policy of their hospital.

Immediately after the death of an infant, parents are usually too overwhelmed to hear much of what the physician or anyone else has told them. It is important that the physician talk to the parents together again before the mother is dismissed from the hospital. This gives the physician a chance to go over what happened, to answer questions, and to give the parents some idea of what to expect during the bereavement process. The physician shares that parents who have had an infant die sometimes experience loss of appetite, difficulty sleeping, loneliness, depression, and feelings of guilt, anger, and hostility. They are also told that some mothers at first hear their baby crying or may even feel fetal movements. Parents feel better knowing that these reactions are normal and that they are not becoming mentally ill. If the physician has any undue concerns about either parent, these can be monitored during a follow-up appointment or a phone call when both parents are home.

Parents also need to be warned that many people will be unaware that their baby has died and will ask if the baby is a boy or a girl or ask, "How's the baby?" A photographer is likely to call to set up an appointment for baby pictures. Coupons for baby food and subscription offers for parents' magazines may arrive. New acquaintances who use conversation starters such as "How many children do you have?" evoke sad memories.

Since the parents have many things to deal with immediately after the baby's death, many physicians have found it beneficial to schedule a final interview with the parents at the time of the mother's postpartum checkup. This is a good time to clear up any unanswered questions, substitute fact for fantasy or speculative information, review obstetrical and autopsy data, and assess whether the mourning process is progressing normally. Any indication of pathological grief prompts referral to a psychiatrist.

It is generally agreed that parents should refrain from having another infant until they have completed their mourning process. The process of attaching to a new baby while giving up another are opposites that are extremely difficult to accomplish simultaneously. Parents are urged to wait 6 months to a year before planning for another baby to allow time to complete their mourning reaction.

By responding to the individual needs of specific parents, health professionals can facilitate mourning by helping parents recognize their loss and work through a normal grief process. One of the most profound examples of the importance of mourning the death of an infant was poignantly narrated by a minister.

■ A young couple who had been married for several years announced at last that they were expecting their first child. This word reached their parents from half a continent away. The child, born not too long after Christmas, was a healthy baby boy, and their families and friends rejoiced with them.

Five weeks later came a hysterical call from the young mother to her parents. Their baby son had died in his crib during the night, and they had found him still soaking in a pool of cold sweat. It was a case of sudden infant death—a phenomenon that still puzzles most medical scientists and a shock unbelieveable to those who never have been touched closely by it.

When the grandparents arrived at the couple's home, the grave had been closed. Neither parent had been present. There was no service. The mother was calmly sorting through the baby's belongings to be given away. The father apparently never did grieve, nor would he allow his wife to express the very real grief she felt. By the standards of many, the couple recovered quickly. They had promptly closed the pages on this part of their life, having never expressed their true feelings.

More than a year passed, and another healthy son was born to this couple. This time the mother was unable to care for or give her love to this baby. In deep depression she sought help but was never able to fully come to terms with her loss and the hurt it left. The father has raised the child since birth. The couple is now divorced.

At this point the minister paused and wiped tears from his eyes before he continued with his story. With an unsteady voice he shared, ''That was 6 years ago, and those were our first grandchildren.'' _____

When perinatal death occurs, the role of medical personnel is the prevention of postmortem psychiatric sequelae in the parents. Failure of parents to work through their mourning following a stillbirth or neonatal death can result in dire consequences for the well-being of the family. The mother may need help in affirming that she was pregnant, that she did give birth, and that the baby has died. The parents may need assistance in saying hello and good-bye to their infant. In some hospitals when the infant's death is imminent, parents are asked if they would like to hold their dying baby until the end. Some parents want to dress their baby in the clothes in which they had planned to take the infant home. When the interval of time between birth and death is too short, the empathy, understanding, and support from caring professionals is paramount.

DEATH OF A CHILD

Life's ultimate tragedy has been called the death of a child. In 1980 the National Center for Health Statistics reported that more than 68,000 children, teenagers, and young adults between the ages of 1 and 24 years died in the United States. Accidents were a leading cause of these deaths, leaving the lives of loved ones shattered by grief. Parents have a psychic attachment to their child, and when the child dies, they lose a part of themselves. Although the principles of bereavement apply when a child dies, grief is intensified because a child's death is not in the natural order of events. Parents never expect to outlive their children.

The grieving family

Numerous factors make the present-day American family vulnerable after the death of a child. The support system has virtually been eliminated by a mobile and characteristically anonymous society. Relatives live too far away, and neighbors

Life's ultimate tragedy has been called the death of a child.
Photograph by John Hennessey III.

are frequently too distant. The church is no longer the source of comfort and support it once was. Medical advances have replaced the supporting family physician with specialists and have left society with little practice in helping family members who have experienced the death of a child. This vulnerability is reflected in the fact that many parents who have lost a child are on the verge of divorce within a year after the child's death.

The intrafamily dynamics are even more affected by the sudden death of a child. There is no time to anticipate the tragedy and have any benefits from grief before the death actually occurs. When the death is interpreted by one or both parents as having been preventable, there is unusually high potential for shame and guilt. Additionally, societal sanction of accusation further intensifies the likelihood of pathological mourning both for the parents and for the children in the family.

Alternatives for care

Those who have been involved in the care of their child during a long terminal illness may be emotionally and physically at their weakest when the child dies. Despite this physical and emotional exhaustion, hospice workers verify that family members involved in the care of their loved one are able to cope more effectively with death.

Three alternatives that allow family members to be involved in the care of a dying child are a children's hospice, pediatric units in hospitals, and home care. Regardless of the alternative the family chooses, the emotional, physical, and cognitive needs of the child and the child's family must be met.

In 1982 there were only seven children's hospice programs within the United States *(right)*, but the National Hospice Organization reports that more hospice programs are beginning to accept children. Hospital care can provide the holistic care needed by both the child and the child's family. At the University of Minnesota Medical Center, daybeds are available for parents' use, and the entire family has unlimited visiting privileges day and night. Children are settled in their beds before admission forms are filled out. Rather than isolating the dying child, there is a growing tendency for the child and the family to receive increased attention in the way of both comfort and support.

Home care has proven to be a feasible alternative as long as there is effective control of pain. Oral methadone makes it possible for children to be pain free so that they can live each day rather than existing in pain. Parents report that they can hold their child once again and that the whole family can get a good night's rest. One mother commented, "It's hard to find peace after a child's death if the child dies in pain."

Whenever there is warning of death, support often begins before the death occurs. Comfort may come from the mother whose child is down the hall in the hospital, a member of the health care team who spends extra time, or the person in the community whose child died a year ago.

A young couple gathered their things to leave the hospital following the death of their child. For 3 months they had taken turns staying at the hospital with their little girl. They experienced joy and sadness with other parents whose children were also victims of life-threatening illnesses. Quietly they said good-bye to those who had shared the last months of their lives. Other parents could only express their sorrow and silently fear that they too might leave without their child. The young woman held the hands of another whose child had leukemia. "Accept her death so that you can share her

CHILDREN'S HOSPICE PROGRAMS IN THE UNITED STATES*

Children's Hospice Program
St. Mary's Hospital for Children
2901 216th Street
Bayside, New York 11360

The Connecticut Hospice, Inc.
61 Burban Drive
Branford, Connecticut 06405

Hospice of Louisville, Inc.
233 E. Gray Street, Suite 800
Louisville, Kentucky 40202

Center for Attitudinal Healing
 (Hospicelike Program)
19 Main Street
Tiburon, California 94920

Boulder County Hospice, Inc.
2118 14th Street
Boulder, Colorado 80302

Hospice of Northern Virginia
4715 North 15th Street
Arlington, Virginia 22205

EDMARC—A Hospice for Children
Box 1684
Suffolk, Virginia 23434

*For a further listing, contact National Hospice Organization, 1901 Fort Myer Drive, Arlington, Va. 22101

life. If you live in fear of her dying, you'll miss out on her living. When the time comes, don't be afraid to let her go.'' These facts were learned from experience, which can either tear apart the lives of those involved or, with the help of family, friends, and the passing of time, blend into the fabric of life.

CHILDHOOD BEREAVEMENT

When a significant person in a child's life is gone, the child hurts. Often this hurt is not recognized or not considered to be of a magnitude to prompt attention. Adults become so engrossed in their own emotions that the youngster becomes just one more thing to deal with, and he or she may be left alone with unanswered questions and unexpressed feelings. Childhood bereavement is included in this section because too often the needs of grieving children are overlooked. More specific suggestions, interventions, and educational resources for helping children understand death are presented in the chapter "Children and Death."

Parental loss

Sociologists have suggested that parental loss is likely to be even more traumatic for the child in the limited nuclear families of today than in the traditional extended family setting of previous years. The nuclear family is without the multiresponsibility dimensions of roles, and role substitutes are not as available as was the case of the extended family. Separation or loss disrupts social order, and the bereaved child faces not only personal loss but also a disrupted vacancy in the social system. There is concern as to the long-term effects of parental loss or separation in childhood.

A large body of psychological literature dealing with this issue maintains that the loss of a parent has serious consequences for the child throughout adult life. In contrast, sociological writers view the absence of a parent as a problem in role loss, with the introduction of a substitute or surrogate parent aiding the child's recovery by filling the social vacuum created by the death.

In 1954 Hathaway and Monachesi[6] gathered a wealth of data from 11,430 ninth-grade students in Minnesota. Although the specific interest at that time dealt with predicting delinquency, the information has been valuable for numerous research issues, including the relationship between childhood bereavement and later behavior disorders.

Bendiksen and Fulton[1] conducted an anterospective study from 256 subjects of the original Hathaway and Monachesi investigation. Their subjects included those from intact homes and those from broken homes caused by parental death or divorce. At the time of this study the subjects were in early middle age. Their analysis of behavioral and attitudinal data indicated that there are differential consequences for individuals who have experienced parental loss in childhood. Subjects from bereaved and divorced childhood families report more major illness and extreme emotional distress than the control group. Data suggest that although children have serious emotional and interpersonal adjustments to make following the death of a parent, adjustments are more severe for children from divorced homes who experience being separated from a parent without loss and desertion without closure. It was concluded that childhood separation from a parent because of death or divorce is a serious personal crisis with possible serious consequences for later adult life.

Separation illustrated
Death

■ Following their mother's death, 7-year-old Sally and her older brother were adopted into separate homes. The nurse-counselor who followed Sally before and following her mother's death made a follow-up call to see Sally at her new home.

Sally was delighted to see the nurse, and because she and the nurse had often drawn pictures together, she quickly ran to get paper and pencil. As Sally drew, she reported, "Everything is fine. I have my own room, and sometimes I get to see my brother."

Figure 11-1 is her drawing, which does not support Sally's saying that "everything is fine." Chap-

Fig. 11-1. Everything is fine?
© *1979 A. Jann Davis.*

ter 5 gives more detail on features and indicators in children's drawings, but a review of relevant points includes: children's figure drawings reflect their self-concept; facial expressions are often very reliable indicators of the child's feelings; rain, flying birds, and clouds may indicate that the child feels threatened by the adult world.

The nurse commented to Sally, "The clown looks so sad."

Sally looked at the picture and answered, "The

clown is sad because he is worried about his doggy.''

"The clown is worried about his doggy?''

"The clown is worried that his doggy will get sick.''

The nurse encouraged, "What will make the doggy sick?''

At this point Sally began to cry. "My doggy's going to get cold outside and get an earache and die just like my mommy did.''

At the time of her mother's death Sally had been told that her mother had died from a serious disease called cancer. Sally was too young to comprehend what she had not experienced. The worst thing she could remember was an earache, and she decided this was what made her mother die.

Before Sally's mother was diagnosed as having cancer, Sally's family consisted of both parents, her brother, and the family dog. Her father disappeared when the mother became ill, later divorced Sally's mother, and refused to have anything to do with the children. Sally had not only lost both parents but she was also separated from her brother. The only remaining member of the original family was the dog, who was required to sleep outside.

Unfortunately, Sally's adoptive parents would not allow her pet in the house. When they realized how important the animal was to Sally, they purchased a dog house, which Sally promptly filled with "warm blankets." They also explained to Sally that as the air grew colder outside, the dog would grow more hair that would be like a coat to keep him warm. _____

Just as Sally had worried that her pet would die the same way her mother had died, sometimes children will experience physical symptoms similar to those that loved ones had experienced before their death. Although most frequently children's grief is worked out through their behavior, sometimes physical symptoms will be substituted for anxieties they are unable to handle. If these symptoms persist despite repeated reassurances, professional help should be sought for the child.

Divorce. Parents as well as children feel guilty about causing divorce. To appease their guilt, parents may overindulge their children, and children may try to nullify their bad thoughts and deeds with model behavior. "I was bad, and my folks split up. I will be good, and they will live together again.''

Children need to be told over and over, through words and actions, that the divorce is not their fault and that it is beyond their control. Until this is accepted, they will spend time and energy entertaining guilt over separation and hope for reconciliation.

Confusion results when a youngster is told only good or bad things about the other parent. The child may think, "If she's so nice, then why aren't you living with her anymore?'' or "She says he's bad. . . . Half of me is Dad. What's going to happen to me?''

Couples going through a divorce are sometimes not aware that they may be treating their children like pawns, moving them here and there, fighting over them, and using them as a way to hurt the other spouse. Fig. 11-2 was drawn by a 7 year old whose parents were in the process of a very bitter divorce. The child's picture includes the heavy clouds, rain, and flying birds that are emotional indicators drawn primarily by children who do not dare strike out at others but turn their aggressions inward. These children feel threatened by the adult world and in effect are standing under pressure from above. When the parents were shown the illustration of their son's feelings, they readily admitted being so involved with their own feelings that they had not really considered their son's.

Parents can help youngsters understand the reasons for divorce by answering their questions honestly and briefly. Facts can be admitted. "We were no longer happy together.'' "We each made mistakes.'' Sordid details are not necessary. The children were there and exposed to the emotional climate if not the direct conflict, and they will ultimately form their own opinions.

Patience, understanding, love, and openness can help children come through the traumatic crisis of

Fig. 11-2. A child's drawing expresses his emotions.
© 1979 A. Jann Davis.

divorce so that childhood memories will not stand in the way of adult years of love and happiness.

Sibling death

Major emphasis has been placed on the child's reaction to parental death with little observation of the effects of sibling death. The exploration of immediate, prolonged, and symptomatic reactions of children following death of a sibling deserve attention. Many clinicians have observed that the loss or death of a sibling during childhood is related to the timing and appearance of overt depression in adulthood, with a depressive episode likely to appear when the adult's own child reaches the age at which the sibling died.

A child's reaction to a sibling's death is influenced by the age and sex of the child and the intensity of the association. There may be strong and exaggerated feelings—either hostility or overidealization—in relation to the lost sibling. Reactions may include depression, anger, anxiety, aggression, defiance, withdrawal, regression, remorse, and guilt.

The sudden death of a sibling creates a situation in which children, like their parents, do not have the benefit of anticipatory grief, or grieving before the actual death. Parents are caught up in their own overwhelming grief and the immediate legal and social details surrounding the death. It is only later that parents reflect, ''I really don't remember much about the other kids those first weeks after the accident.'' Parents sometimes need encouragement to set aside time for their surviving children who too are overwhelmed by the death of their sibling. An 18 year old reflected back on the time his sister died. ''I was only 10 then, but I can remember thinking that Mom had time for everyone but me.'' Children need the opportunity to share their loss, have their questions answered, and be allowed to continue with their lives. Too frequently parents idealize the child who has died, making it difficult for surviving children who may feel they ''could never do anything as good as he did. It was like living with a ghost.''

When a sibling's death follows prolonged illness, the children in the family may still believe that they were not informed honestly about the expected death. In some cases this may be true; however, children may have been told but simply did not stay told. Parents are unable to incorporate detailed information regarding disease and prognosis during the first days after diagnosis, and undoubtedly the same inability applies to siblings when their parents tell them about the seriousness of their sister's or brother's illness.

Recognition of the profound effects of sibling death can prompt helping professionals to provide rapid and skilled intervention whenever childhood grief is delayed, appears in extremes, or persists too long. If children are able to work through their grief following the death of a loved one, they are better able to form loving relationships in the future.

WIDOWHOOD

Widowhood is a time of great change. At the onset the desolation and isolation make it difficult to get through the day. Most people are able to progress from crisis to growth as they regain happiness and develop new interests and relationships. Although most make this adjustment without help, there are many things that can make this experience less painful. An understanding of the problems of widowhood and factors related to adjustment will benefit those who assist widows as they work through bereavement.

Adjustment factors

In the past few years a concept called anticipatory grief has been gaining more attention and is being considered an important factor in adjustment to widowhood. This phenomenon has to do with grieving before the death of a loved one, and there is general consensus that women who expect their husband's death benefit from this anticipatory grief. Although this prior grief does not eliminate the impact of the actual death, it does decrease the overwhelming suffering experienced when there is little or no warning. The exact length of time necessary for anticipatory grief varies among researchers, but most agree that 2 weeks to 2 months is minimum.

Men do not seem to benefit significantly from anticipatory grief, but this may be difficult to accurately determine because they do not have the permission of society to openly express their sorrow. Men are often the quiet victims of their grief. This is not to say that they are more lonely or have more grief than women, but their emotional pain is rarely recognized, and they typically do not get the opportunity to ''unload.'' Many people feel uncomfortable dealing with a man's emotions and hesitate to really get involved with a man in crisis and thus expose themselves to his feelings. The statement ''I'm okay'' may be accepted when coming from a man, whereas the same statement from a woman may not be taken at face value.

Throughout the past 10 years studies have pointed out that widowers seem to adjust better than widows to widowhood. The word ''seem'' is used here because it is difficult to objectively measure two ways of handling grief. Although women are more likely to give in to emotion—to feel, share, and express it—men have a tendency to overcome emotion with motion. They busy themselves with going and doing and ultimately return more quickly to previous roles and functions. However, this social recovery may not reflect emotional recovery. Widowers do express more independence and confidence in recovering from the death of their spouse perhaps because many women have built their identities around their husband's and experience a radical life-style change when their spouse dies. This may become less true in the future as many women are retaining their own identities and becoming more career oriented.

Another factor that helps in social adjustment is that it is easier for men to remarry than it is for women. The average American wife can expect approximately 10 years of widowhood because typically husbands are 4 years older than their wives and women outlive men by about 5 years. Longevity contributes to the fact that widows outnumber widowers 5 to 1, making it increasingly more difficult for a woman to remarry after the death of her spouse than it is for a man.

Independence also makes it easier to adjust to widowhood, and factors affecting adjustment include dependent children, health, money, and personality. Although dependent children offer a great deal of comfort to the widowed person, there is also a great deal of stress from becoming both

mother and father while at the same time dealing with bereavement. Widowed persons who are psychologically, physically, and financially able to live apart from their families after the death of their spouses are apt to make a better adjustment than those who move in with adult children because of insecurity, health, or finances.

The experience of widowhood is difficult for both men and women. It is equally important that members of the interdisciplinary team, such as nurses, chaplains, social workers, and counselors, assist a husband or wife in dealing with emotions while their spouse is still alive. Physicians may promote adjustment in bereavement by informing a spouse of the seriousness of the husband's or wife's condition as soon as it becomes evident. On the surface it is hard to determine if emotional adjustment has taken place. As one widower stated,

The average American wife can expect approximately 10 years of widowhood.
Photograph by A. Jann Davis.

"The only place I hurt is where it doesn't show, and the only time I cry is when no one can see."

Who helped most?

Table 11-2 is based on the experiences of 119 widowed persons between the ages of 28 and 70 years whose spouses either had died in an acute general hospital or were pronounced dead on arrival (DOA) at the hospital. These widowed persons were interviewed after 13 to 16 months of bereavement and were asked which people inside and outside the hospital gave them help (little, some, or great) before and after the death of their spouse. If the widowed person responded "great help" or expressed disappointment in a person or group, he or she was asked why. The following synopsis of this study helps to point out that what is thought to be of great help may be different from what is helpful in reality.

Social workers. Social workers had little if any contact with the majority of the respondents, which helps to explain why only 10 percent reported great help from social workers. The appreciated services were making arrangements for special equipment at home, assistance in securing financial aid, transportation for treatment, and finding people to stay with their spouse during the day.

The 4 percent who expressed disappointment in social workers complained that they failed to familiarize themselves with the case histories of clients.

Physicians. Physicians were rated as offering great help when they were honest, compassionate, available, not hurried, and comforting to the family. Spouses praised them for offering all the information they wanted in language that could be understood. They also appreciated the physician for being honest and at the same time encouraging and for helping with decisions such as taking a spouse off the respirator.

Disappointment in physicians was expressed by 27 percent of widowers and 33 percent of widows. Reasons centered around allegations of failure to be honest; avoiding the family; making the wrong diagnosis; being cold, impersonal, and unconcerned; lacking gentleness; and having a poor bedside manner.

Nurses. Nurses were praised for being solicitous, showing concern, and helping explain tests and equipment when this was not given by the physician. It was also appreciated when nurses extended visiting hours or helped give the spouse confidence about caring for the client at home. One respondent commented that the nurse had put her arms around her, and this gesture had meant a lot.

Table 11-2. Support groups who were identified as being of great help

Support group	Percentage of respondents who said support group was of great help	
	Widowers	Widows
Social workers (most respondents had no contact with social workers)	5%	5%
Physicians	47%	40%
Nurses	56%	55%
Chaplains	44%	71%
Neighbors	56%	68%
Local clergy	56%	62%
Funeral directors	76%	76%
Family	80%	80%

Modified from Carey, R.: Omega **10**(2):163, 1979-1980.

On the other hand, 12 percent of widowers and 15 percent of widows complained about nurses. The major complaint concerned an attitude of coldness and unconcern, and dissatisfaction with overall hospital care was vented onto nurses.

Chaplains. Chaplains were considered helpful and attentive to both the clients and relatives, assisting clients in talking about their approaching death, and consoling the relatives after the death.

Disappointment in chaplains was expressed by only 5 percent of widowers and 7 percent of widows. No specific comments were made.

Neighbors. Neighbors were praised for their help before and following the death of the spouse. Before the death, they visited, helped with the children, and brought in meals. Following the death, they attended the funeral, sent cards and flowers, and brought food to the home. Widows commented that they appreciated neighbors asking them to dinner or to go out.

Only about 2 percent expressed disappointment in the behavior of neighbors, and frequently this centered around the fact that neighbors perceived the widowed person as a "romantic threat." It was necessary for some to leave old social groups and join new ones to avoid these accusations. Other complaints had to do with the sincerity of the phrase "Call me anytime," which was found to last only a few weeks.

Local clergy. Local clergy were praised for their visits both in the home and hospital before and following the death. Appreciation was also expressed for allowing family or friends to take part in the funeral service.

Only 5 percent of widowers and 15 percent of widows expressed disappointment in the clergy. Those who were churchgoers expected a follow-up visit from the clergy after their spouses's death, and when the visit did not occur, the bereaved expressed disappointment.

Funeral directors. Funeral directors were second only to family members in receiving praise from the widowed. They were cited as being helpful in obtaining Social Security benefits and insurance payments and were described as being courteous, honest, and professional. It was also appreciated that they did not try to pressure people into expensive funerals and did not send their bills immediately after the funeral. Only one respondent expressed disappointment in a funeral director, and the specific comment was not given.

Family. Family was rated as being the most helpful group to the bereaved. They were praised for offering emotional and physical support before and following the death. Their phone calls and visits helped the widowed person feel loved and cared for. Invitations to dinner were especially appreciated.[4]

Implications

Members in the helping fields are praised for their humanistic aspect of care as much as their technical competence. Although some negative comments are based on logic, others are based on grief. Anger may be vented at the physician for failing to keep a loved one alive. The nurse may become the object of displaced anger because something completely apart from nursing went wrong. Kind words and touch do not take time away from a busy schedule, but they do convey sincerity and empathetic concern that are so appreciated by hospitalized clients and their families.

Funeral directors are doing much more than directing funerals. They are in a position to truly help people in bereavement. Too frequently they are recognized only for their technical skills surrounding disposal of the body. Their services include support of bereaved individuals during a time of most acute grief.

The communication process is basic to all human relationships, and when someone is prepared to listen, most people want to talk. Whereas a chaplain or other religious leader is welcomed by many, some would prefer having a nonreligious person with whom to share. When this need exceeds the time or the skill of the primary care giver, a social worker or counselor may be able to assist in physical and psychological needs before and following the death of a spouse.

The release of feelings is one of the most valuable components in the bereavement process, and the importance of creating an atmosphere in which bereaved individuals are therapeutically able to express these feelings is expressed by Bowlby:

> If we are to give the kind of help to a bereaved person that we should all like to give, it is essential we see things from his point of view and respect his feelings— unrealistic though we may regard some of them to be. For only if a bereaved person feels we can at least understand and sympathize with him in the task he sets for himself is there much likelihood that he will be able to express the feelings that are bursting within him—his yearning for the return of the lost figure, his hope against hope that miraculously all may yet be well, his rage at being deserted, his angry, unfair reproaches against 'those incompetent doctors,' 'those unhelpful nurses,' and against his own guilty self; if only he had done so and so, or not done so and so, disaster might perhaps have been averted.[3]

Being able to share without judgment or retaliation is a gift of helping that can be extended by all care givers. People who care help the widowed person achieve emotional independence from the deceased spouse. When this adjustment is made, the single person begins to recognize and face opportunities for a creative, wholesome life ahead.

SUDDEN DEATH

It is extremely difficult for survivors to accept the death of a loved one, especially when it comes without warning. The first step in helping a family deal with unexpected death involves properly calling them to the hospital. Support continues as hospital personnel assist family members from the time they arrive at the hospital until they leave. Approximately 1 month after the death, a follow-up call provides the opportunity to clear up any questions and assess the bereavement process. The following are suggestions in helping relatives deal with sudden death.

Notifying the family

When notifying the family of a death, the initial concern is whether to give this information over the phone or wait and tell the family in person after their arrival at the hospital. Some contend that tragic news about a sudden death should be given over the phone so that relatives are spared the rush to the hospital and the chance of being involved in an accident. Others maintain that such facts must never be given over the phone and any questions about the person's condition should be answered with "Everything possible is being done" or "The doctor is with him or her now." Those who favor this approach state that it is more therapeutic to wait until the relatives reach the hospital so that they can be informed in a more controlled and supportive environment.

There are times when either of these approaches would be appropriate and also times when neither will suffice. The safety of the survivors is always an issue but must not be used as a guise for an approach that is less painful for the health care professional. An important consideration is the trust between the health care team and the relative. If requested information is withheld once, relatives may wonder what else they have not been told.

In these two approaches the health care professional takes the lead and makes the decision as to when the relatives are told about the death. If, on the other hand, the family is allowed to take the lead with questions and the health professional responds honestly to their questions, the decision concerning information becomes the family's. The following is an example of this family-centered approach:

■ Mr. Brown was brought to the hospital via ambulance and was pronounced dead on arrival. When the next of kin was notified, the nurse was careful to speak slowly and clearly and verify the relationship with the deceased before any information was given.

> NURSE: Hello, may I talk to Mrs. Brown? Mrs. Brown, this is Jane Smith, and I'm a nurse in the emergency department at Woodward Memorial Hospital. Is your husband's name Max M. Brown?
> RELATIVE: Yes. What's happened?
> NURSE: Your husband has been brought to the emer-

gency department by ambulance and we need for you to come to the hospital.

RELATIVE: What's happened?

NURSE: Your husband apparently has had a heart attack. Would you like for me to call someone to bring you to the hospital?

RELATIVE: No, I can call my neighbor. I'll be there right away.

The nurse responded to the questions and volunteered no more than was asked. Had the relative questioned if her husband was dead, the nurse would have been honest without going into shocking details. Sometimes people do not ask this question because they are not ready to hear the answer. If the individual seems expecially distraught, a friend, neighbor, minister, or taxi service can be contacted for the trip to the hospital. The importance of exercising extreme caution in driving to the hospital is emphasized, the name and address of the hospital are repeated, and directions to the hospital are offered. _____

Supporting the family

As soon as the family arrives at the emergency department, they should be taken to a private room and told that the treating physician will be with them in a few minutes.

Within the hospital there needs to be a room large enough for family members to gather in privacy, where phone calls can be made and a rest room is available. A pot of coffee is usually appreciated. Individuals who have gone through the experience of a relative's sudden death have later shared how difficult it was to call loved ones in the solitude and confinement of a phone booth or within the public space of a hospital lobby. They also missed having a room in which they could express their shock and grief in private. One man commented:

Here I was. My wife just died, and I'm surrounded by strange people. So I asked if there wasn't someplace I could go to be alone and let it all out. They sent me to the chapel! You can't scream in a chapel. Just isn't right. I asked where they stored the mops and brooms. Seemed a more fitting place. When I want to meditate or pray, I'll go to the chapel.

It is best if relatives are not left by themselves. This is of particular importance if the relative is alone and in an emotional turmoil or if the person somehow feels responsible for what has happened. If the nurse is unable to stay, a social worker, the hospital chaplain, a trained volunteer, or another member of the interdisciplinary team can offer support, listen, make phone calls, get coffee, or help in other ways. Although the family may not have to wait long before talking with the attending physician, minutes become an eternity for those who want information about a loved one. The relatives will be anxious, apprehensive, and nervous, and they desperately need kindness, gentleness, and empathic understanding from a support person.

It is the physician who talks with the family members about their relative's death. If this is not done, they will question if a physician was even present when their relative arrived at the emergency room and if everything possible was done. This information coming from another health professional leaves many questions that may linger and doubts that may build. In the case of an unexplained death an autopsy is necessary, and families are usually less resistant if they are assured by the physician that this examination after death is done with dignity and respect and that it will not cause further suffering.

Viewing the body

The family members have the right and need to see the body of their loved one. Ideally this will not take place in the hospital morgue, in an area that is without privacy, or in a room that will be urgently needed. Before the family views the body, tubes and drains are removed but equipment is left in the room. A room without any equipment looks as though nothing was done. Although they may have been told what was done to save their relative's life, they will be more apt to remember what they see than what they hear. Any mutilated areas of the body should be draped. Being able to view any part of the body that is identifiable helps the survivors in their bereavement process.

A woman's husband was crushed in a farm accident. The physician told the woman that the only identifiable part of his body was his left hand. She asked to be permitted to see her husband. His body was draped, leaving his hand uncovered. She held his hand and sobbed, without making any effort to remove the drape. Another woman, whose daughter's body had been draped because of severe and multiple injuries, chose to remove the drape. She looked at her daughter's body and then replaced the drape. "It's not as bad as I had imagined."

Family members should not receive sedation unless a medical condition warrants its use. It is an injustice to the individual to provide sedation when support is greatest and then withdraw it after support is gone, leaving the person to cope alone. People have the right to feel what they feel. Some display little emotion, whereas others cry and scream. This is not the time for words of wisdom. Phrases such as "I know just how you feel" or the sharing of similar experiences are completely out of place. It is *impossible* to know how another person feels. The bereaved may ask, "Why?" which can only be answered, "I don't know." They may want to know "Was he conscious when they brought him here?" "Was he in pain before he died?" and "Did he ask for me?" These questions should be answered honestly. If there are children in the family, parents can be encouraged to tell their children about the death and allow them to participate in discussions and activities surrounding the death.

Often family members share their thoughts, their confusion, and "If only I had. . . . " They need someone who will listen as they relive the last moments they shared with the deceased. They need someone who will respond without making judgments. Grief may be so intense that nothing is able to penetrate but the sense of touch. It cannot be cured with an injection or words. Grief involves hard work that must be completed before people can say good-bye to a part of their lives.

Leaving the hospital

It is unwise for any person to leave the hospital alone after the unexpected death of a loved one. Either a friend or a relative must be located to drive the person home and spend the night, or the person should be admitted to a comfortable room in the hospital during this emotional crisis. The incidence of suicide is high following the sudden death of a long-time spouse. The benefit of having someone stay with the survivor is expressed by a newly widowed woman:

Awakening to face that horrible shock all over again made sleep hardly worth the effort. It was wonderful to have someone there to listen to me talk myself to sleep and help me through those first few days and nights.

Follow-up

So much happens in just a few hours time to those who receive the phone call to come to the hospital. The words "heart attack," "dead," "autopsy," "mortuary," and "funeral" overwhelm details. Questions later arise but may not be pursued. The phone number and the working hours of the support person who has shared this time of crisis help the survivors feel less alone when they leave the hospital. When questions arise, they have someone they know to contact. Immediately after the death, time is filled with details that must be taken care of, such as funeral arrangements, probating the will, and filing important papers. Family and friends provide both physical and psychological support, but as they resume their normal life, the bereaved family members are left to rebuild their lives. Doubts and unanswered questions surface that need to be cleared up before the person can progress. If the hospital support person has not been contacted after about 1 month, a follow-up call is made to check on the family and answer any questions that have developed. Information cards such as Fig. 11-3 are filled out the day of the crisis and will help refresh the support person's memory about the circumstances surrounding the death. Without this information to refer to, inappropriate comments are likely to detract from the effectiveness of the follow-up. Sometimes family members want to return to ths hospital once more; most welcome the opportunity to talk about their loved one and review what happened at the time of death. The importance of this follow-up call is stressed

Date	Medical record No.	Support person	Physician		
Name Last	First	Middle	Date of birth	Age	Sex
Client arrival emr. @		Wheelchair ☐ Car ☐	Ambulatory☐ Ambulance ☐		
Name of nearest relative	Relationship	Address		Phone No.	
Relative notified @	Relative arrived @	Relative left hospital @ with			
Treatment given in emergency room					
Cause of death					
Relative viewed body	Autopsy ordered	Disposition Time Place			

Fig. 11-3. Information on sudden deaths.

in the following situation experienced by a physician:

■ When I came home for lunch, I noticed a woman sitting in her car outside the house. I didn't think much about it until after lunch and the lady was still sitting there. I figured that maybe she was sick, so I went to the car. She rolled down her window, looked at me, and said, "You killed my husband."

I didn't even know who she was. She told me that 2 years ago her husband had died because I hadn't done anything to save him. Frankly, I couldn't remember her husband, but I asked her to come to my office.

I located her husband's record. According to the notes, he was a patient in the hospital when he suffered a massive coronary. We had worked on him for almost an hour. When she came to the office, I asked her what she had remembered.

"They called me to come to the hospital. . . . He had gotten worse. When I got there, he was dead. He was in his same room, in the same bed that he was in when I left earlier. You didn't even move him to intensive care. The room was just the way it had been. You just let him die."

It has taken this woman 2 years to get up enough nerve to confront the physician, and all she was able to do was sit out in front of his house. The physician showed her the medical record and later took her to the hospital to read through her husband's hospital records. Before leaving the hospital, she told the physician, ''I just wish someone had taken the time to tell me this 2 years ago.''

Without question, the woman had received much of this information at the time of her husband's death, but her level of stress may have prevented retaining what she heard. She did, however, remember what she saw, and based her conclusions on a room that showed none of the resuscitative efforts that had actually occurred.

Follow-up provides the opportunity to talk to the family under less stressful conditions, clear up questions, and find out how they are coping. This information is also important to those who cared for the person before the death and for those who spent time with the family following the death. Often care givers do not know what happens after the crisis, and they need to have the chance to bring closure to an experience that may have been a traumatic one for them as well as for the family.

Sudden death leaves no time to find meaning and sense in a tragic happening. This total life disruption can be more humane when families receive psychological support throughout the ordeal that often begins with a summons to the emergency department of the hospital. It is seldom clear that nothing can be done to save the victim's life until that person is dead, and until this time the medical team must place the needs of the family secondary to trying to save the client's life. Family members also have desperate needs that can be met by other personnel or a volunteer who is available around the clock. The survivors today may be the victims tomorrow unless someone takes the time to listen therapeutically, respond without judgment, and protect when necessary.

SUPPORT GROUPS

Living in a complex, technological society has resulted in a loss of the natural support groups that were once created by family and friends. Even though the links that once bound people together have weakened, people still need human fellowship. They need to share, to give, and to feel that they count. For many people a support group answers this need. It is an opportunity for people to come together with others similarly situated and help each other as well as themselves. In the United States more than a half million self-help groups exist, and the number is growing. The National Self-Help Clearinghouse is located at 33 West 42nd Street, Room 1206-A, New York, New York 10036. The clearinghouse has a referral service to help put inquirers in touch with appropriate self-help groups. It also helps people develop and enhance self-help groups and keeps them up to date on new groups and ideas.

Death of an infant or child

Some bereaved parents feel abandoned. Their friends, extended family, clergy, and counselors are unable to console or respond to their needs. Other parents who have ''walked the road'' may be the best source of comfort for these grieving parents. Support groups for parents who have experienced a stillbirth or infant death include: International Council for Infant Survival, Experiencing Neonatal Death, Support for Parents With Empty Arms, and The Foundation for Sudden Infant Death for parents whose babies have died of the sudden infant death syndrome (SIDS). There is often a real curative factor in being able to share with others ''who understand what we are going through better than anyone else.''

There are also groups for parents who have had a child die. These groups include Compassionate Friends and Parent Support Group, and they make it possible for parents to talk about their child's illness and death and share their feelings of sadness, anger, and guilt, They also help mothers and fathers communicate feelings with each other that may have been kept to themselves in an attempt to protect each other. Couples move apart, in particular when the father does not want to share his sadness with his wife. It is not uncommon for a grieving father to take on additional jobs or duties outside the home that may interfere with support and communication between the couple.

Many parents who have lost children traumatically have found that traditional sources of help do not know how to deal with them. Groups such as Parents of Murdered Children (POMC), Mothers Against Drunken Drivers (MADD), and parents such as Art Linkletter against drugs are doing more than helping to alleviate the suffering of traumatized parents. They are banding together and rechanneling their grief and energies to correct the problems of society that contributed to the deaths of their children.

Death of a spouse

Many widowed persons report that friends, family, and the clergy were all very helpful after the death of their spouse, but those who were extremely helpful were others who had been through widowhood. "While everyone else was telling me all the bright things, others who had been widowed understood that I felt like my future was gone. I didn't have to put on a front. With them it was okay to share what I was really going through." Some of the self-help groups for widowed persons include Widows, New Encounters, Solo Parents, Singles Again, Suddenly Alone, and THEOS (They Help Each Other Spiritually).

Implications for helping professionals

Many self-help groups establish links with helping professionals who work cooperatively rather than authoritatively with the groups. For some, mutual aid groups offer a more acceptable kind of help than what a professional can give. If professionals take over, the groups lose their spontaneity and autonomy, which are their appeal. There is a risk that people may use self-help when professional care services are mandated and also a danger that a group facilitator may use a group for personal needs. Some have trouble letting go of a person or couple who believe it is time to leave the group. Although some members stay to help new members, others find the experience too painful. They have worked through their initial crisis and are ready to go on with their lives. A consulting professional may be able to recognize these problems and

deal with them before they cause damage.

Support groups are effective, and they are here to stay. In a computerized age in which people become numbers, support groups help people realize that they are not alone and that they are cared about. During a time of crisis, people need people, and that is what support groups are all about.

AMERICAN AND BRITISH FUNERAL CUSTOMS

Nestled between a grocery store and a bakery on a main street in a small town in England is the funeral parlor (Fig. 11-4). No pomp and splendor, no extras, just the services necessary to dispose of a body according to the laws of that country.

Some American funeral directors contend that England is about 50 years behind the United States. The English find American practices ostentatious. Two countries, sharing the same language and having distinctly different ways of dealing with death, maintain customs of mourning that are appropriate in the culture and time in which they exist.

History

In preindustrial times the funeral was intended to ensure the resurrection of the physical body and the safety of the soul of the deceased. Bells tolled to frighten away evil spirits who might possess the body before it could be buried. By the late nineteenth and early twentieth century, funerals focused more on the benefit to survivors and were turned into elaborate affairs on which people often spent more than they could afford to see that a person was well buried. Rituals surrounding mourning were just as elaborate as those surrounding funerals, and etiquette books went into great detail about what those in mourning should wear and for how long.

Lerner[7] maintains that the differences between the American and British funeral customs were brought about by World War I. During four years of fighting, the British experienced extraordinarily widespread personal loss; three quarters of a mil-

Fig. 11-4. Francis Chappell, a funeral parlor in England.

Photograph by A. Jann Davis.

lion men were killed. Many of the prewar rituals and beliefs were rejected, and a postwar etiquette book reflected the change in mourning clothing. Rather than being shrouded with black crepe for 12 months, the widow dressed in her ordinary clothing, and widow's attire became the exception rather than the rule.

The United States entered the war in 1917 and suffered comparatively fewer fatal casualties. More of the prewar customs were retained in America, although etiquette books suggested that mourning clothing should only be worn as long as sorrow is beyond suppressing.

Differences

Funeral customs in the United States and Great Britain differ in many respects. The British eliminate anything that does not have an essential function; bodies are not routinely embalmed, cosmetics are not used, and the body is dressed in ordinary night clothes or in a shroud rather than street clothes. The British prefer coffins that are tapered rather than the rectangular caskets. The coffin is usually closed as soon as the remains are placed inside, and vaults are not used, so the ground must settle before a gravestone is placed. The majority of Britian's dead are cremated, followed by a memorial service. This eliminates viewing of the corpse at all, preventing what the British describe as unnecessary expense. For example, at St. Christopher's Hospice in England, after the person has died the family views the body before it is taken to a mortuary. The family remembers the person in bed rather than in a satin-lined box.

Another cultural difference between the Americans and the British is the role of the funeral director. The British funeral director is viewed as a tradesman selling a service. He visits the bereaved household and lays out the body in the home or takes it to a funeral parlor. Funeral arrangements are discussed, and a coffin is frequently sold from pictures. A "tea" may take the place of the American funeral dinner. Euphemisms are used less in England. The corpse is referred to as a corpse or a body, not "Mr. Jones," and the word "dead" or "died" is not replaced with "deceased" or "passed away."

The American funeral director is viewed as a professional offering comfort and counsel in addition to products and services. Products include burial footwear, special undergarments, and handmade original fashions to complete the ensemble. Casket styles include classic, colonial, provincial, and a multitude of others. They are equipped with an adjustable innerspring mattress or a soft foam bed and interiors to match the rugged, romantic, or homebody personality. Burial vaults, required by many cemeteries to prevent the grave from collapsing when the casket disintegrates, also come in a variety of colors and designs. Other items include earth dispensers to prevent soiled fingers from the ritual scattering of earth over the casket and artificial grass to conceal the bare earth.

In the United States it is common for relatives, co-workers, neighbors, and casual acquaintances to attend a funeral. This gathering provides a kind of group therapy at this transition between death and life. In England even the closest relatives sometimes do not attend the funeral of a loved one.

The British find American practices of embalming and the use of cosmetics both expensive and death denying. The Americans contend that the British customs are hurried, show lack of respect for the dead, and avoid acceptance of death by eliminating viewing of the body and the failure to attend the funeral.

The best way to evaluate funeral customs is in terms of immediate and prolonged benefit for the bereaved. Research has shown that there is an elevated risk of mortality in the period following the death of a loved one. Customs that facilitate successful mourning and reduce physical or psychological problems must be considered therapeutic, although measurement of such benefits is difficult. It is theorized that attendance at a funeral may provide support for the bereaved, and it is also hypothesized that this benefit comes from the social support of such a structured family gathering.

Any disruption in life that is accompanied by stress increases one's health risk in future years. If a particular type of funeral or mourning custom minimizes disruption caused by death, it benefits the survivors. Funeral and mourning customs in Britain and America differ greatly. Each culture molds its rituals to provide comfort during bereavement, and each custom is appropriate within that culture.

• • •

According to Kubler-Ross, death is the final stage of growth. It is just as normal a part of life as birth, adolescence, and old age, but how to deal with grief is often neglected. People do not grieve in a standardized way—they experience unique feelings when the ending of a loved one's life comes too soon or too late. Care givers respond totally anew with each grieving individual: the parents who cradle their stillborn infant in their arms, the child who asks, "Where's Daddy?" the widowed person who must restructure her way of looking at the world. The work of grief may be the purest pain known to the mourner. It must be pursued and cannot be hurried. Helping professionals who assist others in accepting and experiencing the deep emotion of grief help them face the future without having their lives shattered by the past. By listening and responding to the needs of those who are bereaved, the care giver helps people grow in understanding and wisdom. For some, the grief of bereavement can ultimately be turned into growth.

REFERENCES

1. Bendiksen, R., and Fulton, R.: Death and the child: an anterospective test of the childhood bereavement and later behavior disorder hypothesis, Omega **6:**45, 1975.
2. Blank, R.: Mourning. In Kutscher, A., editor: Death and bereavement, Springfield, Illinois, 1969, Charles C Thomas, Publisher.
3. Bowlby, J.: The making and breaking of affectional bonds, London, 1979, Tavistock Publications, Ltd., pp. 93-94.
4. Carey, R.: Weathering widowhood: problems and adjustments of the widowed during the first year, Omega **10:**163, 1979-1980.
5. Furman, E.: The death of a newborn: care of the parents, Birth and the Family Journal **5:**214, 1978.
6. Hathaway, S., and Monachesi, E.: Adolescent personality and behavior, Minneapolis, 1963, The University of Minnesota Press.
7. Lerner, J.: Funeral and mourning customs in Britain and America: historical perspectives on cultural differences, NRIC National Reporter, **4**(2-3), 1981.
8. Lindemann, E.: Symptomatology and management of acute grief, American Journal of Psychiatry **101:**141, 1944.
9. Powers, C.: Your retirement widowhood guide, Long Beach, Calif., 1974, American Association of Retired Persons and National Retired Teachers Association, p. 3.
10. Schmale, A., and Iker, H.: The effect of hopelessness and the development of cancer. Part I. Identification of uterine cervical cancer in women with atypical cytology, Psychosomatic Medicine **28:**714, 1966.

BIBLIOGRAPHY

Adams, J.: Yesteryear's youngsters, MD **20**(12):31, 1976.

Bowlby, J.: Attachment and loss, vol. 2, Separation, anxiety and anger, New York, 1973, Basic Books, Inc., Publishers.

Cohen, L., and others: Perinatal mortality: assisting parental affirmation, American Journal of Orthopsychiatry **48:**727, 1978.

Engel, G.: Is grief a disease? A challenge for medical research, Psychosomatic Medicine **23**(1):18, 1961.

Faschingbauer, T., Click, M., and Moore, C.: Grief, funeral attendance and illness: an objective evaluation, NRIC National Reporter **3**(4-5), 1980.

Greenblatt, M.: The grieving spouse, American Journal of Psychiatry **135**(1):43, 1978.

Haun, D.: Perceptions of the bereaved, clergy, and funeral directors concerning bereavement, NRIC National Reporter **3**(7), 1980.

Hilgard, J.: Depressive and psychotic states as anniversaries to sibling death in childhood. In Shneidman, E., and Ortega, M., editors: Aspects of depression, Boston, 1969, Little, Brown & Co.

Klerman, G., and Izen, J.: The effects of bereavement and grief on physical health and general well-being. In Kasl, S., and Reichsman, F., editors: Advances in psychosomatic medicine: epidemiologic studies in psychosomatic medicine, vol. 9, New York, 1977, S. Karger.

Klaus, M., and Kennell, J.: Parent-infant bonding, ed. 2, St. Louis, 1982, The C.V. Mosby Co.

Kubler-Ross, E.: On death and dying, New York, 1969, The Macmillan Publishing Co., Inc.

Kubler-Ross, E.: Living with death and dying, New York, 1981, The Macmillan Publishing Co., Inc.

Lewis, E.: Mourning by the family after a stillbirth or neonatal death, Archives of Disease in Childhood **54:**303, 1979.

Lewis, E., and Page, A.: Failure to mourn a stillbirth: an overlooked catastrophe, British Journal of Medical Psychology **51:**237, 1978.

Marris, P.: Widows and their families, London, 1958, Routledge and Kegan Paul, Ltd.

Mitford, J.: The American way of death, New York, 1963, Simon and Schuster.

Parkes, C.: The first year of bereavement: a longitudinal study of the reaction of London widows to the death of their husbands, Psychiatry **33:**444, 1970.

Puckle, B.: Funeral customs: their origin and development, London, 1926, T. Werner Laurie, Ltd.

Rinear, E.: The nurse's challenge when death is unexpected, RN **38**(12):50, 1975.

Satterwhite, B., Belle-Isle, J., and Contradt, B.: Parent groups as an aid in mourning and grief work. In Sahler, O., editor: The child and death, St. Louis, 1978, The C.V. Mosby Co.

Schreiner, R., Gresham, E., and Green, M.: Physician's responsibility to parents after death of an infant, American Journal of Diseases of Children **133:**723, 1979.

Vachon, M., and others: Stress reactions to bereavement, Essence **1**(1):23, 1976.

Please see my need

Take time to hear my words.
Please know that I'm still here.
Outside I'm weak and sick and worn,
Inside my heart knows fear.

I have so much I want to say.
There's much undone to do.
I don't want a world of cold machines,
I just want some time from you.

You check for fever—you check my pulse,
And then you're on your way.
Oh please, just sit and hold my hand
A few minutes . . . can't you stay?

Skip my bath. Don't change the sheets.
Use this time instead . . .
Let me share the fears I know.
Please, sit here by my bed.

Inside I beg, but I can't ask,
Your time is yours to give.
So many need your help and care,
So many—who will live.

I've used up all the life I have.
I now await the day.
So God, I pray You'll see my need,
Please send someone who'll stay.

From **A. Jann Davis**
Please see my need
Supervisor Nurse, July, 1977.

Index